The Dictator's Highway

Patagonian Exploits along the Carretera Austral

Justin Walker

justinwalkerwriter.wordpress.com - stories across borders

© 2015 Justin Walker.

Justin Walker has asserted his right to be identified as the author of this work in accordance with the Copyright, Designs and Patents Act 1988.

All rights reserved. No part of this book may be reproduced in any form without permission from the publisher except for the quotation of brief passages in reviews.

Front cover designed by Caroline Shave.

ISBN 978-1-326-11525-8

Contents

List of Maps 5

Prologue: The South 7

One: The Amadeo 13

Two: Cuerpo Militar del Trabajo 26

Three: Tsonek 40

Four: Los Chicos 53

Five: El Pajarero 66

Six: Padre Antonio Ronchi 80

Seven: Ciprés 94

Eight: Javiera 106

Nine: Tamango 119

Ten: Huemules 130

Eleven: Agua 141

Twelve: Trucha 155

Thirteen: Don Vicente 166

Fourteen: Valle Leones 182

Fifteen: Cerro Castillo 197

Sixteen: Claudia 215

Seventeen: Merluza 229

Eighteen: Queulat 241

Nineteen: Huelga	253
Twenty: Zeta	270
Twenty-One: Colilargo	283
Twenty-Two: Pudú	298
Twenty-Three: Corte de Luz	311
Twenty-Four: Lomo a lo Pobre	326
Epilogue	335
Acknowledgements	340
About the Author	342
Dictating Your Own Highway	343
Appendix 1: Pronunciation Notes	344
Appendix 2: Journey Data	347
Appendix 3: Glossary	349
Appendix 4: Sources and Further Reading	370

List of Maps

Map 01: Chilean Patagonia (Northern Parts) 6

Map 02: Villa O'Higgins 39

Map 03: Carretera Austral - South 79

Map 04: Caleta Tortel 93

Map 05: Cochrane and Tamango 118

Map 06: Puerto Guadal and Puerto Bertrand 154

Map 07: Puerto Río Tranquilo & Lago General Carrera .. 181

Map 08: Carretera Austral – Centre 195

Map 09: Reserva Nacional Cerro Castillo 196

Map 10: Coyhaique 214

Map 11: Puyuhuapi and Puerto Cisnes 228

Map 12: La Junta and Raúl Marín 252

Map 13: Carretera Austral – North 268

Map 14: Futaleufú 269

Map 15: Chaitén 282

Map 16 : Peninsula Huequi 297

Map 17: Hornopirén, Contao and Puerto Montt 325

Map 01: Chilean Patagonia (Northern Parts)

Prologue: The South

Stretched along the western face of South America, there lies an intriguingly shaped land. Surprisingly long and unusually narrow, Chile is unmistakable. She is a bamboo cane; a drainpipe. If she joined a fidgeting queue of nervously excited aspiring fashion models, bulbous Brazil and pot-bellied Bolivia would steal envious glances at Chile's sleek and slender figure. From head to toe, her skinny form extends an extraordinary 4300 kilometres, similar to the separation of London from the North Pole. Measured along the road, rather than in a straight line, the distance is even greater. The capital, Santiago, is a 2000-kilometre drive from northerly Arica and 3000 from Punta Arenas,[1] the largest of the scattered settlements that cling to mainland America's tapering tail.

Beyond Punta Arenas is a remote headland known as Cape Froward, principally noteworthy for its location at the very tip of the tail. Despite that accolade, this inaccessible spot is not the southernmost point of Chile. In fact, it's not even close. Across the Strait of Magellan cluster hundreds of inhospitable islands in an intricate, tangled web of fjords and sea canals. Among the jigsaw pieces are familiar names: Dawson Island, the Beagle Channel and the archipelago of Tierra del Fuego whose ultimate, defiant outcrop, where the Hermite Islands finally cede to the Drake Passage, is Cape Horn. Even the *Cabo de Hornos*, which maintains an expressionless vigil over volatile churning waters long the subject of sailors' nightmares, is not the endpoint. Beyond the horizon the Diego Ramírez archipelago, the

---

[1] It isn't actually possible to drive all the way from Santiago to Punta Arenas whilst remaining in Chile. The 3000-kilometre route includes long sections on Argentine highways. The extreme southern regions of Chile still have no domestic road connection to the capital.

final smattering of land in South America, breaks the surface of the angry ocean.

As far as my friends were concerned, their country projected further still. Maps invariably inset a diagram showing the Chilean Antarctic claim, a 37-degree slice of the icy continent that inconveniently overlaps with the sectors claimed by Argentina and the United Kingdom. Chilean Antarctic Territory also includes the Antarctic Peninsula and the South Shetland Islands. Given their less aggressive latitude, both of these have been selected by numerous countries for their Antarctic research stations, and they consequently rank among the more thoroughly explored parts of the continent. Whenever the topic arose, colleagues spared no trouble in eliminating any doubt I might carelessly have expressed: Chilean entitlement to that frozen land was an accepted fact, not a point for discussion. Accordingly, the mid-point of Chile is marked by a monument at Puerto Hambre, a small Patagonian bay that lies 4000 kilometres from Visviri in the northern desert and 4000 from the South Pole. Which, as everybody knows, is in Chile.

Once I'd arrived to live in Santiago, not long passed before the high regard in which my neighbours and colleagues held 'The South' became apparent. It is *precioso*, stunning, I was constantly told. Consequently, as evenings lengthened in the latter part of that inaugural year, I spent hours poring over maps of southern Chile, my deliberations aided by a glass or two of *vino tinto*. The outcome was a ticket to Punta Arenas, the most southerly destination within range of a domestic flight. When the school year lurched to a close in December, amid award ceremonies, balmy summer evenings and exhaustion, I took my trip to The South. I ate fire-roasted Patagonian lamb, lodged in a pink-painted clapboard house, and slept under canvas around the renowned W-circuit of the Torres del Paine National Park, losing in the process the first and finest of several cameras that disappeared throughout my South American years. These were places that few Chileans visited, I learned, since many lacked the means or opportunity or inclination to do so.

For a novice, it was a commendable first foray into Chilean Patagonia. Proudly returning to Santiago, brimming with tales of fearless endeavour, I was perplexed to discover that I hadn't visited 'The South' at all. No, where'd I'd gone was so far off the map that it didn't count. 'The South' for everyone else meant the regions of Los Ríos and Los Lagos, much closer to the capital but still several hundred kilometres away and, crucially, within a committed day's drive for the procession of chunky four-wheel-drive BMWs that head for rural refuge with the advent of summer.

From roaring waterfalls to belching sea lions, and from rolling hills to towering volcanoes, these are indeed enchanting regions. Eight sizeable lakes line up in a north-south row, like rungs on a ladder, with tongue-twisting names: Panguipulli, Riñihue, Puyehue and Llanquihue. On their shores, smart holiday residences jostle for north-facing aspects. Towards the mountains, there are magical forests of monkey puzzle. Further south is the unenticing port of Puerto Montt, the most populous city in the region. And southwest of there is Chiloé, Chile's largest island, known for its wooden churches, houses on stilts, colonies of penguins and a local cuisine known as *curanto*, still today cooked in a hole in the ground.

In contrast, the North of Chile is dominated by the vast, open expanse of the Atacama Desert, a place so dry that abandoned mining communities stand like ghost towns in the sand, having decomposed hardly at all in 50 years of disuse. Here in the desert, world-class observatories take advantage of constant clear skies, and in spite of plummeting night temperatures, the naked mountains never see snow. The church at San Pedro has a ceiling supported on beams of cactus wood, and El Tatio has the world's highest geyser field. In the Elqui Valley, a local grape brandy is distilled, a potent spirit known as *pisco*. Tiny Pica is a sleepy oasis awash with lemon groves, and when spring conditions conspire favourably around coastal Caldera, there are glimpses of the *desierto florido*: the flowering desert.

The eastern margin of Chile is formed by the ubiquitous barrier of the majestic Andes. In winter, the dreamy view of snowy peaks was a constant distraction outside my office window. The Cajón de Maipo is a spectacular Andean canyon within easy reach of the capital, and the upper mountains are close enough for a day trip to hike, to ride or to ski. High in the *cordillera*, there is a cross-border route known as Paso Los Libertadores, frequently closed by snowfall. On the Argentine side, the road to Mendoza gently descends through striking scenery of rusty red rock, complemented in autumn by amber-leaved poplar: elongated arrowheads pointing to the sky.

Out west are the winelands. Beyond the interminable vineyards and over a second mountain range is the Pacific coast. Every family has its favourite bay or resort, and the lucky ones keep an apartment there: a weekend bolthole and a summer sanctuary to escape the city's roasting heat. Some way offshore is the Juan Fernández archipelago, known for its harvest of rock lobster. Three thousand kilometres further west is Rapa Nui, annexed by Chile in 1888 and also known as *Isla de Pascua*: Easter Island. Most salient of its historic sites are the *ahu*, wide stone platforms on which giant carved *moai* have in modern times been re-erected, their backs to the ocean, watching once more over their devoted peoples as they did of old.

There is much to be admired throughout Chile, but my colleagues were right: The South, in particular, is *precioso*. The lakes and parks of the Near South have a tasteful but somewhat managed charm, and at the continent's utter end, the rugged, remote Far South has an abrasive, untamed splendour. But the South of Chile has more than just these two. In such an elongated land, there is still room for more. Somewhere south of Puerto Montt, Patagonia begins. Slapped in the middle of this region is a town called Coyhaique. I'd noticed that name listed on the airport departures board, but for some reason visiting there had simply never occurred to me. On the map, Coyhaique was phenomenally far from everything else, and I'd rarely heard anyone say that they'd actually been.

The moment I began to read more, I was hooked. In a country already characterised by astonishing variety, Chilean Patagonia raises the standard even higher. It is a place of wonder. Gaping chasms twist between thundering chains of mountains. Mighty glaciers descend from two colossal ice fields, bulldozing through a landscape that, as a result, is even now being formed. Here flow Chile's most powerful rivers, implausibly coloured by glacial sediment. Among uncounted lakes, there is one that goes deeper than almost any other on Earth. Glassy fjords cut the land into ribbons, and the ocean fringe is strewn with islands, each one silently keeping centuries of secrets that will never be known. And spread across it all, one of the greatest temperate rainforests on the planet hems the Pacific coastline. Only in dreams and fairy tales are there places of such staggering beauty.

This bewildering landscape is home to some remarkable wildlife: illustrious condors, unfathomable whales and venerable owls;

prowling pumas, preposterous pelicans and playful penguins. Patagonia has the world's southernmost hummingbirds, a deer that doesn't reach your kneecap, and trees that have stood since before the birth of Christ. And – clutching at straws a little now – in these parts, too, are the largest-ever rhubarb stalks and the world's most vindictive horseflies.

During the presidency of the dictator, Augusto Pinochet, a road was built through this region for the first time. Most of the route remains unpaved; distances are far and facilities limited. Where there are fjords to be crossed, the road simply gives up and onward progress depends on a boat. The single carriageway threads through the Patagonian landscape, enabling access to tiny settlements that time forgot. There's no avoiding it: moving around the region depends almost entirely on this road. Stretching over a thousand kilometres from Puerto Montt to Villa O'Higgins, this is the *Carretera Austral*: the Southern Highway.

I was three years in Chile before I made it to the region, but when my contract in Santiago finally staggered to a close, I headed south again. This time, I made straight for the Dictator's Highway.

Image 01: Hitchhiking near Puerto Bertrand

One: The Amadeo

A vast cityscape. Lofty steel-framed spires in the business district were outnumbered all around by the clunky cuboid forms of apartment towers. Further out, single storey housing spread across an expansive plain; monochrome barracks, endlessly repeating. The river bed, virtually dry, cut a nonchalant sweep through it all and the asphalt band of an urban motorway snaked over and under at will. Above it all, a backdrop of snow-capped peaks soared into a compelling blue sky. For those few moments, Santiago was a magnificent sight: self-assured, forward-looking and aspirational, and baked in January summer sunshine. But within a few rapid seconds, the urban features were overcome, hidden behind a thick haze of choking brown aerial grime.

Fixing a southerly course, parallel to the Andes *cordillera*, our verbose captain periodically announced a series of volcanic peaks on show through the round-cornered peepholes of toughened glass. Antuco, Callaqui and Lonquimay all slid silently by. Several hundred of Chile's volcanoes are considered active; 60 have erupted in the past five centuries alone, a mere heartbeat in geological chronology. Mighty Villarrica followed next, and then the most dramatic of all, the clumsily-named Volcán Puyehue-Cordón Caulle, spewing out material five miles below. A cauliflower of grey ash was clearly visible, rising from the dark fissure. In the initial explosion six months earlier, a hundred million tonnes of material had been ejected, depositing a thick layer of sandy grit across extensive areas of Argentine territory. The airborne debris had completed a full circuit of the globe.

On touching down at Puerto Montt, we taxied past a row of arc-roofed army buildings looking like half-buried drinks cans, surrounded by elderly military vehicles abandoned in the long grass. At the opposite end of the airfield was a swanky modern passenger terminal, a fanfare of plate glass reflecting the perfect sky. Directed across the tarmac and through the door for arrivals, I passed by the baggage carousel to collect my *mochila*, my rucksack, and located a bus into the city.

'Where will I find the Navimag ferry port?' I asked the driver as we arrived at a sprawling transport interchange behind the seafront.

He pointed over my shoulder. 'That way along the *costanera*,' the coast road, he said, 'but it's too far to walk. You'll need a taxi.'

I walked. It took about ten minutes.

The Navimag desk was in a small, wood-panelled office behind the waiting room.

'I have a ticket for the midnight ferry to Puerto Chacabuco,' I explained.

The uniformed *señora* handed me a flimsy boarding card and instructions to return there by ten. The long ocean passage from Puerto Montt to Puerto Natales[2] had always appealed, particularly for the scenery and wildlife of the sea canals of southern Chile. In contrast, four full days on a freight boat could presumably become wearisome in damp weather and low visibility and on this occasion a shorter alternative suited my purpose. A voyage of just 24 hours was sufficient to reach Puerto Chacabuco. Not far inland from there was Coyhaique, the region's principal town. And from there, I could fly to Villa O'Higgins,[3] the southern starting point for a pilgrimage up the long and winding Carretera Austral.

Puerto Montt, named in honour of nineteenth-century president Manuel Montt, is set amongst hills. In fact, it's difficult to think of any place in Chile that is not. A crumbling set of concrete steps veered erratically up a steep slope behind the port. The reward at the top was a 360-degreee panorama dominated by volcanoes Calbuco and Osorno

---

[2] Puerto Montt and Puerto Natales. *Puerto* means 'port' and *puerta* means 'door'. The similarity is not surprising since a port is the gateway between sea and land.

[3] *Villa* and *pueblo* can both mean either 'town' or 'village'. Villa is pronounced *VEE-ya*. In Appendix 1, see Pronunciation Note One: Double-L sounds.

to the north. In the opposite direction was the Seno de Reloncaví, a huge bay, 40 kilometres in diameter, rich blue water under the pale and cloudless sky. The far shore was a parade of hazy headlands, their weathered form resembling the edge of a serrated blade. On the near side, beyond a row of dock warehouses, my room for the night was tethered mid-channel to a pair of tugs. With her bright red hull, white bridge, bottle green decks and a jaunty lemon-coloured funnel, this was the *Amadeo*.

I called at a *peluquería*[4] for a pre-summer hair-shearing and then at the imaginatively named 'Bigger' supermarket for a half-kilo packet of lentils: compact, convenient, nutritious and therefore my camping food of preference. Next stop was a hardware store, where I added a canister of camping gas to an already bulging rucksack. The shop was richly reminiscent of ironmongers from a 1970s childhood, with tools and ropes, pipes and taps, tubs of screws and nails, door hinges and sacks of cement, electrical sockets and enormous reels of fat cable, grease, paint...

It wasn't as simple as taking an item from the shelf and paying the cashier. Completing the transaction involved a three-stage process that had bewildered me since arriving in Chile. With the help of the first assistant I chose a bottle of gas from a selection locked away in a glass cabinet. He gave me a handwritten ticket to take to a second employee at the *caja*, where I paid. Meanwhile, the canister was transferred to a third colleague at the *empaque*, the packing and collection area. Reporting there with my payment receipt, I finally gained custody of the purchase, meticulously wrapped in brown paper. It's easy when you know how. A short distance down the road I realised I might do better with two bottles; replacement cylinders would most likely be difficult to find in small Patagonian *pueblos*. Back in the store we repeated the process, this time with the three assistants exchanging mildly quizzical looks.

Puerto Montt had many of these quaint olde-worlde shops: traditional butchers, bakers, greengrocers and a *cordonería*, a store that sold thread, string, wool, shoe laces and numerous other kinds of long, thin things. Perhaps all retail outlets should be differentiated by the

---

[4] Most words in the Spanish language are emphasised on the penultimate syllable, or alternatively on any syllable with an accent. A more detailed explanation is given in Appendix 1. See Pronunciation Note Two: Emphasis and accents.

shape of their stock. Alongside the *cordonería* might be a shop we could call a *redondería* for spherical objects, with golf balls and tennis balls, pumpkins and oranges, marbles and balloons. There would be another store for wallpaper, kitchen roll, aluminium foil and carpets: the *rollería*. If you wanted to buy a packet of macaroni you would find one in the *tubalería* along with drinking straws and organ pipes, whereas spaghetti would obviously be available back in the *cordonería*. It would be a highly logical system, and you would always know if you were in the right shop; why has no-one ever tried it?

Back in the real world, intruding into Puerto Montt's traditional idyll were shop windows stacked with games consoles and electronic gadgets, and countless stores piled high with imported synthetic clothing. Also, for those with a more cavalier attitude to their loose change, there were cavernous premises with row upon row of electronic entertainment machines, each one a festival of flashing lights, chirruping their persistent electronic refrains, competing for attention like impatient toddlers.

With afternoon drifting into evening, a sharp wind from the bay cut through my fleece, a reminder that conditions in the South would be less friendly than the benign summer beginning in Santiago. A bevy of sleepy drunks was slouched against a wall in the evening sunlight. I needed to eat but the town centre restaurants were either utterly empty or full of stern men in a haze of cigarette smoke, both of which were equally intimidating.

Gathering courage on a street corner near the port, I pushed open the timbered door of the Cirus Bar. Hung in the lobby was a mariners' chart of the seas around Puerto Montt and the nearby island of Chiloé. At the foot of the map was a peninsula named Huequi,[5] its strangely block-shaped outline evocative of The Wirral in northwest England. Four villages were dotted around its trapezoid coast but there was no road apparent by which to arrive. Did people really live in such isolation? How did such communities survive?

---

[5] Words beginning 'hue', like Huequi, usually sound like they begin with W. A brief note is placed in Appendix 1. See Pronunciation Note Three: HUA, HUE and HUI sounds.

A handful of customers were inside. A group were sharing a joke at the bar, and others were seated around square tables throughout the gloomy room. A familiar song by Toto was playing from a black-cased tower system on the bar. I chose a place in a window booth and ordered *lomo a lo pobre*, a popular but calorific tenderloin steak dish that was a favourite of mine. Served with chips, caramelised onions and fried eggs, it had proved adept in equal measure to cheer the downhearted, to comfort the shiveringly cold, and of course to satisfy the hungry. It was just as fitting, I hastily decided, to mark the start of a long journey. I also had a *schop*, a draught beer. This one was a large juggy glass of a brew known as *Kunstmann Torobayo*, a product carefully marketed to give the impression of deriving from long Germanic tradition when in reality, production began as recently as 1997.

Alongside the beer, the waitress brought *pan* and *ají*, bread and red chilli. As is common throughout Chile, the *ají* came disguised as a small dish of *pebre*, a sauce in which the chilli is finely chopped with tomatoes, onion, garlic and coriander in olive oil. It is a tasty condiment, especially for those who enjoy their food *picante*, spicy hot. In a country where citrus grows juicy and large, it is also customary to provide a plate of halved lemons. Although their principal purpose is to add zest and zing to steak or fish, I also developed the habit of squeezing a lemon into my glass of *agua de la llave*,[6] tap water.

Relishing each fibrous mouthful of steak, I ate unhurriedly to consume the empty hours before my appointment with the *Amadeo*. Reminders of my teens boomed from the stereo: songs by The Police, Big Country and Level 42. When the waitress pointedly asked a third time what more she could fetch me, I understood that my occupation of her table could be extended no further so I slunk reluctantly away.

In contrast to the rigid plastic benches of the Navimag waiting room, lining a separate corridor were plush double seats that looked to

---

[6] *Llave* means 'doorkey', but the same word is used for 'tap', so *agua de la llave* means 'tapwater'. However, this expression is local to Chile. On one visit to Buenos Aires I surprised the waitress by requesting 'water of the key'. In Argentina the correct expression is *agua de la canilla*.

have been removed from a bus; even the reclining mechanism still functioned. While a handful of us waited there, one traveller returned his bag to the luggage attendant and disappeared. His timing was unfortunate. At that exact moment we were called forward. A port official wearing a high-viz vest checked our names against his computer print-out and we were shepherded aboard the shuttle bus.

The *Amadeo* was not a passenger ferry. The bulk of her capacity was for vehicles and freight, with only a handful of sleeping berths set aside on an upper deck. The orange-jacketed man led us on foot over the vehicle ramp into her vast hangar-like hold. We rode to a higher level on an impressive elevator designed to lift multi-axle vehicles and were guided to a small dining room where I banged my head on the low doorway. There was a short welcome with a safety announcement and an explanation of meal times, and we were shown to our cabins. I was to share with a truck driver, Helmut, and the guy who'd gone missing. He showed up shortly afterwards, a balding Swiss traveller called Philip.

Having commandeered one of the lower bunks, I explored the passenger deck. At the rear of the ship was a balcony from where it was possible to see the ship being loaded. A rail guarded a yawning opening in the steel floor through which vehicles were being raised on the giant elevator. Many of the trucks were shipped with just the trailer part. It made sense; better to keep a cab and driver at each port than have both sit idle on a long sea voyage. Thick straps were secured over the axles and fastened to heavy-duty brackets on deck.

We sailed in one o'clock darkness, just an hour late. In a conscious effort to set aside the novelty of spending the night on a freight ship, I retired to our cabin after a short while, determined to slip promptly into slumber in spite of the movement of the vessel and her repertoire of unfamiliar sounds.

*

An inspection of the map of Chile reveals something surprising to the south of Puerto Montt. Most of Chile, the northern two-thirds or so, is a single unified whole. This relatively warm and mainly dry territory is delimited by the sea on one side and mountains on the other. Or, making more of this, Chile is washed on its west side by our globe's greatest ocean and has the longest mountain chain on Earth to the east.

Adding the thirsty desert in the north and extensive ice fields in the south, the country is entirely hemmed in by impenetrable obstacles. Ecology and culture have evolved in isolation and *Chilenos* take pride in being quite distinct from their more Latin neighbours.

Nonetheless, and getting back to the point, despite its ribbon-like profile, the mainland part of Chile has the expected characteristic of a regular continental domain: it is integrated as one cohesive piece. In contrast, it is further down the map that the geography of the country becomes rather unusual. In the final third of its length, much of Chile is not connected to the South American landmass. Aside from a narrow strip tucked in beneath the southern Andes, the remainder crops up in the form of isles that gather against the western shore. Identifying where the mainland ends and the islands begin is a perplexing task given the intricacy of the coastline, riddled with fjords and sea channels. The terrain disintegrates into a tangle of impossibly crenelated coastlines resembling crazy paving or like a thousand fragments of pottery swept up against the edge of the continent.

As we slept, the *Amadeo* transported us deep into this territory, an in-between zone where ocean and continent meet in confusion. These lands, crowded with steep mountains and thick with temperate rainforest, are inaccessible places. Aside from a mere handful of communities, most have never supported human habitation, certainly not in modern times. The few *pueblos* clung to the coast as if afraid to venture to the interior.

*

Temperate Rainforest

Dense evergreen forest in areas with reliable heavy precipitation is usually known, unsurprisingly, as rainforest. Such forests are found in both tropical and temperate regions.

Tropical rainforest refers to moist broad-leafed forests within the tropics (either side of the equator). There are tropical rainforests, for example, in the northern portion of South America (e.g. in Peru and Brazil), in Central America, in equatorial Africa, in Southeast Asia and on certain Pacific islands. Areas with tropical rainforest are characterised by high temperatures and very high rainfall.

> Temperate rainforest is less widespread. It can be either coniferous or broad-leafed, and grows outside the tropics. For example, there are temperate rainforests in New Zealand, along the Irish, Scottish and Norwegian coasts, in East Asia including Japan, Korea and southern China, and in southern Chile. Areas with temperate rainforest are characterised by cooler maximum temperatures and moderately high rainfall.
>
> The world's greatest temperate rainforests are both found on the Pacific coast of the Americas. The largest of all stretches from Alaska and California, in North America. The second spreads across Patagonia, extending from Valdivia to Tierra del Fuego.
>
> The northern part of the Patagonian forest is composed of Valdivian temperate rainforest. This includes deciduous species of southern beech,[7] and conifers such as the *alerce* or Patagonian cypress and the *araucaria* or Chilean pine, commonly known as the monkey puzzle.
>
> The southern portion is Magellanic subpolar forest, which is also dominated by various species of southern beech. These are the world's southernmost woodlands. Due to the extreme climate, many are dwarf species, subject to stunted growth and wind shear.

*

My earplugs were almost too successful. Having located the dining room after waking at long last, I scraped the last crispy remnants of scrambled egg onto a plate and helped myself to warm bread and a mug of tea. Fortified, I braved the bracing breeze out on deck. The *Amadeo's* wake was as straight as tram tracks, distantly converging. We'd passed the intriguing Huequi peninsula and the island of Chiloé during the night, and now the Pacific horizon was a perfect line between pale blue sky and deeper blue sea. Occasional vessels crept silently in the opposite direction, sometimes no more than a distant speck of colour on the limitless ocean.

Leaning on the rail, I was joined by my roommate, truck driver Helmut.

---

[7] Ten species of southern beech [Latin: *nothofagus*] grow in Chile. They are listed in Chapter 9.

'What do you have in your lorry?' I asked.

'*Cerveza.*' he replied. 'Thousands of cans of beer. I drive for the Cristal brewery.

'How far do you go?'

'Just about everywhere. This load is for Coyhaique but I deliver all over Chile and Argentina. Some journeys are three days out and three days back. There isn't a place I haven't been with my truck. It doesn't matter where people are, they still want beer.'

'How often do you travel on this ship?'

'It used to be every month but I don't often drive this route any more. I'm usually in Argentina. I like it there. People are much more equal in Argentina,' he said. 'There, the owner of a depot will sit down to eat with his workers. That never happens in Chile. But I like this boat. It gives me a chance to be still. Otherwise, every day I'm driving; all the time, driving. On here, the ferry does the work, and Señor Helmut can rest.'

The Guaitecas Archipelago appeared on our starboard side, the first sign of the island multitudes to come. Beginning with this small group, an unbroken island constellation continues all the way to Cape Horn, mostly uninhabited and rarely visited, hardly even mapped. Insular Patagonia is a bewilderingly unblemished and pristine natural wilderness. It is also very long, 1500 kilometres from one end to the other. For comparison, imagine a corridor of islands extending from London to Stockholm, or from Massachusetts to Georgia.

Further south, we sailed into Canal Moraleda, the broad channel separating continental Patagonia from the archipelago. At this point, the canal was 20 kilometres across, but further south, our ship had to pick a careful course amongst huddled gangs of islets. Some were low mounds that barely broke the surface. On others, towering cliffs plunged into the dark sea. Some of the channels were broad and the shores distant, affording any fugitive a thousand hiding places. At other times, the *Amadeo* squeezed through gaps so narrow it seemed it would be possible to throw a stone from one bank to the other.

Every passing island and headland delivered new scenes to admire. Where the sunshine was brightest, precise reflections were cast in the glassy water of the fjords. In almost the next moment, a chill gust might herald a valley boiling with turbulent cloud, the upper slopes veiled.

'Have you ever seen a whale?' asked Helmut.

'No. I saw a dead one on a beach one time, but I've never seen a whale in the ocean.'

'Keep your eyes on the sea. We often see them in this area, usually far off. Pay attention to the surface of the water and you might see the back of a whale push up above the sea, or even its tail.'

I watched for an hour. The whales were hiding.

A mist of light drizzle began to blow through the air. Penguins swam alongside the ship, splashes of black and white in the translucent green water. The island community of Puerto Aguirre came into view, home to around 2000 hardy souls. The village cluttered the shoreline: boxy homes in white, blue and yellow, corrugated roofs of shiny aluminium and smoke rising from row after row of chimneys, each higher than its neighbour on the steep incline. Boats were moored in the harbour but there were neither cars in the town nor any road on which to drive them.

Sitting in one corner of the green-painted deck, a young couple inclined their faces skywards in worship of the afternoon rays. Regardless of the sunshine, Hervé and Séverine, from France and Belgium, wore smart hiking jackets against the frequent icy blasts.

Hervé described their South American trip. 'We're nearly halfway through,' he explained. 'The next few weeks will be all about hiking. Tomorrow we're going to Cerro Castillo, and after that to El Chaltén in Argentina. I've always wanted to see Cerro Castillo. It's supposed to be beautiful.'

They appeared to have researched carefully. I made a mental note of Cerro Castillo; I would be passing that way.

'Originally we wanted to visit the Torres del Paine' added Séverine, 'but I don't know if it's worth it now, after the fire.' She apologised repeatedly for her English, despite speaking the language almost perfectly.

The Torres del Paine, Chile's world-renowned national park, is a Mecca for thousands of outdoor-minded visitors every year. Hiking trails give access to spectacular upland terrain adorned with blue glaciers, iceberg-filled lakes, glorious peaks and ancient forest. Sharp-eyed trekkers have a chance to see condor and flamingo, the flightless *ñandú*[8] and herds of *guanaco*.[9] Lamentably, the area has suffered fire damage several times, including one occasion just a month earlier, when thousands of acres of forest were destroyed. A tourist arrested on suspicion of negligently starting the fire was later released.

Cheerful passengers eagerly lined the upper deck for the final approach along Fiordo Aysén. Frosted peaks fringed with rich green forest were illuminated by golden beams of late evening sunlight. Chutes of water crashed from hanging valleys, and distant clouds were arched over hills like fluffy white eyebrows. Finally, Puerto Chacabuco came into view, a bland settlement at the tip of the fjord. Easily identifiable by their white walls and blue roofs were the buildings at the port itself. Behind them were large cylindrical tanks for some industrial purpose. An incongruous hotel development stood on a promontory overlooking the harbour. All this was dwarfed by the sheer face of Cerro Blanco rising in a single spectacular step, the summit lost to a ceiling of dark cloud. We dropped anchor as dusk fell and a pair of tugboats, one red and one blue like a child's toys, nosed the *Amadeo* around in a slow arc until her stern rested against the dock.

Hervé, Séverine and Philip boarded a bus to Puerto Aysén. As for me, sleep was a more pressing need than covering a few extra kilometres, so I walked instead to Residencial El Puerto for my first Patagonian night. I creaked up the narrow stairs to a small room above the bar. The low bed was piled high with several blankets, a puffy duvet and a quilted bedspread – and this was summer. I unlaced my leather shoes, threw my clothes on a rickety chair and curled up in the linen nest.

*

---

[8] The *ñandú* or rhea is a flightless bird like an ostrich but standing only a metre in height.
[9] The *guanaco* is a relative of the camel. There are four Andean camelids: the domesticated *llama* was bred from the wild *guanaco* approximately 6000 years ago and the domesticated *alpaca* from the wild *vicuña* about 1000 years later.

Patagonia

The southerly extremis of South America is known as Patagonia on both sides of the Andes. Patagonia is not a country and never has been but the name was in use long before the current nations of Chile and Argentina came into existence. The word is derived from Magellan's use of the expression Patagon (meaning 'giant' or 'big feet') as a name for the people who dwelled there. Explorers with Magellan in the 1520s reported sightings of very tall people at the coasts who, it is now assumed, were indigenous Tehuelche.

Patagonian land accounts for approximately one-third of Chile and one-quarter of Argentina, although the definition of its northern limit is somewhat imprecise. In Argentina, all land south of the Colorado River is generally considered to be Patagonian, namely the provinces of Neuquén, Río Negro, Chubut and Santa Cruz. Chilean Patagonia starts south of Puerto Montt, and therefore includes the regions of Magallanes and Aysén and part of Los Lagos.

The land and climate are quite distinct on either side of the mountains. For many, the word 'Patagonia' conjures images of featureless grassland plains. Such scenes are typical of the semi-desert highland steppe on the Argentine side of the mountains, too dry to support forest. Further east towards the Atlantic are the fertile lowlands of the pampas. The Chilean side is quite different to either of these. It is wetter, greener and characterised by mountains, deep valleys, glaciers, rivers, lakes, fjords and islands.

The human population is meagre, around two million in total, only ten per cent of whom live on the Chilean side. Consequently, whereas Chile as a whole has in excess of twenty people per square kilometre and Argentina averages fifteen, the population density of Chilean Patagonia is lower than one person per square kilometre.[10]

---

[10] For comparison, the UK has a population density of approximately 263 per square kilometre, France 120 and USA 34. Low national densities include Canada at 4 and Australia at 3. High densities include The Netherlands with around 500 and Bangladesh at nearly 1200 people per square kilometre. The global figure excluding Antarctica is 53 people per square kilometre of land (2012 figures). South America is known for its empty wilderness areas. The incomprehensible Amazon, the grassy pampas of Argentina, and the desolate Andes are just three of many. Very approximately, allowing a generous degree of statistical leeway, South America has twice the land area of Europe but is filled by only half the population, or rather, not filled. Without any difficulty there are sufficient attractive, secluded, unspoiled and off-the-

Image 02: Canal Moraleda

beaten-trail places to satisfy for a lifetime even the most demanding of travellers. Approximate population in 2014: Europe 742 million; South America 407 million. Approximate surface area: Europe 10 million km²; South America 18 million km².

Two: Cuerpo Militar del Trabajo

Although the shower ran deliciously hot, the plumber responsible for positioning the outlet must have envisaged a cubicle occupant rather shorter than me. Adopting a genre of yogic deformation better suited to someone considerably suppler, I bent my limbs one by one under the stream of water to rinse away a day's accumulation of ferry gunk. A stretch between each contortion relieved the aching of a compressed spine, but absent-mindedly neglecting the proximity of the ceiling, I smacked my head every time on a sharp-edged ventilator cover.

Descending the uneven stairs in search of breakfast, I discovered a room cluttered with small round tables. A woman bustled in, turned on the television and promptly left. I tiptoed over to the set and quietened the volume a notch or two, but I was rumbled – she shot back at once and turned it up again with a confident flourish and an authoritative glare in my direction. The breakfast show was running a piece on celebrity couples, featuring most prominently 'the most operated woman in Chile' and her footballer boyfriend. Two other guests joined me in the breakfast room for some slices of bread and processed ham. We hardly spoke, all three quite distracted by the cosmetically enhanced equipment amply filling the screen.

The day ahead promised to be free of anxiety. After the midday flight and midnight sailing, indeed after three years of timetables and schedules and priorities that trampled all over each other, there were no longer any strategy meetings or performance reviews or disciplinary hearings, and no pressure to achieve any particular thing by any specific moment. All I had to do that day was reach the town of

Coyhaique, a mere 80 kilometres away at the other end of the Simpson Valley.

There, I had a minor quest to fulfil. It wasn't essential, but a vague aspiration had sprouted during my prior research and planning. My idea was to call at the base of the *14º Regimiento Reforzado*,[11] the 14th Reinforced (Aysén) Regiment of the Chilean Army. Given the important role that the military had played in the history of the Carretera Austral, it seemed appropriate on passing to pay homage at the Coyhaique barracks. I wasn't expected there, but with a measure of good fortune I wouldn't need to proceed any further than the gate. If my information was correct, the exhibit I wished to see was parked outside.

*

On the fringe of Puerto Chacabuco, I set down my weighty *mochila* outside a petrol station. The day's short journey provided an opportunity to judge whether hitchhiking really would be a satisfactory means to move around the region. Would there be enough traffic? How many would be inclined to stop? This was a chance to polish stylish thumb-waving techniques and to perfect an earnest facial expression that no driver with any heart could possibly snub. There were also a handful of sites worth visiting along the road. If nothing else, the guidebook recommended two separate *cascadas*, waterfalls. Conditions overhead looked promising for a day of experimental thumbing. Well, in truth, the sky was overcast but didn't threaten imminent rain, and it was somehow light in spite of the greyness.

After the first few vehicles sailed by, a white four-wheel-drive Toyota drew up and Elena offered a ride to the next town. I lifted my rucksack onto the rear seat and sat back contentedly as we pulled away from the forecourt. Elena had lived in Puerto Aysén three years, she said, since taking an office job in the salmon farming industry.

'My children call it *Muerto Aysén*,' Dead Aysén, said Elena. 'They preferred living in a city with cinemas and burger bars and shopping malls. I've not adapted yet either,' she admitted. 'It's strange to live in

---

[11] The ° symbol after the 14 in *14º Regimiento* is actually a letter O. It has the same purpose as the TH in 14th Regiment'. The Spanish word for fourteenth is *decimocuarto* (or *decimocuarta* for a feminine noun), and is written in figures as *14º* or *14ª*.

such a small town. Our supermarket runs out of food at the end of each month. The cashpoint empties too, every payday. You wait all month to get paid and then there's no cash in the machine.'

After a few minutes we turned off the road into some kind of industrial premises.

'I hope you don't mind,' she explained, 'but I have to stop for my *Revisión Técnica*. The mechanics come here only a couple of days each month; otherwise, we have to go to Coyhaique.'

The *Revisión Técnica* was the annual certificate of roadworthiness, equivalent to the British MOT. My heart sank; how long was this going to take? Was I somehow committed to wait with Elena? Would it be ungrateful to excuse myself and try for an alternative ride? I paced up and down, reviewing my rather limited options and attempting to summon up the resolve to take my bag and leave. Luckily I was soon released from my anxious indecision. The garage was processing only heavy vehicles that day, not cars, and we were promptly underway again. It wouldn't take long to reach Puerto Aysén; it looked very close on the map.

A distinctive tangerine-coloured suspension bridge soon came into view, Puente Presidente Ibáñez,[12] marking the entrance to the town. It used to be the maritime gateway to the region, until silt deposits reduced the navigability of the Río Aysén and the port was moved downstream to Puerto Chacabuco. The name of the bridge honoured General Carlos Ibáñez del Campo who was twice president of Chile during the twentieth century. At over 200 metres, it ranked amongst the longest in the country. Orange cables curved pleasingly between the tall towers on either bank.

Elena dropped me in front of a row of dilapidated premises beyond the bridge. Flaking painted signs drew attention to the *Salon de Pool King* and *Triple 7 Juegos Electrónicos*, electronic games, rather reinforcing her views about the quality of entertainment locally available in 'Muerto Aysén'. An exceedingly polite beggar slipped out from between the derelict cabins and asked for 500 *pesos*, about one US dollar. His courteous manner was enough to win his desired reward. I ambled around a couple of blocks of the small town, but restlessly. It felt too soon to be stopping, and I was eager to see those *cascadas*. Back

---

[12] The letter ñ is pronounced 'n-y', as in *señor*. *Ibáñez* is therefore pronounced ee-BAN-yez. In Appendix 1, see Pronunciation Note Four: The letter ñ.

at the main road, the beggar tried his luck a second time. Perhaps he had a poor memory for foreign faces.

When a white van responded to my outstretched thumb a few minutes later, I gratefully climbed in, placing my *mochila* in the rear next to a stack of boxes. The driver seemed rather young – at first glance I thought he should have been at school. He was delivering machine parts, but I never fully comprehended his explanation of what they were. As he drove, the boy told me about his *galgos*. That was not a word I recognised either, but over the course of the conversation it became apparent that they were probably greyhounds.

'Yes, they are *flacos*,' he confirmed, as I tentatively suggested distinguishing greyhound features, starting with skinny.

'Do they run quickly?' I tried, after which I wasn't sure whether to ask if these dogs were raced for betting by chasing an electric bunny around a track; such details don't necessarily transfer from one cultural setting to another. In spite of possessing reasonable spoken Spanish, I was unable to muster convincing translations for 'elongated muzzle' or 'double suspension rotary gallop', either of which might have helped.

The young driver with the mystery machine parts dropped me at a turning for an alternative route labelled '*Camino Turístico*': Tourist Road. After securing the straps around my tent, I started down the riverside track. It was an outstanding setting: long grasses on the verge, green pastures bathed in bright sunshine, tall mountains on all sides and a waterfall spraying from a nearby cliff. I walked through a clump of nose-tingling pine, beneath which stood a row of houses. One had a flock of black-fleeced *llamas* in the yard including a *cria*, a *llama*[13] lamb.

It was walking this stretch that the full horrific reality of the debilitating weight of my backpack began to dawn on me. Before long I sat to rest between foxgloves and fuchsia on the bank of the invitingly cool Río Aysén. Across the river, a troop of stocky birds scavenged in a field, slowly edging forward shoulder to shoulder like a team of police officers conducting a search. These noisy creatures were *bandurria*, the black-faced ibis. On stout red legs their sturdy bronze bodies were

---

[13] Following the same rule as *Villa*, the word *llama* is pronounced *YAA-ma*. See Pronunciation Note One: Double-L sounds. All pronunciation notes can be found in Appendix 1.

partially concealed beneath dull slate wings. Each one drilled in the soil for bugs and worms with a strong curved beak.

Once the short *Camino Turístico* came to an end, the main road divided at a junction known as Viviana: left for the northern part of the region and straight on for Coyhaique and the South. Unusually both directions were paved, for the first part at least. Once again I had little trouble getting a ride, another encouraging sign that hitchhiking in Patagonia might present no difficulties at all.

The bearded driver, Augustino, originated from Santiago but preferred to live in Coyhaique, 'away from the delinquents, drug addicts and thieves,' in his words. 'Down here,' he asserted, 'you can leave your door open and no-one will steal anything.'

I braced myself in the passenger seat as Augustino demonstrated the formidable speed his blue pickup could attain as the road twisted through the Simpson Valley. Part of the time we were even on the correct side of the white line.[14] It was with some relief that I spotted a sign for the waterfall Cascada de la Virgen.

I was travelling with two guidebooks. One was a Spanish-language booklet produced in Chile, and the other one was printed in English. The latter was so full of errors that it must surely have been written by someone who'd never actually visited the places described. Although the local book was more reliable, it was aimed primarily at motorists and repeatedly made suggestions only feasible by car. 'Drive up a track for six kilometres and you will see the entrance to a disused mine' – that kind of thing. No doubt each of these sites had its merits, but it simply wasn't practical for a hitchhiker to stop for them all. However, still green and uninitiated on this first day, I foolishly attempted to heed all the recommendations in the book to an unrealistic degree.

The Cascada de la Virgen was a simple waterfall in two steps. On the bank there was a shrine to the Mother of Jesus, surrounded by vases of artificial flowers and drips of melted candle wax. A messy mosaic of marble plaques inscribed with short prayers of thanks and devotion had been pasted to the cliff. I wasn't detained there long and soon regretted not having asked Augustino to wait. Fortunately there was another attraction listed nearby. A short walk back up the road was the entrance to the Reserva Nacional Río Simpson. Here, the

---

[14] The 'correct side' of the white line was the right. All territories within mainland America drive on the right side of the road, except Guyana and Suriname.

guidebook recommended viewing a *gigantesco tronco de mañío*, a giant mañío tree trunk, which had various events from the history of Chile marked against its 392 rings. Compared to the time an average office block stands, it was astounding how long this tree had lived. A noticeboard disputed the information in my book, stating that the trunk was not *mañío* after all but *lenga*, one of the many varieties of deciduous southern beech. The polished surface of the wood had been cut at an oblique angle, emphasising the rings. A label, pointing very nearly to the centre, indicated that the tree pre-dated 1578, the year that Francis Drake navigated the Aysén sea channels. Moving out, wider rings were labelled with various events of relevance to the region, some of which subsequently surfaced again during the journey.

1818 Chilean Declaration of Independence
1826 and **1833** Charles Darwin in Patagonia
1881 Boundary Treaty with Argentina
1940s Settlers clear millions of hectares
of Patagonian forest by fire

The *guardaparque* approached.
'What is there to see around here?' I asked him.
'Not much,' he replied with disarming honesty.
Still dutifully heeding the guidebook, I took a fourth ride only as far as the Cascada Velo de la Novia, the Bride's Veil Waterfall. Pushing through thick undergrowth, I emerged at the rim of a shallow plunge pool, where a family of six were soaking their feet in the cold water. With the wide falls crashing onto rocks, bright sunlight cast rainbows in the spray. Another couple appeared momentarily, long enough only for each to snap a hasty photograph before retreating along the overgrown path. People can be quite unsure how to respond to simplicity or quietness. Were they hoping for a gift shop?
The family left too, and I rested there in that peaceful place. The constant thundering of the *cascada* drowned out any sound from the road. The irregular cliff face trapped the warmth of the sun, and it was good to doze a while. I ventured around the perimeter of the pool, taking care on the slippery rocks, and drank from the falling water, becoming thoroughly soaked in the process. The tranquil experience was tainted only by my first encounter with *tábanos*, aggressive

horseflies with a nasty bite. A trio were determined to feast on my arms, but at this stage I gave them little thought, as yet unaware what a pest these creatures were to become.

Back at the road once again, I was picked up this time by a couple from Santiago, in Patagonia for a week's holiday. Having arrived to the region by air, they'd driven a hired 4x4 to Puyuhuapi and back, pre-booked in comfortable rooms every night, tackling the Carretera Austral in a refined way.

We caught our first glimpse of Coyhaique from high on a hill. The town swept across a wide plain far below at the foot of the impressive cliffs of Cerro MacKay, surrounded by fields and forests. Descending into the valley, the couple telephoned their agent to check the location of their hotel even though the hire car had Sat-Nav. The wife dialled the number and waited for a response. 'Just a moment,' she said into the handset, immediately passing it to her husband. Clearly, *la Señora* was not sufficiently qualified to make complicated enquiries like 'So, where is our hotel, then?'

*

On the northern perimeter of Coyhaique we finally arrived at the focal point of my minor quest: the army base of the *14º Regimiento Reforzado*. An octagonal gatehouse guarded the entrance, where the statue of an advancing infantryman was raised on a pedestal, but the barracks themselves were hidden from view behind tall trees. The 14th was established in 1948 as an Infantry Regiment. A signals (communications) division was added in 1999 and the current name dates from the 2003 incorporation of the 26th Infantry Regiment.

The couple dropped me outside and drove off to their hotel with a cheery wave. On the grassy verge beside the main gate sat two decommissioned vehicles. One was a Sherman tank, its short gun barrel pointing threateningly forward. The mechanism for turning its caterpillar tracks was open to view, all manner of interconnected cogs and cranks, heavy and robust. But the exhibit I'd particularly hoped to see was the other appliance. It had a driver's cab above its rear wheels, a long narrow frame arching forward to support the front axle, and a wide slightly concave steel blade slung below. A sign emphasised the significance of the contraption:

Esta máquina desarrolló su trabajo en la construcción de la Carretera Austral... colaborando... a la conquista de las fronteras interiores.

This machine worked on the construction of the Carretera Austral... collaborating... in the conquest of the internal frontiers.

The vehicle was a 1962 Austin-Western motor grader, an appliance used in road construction and maintenance, known either as a road scraper or simply an earth mover. Early versions of road scrapers were hauled by horses, the heavy blade set at an angle to level the ground. Later, the FC Austin Manufacturing Company and the Western Wheeled Scraper Company began to develop powered models at their factories in Chicago. The new vehicles, known as motor graders, were heavier and stronger than the horse-drawn variety and were further improved with the incorporation of two separately steerable axles. The Austin-Western name followed the eventual merger of the two companies.

The modern motor graders that subsequently became a common sight throughout my journey were all painted in road maintenance yellow. This one, like the tank, wore green combat livery. That this apparatus was displayed outside the barracks was a sign of the importance of the Chilean Army to the Carretera Austral. It was the engineers of the *Cuerpo Militar del Trabajo*, the 'Military Works Corps', who built the road. On the instruction of President Augusto Pinochet, the dictator whose military government ruled from 1973 to 1989, army engineers established a route around fjords, lakes and mountains, crossing marshland and torrential rivers, largely without the benefit of sophisticated technology. The terrain was smothered by virgin forest and two enormous fields of ice. Rain could be unrelenting at any time of year, and daytime temperatures regularly fell below freezing point.

Commencing in 1976, 10,000 army personnel dug, hacked and beat a path for 1247 kilometres of Carretera Austral and over 200 kilometres of side roads. With the help of 500 tonnes of explosives, they shifted 12 million cubic metres of earth and rock. Eleven workers lost their lives in the process. Though the Chaitén to Coyhaique section was open by 1982, it was not until 1996 that one of Chile's most audacious engineering projects was eventually completed, with a single lane of unpaved track unfurled from Puerto Montt to Puerto Yungay. The long and lonely connection to Villa O'Higgins subsequently opened in 2000, and the spur to Caleta Tortel in 2003.

This new highway connected the capital to northern Patagonia for the first time, and a proposed extension all the way to Puerto Natales would secure access to further territory of strategic importance. From the outset of planned settlement in the region, communications across the Andes into Argentina had always been more straightforward than those to north and south within Chile, an uncomfortable reality for politicians in Santiago. Compounding their unease, this was an era in which territorial ping-pong caused frequent stand-offs between the two countries, most notoriously the simmering tensions over a set of islands in the Beagle Channel, which spiralled perilously close to a military conflict in 1978.

Overland travel was a forbidding prospect for the early pioneers, involving long, uncomfortable hours in the saddle or days on end pounding mountain paths on foot. Even a journey between the two largest towns of the region, Coyhaique and Cochrane, required a lengthy crossing of the huge lake Lago General Carrera. An expedition like mine would have been unthinkable without the Dictator's Highway. Formerly named the Carretera General Augusto Pinochet, it is now known as the Carretera Austral or simply *Ruta 7*.

For residents of far-flung Patagonian communities, the impacts have penetrated considerably deeper than simply facilitating travel. The Carretera Austral has triggered the provision of services such as electricity, drinking water and sewers. It has contributed to rural health levels, enabling doctors to visit homes and residents to access clinics. It has enhanced opportunities for education, helping children attend school. It has provided new openings for commerce and has multiplied opportunities for tourism.

*

I found lodging at Hospedaje Marluz. The owner, Nomi, led me upstairs, shouting a warning just in time about the low beams. She showed me into a small square room with freshly painted cream walls and recently varnished floorboards. A metal-framed bed along one wall had a cover with a cheerful design of large rectangles in green, white and pink. The window had been pushed open, and a breeze lifted the nets momentarily, revealing a mechanic's workshop next door. I rested my *mochila* on the floor and sat on the edge of the bed, my feet on a fleecy rug. The room was perfectly adequate for a couple of nights, so long as I remembered to stoop when passing through the doorway.

I ate that evening at the *Casino de Bomberos*. It wasn't a venue for roulette and black jack; *casino* in this context means 'dining room'. The *bomberos*[15] are fire fighters. This is a volunteer force in Chile, where it is common to see uniformed officers shaking collection tins. The *bomberos* in Coyhaique supplemented their funds with a restaurant that operated inside the fire station premises, and Nomi had recommended their excellent food.

As I tucked into a bowl of *pastel de jaiba*, a delicious crab dish, the sole waitress dealt patiently with a table of six smartly apparelled North Americans. The three men carried on an over-dramatized conversation about fly fishing, seemingly the reason for their visit to the area, whilst the women exchanged sympathetic looks. Only one had any Spanish and she loosely interpreted the menu for her five friends. I later caught snatches of her apologetic comments.

'Oh, I'm so sorry,' she said, as her neighbour's plate was delivered, 'it's not avocado after all. It appears to be a sauce with capers.' And later, on commencing her main course, 'I have news for you,' she announced, 'this is not gammon; I think it must be trout.'

*

Castellano

To be absolutely precise, 'Spanish' is not the correct name for the language. Spanish, like British, is a nationality. The language sometimes referred to as Spanish is more accurately called Castilian or *castellano*.

Several native languages are spoken in Spain. Over the centuries, *castellano*, which originated in the large central region known as Castile, became dominant. However, it is not the only native language spoken in Spain. Even today, one in ten of the population have a maternal language of Catalan, Galician or Basque, with smaller numbers keeping other regional languages alive.

---

[15] The word *bombero*, fire fighter, is derived from *bomba*, meaning pump. A *bomba* can also be a fire station or petrol station.

> The linguistic complexity of Spain is not unusual. Even discounting modern patterns of immigration, many countries worldwide have mixed populations of various native tongues. Even in Great Britain, linguistically dominated by English, there are also those whose native tongue is Welsh, Scots, Scottish Gaelic or Cornish.
>
> *Castellano* has 400 million native speakers, more than any other language on Earth except Chinese Mandarin, and is an official language in 20 countries, most of which are in Latin America. In Chile, a number of native languages are also in use including Mapudungun (the Mapuche language), Aymara, Quechua and Rapa Nui.
>
> Students who have learned 'Spanish for Spain' often take time to adjust to 'Spanish for Latin America'. It can be difficult to become accustomed to the confusing variations across Latin America, and the many differences between there and Spain, which complicate pronunciation, grammar and vocabulary.

*

I woke to the dull chimes of a church clock. In place of a window, the downstairs shower room had a gaping hole in the wall, beyond which there were chickens pecking in the dusty yard. That morning I was able to supplement the guest house breakfast of bread, cheese and jam with a mug of very fine tea. A friend had kindly given me a luxury box of Fortnum & Mason Countess Grey to cheer me on cold Patagonian mornings. One other guest shared the large dining room table. Paloma, from Villa O'Higgins, was in Coyhaique to register for a degree course in Diet and Nutrition.

'What's that about?' I asked.

'They teach us how to turn fat people into thin people,' she bluntly replied, adding extravagant animations to ensure I understood.

I carefully kept my counsel, the reason being an unfortunate recent personal discovery. A former friend had pointed out, and a set of bathroom scales had confirmed, that I'd unwittingly been stashing away a glut of surplus bodily kilogrammes. To my distress, I had graduated to a bulkier-than-ideal category on those height-weight charts you see in doctors' surgery waiting rooms and in vanity magazines. Having always been the lanky kid at school, this news had come as quite a shock. In order to dispense with a few of those charlatan kilos, I'd made a commitment to a regime of nutritional restraint, and to this end was permitting myself one solitary cooked meal per day.

Although she was completing the registration paperwork in Coyhaique, the university was actually located in distant Santiago. Travelling away from home for education would not be new to Paloma. She'd already lived in Coyhaique for her four years of secondary education, she explained, since Villa O'Higgins only had a primary school.

'There are loads of us like this,' she told me. 'You have to leave home when you start secondary school. You can't even go back for a weekend; it's too far. I only saw my family twice each year: for the short winter holiday and in the summer.'

It was to Paloma's hometown of Villa O'Higgins that I was headed next. Having flown to Puerto Montt, sailed to Puerto Chacabuco and hitchhiked to Coyhaique, the following day I would complete the final leg of my outward journey to the furthest point of the Carretera Austral.

Image 03: Motor grader at Coyhaique army base

Map 02: Villa O'Higgins

Three: Tsonek

Aside from a pilgrimage to the barracks of the *14° Regimiento Reforzado*, the principal reason for visiting Coyhaique was to present myself at the desk of Transportes Aéreos[16] Don Carlos. Amongst diverse Patagonian routes offered by this small private airline was one connecting the regional capital to Villa O'Higgins. At the office just off the *plaza de armas*, the town square, I was furnished with two salient pieces of information. First, rather disappointingly, I was reminded how reckless it would be to take bottles of camping gas on a plane. Although this familiar regulation routinely applies on passenger jets, I'd imagined the rule might be more relaxed for a lower-altitude flight. But no: '*Es altamente peligroso, señor,*' the Don Carlos clerk spat: highly dangerous.

The second useful morsel was the maximum baggage allowance: just ten kilogrammes per passenger. When I'd telephoned some weeks earlier to ask specifically about this, the only guidance I'd received was 'make sure your bag isn't too big'. Now it transpired that 'not too big' actually meant that a charge would apply to anything over ten kilogrammes. Although the printed ticket stated 15kg, the assistant struck a neat line through it and wrote '10kg' by hand. That must have been the penalty for asking naïve questions about flying with gas bottles.

In view of the remote location of Villa O'Higgins, discovering the small planes of Transportes Aéreos Don Carlos had been an unexpected bonus. Regular passenger services with the principal Chilean airlines, Lan and Sky, flew only as close as Coyhaique or

---

[16] *Aéreos*. Say all the vowels separately: a-AIR-ay-os. All pronunciation notes are in Appendix 1. This one is Pronunciation Note Five.

Puerto Natales. Coyhaique was 600 kilometres north by road and ferry and Puerto Natales a similar distance south, but Don Carlos could deliver me directly to the village.

'How frequently do you fly into Villa O'Higgins during the summer?' I'd asked them by telephone.

'Twice each week. But there's only room for four passenger in the plane.'

'Can I reserve a ticket?'

'Not really. The route is subsidised for the benefit of villagers, not tourists.'

'Is there sometimes an extra seat?'

'We don't plan very far in advance, because the subsidy comes from the national government on a month-by-month basis. Your best bet would be to contact us at the end of December to ask if we have any spaces left on the January flights.'

I did, and there was: one place. As long as I could get to Coyhaique, I had a passage to Villa O'Higgins. One good reason for starting there and not at the northern end of the road was to benefit from a better climate. It is difficult to predict how much the weather might deteriorate by late February, which is the latter part of the short Patagonian summer. Given the choice, it was probably preferable to move away from the extreme south before autumn came.

I began an urgent reappraisal of my kit, discarding all but the essentials. In truth the weight limit was probably a blessing in disguise. How many t-shirts did I really need, and how many pairs of socks? Which was more important: a torch or a multifunction tool; a camera or binoculars; a novel or a notebook; a scarf or a woolly hat? Did I need sandals as well as leather walking shoes? Could I manage without my warm fleece? Nomi kindly offered to store my rejected bits and pieces at Hospedaje Marluz until I passed through Coyhaique a second time, later in the trip. My tent alone was over four kilogrammes so I was never going to make it, but wishing I'd been more ruthless before leaving Santiago, I eliminated as much as I dared.

*

Coyhaique had been a useful stepping stone, a base camp for the approaching expedition. By far the largest town in the region, it had modern comforts that were harder to find elsewhere. There were restaurants, plentiful options for accommodation and several shops. In the countryside around the town, various destinations probably merited further exploration, but other than the barracks with their green Austin-Western motor grader, these could wait. Given that the Carretera Austral had Coyhaique at its midpoint, I was due to return here after two or three weeks on the road.

I strolled into town that evening for a valedictory meal, a gastronomic send-off to start the adventure. With commendable foresight I'd consumed only fruit for lunch, permitting me an evening feast. I don't enjoy solitary dining: jovial restaurant groups can be a sharp reminder of one's aloneness, and even entering the room unaccompanied can be surprisingly awkward. As I paced the town centre streets that evening, bypassing what must have been half the restaurants in Coyhaique, I couldn't find a suitable place. They were too touristy or too local, too expensive or too cheap, too fancy or too simple… but finally I spotted a place called El Duendecito de la EME, the meaning of which I'm still uncertain. Inside, there was cheerful music playing, a welcome from friendly apricot t-shirted staff and a pizza oven fired up and eager for action.

I took a table, '¿para una persona, señor?' and selected the *Rodizio de Pizzas*, the all-you-can-eat buffet. A succession of waiters circulated, proffering platters stacked with piping hot slices of every conceivable variety: pizza with mushroom and *chorizo*, pizza with bacon and caramelised onion, with chicken and *merkén*, with salmon, a Mexican pizza topped with nachos and guacamole, and more. There followed two types of *pizza dulce*, sweet pizza. One was a crepe with chocolate sauce on a sweet base and the other, more conventionally coloured for a pizza, was topped with jam, gratings of white chocolate and peach segments. I halted at fifteen tasty slices. Sixteen would have been equivalent to two whole pizzas, but given that I was eating for lunch as well as dinner, my regime cannot have been compromised too gravely. Moreover, the next day I was heading into wild and desolate country, and it would have been reckless to start out undernourished. In any case, what is the point of all-you-can-eat if you don't eat all that you can?

*

> **Merkén**
>
> A popular seasoning in Chile, *merkén* is a spice long used by the indigenous *Mapuche* people. It is made from *ají cacho de cabra*, the goat's horn chilli pepper, which is smoked, dried, and mixed with cumin and coriander seeds. It is highly *picante* and very tasty.

*

Despite efforts to economise, my *mochila* was well over the limit. As I heaved the rucksack onto a huge set of scales on the morning of the flight, I waited nervously to see how much the excess would eat into my miserly travelling budget. In the event it wasn't much: just 3500 *pesos*, approximately seven US dollars. I was directed to a van waiting outside, loaded with boxes and packages, where another three passengers waited.

The first hand I shook belonged to a man whose accent was a struggle to interpret. He was returning to his home in Villa O'Higgins, I gathered, but any details beyond that were lost in a muddle of rapid consonants. The second man was an immigration official working on Lago O'Higgins, an immense lake[17] extending for 1000 square kilometres within several connected valleys. Locals told me it was shaped like a hand, with five linear once-glaciated valleys forming the extended fingers. Villa O'Higgins was located at the tip of one finger.

'The *frontera* passes through the lake,' the officer explained. 'We monitor Chilean waters, and there are Argentine patrols on their side. They call it Lago San Martín.'

'So you have to stay there overnight?' I guessed. 'How long is each shift? One week? Two weeks?'

'Fifty days. We work fifty days in a row and then have ten days off'.

Travelling to and fro was such a protracted undertaking that shorter shifts would have been inefficient, he said. As a consequence, this man saw his family in Coyhaique for only seven days in every two months.

The third passenger was Luci, who sounded North American. How had she got herself on a flight for residents?

---

[17] England's largest, Lake Windermere, covers just 15 square kilometres.

'I work at an ecocamp in Villa O'Higgins,' she volunteered. 'We have plenty of space for camping; you'd be welcome.'

The idea was appealing in theory, but something held me back. Preferring to keep my options open, I muttered a non-committal response and angled for more detail.

'As much as possible is built from recycled material,' she offered eagerly.

In my mind I saw tepees crafted from discarded fertiliser sacks glued together with dung and supported on pillars of rusty oil drums.

'And we have composting dry toilets.'

I was not yet persuaded.

The four of us climbed into the van along with a man who, it later transpired, was the pilot. We drove to a small *aeródromo* at the edge of the town, where we sped along the runway before stopping outside a pair of hangars. The tall, heavy doors shuddered aside to reveal a small white aircraft. Two stripes, red and gold, emphasised the elegant form of the plane's streamlined fuselage, and bold red characters spelt out the words Aerotaxis del Sur.

I looked around for the ground crew. Ah – of course, *we* were to be both ground crew and baggage handlers. So we set to unloading the van and packed boxes and bags into the plane as directed by the pilot. Hatch covers lifted to reveal a variety of storage spaces, from a long locker near the tail to a secret cubbyhole in the nose. My *mochila* was stuffed into a nook in front of the pilot's feet. Having loaded up, we pushed the plane out of the hangar. Sunshine glinted off her windows, and the wheels crunched over the gravel.

In turn, each of us climbed aboard over the wing and sat where instructed. As the smallest, the Villa O'Higgins resident was selected to sit alone in the narrowing rear of the cabin. The official shared the front seat with the pilot, a decision that, I suspect, owed as much to the weight of his authority as to that of his body. That left two foreigners on the middle bench: I was on the left, with Luci alongside.

The engine squealed excitedly, and our twin propellers span into a blur. Donning a headset, the pilot began a routine of checks against the dials, conversing over the radio with a controller somewhere. We began to crawl forward. Our little craft bumped onto the asphalt runway, paused, accelerated, and rose above the Patagonian countryside. Flying almost due south, we climbed towards the magnificent form of Cerro Castillo whose dark, jagged, frost-shattered peaks grew large through the front windscreen. Ice and snow lay in depressions between razor-sharp ridges of rock. The plane's trajectory barely cleared the mountain, close enough, it seemed, to reach down and scratch in the dust with a stick. Passing the craggy summit, our tiny cabin rolled sickeningly to the left – whether by pilot choice or due to a gust of wind wasn't clear – and the wingtip dipped alarmingly close to the lip of the pass.

Our seats in the sky commanded a stunning view: pastel pastures, sprawling forests that from such a height resembled a covering of moss, mountain slopes in varied shades of brick and basalt, peaks topped with Royal icing, timeless glaciers and turquoise lakes. All this was set against a cobalt sky flecked with wisps of cloud. Barely perceptible, a sandy trail snaked through the valleys: the Carretera Austral. When the altimeter needle held still at 11,000 feet (3350 metres) the peaks were passing beside us, not below. In the absence of a pressurised cabin, our breathing was slightly laboured, but I suspect the cylinder of camping gas would probably have been fine.

The largest of many lakes was the vast acreage of Lago General Carrera, part Chilean and part Argentine. Another feature straddling the border was the bulky mass of Monte San Lorenzo. The colossal mountain's multiple summits were thick with unblemished snow. Unrelenting winds had folded a layer into a leering cornice along the ridge, and disturbed mounds beneath were evidence of earlier avalanches. The huge glacier Ventisquero Calluqueo clung to the mountain's Chilean face, its surface cracked into ridges and ruts and etched with rust-coloured debris in precise parallel curves. Virtually lost amidst the mountain wilderness was a tiny grid of streets: the town of Cochrane.

Clouds began to accumulate. Scattered summits became conical islands in a grey sea. How would the pilot manage to land safely? How would he know where to find valleys and in which places the mist concealed solid and unforgiving mountain walls? Happily, his clairvoyance was not put to the test. A gap opened up, and we banked to dive through, ears popping with the rapid descent. Straight ahead was the Río Mayer, flowing into the northeast finger of Lago

O'Higgins. We passed low over the airfield, and swooped round in a steep, dramatic about-turn. Finally, our pilot returned us skilfully and softly onto the ground, bringing to a close a breathtaking flight.

*

O'Higgins may not seem an obvious name for a Chilean lake and village. Nonetheless, this moniker appears everywhere. Streets, buildings and parks throughout the country are named after Bernardo O'Higgins Riquelme,[18] an independence hero. Bernardo was born in 1778 in a town called Chillán, 400 kilometres south of Santiago, to the unmarried pairing of Ambrosio O'Higgins and Isabel Riquelme. Ambrosio was a Spanish military officer of Irish descent who later became Viceroy of Peru.[19] Since Isabel was 40 years his junior, the coupling might not have served the aspirations of her wealthy family. Or perhaps it was just a holiday fling.

Following early childhood in Chillán, Bernardo attended school in Lima before continuing his education in London. Accordingly, there is a monument to Bernardo O'Higgins beside the Thames at Richmond Bridge. There in the British capital, he learned about campaigns for independence in the United States and met others who harboured similar desires for Latin America.

O'Higgins became a central figure in the struggle against Spain. Independence was declared twice. The first occasion was on 18

---

[18] As is common in the Hispanosphere, Chilean people tend to inherit two *apellidos* or surnames, one from each parent. Bernardo O'Higgins Riquelme, for example, has O'Higgins from his father and Riquelme from his mother. He is generally known simply as Bernardo O'Higgins, but writing his name as Bernardo O'Higgins R. is also correct.

As another example, the full name of Chilean tennis player Marcelo Rios, the first Latin American to top the ATP world rankings, is Marcelo Andrés Ríos Mayorga. Marcelo and Andrés are his forenames whereas Ríos and Mayorga are his paternal and maternal *apellidos*. The full name of Chile's first female president Michelle Bachelet is Verónica Michelle Bachelet Jeria. Chilean women do not take their husband's name at marriage, but instead stick with their birth surnames throughout life. Some women may like this idea but it's not as gender-equal as it first sounds. A daughter will inherit one *apellido* each from her mother and father but which one? It is the grandfather's paternal surname in both cases. Although a woman's *apellido* survives her by one generation it is her father's surname that endures, and not the maternal name.

[19] 'Peru' in this context was a larger territory than the modern country of the same name. Administrative structures in Spanish-controlled South America evolved throughout the colonial period. At the time of Ambrosio O'Higgins, the Viceroyalty of Peru included modern Peru plus regions that now lie within the borders of Chile, Bolivia, Argentina and Brazil.

September 1810, when the Government Junta of Chile unilaterally announced that the country would cease to be a colony of Spain, claiming a new status as an autonomous republic under the Spanish monarchy. There followed seven years of war, through which O'Higgins rose in prestige and power. His leadership qualities and military tactics are both subject to debate, but he is said to have won Chilean hearts with charisma, enthusiasm and bravery. In 1817 he became Supreme Director of the country and was instrumental the following year in establishing the new independent republic.

The earlier date is retained as the National Day, known as the *dieciocho*. Therefore, Chile celebrated a second century as an independent nation on 18 September 2010. A year of festivities began in tragedy with the central regions rocked by a massive earthquake in February. In contrast, October the same year saw widespread euphoria for the rescue of 33 miners trapped underground at the San José mine in the north of the country. The bicentenary arrived during the course of their ten-week ordeal. That day, *Los 33* raised a Chilean flag, sang the exceedingly rousing and rather lengthy national anthem and danced the traditional *cueca*.[20]

For his role in winning independence, the name of Bernardo O'Higgins is greatly honoured in Chile. The principal street through the centre of Santiago bears the title Avenida Libertador General Bernardo O'Higgins. There are further O'Higgins streets in many towns. His statue is displayed in plazas the length of the country. The Chilean research base in Antarctica and various ships of the *Armada* have been named after him. And in Patagonia, within Parque Nacional O'Higgins, a lake, a glacier and a *pueblo* are all named in his honour.

*

This time there were baggage handlers to receive us. Or rather, the three other passengers all had friends meeting them, who pulled bags and boxes from the plane and transferred them to waiting vehicles. Luci was greeted by Mauricio, who'd arrived in his veteran Land Rover. He offered me a ride too, and in a moment of uncharacteristic decisiveness, I climbed into the back of the vehicle. We exited the airfield directly onto the principal road, the only road really, and

---

[20] The *cueca* is described in Chapter 5.

located *Tsonek* ecocamp just outside the village to the north. After reversing the vehicle off the gravel road, Mauricio led us on foot up uneven stone steps to a path through the trees.

He was young, mid-thirties I would imagine, and was long-haired and bearded as any self-respecting forest dweller should be. Originally from Talca, he had purchased a hectare of woodland from a *gaucho*, a Patagonian cattle herder or cowboy. There was a small shack at the entrance, and a larger communal kitchen, more recently completed, was located further along the narrow path. Its walls were made of planks stood upright with one end buried in the soil, attractively arranged with bark on the outside to mimic the appearance of a log cabin.

'We didn't fell any trees,' Mauricio explained. 'Everything here was built using material from the forest floor, and with waste scavenged from other construction projects in the town. I've been out begging quite a lot!'

He had procured some fortuitous discards: large chipboard sheets for the floor, plastic panels for the roof and panes of glass of varying dimensions to glaze the windows on three sides. There were shelves, a sink and a table, purportedly all fashioned according to the same rules of 'forest floor or recycled', and an *estufa* or log-burning stove. A cylinder set above supplied hot water to both the kitchen tap and a shower room behind a dividing wall.

'How long have you lived here?' I asked Mauricio.

'I bought the land three years ago. I've stayed here most of that time, all year round. I began under canvas and then built the cabin at the entrance. But Luci sleeps there now, so I'm back in a tent.'

'And when did you open as an ecocamp?'

'Only this week. Just a few days ago we had our first guest.'

Around the site were a number of platforms on which to stand tents. Preferring soil to hard planks, I cleared twigs and stones from a patch of ground and pitched my tent there. Then it was time to try the dry toilets. Mauricio had already mentioned them a number of times and it was with conspicuous pride that he led me to the block of three cubicles and ceremoniously opened the door. Empty bottles of green, brown and clear glass were set into mud walls, allowing light through. Each of the three toilets comprised a plastic seat mounted on a frame above a metal drum. There was a funnel to channel liquids away and a bucket of woodchips to sprinkle over anything else I might have the urge to deposit. I was relieved, not only by using the seat for the necessary duration, but also from the knowledge that it wasn't my role to empty the drums.

*

On one side of Villa O'Higgins, through a smart arched gateway and across a narrow field in which a horse nibbled at the short grass, a long set of steps climbed to a hillside *mirador*, a view point. From the elevated position of the covered platform, it was possible to see the whole village, arranged in regular square blocks beside the airfield. The older part, begun in the late 1960s, had small houses in a style typical of rural Chile: colourfully painted metal sheets pinned to a timber frame, three or four rooms inside, floors raised above the dirt on short pillars, and a corrugated metal roof with a chimney spewing smoke from a stove within. Another block had more recent construction: fifteen identical dwellings in blue and burgundy. It looked like a West Ham United supporters' convention. In the next block, another development was underway, this time with walls of egg-yolk yellow. These bungalows were the most substantial of all – the design even incorporated wall insulation – but on the negative side the occupants were going to need sunglasses whenever they looked at their houses.

One of the streets was being paved. Most others had a surface of sand and dirt, and the occasional vehicles raised dust that blew into clouds, depositing a thin layer on windows, roofs and sills and even on garden plants. Beyond the town, the black strip of the runway baked in the afternoon sun. An aircraft materialised from the northern sky, banked over the river mouth as we had done and touched down. Two planes in one day: a busy time at Aeródromo Villa O'Higgins.

The *plaza de armas* in the village centre took up a whole block. Although this was a habitually rainy place, the square was yellow with parched grass and brittle vegetation. Another block was dominated by the modern primary school, the charmingly named Escuela G-47, with its green steel frame and matching roof. This must have been the school that Paloma, the soon-to-be nutrition student I'd met in Coyhaique, had attended as a child. The teachers, all from outside the region, were paid an additional bonus for living and working in these outlying parts. Although the supplement must have been welcome, the regular salary in a Chilean government school wasn't hugely motivating to start with. In the neighbouring block was a large gymnasium with a striking blue roof, and a church and museum shared another plot nearby.

So this was Villa O'Higgins, the end of the Carretera Austral. In terms of my adventure, this was not the end at all, but the beginning. From this tiny village, I would start my northward journey, a thousand kilometres and more, all the way to Puerto Montt.

A diminutive blonde appeared at the *mirador*, out of breath from the many steps. She settled herself at the opposite end of my bench and fired off a rapid volley of questions: who was I, from where, why was I here, how long had I lived in Chile...? Responding with similar enquiries, I gathered only that this lady was Quebecois. Before there was a chance to delve any further, raucous voices and heavy footsteps carried from the walkway below. A gang of six leather-wrapped bikers stomped onto the platform. They were from various parts of Chile – Santiago, Valparaiso, San Pedro de Atacama – and their group membership had enlarged as they'd met along the road. Miss Quebec became somewhat distracted – one gentleman in particular afforded her devoted attention.

'You don't see much scenery,' the handsome biker told her. 'You have to watch the road the whole time. It's easy to slide off where the gravel is deep and loose.'

'It's a long journey, too,' added another. 'Hundreds of kilometres. And it's quite slow; we rarely get above 40 kilometres per hour. I've spent my whole holiday in the saddle.'

'Can you carry two on your bike?' asked Miss Quebec.

'Not really,' said the handsome one. 'With all my gear, there's not much room for a passenger. But Mario could probably take you with him,' he added, indicating one of the group who hadn't yet spoken.

'Yes, Mario will make space for you,' the others agreed readily, and a contagious laughter spread quickly amongst them. The unfortunate friend who'd been singled out smiled awkwardly, shaking his head, before turning away to the valley view.

A third plane landed. It was much busier than I'd imagined possible, that airfield.

'My ex-husband had a bike,' said Miss Quebec, 'a Harley Davison,' but they were no longer paying attention. Instead, they had become embroiled in a lively discussion about *cordero*, Patagonian lamb, and more specifically how they could acquire one.

'Eighty thousand *pesos* is far too much,' one of them complained. 'We are just six people. How can we eat a whole sheep?'

'I've spent more on fuel than I'd anticipated,' added Mario, piping up at last. 'A tank of *gasolina* costs much more here than in the rest of Chile. I'd rather eat cheaply and spend the money on beer.'

'There's nothing to do here,' another complained.

The next day, they rode 220 kilometres back to Cochrane.

Searching for provisions later, I located a bakery and three grocery stores dotted around in various streets. Stacked next to a basket of shrink-wrapped horseshoes were canisters of camping gas, but not being of a resealing design, they didn't suit my stove.

One of the blocks at the edge of the village was dominated by Hostal El Mosco, a substantial timber building. Judging by the number of bikes and tents in the yard, El Mosco was the accommodation of preference for many of the cyclists who tackle the Carretera Austral. Opposite was the Robinson Crusoe Lodge, recently opened, from which Mauricio had scavenged building materials. Gleaming white and with opulent black-framed double-glazed windows, this was the exclusive alternative for tour groups with organised itineraries and those preferring a certain standard of comfort. The guests going in and out, most of them sporting the latest breathable and wind-resistant trekking gear, had the contented air of people with reliable access to soft pillows, hot showers and three-course dinners.

Such comforts as these were going to be hard to come by on the six-week trek ahead, but if the first day was anything to judge by, it seemed there would be no shortage of company. Still without gas, I resorted to cooking on the *estufa* that evening, pasta in tomato sauce and a lump of cheese providing a lingering connection with the rapidly fading familiar world.

Image 04: Chilean Patagonia from the air

The writing in the lower right corner
is on the inside of the aircraft window.

Four: Los Chicos

Of Mauricio's ten brothers, eight still dwelled in their hometown, Talca. Just one, Enrique, had joined him at Tsonek. With construction of the kitchen completed, Enrique spent his days on maintenance and improvements. In common with his brother, Enrique was placid and unassuming, but other than a shared slim build there was not much in their physical appearance to suggest a family connection. Twenty years senior, Enrique lacked his younger brother's height and wore his hair short with a greying beard. Also, whereas Mauricio was conversant in English, Enrique's rare and measured discourses came only in *castellano*.

'I became tired of the city,' he announced that evening after dinner. 'I prefer it here. Life in Patagonia is so much less complicated.'

That was easy to believe. Arriving in Villa O'Higgins had been like stepping into a different century. It was a world away from Santiago with its high rise apartment blocks, underground car parks, multi-lane highways clogged with bendy buses, traffic lights, advertising billboards spreading like a rash, the spider's web of cables slung across every intersection, a pharmacy on the corner of every block, department stores, hypermarkets... Santiago was not dissimilar to modern cities the world over, aside from a phenomenon known as *café con piernas*, coffee with legs, which it is probably best to set aside without further discussion.

The key difference wasn't the absence in Villa O'Higgins of these luxuries and conveniences. The real distinction between the two places was not anything concrete and visible. It had less to do with physical infrastructure and municipal provision but instead related to what took place inside people, within soul or psyche or spirit. For sure, there was less going on in Villa O'Higgins than in a city of seven million, but what seemed more significant in this remote outpost were the differences in approach and values. Santiago had momentum, materialism, a competitive edge, self-indulgence and a hint of aggression. Villa O'Higgins was contented, peaceful, plain, and unpretentious.

It was this step-change in attitude that required the newcomer to adjust, not the lack of internet access or the non-existent fast-food joints. Surviving in a place like Patagonia involved thinking and acting differently. It meant making fewer demands, having fewer preconceptions and preoccupations, choosing to be adaptable and flexible, and remaining calmer and less highly strung. Since these were internal changes that took time to ripen, the backpacking foreigner plucked straight from the city was unavoidably conspicuous. We are coloured by the dye in which we most regularly bathe, and it would take more than a short while to rinse it out. For example, however much I understood the appeal of the slow pace, the serenity and the calm, the impulse to achieve and get things done arose repeatedly. I'd climbed to the *mirador* so what was next? Where could I go? What could I see?

Arbitrary goals like these appeared not to be priorities for Enrique. Whatever he did, whether sweeping the path with a palm frond, chopping firewood or washing the windows, he was never hurried. Whatever could be achieved, that would be done. There was little point in feeling guilty about anything that remained unfinished; whatever it was could wait. It wasn't about being lazy; neither Mauricio nor Enrique could be described as idle, but both had learned a more measured rhythm.

'Take our diet,' Enrique continued. 'I never have to think about what to cook. We just eat whatever is available.'

'For example?' I probed. 'What kind of meals do you usually have?'

He pointed to the empty dish on the table in front of him. 'Most days we eat pasta. They always have pasta at the *almacén*,' the grocery store. 'Vegetables are more difficult to find. Recently the *pueblo* ran out of potatoes, too. That was a difficult week.'

'Are the vegetables grown locally?'

'Not many. The climate is difficult here for agriculture and the ground is very rocky, but along the river are a collection of smallholdings called Las Chacras. We buy fresh foods there, but only in season, of course. Most food products are delivered from Coyhaique. When the truck arrives, some villagers run to the shops and start queuing. They're always the same ones; you know who'll be at the front of the line. They take the best pieces and by the time I get there, quite often only the bruised or damaged produce is left.'

'What about meat?' I asked. 'Where do you buy meat?'

'There's no *carnicería*,' he explained. 'The *gauchos* sell *cordero* but you have to buy the whole lamb. Sometimes you can get a half or a quarter but nothing smaller than that.'

On another occasion, Enrique showed me their eco-bricks: plastic bottles filled with discarded wrappers and packets, pressed in tightly through the unscrewed top. There were only a few; not yet sufficient to build with.

'We have solar lanterns and lights,' he explained, in keeping with the environmental theme. 'Also, we smoke roll-ups so there is no waste.' Then he, too, boasted about their dry toilets. It must have been a family obsession. Perhaps toilets were very wet back in Talca.

*

The Campo de Hielo Sur

The Campo de Hielo Sur or Southern Ice Field is an enormous elongated lump of ice up to a kilometre thick, whose northern tip is not far west of Villa O'Higgins. Imagine donning a pair of ice skates in Middlesbrough and setting off south. If the Campo de Hielo Sur was laid on top of England, you would be able to skate all the way to London. In reality you wouldn't get very far as the surface is rutted with crevasses and ridges.

Eighteen thousand years ago, the Patagonian Ice Sheet extended across 400,000 km^2 (that's larger than Germany), covering the whole of southern Chile and encroaching across the Andes into Argentina. The ice has since retreated and diminished until today there are two separate ice fields. The Campo de Hielo Sur has an area of 13,000 km^2 and its smaller sister, the Campo de Hielo Norte, covers 4000 km^2. The two pieces are a mere fraction of the former vast sheet but they still rank among the most extensive unbroken areas of ice in the world.

> Strictly speaking, these are ice fields and not ice sheets. The area must exceed 50,000 km² to qualify as an ice sheet. In the present day, continental ice sheets of such enormous dimensions exist only in Greenland and Antarctica.

*

Mauricio and I drove several kilometres along the lake to a *muelle*, a tiny quay named Puerto Bahamondez. His idea was to coincide with the evening ferry in the hope that it might bring backpackers needing accommodation. His self-belief was commendable, particularly in view of the rather basic facilities he had to offer. We passed alongside the smallholdings at Las Chacras and crossed an impressive suspension bridge. A single-lane vehicle deck hung from chunky cables slung over tall H-shaped steel towers. Beyond, work had begun to widen the unpaved road that squeezed between the lake shore and a tall cliff, the rock being blasted with explosives and the resulting debris being stacked up to reinforce the lower bank.

Adjacent to the dock was a steep track that led to a hydroelectric station. This small facility has been the sole source of electrical power for Villa O'Higgins since the turbines were switched on in 1983, seventeen years after the village was founded.

'I wish the residents had built it themselves,' Mauricio admitted. 'We could all have benefited from cheap renewable electricity. As it is, villagers here pay a high price for power, more than it costs elsewhere in Chile.'

Through the open gate, a dilapidated staircase climbed to the baby reservoir, confined within a narrow creek only a few metres across. Rather spookily, somewhere beneath there must have been a giant plughole. The green outlet pipe was narrow, only 40 centimetres in diameter or thereabouts. The pipe descended the creek to a squat stone building where it divided in two. Both halves penetrated the exterior wall of the station to feed a pair of bright yellow turbines. Water gushed from both of these into the lake.

Across the open water, the compact blue-and-white passenger craft emerged from behind the nearest headland, so we hurried down the steep track to the *muelle*. Moments later, with a crunching of wheels on loose stones, a plush bus from the Robinson Crusoe Lodge followed us into the small parking area and blocked the exit.

The ferry tied up at the low concrete quay. Her name, the *Quetru*, was written in capital letters on her blue fibreglass hull, in honour of the magnificently named Magellanic flightless steamer-duck, which is native to this part of Chile. Not unlike the heavily built duck, the boat was short and fat, 20 metres from bow to stern and a 5-metre beam combining to give it a stubby appearance rather like an ice-breaker. Behind slanted windows was a comfortable cabin with several rows of cushioned seats. The upper deck was completely open, and must have afforded great views.

In addition to shuttling passengers across Lago O'Higgins, most ferry sailings also visited a western finger of the lake to see Ventisquero O'Higgins. This glacier, descending from the Campo de Hielo Sur, is an enormous 45 kilometres in length, and the snout is 3000 metres wide. This pale blue wall of ice rises 80 metres above the surface of the lake but vastly more lurks beneath. With the lake bed fully 800 metres below, Lago O'Higgins is believed to be the deepest in the Americas.[21] If multiple copies of London's Gherkin were sunk into this depth, four would disappear without trace and only twenty-or-so floors of the fifth would be visible. Alternatively, this depth would easily swallow two Eiffel Towers or two Empire State Buildings and very nearly three London Bridge Shards. Even the ridiculously tall Burj Khalifa in Dubai would be fully submerged.[22]

Two sets of backpackers trudged along the gangplank. A trio of French tourists togged up in colourful Gore-Tex fussed aboard the Robinson Crusoe bus. Behind them, gathered around a map and looking bewildered, were four young *chicos*.[23] Seizing his opportunity,

---

[21] Only three freshwater lakes anywhere in the world are thought to go deeper than Lago O'Higgins: Lake Vostok (900m), a sub-glacial lake in Antarctica; Lake Tanganyika (1470m) in the East African Rift Valley; and Lake Baikal (1637m), another rift valley lake located in Siberia, nearly twice the depth of Lago O'Higgins (836m). This list refers to the maximum known depths of the lakes, whereas calculating the average depth of each one produces a different list.

[22] Lago O'Higgins depth 836m. Burj Khalifa (1 Mohammed Bin Rashid Boulevard, Dubai) height 829.8m. Empire State Building (350 Fifth Avenue, New York) height 381m. Eiffel Tower (Champ de Mars, 5 Avenue Anatole France, Paris) height 324m. Shard (32 London Bridge Street, London, SE1 9SG) height 306m. Gherkin (30 St Mary Axe, London, EC3A 8EP) height 180m.

[23] *Chico* usually refers to a young person or teenager, although the expression is widely

Mauricio lured them into his Land Rover with the promise of hot showers and comfortable wooden platforms. They were students from Santiago's Universidad Católica, three boys and a girl.

'We've been walking for absolutely ever,' said the girl, unlacing her boots. She extended her leg towards one of the boys who, appearing to know what was required, gently slid the boot off as she grimaced.

'Where did you start?' asked Mauricio.

One of the boys took up the narrative. 'We came from El Chaltén,' he explained. 'We ran out of Argentine *pesos* so we had to hike for two days instead of getting the bus. Then we took the ferry along the Laguna del Desierto.'

'And then another day of walking,' interrupted the girl. 'I've been wearing these boots for three days. My feet are burning… ow… be gentle… owwww!' at which point her helper took a sharp slap for his troubles.

Their journey from El Chaltén had crossed an inhospitable landscape devoid of facilities. Although most travellers use the bus and ferry, the final dozen kilometres can only be made on foot or with hired horses or, for the foolhardy, by bicycle. At the end of their epic trek, the *chicos* had arrived at Candelario Mancilla on the south shore of Lago O'Higgins, an *estancia* or ranch named after the family who'd established it. Travellers waiting for the ferry can find accommodation and meals there, and horses can be hired by those heading in the opposite direction.

Between the two lakes, Laguna del Desierto and Lago O'Higgins, a wild track crosses the Chile-Argentina border. This part of the *frontera* was agreed only recently, following a long history of opposing claims, map-drawing exercises and international arbitration. A conflict flared in 1965 when a Chilean border patrol unexpectedly met their Argentine counterparts in this area. Each believed the other had illegally entered their territory and shots were exchanged. One Chilean officer was killed, Hernán Merino Correa, and three others were captured. The following year, Chilean authorities advanced plans to secure the territories lying north of Lago O'Higgins and began the

---

applied to persons either side of this agegroup, too. Depending on the context, *chico* translates variously as boy, lad, guy, buddy, youth or similar expressions. Whereas the feminine plural *chicas* exclusively refers to girls or young women, the masculine plural *chicos* can describe either a group of boys or a mixed group.

construction of Villa O'Higgins. Nonetheless, the disputed land around the small Laguna del Desierto was eventually awarded to Argentina in 1994.

*

> **The Chile-Argentina Border**
>
> The *frontera* shared by Chile and Argentina is the third-longest two-nation land border in the world. In the mid-nineteenth century, both countries were vigorously staking claims on Patagonian land, leading inevitably to a proliferation of border disputes. Article One of the *Tratado de Límites*, or Boundary Treaty, of 1881 offered two rules of thumb to guide the process of resolution. The first stated that the *frontera* should link the tallest peaks throughout the *cordillera*. The second rule governed bodies of water: streams and rivers emptying into the Pacific Ocean would be considered Chilean and those flowing to the Atlantic were Argentine.
>
> Though the guidelines were frequently helpful, in a scattering of places the line joining the highest peaks did not coincide with the Atlantic-Pacific watershed, a confusion that arose with particular frequency in Patagonia. Arbitration in 1902 overseen by the British monarch, King Edward VII, settled a number of these disputes and led to the splitting of a number of lakes between the two countries, a situation that remains today. Further disagreements concerned Cape Horn, the Magellan Strait, and most notably some differences of opinion over the sovereignty of the Beagle Channel, which required papal intervention to avoid a serious conflict in 1984.
>
> Occasional wrangles continued to fester over a scattering of Patagonian lands. One way to assert rights over territory was to occupy it. Chilean and Argentine authorities constructed *pueblos* in remote valleys, offering incentives to families willing to inhabit them. Villa O'Higgins was established on the Chilean side in 1966, although pioneering families had established tentative colonies around the lake in earlier decades. In turn, Argentina founded El Chaltén in 1985. Benefiting from a stunning location beneath the Fitz Roy mountain range, this small town rapidly became a popular destination for hikers and climbers.

> Beneath the ice of the Campo de Hielo Sur, between Mount Fitz Roy and the summit of Cerro Murallón, a 50-kilometre section remains where the course of the frontier is not yet precisely confirmed. Maps generally box this portion with an explanatory note about the uncertainty.

> **The world's longest two-nation land borders**
>
> **8893km** Canada and United States of America (including Alaska)
>
> **6846km** Kazakhstan and Russia
>
> **5300km** Argentina and Chile
>
> **4677km** China and Mongolia
>
> **4053km** Bangladesh and India

*

The following morning was fresh. In fact, cold might be a more accurate word. With the forest canopy obscuring the sky, it was difficult to ascertain what kind of day was promised but I opted to tough it out and chose a pair of shorts… and a sweatshirt; my arms are wimps.

Mauricio was in the kitchen with the *estufa* lit and a kettle warming.

'Let's drink *mate*,' he offered.

Mate, pronounced *MA-tay*, is a green tea-like infusion usually associated with Argentina but just as popular on the Chilean side of Patagonia. It is brewed with *yerba*, the dried leaves of an understorey tree from subtropical and temperate forest. The plant itself goes under various names including Paraguay Tea, South American Holly and also Yerba Mate.

Mauricio tipped the dusty fragments from a packet and shook the *mate* until the *yerba* formed a sloping surface at the bottom. Confusingly, that's a second use of the same word, *mate*. Although commonly understood as the name of both the drink and the overall concept, the *mate* is actually the pot, traditionally crafted from a dried hollow calabash gourd. Next, Mauricio inserted the metal straw or *bombilla*, pushing the bulbous filter at its lower end under the *yerba*, before pouring a trickle of hot water, but not boiling, down the side of the *mate*, making the *yerba* wet from beneath but not inundated.

The first brew is always considered too bitter so like any *gaucho*, Mauricio sucked through the *bombilla* and spat the liquid onto the ground outside. It's quite normal for the host to take the second drink as well, checking temperature and taste, before refilling the *mate* with hot water a third time. The same *yerba* can be used several times, until the flavour becomes too weak. The host retains the kettle and passes the *mate* to each person in turn, always using the right hand, and with the *bombilla* inclined towards the recipient.

'Never say *gracias*,' Mauricio instructed me. 'If you want to compliment the host, you can say something like ¡Qué rico! But if you say *gracias*, it will be understood that you've had enough.'

Anxiety nagged at me. Tickets for buses on infrequent rural routes sometimes sold out days in advance. Though it was only my first morning, I was keen to ensure I had a way of travelling out of Villa O'Higgins. Complicating the issue, I wanted to hitchhike some of the road, or all the way to Puerto Montt if things went well. In view of the virtually non-existent traffic, I asked Mauricio about the likelihood of finding a ride.

'It will be fine,' he said. 'You can hitchhike anywhere… if you're prepared to wait.'

Waiting wasn't necessarily a problem. Anything less intense than the multiple demands and indecipherable staff room politics of my former routine was a welcome prospect. My habits and expectations had become strongly influenced by the over-hectic world. This was a chance to adopt a gentler pace and rhythm.

'In fact,' added Mauricio, 'I have a friend who makes deliveries to Villa O'Higgins from time to time. I'm expecting him to bring a solar panel in the next couple of days. He might be able to take you back with him.'

'I assume he'll stay here overnight?'

'It's best not to assume anything until you have the exact information,' were Mauricio's wise words.

It isn't easy to step out of the world in which we habitually dwell. For me, a goal-orientated attitude was deeply embedded, however much I may have wished otherwise. It had required a deliberate effort to sit with Mauricio an hour or more that morning, sharing *mate* and conversation, and I was already restless about what I could accomplish that day. My mental checklist was crowded with unticked boxes.

Eventually, though, I started achieving. In a place like this, even taking a morning shower qualified for a tick, especially one taken under stove-heated water. Moving to the next item on the list, I walked into the village to call at the museum, where exhibits portrayed the life of the locally-cherished priest Antonio Ronchi.

'If you want to understand this part of Patagonia,' Luci had told me, 'you have to know about Padre Antonio Ronchi.'

Two men occupied a bench outside the bolted museum door. '*Un momentito*,' one advised.

No problem, the new me can wait a moment… but then I thought it best to enquire deeper. After much discussion between the two, it became clear that this particular *momentito* was likely to be as long as half an hour. I would return later.

Unimpressed at the meagre offering of *mate*, my stomach reminded me about breakfast. Around the corner, the bakery door was locked but this too, I was told, would open in half an hour. Was the baker in a meeting with the curator of the museum? With fresh bread inaccessible, I resorted to vanilla cake, bananas, a tomato the sized of a grapefruit, and some plums, all from an *almacén*. Taking brunch to the *mirador*, I kept watch on the museum door through binoculars but it stayed resolutely shut. My interview with Padre Antonio Ronchi would have to wait.

Next on my checklist was a hike to a glacier at the head of the Mosco Valley. Beginning under the shade of trees, the trail continued across scrub under a hot sun, gently ascending. Gently, that is, until it scaled a huge moraine mound in a steep, punishing climb. There was evidence of a widespread scrub fire. Naked, weathered trunks stood like totem poles. Others had fallen and littered the ground, some of them heavily charred. It was difficult to tell how long ago the fire had destroyed the former woodland, but it was time enough for juvenile beeches to have taken hold.

Across the valley was a mountain that appeared to be an extinct volcano. Its shape was conical, viewed from the northern side at least, and completing the deception was what appeared to be a volcanic plug at the top. Mauricio subsequently corrected me: it was a regular mountain, not volcanic, he insisted. That became more obvious from a later side view. It was not cone-shaped at all but had an elongated, slightly humped and smoothly curving profile giving rise to its local name: The Submarine.

Volcanic or not, *El Submarino* was painted in broad strokes of incredible colour. The lower slopes were wrapped in deep green forest. Fire-razed patches were evidenced by pale open expanses specked with silver-grey trunks like scattered matchsticks. The shoulders of the mountain were warm red rock, convincingly volcanic, and the plug at the top was purple. A thin vertical slash cut through it all, a mountain stream glistening in the sunshine as it tumbled over the rocks, resembling a snail trail. It was a beautifully photogenic mountain and it seemed a missed opportunity not to have a route marked out by which to climb it. I scanned up and down, left and right, trying to locate a suitable course. Parts were steep, but an ascent seemed possible, with an attractive waterfall to visit halfway up.

Such an expedition was not for today, so remaining on the opposite side of the valley, I scrambled further up the heap of moraine as far as a second *mirador*. The path had rapidly gained altitude, resulting in expansive views of Lago O'Higgins and the mountains beyond. A dynamite blast boomed from the road-widening works accompanied by a cloud of dust that drifted over the lake. When the trail beyond became indistinct, I backtracked and took another branch. This one petered out in a bog, and I resorted to leaping from one prone tree trunk to another, employing a variety of gymnastic techniques. I soon gave up on that idea and located some shade in which to enjoy the rest of my lunch, admiring a succession of bright orange bumble bees loading up on goodness from a carpet of wild flowers.

It wasn't easy to sit still as I was persistently bothered by *tábanos*. These were the aggressive horseflies that had previously introduced themselves at Cascada Velo de la Novia. There in the Mosco Valley as I munched a cheese sandwich, I discovered more about their persistence and potency. The *tábanos* hunted in packs and were attracted to anything or anyone who sweated. Even as I sat still, they swarmed around my face, taking a bite whenever they could. I later learned how to fight them off, but at this early stage I just flapped my hands at them quite ineffectively. Feeling increasingly persecuted, I resorted to any means I could think of to escape their attentions. I stood in the open, hoping any slight breeze might blow them away; it didn't. I experimented to see if it would be different in the full sun or in the shade; it wasn't. Walking provided some respite – the buzzing cloud seemed reluctant to touch down when I was on the move, but each time I stopped, their numbers multiplied and they took bites from my arms and legs. When in desperation I removed my t-shirt to replace it with long sleeves, and forsook fashion dignity by tucking trousers into socks, the abhorrent *tábanos* bit through the fabric.

Hurrying to descend, I spotted a pair of figures at the upper *mirador*, pirouetting in aggravated circles, swatting insects with scarves and hats. On approaching it became clear that the dancers were a mother and daughter pair I'd met at Tsonek camp. Following a route described in their guidebook, Serena and Heather had taken a lower path.

'We went as far as a refuge,' said Heather, continually swirling a scarf around like a lasso. 'After that the path was blocked by a rockfall, so we didn't reach the glacier.'

'The creeks are quite deep further up the valley,' added Serena, 'and the book says you have to be careful crossing meltwater streams. They might only be a trickle in the morning but some grow to a torrent in the heat of the afternoon.'

The museum was still closed, so instead I turned my attention to dinner: pasta with tomato sauce and cheese once again; why change a winning combination? This time, the recipe was enhanced by the addition of a real tomato, selected from a box at the *almacén*. In addition, I bought a large carton of Don Simon wine, anticipating that it might be appreciated by the *chicos*. Indeed it was, but it may have been surplus to their true needs. They had already spent the afternoon diligently working through a drum of *chimbombo*, cheap white wine, but selflessly agreed to wash it down with some red.

Hiking in the Mosco Valley had settled my fidgety inclinations somewhat. It was satisfying to have achieved something. Learning the intricacies of *mate* preparation and visiting the *muelle* awarded me two further ticks for my checklist. But in my restless mind a new set of objectives was already taking shape for the following day. So few days and so much to get done.

'You've had a busy start here,' Mauricio remarked that evening. 'Don't do too much. Take time to relax and be still.'

'I *am* relaxing,' I protested, 'but I still want to make the most of being here.'

'We have a saying,' he replied. *'En Patagonia, el que se apura pierde tiempo.'*

In Patagonia, he who hurries wastes his time.

Image 05: Lago O'Higgins

Five: El Pajarero

Peep peep peep peep peep peep peep peep!
05:45.

As I unzipped the tent, an icy draught blew in. Plundering warm clothes from my *mochila*, I wrapped up against the chill.

Mauricio was locally known as *El Pajarero*, the Bird Man. His ornithological pursuits were regarded as something of an oddity.

'The *gauchos* may notice the birds,' he told me outside the kitchen block, 'and they may even find them pretty, but it would never cross their minds to spend time peering through binoculars. They think I'm very strange.'

Of course, outsiders and new arrivals in any place commonly face scrutiny; either that or indifference.

'Three years I've lived here now,' he said on one occasion, 'but it takes longer than that to become accepted. The thing is, I'm not from here. They're suspicious of anyone from The North.'

That was a telling expression. Referring to Mauricio's hometown of Talca as 'The North' seemed peculiar when it was as far south as many of my *Santiaguino* colleagues had ever travelled.

'I'm no different to you,' he concluded. 'To my neighbours here I'm a foreigner. I will never be Patagonian.'

He coaxed the Land Rover into life and drove us to the suspension bridge over the Río Mayer. Our breath made puffs of vapour in the bitter air. I was relieved to have packed my fleece and gloves, and for the presence of mind not to have dispensed with them in Coyhaique. Mauricio erected a tripod at the end of the bridge and fastened an impressive birdwatchers' spotting scope to it, but however professional it looked, these things are only useful for viewing wildlife if any shows up. Unfortunately, someone had forgotten to remind members of the local avian community that they were expected. The early bird was apparently more interested in taking a lie-in than catching worms. It wasn't a great surprise; given the choice I would certainly have stayed in my snug nest, too, cowering under an extra blanket. Breaking up the birdless monotony, a pair of nondescript grey fluffballs flitted agitatedly, and a pitiful yellow chick shivered on a fencepost. Then a lone goose spiritedly lumbered over, but I only saw its disappearing rear.

Steely water slid beneath the bridge, but no feathered life was in evidence there either. Dry land was quite cold enough, and the ducks had clearly decided there was no need to make things worse by taking a plunge in that chilly river. Beyond the bridge, we turned along the riverbank path, wetting our shoes with dew. At last, our early rising reaped some reward: a *chucao*, a bird with both the appearance and personality of an overgrown robin. First, unseen, secluded within a bush, he sang out his cheerful refrain. Then, gaining confidence, he sprang out onto the path, displaying his brown back, red throat and breast and a distinctive upright tail. This was the first of many *chucaos* to make an appearance over the weeks that followed.

Downstream, an eerie mist hung above the thicket, mysterious and moody. At second glance it became apparent that it wasn't mist at all, but dust from the road. The Robinson Crusoe bus came into view, carrying passengers for the dawn sailing of the *Quetru*. The heavy vehicle edged across the narrow bridge and was gone, the low growl of the engine fading to nothing. The haze gradually cleared from above the dark tangle of thicket. The morning sun was yet to find its way into the valley, and the icy air was heavy and motionless.

In an instant, the silence was broken by an urgent series of hollow staccato thumps.

Tap tap tap tap tap tap tap.

Clinging to the textured bark of a thick trunk, wearing a smart, sophisticated black suit and easily identifiable by his striking red head, there was a male Magellanic woodpecker.

Tap tap tap.

The *carpintero* had chosen a tree in full view beside the riverbank path.

'Look how he stands,' whispered Mauricio. 'He inclines his thumb either up or down to get a good grip and uses his stiff tail for support, almost like a third limb.'

Tap tap tap tap tap.

'His tongue is very long, coiled inside his head like a tape measure. When he finds a bug, his tongue shoots out like a lizard's.'

The woodpecker made short work of the trunk, pale chippings spraying in all directions. A female flew in to vandalise a neighbouring tree, the pair hammering a percussive duet.

'Each male normally has two mates,' Mauricio told me.

We waited and listened... and heard the other mate some way off, excavating another tree. Creeping along the path and searching deep into the shadowy web of branches, we located her at last in a uniform dull green costume.

From that moment, the early morning bird-watching experience improved enormously. Chastened by the sociable *chucao* and the stately *carpintero negro*, an impressive array of woodland birds strove to take centre stage. Among the memorable characters were some *rayaditos*, gregarious small birds with stripy heads whose voices resembled unwinding clockwork toys. Another song repeating frequently was that of the white-crested elaenia, a slender fly-catcher whose onomatopoeic local title is *fío-fío*. The buff-winged cinclodes also has a descriptive Chilean name: *churrete*, meaning diarrhoea. Lacking social graces, the unfortunate bird defecates constantly.

Returning through the village centre, Mauricio persuaded the bakery to open. The baker was also the *alcalde*, the mayor.

'The *alcalde* cherishes the traditional ways of Patagonia,' Mauricio told me. 'He doesn't yet appreciate the benefits that visitors could bring to his town. Whenever we talk about it, I cannot make him understand that tourism can generate income, and people would have more work. We could do so much more here; just look at the natural environment. There could be twice as many visitors; maybe ten times as many.'

We breakfasted on fresh warm bread and cheese. The *chicos* had still not risen, no great surprise after downing a barrel of *chimbombo*.

'I could help wake them up,' joked Enrique, standing in the doorway and cradling a chainsaw.

Luci laughed. 'Leave them alone,' she said. 'They're only kids.'

Instead, we ploughed through a bird book and I made a note of all those we'd seen that morning.[24]

***Chilean Name* – English Name**
cachudito – tufted tit tyrant
carpintero negro – Magellanic woodpecker
churrete – buff-winged cinclodes
chucao – chucao
fío-fío – white-crested elaenia
golondrina chilena – Chilean swallow
jilguero – black-chinned siskin
pato real – Chiloé widgeon
rayadito – thorn-tailed rayadito
zorzal – austral thrush

'Didn't you see a *huet-huet*?' asked Enrique.

'No. What's that?'

'You're bound to see them, even here around the camp. They scavenge on the ground and call out their name: *wet-wet*.'

'They have long legs and a very upright tail,' added Mauricio, 'a bit like an oversized *chucao*. But they're not as friendly; a *huet-huet* won't come so close.'

*

At midday, we visited Mauricio's *gaucho* neighbour to buy a *cordero*. The deal had been struck on a previous occasion, but our visit was an expected courtesy to confirm the purchase and a necessary reminder to ensure the lamb would be ready that night. Mauricio was hosting a party to celebrate the opening of his camp.

The neighbour's name was Pancho. I guess he was about 60 years old. Pancho and his wife lived in a small house, a kilometre or two outside the village, up the Carretera Austral. A large log-burning *estufa*

---

[24] A more complete bird list from the journey as a whole is given in Appendix 3: Glossary.

dominated their main room. Mauricio and Pancho sat at either side of a small table, occupying the only two chairs. Mumbling something unintelligible, Pancho gestured towards a stool in the corner, so I settled there.

One wall was lined with sheets of shiny-faced hardboard. Others had the timber frame exposed, doubling as narrow shelves. A bare bulb dangled from the ceiling, and a two-way radio sat on a small chest below a lopsided painting of two hens. An assortment of calendars hung from three nails, the type distributed by companies publicising products: animal feed or tractor parts, for example. The years 2012, 2011, 2010 and 2009 could be seen, and many more were hidden beneath.

When the conversation reached a lull, I gathered both nerve and vocabulary in order to speak.

'How much difference has the new road made to your life?' I asked Pancho.

'Ante, psaroslmntecabllogaucho,' he replied with a sigh. 'Hoydímira, aimuchtrafco,' he added slowly, deliberately and utterly incomprehensibly.

I asked Mauricio later for an interpretation. Pancho had described a time when the trail was narrow and the only movement amounted to three or four *gauchos* on horseback per week.

'Look at all that traffic now,' he'd said.

Traffic?

Pancho had wool to sell at the exchange in Coyhaique. With the truck due to arrive in the days ahead, he'd become concerned about his shortage of sacks. I wondered how this genre of eleventh-hour planning related to 'he who hurries wastes his time'. It sounded more like 'he who isn't organised won't sell his wool'. Surely he'd known all year to prepare for this moment.

'I'll put in a request to Coyhaique,' Mauricio promised. 'Maybe they can send sacks for you.'

Turning on his radio must have been too much trouble for Pancho. Nonetheless, Mauricio seemed glad of the opportunity to help a neighbour.

With a lamb promised we also needed salad, so after dutifully inspecting the mountain of unbagged sheepswool shearings, we took a trip to Las Chacras. Like Pancho's place, the farm had a wooden house on a large plot of land. A pair of tractors stood idle and there were three long greenhouses, each constructed around a frame of rough-hewn timber. The farmer took us inside one of the plastic tunnels, hot with moist air, and cut three giant green *lechugas* from the dark soil.

Across the road, multiple shallow channels of the Río Mosco criss-crossed a wide expanse of large, smooth pebbles. Riverbed rocks had been bulldozed into three enormous levees angled obliquely across the flow to dissuade any further encroachment towards the farms; erosion already threatened the narrow highway. Against a cloudless sky, three large birds of prey were circling: two condors and a buzzard eagle. Each species had its distinct pattern of flight, the condors soaring effortlessly whilst the eagle flapped busily to stay aloft.

*

A bucket of water sufficed to keep the lettuce fresh until evening, the green tips poking above the rim like pond plants. Enrique was varnishing the kitchen table, a chunky frame of logs topped by a sheet of plywood cut to an irregular curved form like a textbook amoeba. A large flat box rested against the wall: the new solar panel. With the camp set beneath thick canopy, the most suitable location for the equipment was not easy to decide, but the delivery had arrived that morning all the same and with it, my easy ride to Tortel had come and gone.

The *chicos* surfaced, surprisingly animated, and set off through the woods on foot to find their way to a nearby *laguna*. I declined their invitation, having already planned a hike to the *bandera*, a Chilean flag displayed on a high hilltop where the views of the valley, Enrique assured me, were *espectacular*.

I paused at the museum on the way, but Padre Antonio Ronchi still appeared reluctant to receive visitors. Calling at the shop instead, I couldn't help noticing an enticing block of cheese on the counter.

'Just a small piece, please,' I requested, my resistance cracking with disappointing ease. The assistant's interpretation of *un poco* was different from mine. Not to worry; I'm rarely one to decline an extra helping of cheese.

The route to the *bandera* began on the same familiar steps that climbed to the *mirador*. I stopped at the platform for lunch: bread, plenty of cheese, two tomatoes this time and a banana. Beyond the shelter, the trail divided. To the right was the path up the Mosco Valley, but this time I chose the left fork across a series of boardwalks over saturated ground. It was a corridor through hordes of stunning red and purple native fuchsia. Charles Darwin's rather practical opinion, recorded in *The Voyage of the Beagle*, which refers to his travels in these parts, was that although they had beautiful drooping flowers, most fuchsia were difficult to crawl through.

After the swamp was a punishing two-hour relentless ascent. Hillwalking inevitably involves some upward sections but this route had no respite at all. Where the climbing was steepest, makeshift steps had been driven into the earth and there were ladders fastened to nauseatingly vertical rock faces. The narrow path traversed exposed ledges. A careless step could have initiated a rapid and troublesome descent. The less adrenaline-inducing parts came as a relief, where the path cut away from the precipice and passed through long grasses, and within woodland where the drop remained out of sight.

Tábanos accompanied me to the summit. One landed on my glasses, his undercarriage wiggling across the lens: white, nasty, fat and maggot-like. Spinning arms around my head like a windmill proved to be a wholly unsuccessful method of swatting them away, not to mention making it difficult to clutch onto my binoculars. With patient experimentation I learned an improved strategy: a waiting game. Allow the *tábano* to land and then smack him over the head with a sharp slap. That was not so easy for the few that attacked the back of the neck, but most of them fortunately demonstrated a preference for arms and legs. Moreover, instead of biting immediately they paused momentarily to say grace, a few crucial moments of delay between touchdown and first incision. When the *tábano* had the scent of flesh in his nostrils and was licking his lips expectantly, that was the moment to strike the fatal blow. I became quite proficient at *tábanocide* and considered it a service to humanity. After a slap to the head, they span satisfyingly to the ground like a sycamore seed. Vigilance was especially important at this point for the few who deviously played dead before flipping back onto their feet and buzzing off drunkenly. Therefore it had to be hand and foot, slap and squash, to ensure that extermination was fully accomplished.

Walks came to be scored by the tally of corpses left on the hillsides. I swatted twenty or more that day. It reminded me of a story from infant school in which a tailor grew tired of the flies that swarmed around his jam pot and struck out at them with his handkerchief, killing seven. In celebration, he made himself a tunic embroidered with the phrase 'seven in one blow'. Another day he had an argument with a giant, somehow persuading him that the seven referred to slaughtering giants. Wholesome stuff for impressionable infants. Stopping for every *tábano* slowed my upward progress but provided an excuse for frequent short rests that were welcome because the climb was hard going.

The final leg was steep, exposed and exhausting, but led ultimately to a high plateau under twisted trees. Mercifully, the *bandera* came into view, mounted upon a large protruding rock, snagged around its own mast and tugging impatiently in the brisk breeze. When not wrapped around a pole, the Chilean flag is a striking and attractive one. Above a plain red lower half, the upper part has a white portion to the right and a bold white star set against a blue square at the left. All homes are required to display a *bandera* for the national day in September. Whether the flag hangs lengthways or sideways, the star is positioned at the top left corner. If you have a mind for such things, you'll realise that switching between the two orientations requires turning to the reverse side of the cloth. Red signifies the blood that was shed in the fight for independence, blue is for the Pacific, white for the snow-capped Andes *cordillera*, and the star is to guide the journey of progress.

In rare interludes between killing *tábanos* I admired the *espectacular* view, covered as far as the eye could see by a carpet of treetops in a remarkable range of greens. I hadn't realised that such a multiplicity of greens even existed. The trees on one hill were closer to yellow, and in other places the colour was somehow akin to purple or brown. Reassuring my bewildered eyes, some of the landscape was painted in familiar greens, too. The forest, thick on the valley floor, continued even up steep mountains. Not far from the *bandera*, a file of trees processed up an impossible ridge, awkwardly leaning far from the perpendicular to stand in orientations that loosely conformed to vertical.

Far below, Tsonek ecocamp was secluded beneath the trees. An irregular hole in the canopy revealed the waters of the *laguna* to which the *chicos* had walked. One finger of Lago O'Higgins stretched away to the south, my left, with Chilean and Argentine mountains confronting each other from either side like hunched rows of opposing forwards in a game of American football. Further west, successive ridges were orderly ranks of soldiers standing to attention on a parade ground. To the north were a haphazard cluster of lakes and then yet more mountains draped in unending forest.

Directly below the *bandera* was tiny Villa O'Higgins. The messy gathering of rainbow roofs resembled a scale model. From my lofty vantage point, certain village facilities were apparent for the first time. The *cementario*, the cemetery, was the solitary installation beyond the black stripe of the runway. Also, on a triangular patch of flat ground near the lake, two other features caught my attention. One was a football pitch encircled by an imprecisely-marked running track, and the other was a rodeo *medialuna*.

Every rural community up and down Chile has its *medialuna*, typically of timber construction and ringed by tiered benches. A popular sport in Chile, *rodeo* attracts large crowds. In this sport, a calf or bullock is chased around a semi-circular enclosure by a pair of mounted *huasos*,[25] cowboys, whose aim is to pin the animal against a cushioned strip on the wall. The horses work in tandem to block the escaping calf. One *huaso* moves forward to catch the animal under the chest of his horse, and traps it against the wall. Points are awarded for accuracy and it appears to be of particular merit to lift the calf's feet from the floor.[26] The calves and bullocks become mildly distressed, as any of us might if we were chased around a stadium by two muscular horses, but they otherwise remain unharmed. The arena is named for its shape; *medialuna* means 'half-moon'. Another type of *medialuna* is sold at the bakery; the word can also mean 'croissant'.

It is common to see *huasos* at work throughout Chile, usually on horseback, costumed in colourfully striped woollen ponchos and the characteristic wide-brimmed straw *chupalla* or sombrero. The cowboy history of Chile is commemorated on the *dieciocho*, 18 September, when *huasos* and their steeds play a conspicuous part in patriotic

---

[25] *Huaso* is the common Chilean word for a cowboy, whereas *gaucho* is an expression from Patagonia.

[26] This not-so-informed interpretation of Chilean *rodeo* stems from having watched a handful of events both on television and in person at the *medialuna*. My apologies if I have misrepresented the finer aspects of the sport.

celebrations, expertly demonstrating cattle-herding feats and competing in *rodeo* contests. This same day, every man and boy has the chance to be a *huaso* for the day, or at least to dress like one, if they are willing to set inhibitions aside and dance the *cueca*.

*

> **The Cueca**
>
> The *cueca* is the national dance of Chile. Although it is performed by partners, their respective moves ensure that they hardly touch until the end. The man sports the traditional outfit of the *huaso*: a *chupalla* on his head, tailored shirt, flannel poncho, dark trousers and riding boots complete with polished spurs. The woman wears a colourful dress and an embroidered apron. They both carry lace handkerchiefs, waving and holding them aloft throughout the dance.
>
> The distinctive music is played by a band of guitar, accordion, percussion and two voices, sometimes with the addition of other instruments such as the *guitarrón*, piano or harp. The *guitarrón* has the appearance of a guitar but with 25 strings, and is generally plucked, not strummed. On hearing the opening chords, spectators accompany the band with rhythmic clapping.
>
> The *cueca* is an intricate dance that requires considerable practice. The movements are abrupt and agitated, not smooth and flowing. First there is a slow promenade with arms linked. Partners then pirouette around each other back and forth in semicircles (known as *medialunas*, naturally), alternately turning towards and away from each other, not forgetting to twirl the handkerchiefs.
>
> While the lyrics of the song describe a violent disagreement in a bar, the interaction of the two dancers is said to represent a cockerel courting a hen. It usually ends with the man on one knee and his partner standing over him, her foot planted triumphantly on his raised knee.

*

I once spent the evening at a *medialuna* for a sporting event that was not *rodeo*. In 2009, Chile hosted a World Group elimination playoff versus Austria in the Davis Cup. The Chilean tennis team[27] had opted to play on the clay of the *medialuna* in Rancagua, 90 kilometres south of Santiago. The various pieces of *rodeo* paraphernalia had been cleared away, leaving a circular terrain of appropriate dimensions for a tennis court. Stadium staff had been tasked with painting white lines, setting up a net and clearing away cowpats. It just so happened that the match was scheduled for the weekend of the *dieciocho*. Partisan spectators, already hyped-up from the one-hundred-and-ninety-ninth birthday celebrations of their nation, arrived to Rancagua with flags, whistles and trumpets, and could not contain themselves. Regardless of the umpire's appeals for calm, the crowd erupted in wild and disorderly celebration each time one of their gladiatorial heroes won a point. They whistled and jeered the Austrian serves to such an extent that the umpire interrupted the game to deliver a lecture in tennis-watching etiquette. Embarrassing though this was, in the context of the *dieciocho* weekend, such merriment was not a great surprise. With all this misbehaviour slowing play, it was not until the early hours that the Chilean team finally secured the second match of the night, guaranteeing their survival in the World Group for another year.

That period of my life in a quite distinct part of Chile felt a million miles distant from the *bandera* hilltop. Nonetheless, my step-by-step return towards that other world was about to begin with a first stride up the Carretera Austral. In the valley below, the road trailed out of the village like a narrow ribbon, winding far into the distance between hills and lakes and through wetlands and woodlands. However, I wasn't finished with Villa O'Higgins yet. For one thing, I still hadn't seen inside the museum. Secondly, another event was looming: slowly and sedately as befit Patagonia, Tsonek ecocamp was gearing up for a party.

The descent was steep, and I slid frequently on the dusty ground. The pale rock reflected the heat of the sun, and it was a relief to move

---

[27] Tennis is popular in Chile where, as in Spain, it is usually contested on clay courts. Marcelo Ríos of Chile became the first Latin American man to top the ATP world rankings, in 1998. In the 2004 Summer Olympics in Athens, Nicolás Massú won the Men's Singles gold medal, and Massú with Fernando González won the Doubles. To date, these are the only Olympic Golds ever won by Chilean athletes.

into the shade of a copse that clung tenaciously to the incline. Amongst the birds that made a home in these branches were some I recognised from the ornithology class that morning. Most frequent were *rayaditos* and *fío-fíos*, whose distinctive whistles were unmistakable. Then I heard a new voice.

'*Wet-wet! Wet-wet!*'

The call was modestly and precisely enunciated. Was this the creature that Enrique had described?

After a short pause, the sound repeated further down the trail.

'*Wet-wet! Wet-wet!*'

I padded along as lightly as I could, eyes on the forest floor. There he was! Scuttling across the path was a dark bird. He had rufous markings and long black legs. Rather like the smaller *chucao,* he had a pronounced upright tail. He was unmistakably a *huet-huet*.

Image 06: The Bandera

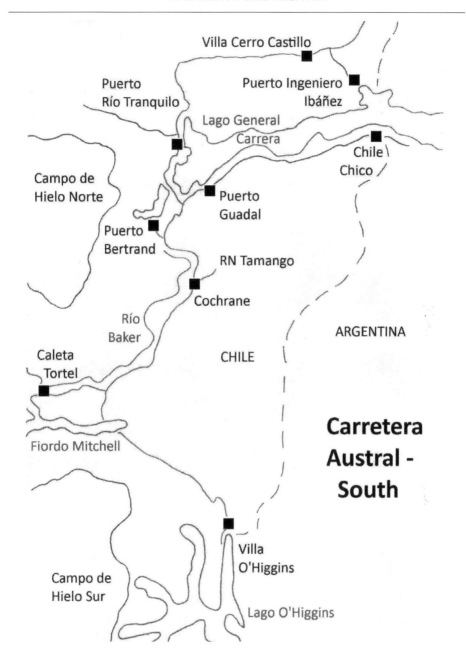

Map 03: Carretera Austral - South

Six: Padre Antonio Ronchi

It was the afternoon prior to the Tsonek party. Mauricio and Enrique had gone out, and the *chicos* were sleeping. Busily cleaning the communal kitchen, Luci appeared to be the only person getting anything ready in spite of her claims that *everyone* was helping. A detective calling by that afternoon would have struggled to find many clues that a celebratory feast was imminent. With the party almost upon us, there was neither fire pit, nor logs, nor meat. In the belief that roasting *cordero* over an open fire was surely not a short process, I shared my concern with Luci.

'I've learned to let the two brothers run things as they judge best,' she confided. 'They usually have a plan, even if it's hard to detect.'

The homeliness of Tsonek ecocamp was probably down to Luci's influence. She demonstrated a level of maternal care not only towards Enrique and Mauricio but also to Tsonek as an entity. She occupied herself with domestic chores and had brightened up the kitchen with colourful fabrics.

'I've been married twice,' she told me on a different occasion, 'but now I'm living just as I want to. I'm quite happy at Tsonek for the time being. I have a role here.'

Luci's post-matrimonial freedom had brought her to Chile, and more specifically to Isla Negra where she visited one of the homes of the poet and Nobel laureate, Pablo Neruda. It was there that she'd crossed paths with Mauricio.

I took charge of the *lechuga*, washing the oversized leaves in an outdoor sink and arranging them artistically in the most suitable receptacle I could find: a wok. As I did so, Mauricio marched up the forest path with a sack slumped over his shoulder.

'Brave hunter bring meat,' he announced, dropping the sack to the floor where it wriggled and bleated.

The poor animal was to be slaughtered on site prior to roasting. Mauricio departed to fetch the *gaucho* who would commit the deadly deed, and I returned to washing lettuce. It was tempting to offer some to the lamb.

It was at this point that the tap ran dry. It rotated freely one way and then the other but nothing came, not even a drip. The water pipes were connected to a large tank high on a tall timber tower beside the kitchen block. I'd assumed that whichever source fed this tank did so automatically without human intervention. I was mistaken.

Enrique fetched a frail homemade ladder.

'Hold the base for me,' he requested, hopping adeptly from rung to rung.

It briefly passed through my mind to be concerned about what might happen to him if he fell but in truth I was more worried about what would happen to me, given my vulnerable position directly beneath. He lifted the lid of the tank.

'*¡Pucha!*'

In some respects the empty reservoir was good news. At least it ruled out a more intractable problem like a blocked pipe or a faulty valve. Enrique performed some high altitude acrobatics to remove himself from the tower and then he was down the ladder, relieving me of responsibility for his life. With the hour already approaching eight in the evening, we had no fire, our dinner was still alive and the taps had run dry. On the positive side, at least we had a wok full of salad.

Having changed into swimming shorts, Enrique fetched a small pump, a roll of gaffer tape and a canister of fuel. Beside the road, a spring emerged from an underground stream. A plastic pipe had been installed there, leading all the way uphill and up-tower to the empty water tank. Enrique began by fastening the open end of the pipe to the pump. It was a clumsy fit but the seal was eventually affected with the help of several strips of sticky tape and some widely distributed energetic swearing. He topped up the small tank with fuel, screwed on the cap, and immersed the water-intake in the stream. Holding the small machine down with one foot, Enrique pulled the cord to start the engine… and pulled it again… and again. Nothing.

'*¡Pucha!*'

He fiddled with the fuel valve and tried once more. A brief splutter but nothing convincing. More expletives. After a further succession of brutal but unsuccessful tugs on the cord, Enrique telephoned his brother to explain the problem. At the very same moment, the Land Rover appeared around the bend in the road, bringing Mauricio and the *gaucho*. All three stood around the pump and scratched their heads but neither of the younger men volunteered to step into the icy stream. At length, the pump shuddered into life in a cloud of blue fumes and the water tank began to fill. Crisis averted.

*

Assisted by the morbidly fascinated *chicos*, the *gaucho* slit the throat of our main course and removed her dirty fleece. There was still no sign of a fire.

Guided through the darkness by an impressive trail of orange solar lanterns, guests began to arrive. It was the first visit for most, but in the gloom it was difficult to inspect much of the property. Mauricio could be heard somewhere in the obscurity playing his drum. Although I could appreciate his need to take a moment to compose himself, his timing appeared poor. Or it could be that those five minutes were precisely what Mauricio needed to collect his thoughts and morph into a genial host. He who hurries wastes his time, as is well known.

The gutted carcass was stretched onto an X-shaped metal frame. Over the hubbub I caught a comment from the *alcalde* – something about roasting for two hours. I recognised another guest, Marcelo, a shop proprietor from whom I'd been purchasing my lunchtime snacks.

'I'd had enough of living in Santiago,' he told me. 'I'm so much happier here in Patagonia.'

That seemed to be a recurring theme. Villa O'Higgins also had the advantage of being a long way from his ex-wife. His children were attending schools in the capital but would shortly arrive for the summer vacation.

The mayor stepped over to join us. Prompted by Mauricio's earlier comments, I raised the subject of tourism.

'Yes,' he agreed, 'we need to do everything we can to attract visitors.'

'How about a path up *El Submarino*?'

He laughed. 'You're not the first to suggest that. It's a beautiful walk. I'm sure we will build a trail up there one day.'

Standing in the flickering firelight were a French couple. 'We're working at Hostal El Mosco,' they explained, 'but initially we arrived as tourists. We came from Colombia on our bikes. When the season ends, we'll ride to Santos in Brazil to get a ship to Lisbon. Then we can cycle back home to France.'

'That's a long way on a bike.'

'The final part across Portugal and Spain will be almost nothing,' they told me. 'The map of Europe is so compact compared to the routes we've pedalled in South America. Here, we've already covered the same distance as Paris to Delhi.'

Later, much later, we ate *cordero* accompanied by potatoes and a most excellent salad. I took a large chunk of the succulent roast, dripping with dark juices. It tasted divine. A subtle hint of smoke and ash even enhanced the flavour of the tender fibres. The *alcalde* had slipped away, but aside from mayoral absence, the party was a success. Guests were numerous and they ate and drank plenty.

In the early hours I escaped the crush of people in the kitchen and waited a while by the glowing fire. The journey was beckoning. It was far shorter than cycling from Colombia to Patagonia but my road was waiting all the same, the Carretera Austral. It was the reason I'd come here, after all. Cochrane, Río Tranquilo, Cerro Castillo, Chaitén... all these unknown places lay ahead. First of all, I had to get to Caleta Tortel. It was time to make a plan.

*

The following morning, I called at Marcelo's shop. He kindly took my camera battery to recharge, and I stocked up on travel food, there being neither village nor shop nor petrol station nor itinerant cookie merchant anywhere along the road. Returning to Tsonek with my purchases, I discovered the four *chicos* in a heap at the side of the road, sprawled against their bulging *mochilas* in the shade of a large tree.

'We've been here ages already,' they admitted. 'One car did stop, but he would only take two of us.'

What did their difficulties imply for my plans? I was not averse to taking advantage of the twice-weekly bus, but giving up on hitchhiking without so much as a single attempt felt like a betrayal. A solitary traveller must have a better chance of getting a ride than a group of four, I reassured myself. With no particular deadline to meet, what would it matter if I had to wait a few hours? Going slowly might even be beneficial, casting aside the frenetic march of the city and responding instead to Patagonia's gentle heartbeat. After all, he who hurries in Patagonia wastes his time.

When I mentioned my bus versus hitchhike dilemma to Luci, she dispensed a measure of perceptive advice.

'Why is it such a big deal?' she asked. 'Why would you put yourself under pressure? You can travel out of here in whichever way you like but you seem to have made hitchhiking into some kind of sacred goal. Is it really so bad to go by bus?'

'I just thought I'd like to try. I'd prefer not to use the bus unless I've tried to hitchhike first.'

'Of course you would. But what if you don't get a ride? Does that make you a failure? Is that how you want to treat yourself? It's the journey that matters, not the transport. Go ahead and travel. Hitchhike if you want, or take the bus. Or you can skip, or roller-skate, or walk on your hands; what does it matter? Get in tune with your spirit. Listen to the whispers in the air. Enjoy the road, and stop worrying so much.'

How insightful. I should have listened.

'Incidentally,' she added, 'did you get to the museum?'

'No. Or at least, yes, I got there. I've been there several times. It's always closed.'

Luci laughed. 'It's often closed, yes. That's the way things are around here; it's difficult to fix a plan. Well, keep trying; it's worth a visit.'

'I'm running out of time. I want to leave tomorrow.'

'I see. Well, that's up to you. I guess it depends what you decide is more important, doesn't it?'

'I need to start my journey. I have a long way to travel.'

'Sure, of course you do. Like I say, that's for you to decide. It's a choice isn't it? Who is making you leave? You can get started if that's what will make you happy. But if there are still things you want to do here, then what's the harm in staying?'

*

Since discovering the road beyond the village to Puerto Bahamondez, I'd had it in mind to return to that lakeside quay and commence my expedition there, at the absolute end of the Carretera Austral. With that in mind, I changed into shorts and t-shirt, slathered on a layer of sunblock and set out on Enrique's bike. Cycling proved to be a demanding pursuit, the thick tyres sinking into the soft road surface. It was only a short ride, but the elderly bicycle had a way of exaggerating every bump and incline. Each one was an unpleasant surprise considering how flat it had seemed from the cab of the Land Rover. If riding uphill was hard work, then the downhill stretches were perilous. Contending with a loose, potholed surface, it wouldn't have taken much to lose grip altogether and end up sprawled in the dust.

The *Quetru* was nowhere to be seen, but two large fishing vessels were docked at the *muelle* with their nets hung up to dry. A short, stocky man was repairing an upturned rowing boat. Construction materials had been delivered for some intended project: a stack of steel beams, two barrows leaning against the fence, and sacks of cement on a pallet.

At the back of the dock, there was a varnished notice board:
Fin del Camino Carretera Austral 1247km.
End of Carretera Austral Road 1247km.

Having wheeled Enrique's bicycle level with the sign, I took a deep breath and began to pedal. The entire Carretera Austral lay ahead, weeks of adventure and surprises. The gravel track began beside the lake, rising and falling with the contour of the land and squeezing beneath the cliff where the road-widening works were underway. I rode across the suspension bridge and passed the vendor of fine lettuces in Las Chacras. On reaching the airfield, I was tempted to cycle along the runway but lacked the nerve. It isn't easy to justify such antics through a foreign language, and it's worth bearing in mind that an unobtrusive rural *aeródromo* could actually be a military installation. It was just a short ride but I was already sore by the time I arrived back, and not at all envious of those who cycle the full length of the highway.

The *chicos* had returned to Tsonek, having failed in their bid to leave the village. Not only did that confirm the difficulty of hitchhiking from Villa O'Higgins but it also put us in direct competition for a ride the following morning. Nonetheless, trying to put into practice the advice

I'd recently received from Luci and Mauricio, I was determined to respond to obstacles like these with calm and composure. I would embrace whichever circumstances Patagonia saw fit to supply. If that meant moving slowly, it would be a gift and not a trial. Disappointingly, such positive resolve can be simpler to adopt in principle than in practice.

Discerning that the disconsolate young explorers were in need of mothering, I fried the few left-over party potatoes in a fiery cocktail of spices: bubble and squeak à la Patagonia. There also remained a small mountain of steak and *chorizo*, half a wok of salad and a quarter of the *cordero*. We ate hungrily, and the *lechuga* was especially fine.

I sat with Mauricio that final evening, ruminating on our varied life stories and lubricated by a glass or two of wine. Or it may have been three. After a good while, he offered me a whisky. Never having had a happy relationship with that particular poison and demonstrating uncommon good sense, I declined and retired to bed.

*

Vehicles taking the Carretera Austral between Villa O'Higgins and Caleta Tortel cross the Mitchell Fjord on a ferry. It sails each day at 11am, 1pm and 7pm. Estimating that those aiming for the first crossing would depart between eight and half past, I woke early and was impatient to get to the road. Unexpectedly, in a test of my new relaxed attitude, my host had prepared coffee and toast. Which was more important: hurrying to meet an arbitrary deadline or enjoying some moments with a friend? Fighting every urge to get moving, I sipped a strong *espresso*. As Mauricio and I chatted, the faint grumble of a vehicle filtered almost imperceptibly through the trees, followed some minutes later by another… or was it my imagination?

As soon as the two of us made it to the road, a large truck from the construction site stopped and the door swung open. That was quick; I hadn't even put down my bag. Unfortunately he was only going halfway, to fetch gravel from a quarry. Satisfying though a quick start would have been, I had no wish to be abandoned midway. Better to be stuck in Villa O'Higgins than marooned in the middle of nowhere. So we walked instead to the edge of the village and Mauricio left me there. I wasn't the first to have waited eagerly at that spot; a small carved sign was hung from the fence with an inscription in English:

Good Luck to Hitchhikers.

The carver, at least, had waited there a while.

The battered Cochrane bus passed, scattering grit and sand, and four smiling *chicos* waved through the filthy rear window. My mind was suddenly overrun by doubts and second thoughts, but there was nothing I could do; the bus had gone. I was committed to hitchhiking, or else wait for the next departure in three days. Sitting on a mound of stones, it was hard not to fret. It was getting late for the first ferry, but at least there were two more to follow. In an hour or two, vehicles would pass to meet the second sailing.

Birds flitted through the branches hanging above. An electric-blue dragonfly hovered inquisitively before zigzagging away. A trio of hens clucked through a hole in the fence and pecked in the dust.

I was startled by a sudden sound, the rattle of the cattle grid a short distance away at the edge of the village. A black car was approaching. Clambering quickly to my feet, I fixed a friendly smile and held out my thumb. They slowed, apparently in conversation, slowed even more, and then drove by without even a glance in my direction.

Forty tedious minutes seeped away before another vehicle came. I leapt up energetically. The van was ancient but that hardly mattered, as long as it could survive as far as the ferry ramp. With enthusiastic expectation I signalled boldly and cheerily.

This could be it, the start of the adventure.

It could be…

Could it be…?

It wasn't.

Backfiring constantly, the van turned off the road and spluttered to a halt.

A surprising number of vehicles did pass during the course of that morning. Almost every driver made a gesture of some kind to indicate that they were full or that they were turning off the road shortly ahead. Others called at a building supplies yard a stone's throw from where I sat. One of these was a green pickup that reappeared several times during the morning. On each occasion, I sprang into the road eagerly, by this stage begging a ride, and each time the driver grinned and shook his head. Such disappointments felt like personal insults, or like false promises intended to distress: the delusion of persecution.

By midday, it was too late to catch the second ferry. The final chance to cross Fiordo Mitchell was the 7pm sailing. Would anyone depart Villa O'Higgins for the evening boat? Who would choose to drive through such a wilderness at night?

In a flash of red and black, a *carpintero negro* darted across the road, swiftly followed by one of his two green mates. Interpreting this as a positive omen, I resolved to face the afternoon with renewed determination.

A family of three were packing their holiday kit into a car outside a rented *cabaña*. When it finally became apparent that they were ready to leave, I sauntered across to ask a tiny favour.

'*Señores*; is there any chance you might have room for me?'

The hitchhiker's frame of mind rages agonisingly between ecstatic highs and deep lows.

'Just look at all the things we're carrying,' the woman said. 'Our car is already full.'

It's not for me to suggest that motorists should always pick up hitchhikers. Plainly there are reasons why a driver might be hesitant. What it did cause me to ponder, as I sat on that pile of Patagonian stones, was the occasions when I had driven disinterestedly past someone holding out a thumb, metaphorically speaking, and had chosen to ignore them: the beggar asking for coins, obviously; the disorientated foreign visitor at the railway station; an out-of-sorts colleague; the habitually depressed acquaintance yearning for someone to listen; the alone one; the unpopular one; the guy sleeping on a flattened cardboard box in a doorway. How often had these people appealed to me and how many times had I bothered to find out what it was they needed?

I was tense and frustrated, unnecessarily so. A poor mood was hardly going to help. Once again I was wasting energy on regret: why had I not taken the bus; why did I delay for coffee in the morning rather than come directly to the road; why had I not made more effort to contact someone in the village who might be travelling my way? Not only did these things bother me, I was also upset that they bothered me, and irritated at being unable to accept my lot more graciously. It's not as if the schedule was tight. I had six weeks to reach Puerto Montt, a period beautifully free of deadlines and responsibilities. What harm would come from a postponement of one day? I read my book for a few minutes and then, not able to concentrate, tried another. Pangs of hunger came, or possibly dejection, so I shuffled back to Tsonek and mournfully chewed on a cold chunk of rubbery *cordero*.

Reinvigorated, I hurried back to the road where the shade had moved to the opposite side. *Tábanos* taunted me. A few cars passed but nothing for Fiordo Mitchell. A man arrived on a bicycle, leading two horses attached to a frayed length of rope. He released them to join others grazing beside the road. Suddenly another horse thundered in, galloping in wide circles around the herd. This strange equine harassment agitated the group and they took flight together and disappeared into the copse.

Eventually I quit. Like the *chicos* the previous day, I'd failed to hitchhike away from Villa O'Higgins. Would I have to wait for the next bus, still two days away? Although I knew the delay hardly mattered, I felt sorely discouraged, as if the setback were a silent remark on my competence and worth. The kindly sympathy expressed by Luci, Enrique and Mauricio only made it worse.

I needed a distraction; I couldn't mope around the camp all evening. A good meal would set me right, so I visited the village to purchase ingredients. As I was passing Hostal El Mosco, the French cyclist Frédérique hurried outside with a message for Mauricio.

'Are you still here?' she chuckled. 'I thought you were leaving.'

'I tried to go. I sat all day by the road, but didn't get a ride.'

'I'm sorry; that sounds no fun. You need a bike. That way you can travel any day you wish.'

'I should have used the bus. It went this morning.'

'Should have? I don't trade in should haves. Each day has enough to cope with without wasting your energy on what might have been. Deal with what you have – you'll find life a lot easier.'

'Wait a minute,' she interrupted herself abruptly. 'Come with me and meet our boss, Jorge.[28] I'm sure he said he was driving to Coyahique tomorrow.'

Perfect. Problem solved.

*

---

[28] *Jorge* is pronounced something like HOR-hay. In Appendix 1 see Pronunciation Note Six: J and G.

I gave the museum one final try late that afternoon. It was open, of course. Inside was a single main hall containing a limited number of artefacts and various display panels relating to the short history of Villa O'Higgins. Half of the museum was dedicated to the story of the priest that Luci had mentioned, Padre Antonio Ronchi.

Antonio Ronchi, the panels described, had been ordained in his native Italy to serve in a congregation known as the Servants of Charity (*Servi della Carità* in Italian and known in Chile as *Obra Don Guanelli*). This group was founded in the early twentieth century by the priest Luigi Guanella. The 'Guanelliani' combined their Catholic faith with an emphasis on serving the poor. You access the soul, Guanella believed, by attending to the body. He died in 1915 and was canonised (as a Saint) in 2011 by Pope Benedict XVI when a relic holding fragments of his bones was associated with the miraculous healing of a Pennsylvanian man who had suffered serious head injuries while rollerblading.

The Servants of Charity developed a global reach, working through 150 centres in Asia, Africa and Europe but predominantly in Latin America. The young Padre Ronchi was sent to Chile. He began at the Obra Don Guanelli community in Rancagua but moved before long to the Patagonian village of Puerto Cisnes[29] where he lived at the Hogar San Luis, the local home of that congregation. The boards described that, during an initial seven-year stay, he visited every hamlet in the area, witnessing first-hand the harsh conditions: nylon tents inhabited by fishermen and peasant farmers in woodland shacks. Following the tradition of the Servants of Charity, he attended not just to spiritual matters but also used his influence with authorities and businesses to improve the lives and livelihoods of ordinary people.

After a five-year posting in Rancagua as Parish Priest, Padre Antonio Ronchi began a second spell in Puerto Cisnes in 1972, which lasted almost twenty years. From his base at the church Nuestra Señora del Trabajo, he dedicated his work to the development of the region. In addition to various social projects, he organised the construction of boats and wharfs, chapels and hostels, and workshops for artisans. He also established Radio Santa María and a network of FM antennae that came to be known as MADIPRO, Madre de la Divina Providencia.

---

[29] Puerto Cisnes features later in this journey.

Later, television transmitters were installed for the broadcast of news, films, and literacy programmes.

Regardless of high local approval, dissenters suggested Ronchi's ambitious projects exceeded the remit of his organisation. Church authorities recalled him to a new position in Santiago in 1992. Following protests, he returned to Patagonia where he was based in Ancud on the island of Chiloé, over 300 kilometres from Puerto Cisnes. For the residents there who held him dear, he might as well have flown to the moon.

He continued to reach out to those in isolated parts of Patagonia. Having opened a school on Isla Toto in 1993, he helped organise that same community for mussel farming, and then founded another school on Isla Magdalena. In 1994, Antonio Ronchi was awarded Chilean nationality in recognition of his dedication to impoverished communities.

At the rear of the museum, the curator showed me a replica of the cell in which Padre Ronchi had lived. It was modestly furnished with just a low bed, a chair and a rudimentary desk. His ministry earned him few luxuries and many hardships. One thing that struck me was how recently all this had taken place. These were the closing years of the twentieth century but the conditions in which Father Ronchi had chosen to live were far removed from the world of modern comforts. Those disobliging conditions may have contributed to the ill health he suffered in the latter part of his life, culminating in his death in 1997.

*

Luci baked an apple dessert in the log oven to complement my offering of macaroni cheese. It was a tasty farewell dinner, washed down with '*buen viaje*' glasses of wine. Tsonek had been a gift, and so had the people I'd encountered there. My timing had been fortunate; a day or two either side, I would have missed the opening party and wouldn't have crossed paths with the entertaining *chicos*. I suppose it's always that way when travelling.

That night I unrolled my mat on the kitchen floor. The next morning I would follow the *chicos* up the Tortel road. It wasn't really hitchhiking but I could pretend – who was ever going to know? This time I could afford to be confident: my journey up the Carretera Austral really was about to begin.

Image 07: The Carretera Austral near Villa O'Higgins

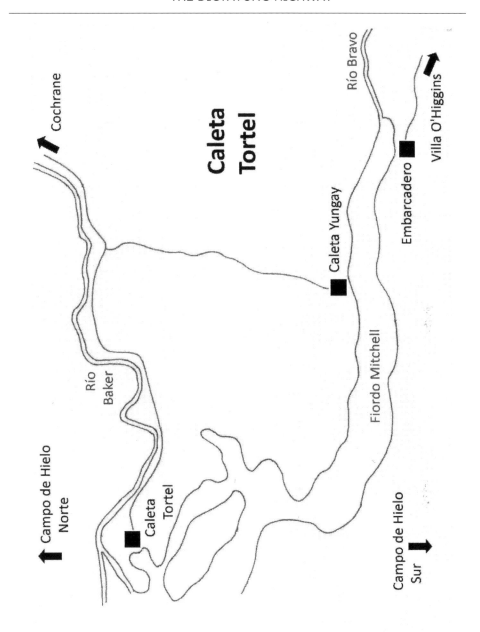

Map 04: Caleta Tortel

Seven: Ciprés

A sound, somehow familiar.
There it was again.
My semi-conscious mind reluctantly stirred.
The third time, the repeating tones took on a tuneful quality.
Wet-wet! Wet-wet!

With the kitchen floor hard against my back and head resting on a thin makeshift pillow of yesterday's clothes, I tracked the path of the ground-dwelling bird, following the direction of her flute-like voice. It curiously resembled the wooden sound of a cuckoo clock. The soothing song was far preferable to the more common dawn alarm of Patagonia: the cockerel's piercing cry.

Once the *huet-huet's* call had faded into the forest, I wriggled out of my nylon quilted cocoon and prepared a fire in the *estufa*. Breakfast was a slice of cake and a mug of Countess Grey, this being an occasion that deserved to be distinguished by a superior tea. Given its negligible weight, the box of teabags had survived the Coyhaique pack cull. I'd never heard of Fortnum & Mason previous to receiving this gift – there appears to have been an oversight in my upbringing – but I'm assured that they purvey only the finest products. I don't fully comprehend why Mr Fortnum and Mr Mason cannot call it Lady Grey like everyone else. 'Lady' is possibly not grand enough for those who shop on Piccadilly.

I was all set for departure when Jorge telephoned. His news of a two-hour delay made me fidgety and restless and I toyed with the idea of thumbing to the first ferry, but in the event my fleeting roadside vigil was as half-hearted as my mood. One car came and went before I returned to the kitchen, drank more tea, studied the map and read for a while.

Then another call: time to go.

*

Jorge flung open the driver's door and leapt out.

'We need to stay ahead of the Robinson Crusoe bus,' he urged, wrestling my rucksack through the sliding rear door of his minibus. 'On this road, the last place we want to be is stuck in a cloud of dust.'

With a 600-kilometre drive ahead, Jorge seemed glad of the company but he still charged me equivalent to the bus fare, something he'd neglected to mention the previous day.

'I can't take you all the way into Caleta Tortel,' he confirmed, 'but I'll drop you nearby. It won't be difficult to get a ride from the junction to the town.'

'Have you been to Tortel?' I asked.

'Yes. It's very pretty; you'll like it. I run a bus service to bring travellers to Hostal El Mosco so I've been there several times. When I discovered that backpackers didn't bother coming to Villa O'Higgins because the journey was so difficult, I set up a shuttle.'

It was good to get started. One thousand, two hundred and forty kilometres of Carretera Austral stretched into the future; probably five or six weeks of hitchhiking and bus rides. First of all, we crawled through terrain that had been visible from the *bandera*: thick forest, scattered lakes surrounded by dry grassland, and the road turning this way and that to negotiate a route through it all. After a while a narrow side road divided off.

'That goes up to the Sheep Bridge,' said Jorge.

The Sheep Bridge was one of the crossings into Argentina, high in the mountains. On we drove, bending around L-shaped Lago Cisnes,[30] after which the road settled on a more promising direction towards the northwest, a thin band of rolled gravel negotiating two back-to-back valleys and vaulting the pass between them.

Half an hour into the journey, we crawled to a halt. In the process of widening a corner, a number of boulders had been blasted from a cliff

---

[30] *Cisnes* are swans, so *Lago Cisnes* means 'Swan Lake'. However, Tchaikovsky's ballet goes under the title *El Lago de los Cisnes*.

and had come to rest in the road. As we waited for a yellow excavator to shift the large rocks, a short line of vehicles built up, including the bus that Jorge was keen to avoid. Even without tailing another vehicle, everything inside Jorge's minibus was now clad in a layer of dust. The seats, the dashboard, our clothes and my bag were all dressed in fine white powder. No doubt we had inhaled plenty, too.

On the move again, we began to gain altitude. In the valley floor, a glistening blue lake was lined with a rim of golden reeds. The slopes opposite clambered through forest to icy peaks. Climbing above, our road twisted around a dizzying sequence of hairpin bends.

'We'll soon see vehicles from the first ferry,' predicted Jorge as we approached the highest point. He was right. One of them was an underpowered city car quite unsuitable for the rough terrain, its roof stacked high with dusty luggage.

We raced down the far side of the pass, crossing the deep gorge of the Río Bravo on a narrow bridge. 'I must get further ahead of the bus,' explained Jorge. 'We need to stop in a while to pick up some timber.'

Having parked above the river a few kilometres later, we slid down the bank. A rowing boat was pulled up on the opposite side.

'The *gaucho* lives there,' said Jorge, pointing out a low, rambling property. 'He said he would leave some *mañío* somewhere under these bushes.'

We located two thick planks amongst riverside undergrowth, hauled them up the slippery bank and slid them beneath the seats in the back of the minibus. *Mañío* is a tree native to Patagonia, misleadingly known as Prince Albert's Yew for its small and convincingly yew-like leaves. The yellow timber is popular in furniture joinery, which is what Jorge had in mind. Wood is indispensable in Chilean Patagonia. In addition to houses and carts, numerous daily objects are of timber construction. It is also the principal fuel for heating and cooking. With forests threatened, the cutting of trees has become increasingly regulated.

'It's forbidden to fell any living trees,' Jorge explained, 'but the people find ways around the rules. Sometimes they light fires to kill the trees. You see, you're allowed to cut them once they're dead.'

We stopped again later, at a ramshackle farmhouse, this time for some *ciprés*. 'Cypress is good for building,' Jorge told me. 'It's light and strong, and slow to decay even if it gets wet.'

For that reason, cypress is preferred for house pillars that stand in soil. Caleta Tortel was constructed almost entirely from *ciprés de las Guaitecas* that grows abundantly nearby. This particular species is also the southernmost conifer in the world, owing to the unlikely patches that bravely endure Tierra del Fuego's harsh conditions.

In the yard beside the house, strips of beef hung on a rack of thick bamboo poles in an open-fronted shelter. A wheelbarrow beneath contained the ashes of an expired fire. Nearby, a brown-and-white cowhide was draped over a wire fence. When Jorge's urgent rap on the door elicited no response, we continued empty-handed. In any case, surely it made more sense for Jorge to collect the heavy planks on his return.

At the wide concrete ramp of the ferry *embarcadero*,[31] a modern waiting room had been built beside a small parking area. The dusty, rocky ground was thick with stubborn low vegetation. A short distance back, a promontory offered an ample view of the valley. Sheer mountains rose on either side of the water. To the right, the Río Bravo emptied into Fiordo Mitchell in indecisive channels, lattice-like through an uneven platform of alluvial deposits. The shallows nearby were cluttered with a floating mat of organic debris including hundreds of sizeable tree trunks. Presumably all this had washed down the river – unless it had drifted from the opposite direction, propelled by wind and tide along the fjord.

The ferry arrived, gliding across the glassy water, and proudly bearing the name *Padre Antonio Ronchi* in white letters across her red hull. She eased up to the concrete *embarcadero* with a dull metallic clunk. A ramp was lowered from her bow and a small clutch of vehicles reversed aboard. The 20-seater Robinson Crusoe bus took a central position with cars either side like a police escort flanking a limousine. A troop of leather-jacketed motorcyclists lined their chrome-piped machines against the steel inner walls of the hull. Jorge slept in

---

[31] The *embarcadero* is the place where you embark, the ferry ramp or landing stage. The word embark (or *embarcar*) is derived from the Latin *barca*, meaning boat (or *barco* in *castellano*).

his minibus throughout the smooth crossing. He still had a long journey ahead.

The mouth of the Río Bravo receded behind us. In common with most Patagonian fjords, Fiordo Mitchell is a narrow sea corridor extending along a previously glaciated valley. Out towards the ocean, it connects to a labyrinth of sea canals woven amongst the thousand islands that form the southern buffer of Chile's Pacific coastline. But we didn't need to go that far; this passage, an hour's sailing or thereabouts, would deliver us to Caleta Yungay,[32] just a few kilometres down the fjord on the opposite bank. One day the ferry might be superseded by a road. It would be a huge job to cut and blast a suitable route through the mountain slopes, but eliminating the boat would reduce the isolation of Villa O'Higgins and increase opportunities for trade and tourism.

When the mist of drizzle strengthened into rain, I retreated to the passenger cabin and chatted with the Robinson Crusoe driver. It might have been sensible to request a ride but I couldn't bring myself to ask; it was too early in the trip to sell my soul. Instead I returned to the passenger seat of the El Mosco bus and accompanied Jorge until our roads divided. A green arrowhead signboard marked the junction:

Caleta Tortel 22km

The minibus rattled away down the gradient and was swallowed up by the forest. I stood for a moment and listened. All was still, save for the intermittent woodland sounds that drifted indistinctly on the still air: the high-pitched whistle of some small bird, a faint leafy rustle and a sudden flurry of beating wings. After slapping on some sunblock I secured my *mochila* and began to walk, pleased to be breathing dust no longer. The road followed the valley of the Río Baker (locally pronounced 'Backer'), but the waters were hidden some distance below, shielded by thick forest.

Walking on the rough track wasn't easy. Loose material swallowed my striding feet and the matter wasn't helped by road repairs on that stretch. The surface had been churned up but was yet to be levelled or rolled. It was like a ploughed field. Adding to the load in my pack were two extra bottles of water. According to Mauricio, the main supply in Tortel had run dry and the back-up reservoir had somehow

---

[32] *Caleta* (as in Caleta Tortel and Caleta Yungay) means 'cove' or 'inlet'.

become contaminated. Visitors had developed stomach problems, he'd said.

Robinson Crusoe cruised by with a friendly toot of the horn, raising a cloud of dust. As soon as the bus disappeared out of sight, I regretted not having requested a ride. Rebuking my wayward mind, I urged myself to enjoy each step and count down the kilometres. On a bus, everything passes in a blur, I reminded myself. At walking pace, I could enjoy the entrancing forest, the sunlight catching on thousands of shimmering leaves, the chuckling of the streams that ran through concrete conduits beneath the road and the cheerful songs of the forest birds.

The low throb of an engine caused me to turn and look back. A motor grader was wobbling slowly towards me. It was all legs and no body, a giant yellow insect with its heavy blade slung beneath. Its pace was not much greater than mine but when it finally crawled alongside, I extended a petitioning arm. Two men were already squashed into a cab designed for one. To ride with them would have required clinging to the exterior frame of the vehicle. Tempting though it was, the decision was taken out of my hands in any case when they passed by without halting.

I continued on foot, opting for the centre of the carriageway where the motor grader had smoothed a flattened pathway. As a result, I was rather recklessly right in the middle of the road when another vehicle took me by surprise on a bend. I swivelled round and instinctively held out a thumb. Too late I saw that the van was painted in the distinctive green and white of the *carabineros*. I had flagged down a police car.

'Are you going to Caleta Tortel?'

'Of course, *señor*. There's nothing else down this road.'

'Do you have room for me, *por favor*? I mean… if that's okay?'

The driver laughed. '*Ningún problema, señor*. Jump in.'

My *mochila* was locked in the secure but petrol-scented cell in the rear part of the van, and I climbed into the back seat of the double cabin. As we chatted amicably, they seemed impressed that I'd taken the trouble to get all the way to Villa O'Higgins. I chose not to admit that I'd done so by plane, which might have been considered cheating.

Approaching Tortel, we paused at a rise in the undulating road where the *carabineros* showed me two sights. One was a mountain with a pleasing fulsome rounded appearance and an intriguing nipple-like rock formation at the crest. The younger man became particularly animated at this point. Secondly, there were two large boulders wedged in the Y-shaped boughs of a roadside tree. A blast of dynamite during highway construction had propelled the rocks into the basket formed by the branches, where they remained trapped.

In the parking area above the town, I concentrated my initial efforts on buying a bus ticket out. Hitchhiking from Tortel would probably have been more straightforward than the day I'd tried to leave Villa O'Higgins, but I'd already lost the desire to put that theory to the test. With no bus scheduled the next day, I booked a seat to Cochrane the subsequent morning. Passenger names were recorded by hand in a book, one page per departure. My confidence in the system started to seep away when the assistant began quizzically turning back and forth from one page to another, and even more so when she wrote my name at the top of a blank page headed by neither date nor destination. Holding up a diagram, she invited me to choose a seat number. I received a thin torn-off ticket, and kept my gnawing doubts to myself.

The tourist information booth, a small shed in the parking lot, operated a centralised reservation system for accommodation. Behind the open hatch, an assistant sat at a desk with a toddler on her knee.

'*Buenos días*,' I began, offering a friendly smile.

The child gave a gleeful, mischievous snigger and slid the window shut. Given the trouble I'd taken to reach Tortel, it wasn't the welcome I'd anticipated. I shot a stern headmasterly glare in the boy's direction. The woman drew her son protectively into her embrace, ruffled his hair and turned away. A poor start.

'Um... I'm looking for lodging, please. I need a single room.'
'There are no single rooms.'
'I see. What about a cheap double room? Are there any of those?'
'Nothing here is cheap. This is Tortel.'
'Ah. Is there anywhere I can pitch a tent?'
'Yes, you may camp *gratis* on the beach at the far end of town.'
'Ah, that sounds great.'
'There's no water. Lighting fires on the beach is prohibited.'

I pondered the options momentarily. 'Are you sure no-one has a cheap room?'

She relented. 'You could try these,' she said, scribbling two circles on a map. 'They're quite basic but probably have rooms available.'

Tortel had no roads. Beyond the cliff-top parking zone, the town spread over steep banks surrounding a bay. Houses were linked up by *pasarelas*, pedestrian boardwalks constructed of thick *ciprés* planks. The two recommended hostels were conveniently close by, at the foot of a long stairway. The assistant pointed me in the right direction and I traipsed down the steps.

I banged on the door at Hostal Tania. A powerfully proportioned woman spoke to me through the adjacent window without bothering to open it.

'What do you want?'

'Do you have any rooms available tonight, please?'

Reluctantly, she opened the door. I was offered a bed in a shared room. The covers were made of colourful knitted squares, reminding me of a blanket I had as a child.

'Do you have any single rooms?'

'We have a *matrimonial* for 14000 *pesos*.'

'Only doubles? That's a shame, I prefer a single room.'

'We do have one single upstairs,' she grudgingly conceded.

'May I see it?'

With an audible sigh, she led me up the narrow stairs, my *mochila* scraping the walls on both sides. The only colour in the sparse room was another squared woollen blanket. Then she led me into the communal kitchen where members of a family were eating at a small round table. The woman treated them to a detailed account of our entire negotiation and plenty more besides. I wasn't sure if she assumed I wouldn't follow the conversation, or whether she was deliberately being rude.

'It's okay,' I said. 'I think I'll look elsewhere.'

The other option circled on my map was Residencial Hielo Sur. The hostel was an old building faced with shingles.[33] On the decking in front was a bench, a signboard and a pile of logs against the wall. It was a safe bet that all this weathered grey wood was *ciprés*.

Renata fussed over me from the moment I arrived and was delighted to offer a cosy single room. The door banged against the foot

---

[33] Shingles are thin wooden tiles used to cover walls and roofs, and are common in Chilean Patagonia.

of the bed, leaving a space barely wide enough to squeeze through. A bent nail on the frame was the only latch.

'Or you could have this one,' she offered, indicating an alternative, 'if you want to see the estuary.'

The view was much more interesting on that side of the house but the room was hardly wider than the bed within it, so I stuck with the first choice. It had pink hardboard covering the walls and an unshaded electric light.

'We have *luz*[34] from seven in the evening until three in the morning,' Renata boasted. 'And the shower is in here;' she pushed open another door. 'We have hot water.'

'*Gracias.* I'll take it.'

At that point I made a mistake. 'I understand there's been a problem with the drinking water,' I began.

Renata's face clouded over. 'Not that I've heard of,' she said, turning her back and teetering down the stairs.

I could have phrased that more gently, something that sounded less like an accusation. It was a redundant point in any case. I had no intention of drinking the water no matter which way she might have answered.

A torn sheet of paper on the wall instructed:

Por favor no fumar ni dejar mochila-s sobre las cama-s. Gracia-s.

Please don't smoke nor place rucksacks on the beds. Thank you.

The S letters had been added later with a different pen. Chilean *castellano* tends to be pronounced quite economically and the letter S at the end of words is commonly unheard. In its non-amended form, the notice had been expressed the way it would be spoken.

I abandoned my *mochila* on the floor, latched the door with the bent nail and left to explore the town. Along the *pasarelas*, everyone gave a friendly greeting, tourists and locals alike. A main precinct clung to the shore around the bay. A renovated section with an attractive rail had the terracotta colour of freshly sawn *ciprés de las Guaitecas*. Steps down from the *costanera*, the 'coast road', gave access to jetties where colourful boats were moored. Tall staircases up the hillsides gave

---

[34] *Luz* means 'light', but here it implies electrical power.

access to further sets of *pasarelas* lined by ornately decorated houses clinging precariously to the steep slopes.

Whereas parts of Villa O'Higgins had given the impression of temporary cabins erected in a field, Tortel had an air of permanence. It was also a labyrinth, both confusing and intriguing to explore. Here and there, the narrow boardwalk avenues opened into wide public areas of cypress decking, Tortel's alternative to the plazas universally found in Chilean towns. One had a carved statue of Padre Antonio Ronchi and another included a children's playground complete with swings, see-saw and slide, all in sanded cypress. There were occasional shops, two churches, a playgroup with a notice in the window advertising a talk on brushing teeth, and the fire station. Rapid response to fire must be a high priority in a place where even the streets are made of wood.

The *Centro de Eventos Comunitarios* was under refurbishment but according to the date on a signboard the project was already overdue. A handwritten notice on the door suggested a reason:

Se necesita carpintero.

Carpenter required.

It was a trade that must always be in demand in Tortel. Unless it was a woodpecker they needed.

At last, surprisingly distant, the final *pasarela* looped back towards the town. Even homes out at the far end were offering guest rooms. Most looked decidedly more upmarket than mine but I was pleased to be lodging close to the road terminus, especially with an early bus to catch.

Returning to Hielo Sur, I extended an olive branch after my ill-advised comment about contaminated water.

'*¡Qué lindo es su pueblo!*' I gushed: how beautiful your town is.

Renata seemed to like that. We chatted a while before I climbed the creaky, wonky stairs to my pink room. There was no vertical or horizontal surface in the whole building; everything was sloping or crooked. A slab of powder fell to the floor as I shifted my bag. Conscious of the same dust all over me I decided to try the shower.

First, I broke the toilet. Water kept flowing after I flushed. The mechanism inside the cistern had stuck open. A rubber flap at the base should have closed to seal the tank. The simplest solution was to reach inside and close it manually, which had the subsidiary time-saving benefit of simultaneously washing my hands.

I was sceptical about whether the shower would be hot, as promised, but my doubts proved unfounded. The water was exceedingly hot – much too hot, in fact. The nozzle squirted a jet of scalding water impossible to stand beneath. I shut off the hot tap and tried the cold: hardly a drip. The tap twizzled freely and the water alternated from off to trickle, to off, to trickle with each 360 degrees. It was devoid of utilisable pressure, even with the cistern now repaired and therefore no longer pilfering the cold supply. All I could do was reduce the hot tap until it produced no more than a dribble, mix it with the cold, and wash the dust from my hair that way. All the same, it was a relief to feel clean.

Although evening had come, many more hours of daylight remained, making possible another exploratory walk. I also needed a somewhere to eat. As I pulled shut the flimsy door of my room, the evening that was in store turned out to be greatly more frenetic and unusual than the relaxed and peaceful sojourn I had in mind.

Image 08: The ferry to Yungay: the Padre Antonio Ronchi

Eight: Javiera

'I lock the door at eleven,' Renata called out as I left. 'If you're back any later, you can sleep outside.'

I took a different route this time, divining my way through the warren of cypress *pasarelas* raised on the hillside. The upper walkways were much narrower than the broad sea-front *costanera*. Two pedestrians would brush shoulders as they passed.

Some way along, a husband and wife were stumbling home, weighed down with their shopping. 'Weighed down' is probably an exaggeration but they appeared to find a pair of carrier bags each a surprisingly troublesome burden.

Suddenly, the sound of urgent footsteps thudded along the boardwalk. A child sprinted by, yelling to another, 'Quick, go to your house and get some wool!'

The boys acted with such intensity that it appeared to be an emergency of some kind, but... wool?

Moments later a girl thundered into me, arms and legs flailing. She must have been around eight years old. '*Señor*, please do you have some wool?'

'No, sorry, I don't.'

I'm sure it was wool. Wool is *lana* and firewood is *leña* so confusion is possible, but this was definitely *lana*.

At Restaurante Mirador, two huge windows overlooked the estuary. No other diners had yet arrived, but there were two long tables prepared for a group. I chose a square corner table which had been set with chunky cutlery, tall wine goblets and two large white plates. Hung on the wood-panelled walls was a framed photograph of a cruise ship in the bay. It must create madness on the *pasarelas* when those vast vessels visit.

The chef appeared through the kitchen door, wiping her hands on a towel tucked into her apron.

'What do you have?' I asked, recognising that this was the kind of place to serve up whatever they happened to be cooking, rather than offering a comprehensive menu.

'If you wait half an hour you can have salmon,' she offered, 'but if you want it now, it will have to be chicken.'

We were interrupted by another young girl rushing in. What was going on with the children of Tortel? Had they all been taking amphetamines? She spoke some garbled words to her mother, the chef, and then turned to me.

'*Tío*,' she began.

Tío means 'uncle' but children use it with any adult, especially when they want something. I always found it rather endearing. It evokes an era when relationships and loyalties were close and you would refer to any man in the village as your uncle and any woman as your aunt (*tía*, as in *Tía María*) because either they really were or alternatively they were familiar enough to be treated that way.

'*Tío*,' she said. 'Please come to the *gimnasio*. The tug-of-war is starting and we all need adults to join our *alianzas*.'

As we hurried there, the girl, Javiera, explained what was happening. It was the end-of-year school party with inter-house games. Javiera was in the *Alianza Blanca*, the Whites. The tug-of-war was the final event and they needed to win. Each *alianza* or house team could nominate two adults for their squad. I imagine there are schools that would be more circumspect about sending their pupils to lure strangers out of the pub to participate in team games, but evidently such inhibitions had not arrived in Tortel.

On the way, we saw the shopping couple again, exhausted at the top of a long flight of steps. The man had decided that he deserved some sustenance. He was slumped against the rail necking a can of beer, a crafty strategy that not only provided refreshment but had the additional benefit of reducing the load in his bag.

At the gym, Javiera dumped me in the middle of a crowd on tiered seating and promptly disappeared outside. Like everything else in Tortel, the gymnasium was completely made of wood: the floor, the bench seats, the walls and wall-bars, the ceiling and the roof. Loud pop music was playing and the younger children careered back and forth. A ball-shaped woman, the headteacher perhaps, tottered here and there directing proceedings. A party with team games, I realised, might explain the urgent search for wool earlier that evening.

Twenty minutes later the tug-of-war appeared to have come no closer. There was a thick rope snaking across the polished floor, but the only people interested in pulling on it were a melee of four-year olds in ballet tutus. There was no telling how much longer would pass before the contest took place, and I hadn't yet placed an order for dinner.

I passed Javiera outside the door, hanging out with her posse in a casual teenage way.

'Sorry,' I said. 'Nothing's happening in there.'

'Yeah, I know,' she said, chewing.

Returning to Restaurante Mirador, I felt mildly guilty for letting down the *Alianza Blanca*, but not sufficiently to keep me from my food.

'Has the salmon arrived?' I asked the chef through the kitchen door.

'No, not yet.'

'In that case, please can I order some chicken?'

'Yes, of course.'

The two long tables had been colonised by what appeared to be a tour party. Most were of relatively advanced years except for two in their thirties. The guide was doing his best to sustain coherent conversation between rival factions. One woman, who had already enjoyed a glass or two of wine, was raising a toast to just about anyone or anything that she could remember. A television was brought in and the guide introduced a tourism publicity video about Caleta Tortel. It kept Madame Toastmaster quiet for ten minutes. During the show, a waitress removed my plate, which I took to be a hopeful sign. On conclusion, the DVD returned to a menu page with a short melodic refrain on a repeating loop. Delightful though it was, after sixteen cycles I judged that most of us had probably enjoyed it for long enough, so I smuggled the remote control back to my table and discretely turned off the machine.

At that point, two more children pushed excitedly into the dining room.

'*Tío,*' one of them begged me. 'We are going to *tirar la cuerda* and we need you on our team. All the *alianzas* need two adults under the age of 35.'

The age limit ruled me out, but I wasn't about to admit it. Then, to my horror, the chef sided with them. 'They need you at the *gimnasio,*' she curtly informed me, as if reports of my earlier escape had reached her. 'Javiera has already asked you, and now these two. You must go with them.'

'Will the chicken be ready soon?'

She dropped her eyes. 'Ah, no,' she said, turning suddenly apologetic. 'I'm waiting for the salmon to arrive. I thought you would prefer that.'

'But I asked for chicken!' I repeated. 'If I go to the gym and pull this rope, will you please cook me something to eat?'

Making our way to the gymnasium a second time, I was twice petitioned to join the *Alianza Verde,* the Greens.

'Very sorry,' I said each time. 'I'm already in the *Alianza Blanca.*'

One of the younger members of the restaurant tour party was also selected for my team. Within ten minutes we were organised into a line and instructed to take the strain and pull. With the rotund headteacher adjudicating, the contest was over in seconds. We were humiliated. I don't even know which *alianza* was at the other end of the rope but their team seemed more numerous than ours and included several large men.

'Is that it?' I asked. 'Any more heats?'

No, that was all. The *Alianza Blanca* was eliminated. *¡Qué pena!* Now dining could resume without further interruption.

Back at Restaurante Mirador the chef welcomed me as if we were best friends. Two hours had passed since I'd first chosen my corner table.

'Is there any chance you can make me something to eat?' I asked, anxious about my curfew and keen not to sleep in the shed.

I received the same meal as the group: chicken and chips with salad. Accompanying a lemon pie dessert, there was a choice of coffee or tea. Restaurant tea in Chile is usually of the herbal variety, not regular black tea, so I asked for *manzanilla,* camomile.

As I left, everyone said goodbye: the tourists, their guide, the waitress and the chef. She even dragged her husband out of the sitting room to shake my hand. Javiera's gang were loitering along the *pasarela* but they ignored me. It was probably for the best. Between us we'd failed to secure a win for the *Alianza Blanca*, having shamefully been beaten by a gang of bearded fishermen.

*

Morning heralded a second fight with the hot water. There was a notice on the bathroom wall with instructions not to wash clothes in the shower:

Atención. Sr Cliente. No deven Lavar. Ropa. En la Ducha. Gracia.

It exhibited an overwhelming proliferation of full stops, and again the words had been written as pronounced, hence *deven* and not *deben*.[35]

I was growing in proficiency and confidence with the water controls when I heard loud music from below. Might this have been Renata's hint that the breakfast hour had passed? I tiptoed down the stairs, arriving directly into the main room. Of four small tables, only one was set for breakfast. Was I the only guest in residence? Or had everyone else begun their day hours earlier?

The tables had lace coverings, although mine had a more practical cloth with squares in pastel shades of green, pink and yellow. A colourful assortment of cushions had been distributed around the eclectic set of wooden and plastic chairs. A lino on the floor had a woodblock design and was nailed around the edge with broad-headed pins. Sunlight streamed through striped yellow-and-white curtains either side of the front door. More windows in the side wall overlooked an ante-room that served as a shop. It was never kept open as such but Renata would attend when someone rang the bell. A bar at the rear of the main room was also finished in matching lino. Behind it were some drinks on a shelf: bottles of *pisco*, cans of beer and some Tetrapacks of wine. At the midpoint of the side wall stood a white enamel log-burning *estufa* that would have been a costly special feature in London or Santiago but here was commonplace. The electrical circuitry appeared to be a later addition – bendy conduit wound

---

[35] B and V sounds can be fairly confusing to the foreign ear. An explanation is given in Appendix 1. See Pronunciation Note Seven: B and V.

around the walls and ceiling with no attempt to conceal it. Tacked to the wall were a list of bus times and a handwritten notice forbidding smoking.

Renata served breakfast: *pan* and *mermelada*, bread and jam, and *té*, black tea this time. Familiar songs were playing on the Tortel local radio station but with translated lyrics. The voices convincingly resembled those of the original singers, unless someone had really persuaded Chris de Burgh to sing Lady in Red in *castellano*, and Bonnie Tyler to croak away about her *Eclipso Total de l'Amor*.

Standing on the shoulders of Padre Ronchi's pioneering efforts, community radio in rural Patagonia commands more extensive coverage than the internet and enables the rapid transmission of information, even to families in isolated locations.

Between songs there was an announcement about a forthcoming workshop on the subject of healthy eating. 'Aysén has the highest levels of obesity of all the regions of Chile,' the presenter explained. An image of the beer-swilling man on the *pasarelas* flashed through my mind. Unfortunately she stumbled over the email and telephone details rendering them barely intelligible. Then she left the microphone channel open during the next song (*Vientos Nuevos*, Winds of Change) and a muffled conversation could be heard in the background, after which a door squeaked open. Slick radio does not come easily.

Renata recommended a circular walk with views of the river valley and its airfield.

'Might dinner be available at Hielo Sur this evening?' I enquired.

'Let me see whether I can get some fish.'

'*Confirmemos cuando vuelva*,' I offered: let's decide when I return.

'¡*Muy amable!*' she replied, apparently warming to my emerging Patagonian flexibility.

It was late morning by the time I set out up the long flight of steps. Beyond the parking area was the school, constructed in *ciprés*, naturally, with the various buildings connected by *pasarelas*. The ground here was probably flat enough for regular paths but with the bulk of the town built this way, I guess boardwalks had become a habit. The walkway crested a hill and cascaded steeply down the other side. The *pasarela* continued across the valley floor far below, a silver streak across the marsh. With a flat base characteristic of a glacier-hewn valley, it was no surprise that this was the site selected for the *aeródromo*. In time, the grassy runway came into view.

On the bank of the Río Baker was a large redbrick house with a drooping windsock outside. Stretching away was a rough landing strip with white-and-orange perimeter markings visible from the sky. With a precautionary glance around, I started along the edge of the airfield towards another windsock in the distance. At the far end of the runway, over a wire fence with orange high-visibility posts, I dropped onto the bank of the grey-blue river. Opposite, partially secluded by trees, a farmhouse stood on an elongated island in the river. The view beyond was dominated by the pleasing bulbous mountain that had excited the younger of the two *carabineros*.

I lay on the bank to read, relishing the sunshine. Birdsong melodies, a light breeze and the gentle movement of the river made for an enchanting setting. A boat chugged into view, carrying a payload of tourists. Distant movement attracted my attention: a man and boy were herding cattle along the opposite bank. Expertly directing a pair of dogs, they separated two from the herd and drove the rest into a pen. A second craft pushed upstream against the current and stopped at the farm. The two occupants stepped ashore and joined the first pair under a tree, where they shared lunch. At length, the peace was disturbed by the faint hum of an incoming plane. As the sound intensified, I scanned the skies, looking forward to witnessing the landing from my close vantage point. At last it came into view but promptly swooped into an adjacent valley and disappeared behind a ridge.

After several hours of peace and contemplation on the riverbank, I began the return towards Tortel. Once across the marshland, I took the route recommended by Renata, trekking high above the town. The hilltop captured unrivalled panoramic views: mountains, the river, the pale winding road, numerous islands in the west and the first reaches of the Pacific Ocean. The islands were all steep slopes and tumbling cliffs. In fact, there wasn't much to distinguish them from the mountains. Islands were simply mountains whose valleys, carved out 18,000 years ago by the glaciers of the Patagonian Ice Sheet, were deep enough to have been inundated by the encroaching sea.

The village and its elliptical bay lay to the south. A long pier protruded over the water. The recently restored rusty red *costanera* skirted a small headland where a pocket of houses gathered under tall trees. The bay was a pool of opaque turquoise with two vessels moored at the centre: a red fishing boat and a white yacht. Around the smoothly curving shoreline, the slopes were covered with low scrub where *ciprés* forest had long since been felled.

*

My foreign guidebook blandly described Tortel as a fishing village. Fishing may indeed take place there but it's rather narrow-minded to assume that every community having a harbour and some boats must have been established for that purpose. Hamburgers are sold at Wembley Stadium but that doesn't make it a fast-food restaurant. Modern Caleta Tortel was founded in the 1950s, but activity began there much earlier. The first records of the area date from early European explorations that were drawn to its location at the mouth of Chile's largest river. One pair of visiting vessels was *HMS Adventure* and *HMS Beagle*. The crew of these two ships spent the years 1826 to 1830 on a hydrographic survey of the sea channels around Patagonia and Tierra del Fuego. The charts they produced continued in use throughout the nineteenth and twentieth centuries. In the course of those early expeditions, the river was named in honour of Rear Admiral Sir Thomas Baker, who at the time was commander-in-chief of the Royal Navy South American Station.

Although the lead boat of the expedition was the 380-ton *Adventure*, the 235-ton *Beagle* is better remembered. Whilst mapping the Patagonian coastline, *Beagle* captain Pringle Stokes reportedly became depressed with the bleak landscapes, dreary climate and gruelling work, and opted to curtail his difficulties by turning a weapon on himself. Although the pellets that lodged in his skull failed to complete their gloomy mission, Captain Stokes finally succumbed to gangrenous infection some days later. His death left Robert FitzRoy in charge of the *Beagle* at the tender age of 23. FitzRoy subsequently returned in charge of the *Beagle's* second voyage from 1831 to 1836, with Charles Darwin aboard.

The first Chilean exploration took place six decades later when a vessel known as the *Toro* explored the Baker fjord and the rivers Bravo and Pascua. Around the turn of the twentieth century, Chile and Argentina both engaged in further expeditions as they established their territorial limits. The Chilean government offered a concession to whichever company would organise colonisation of the Baker estuary. As a result, the Sociedad Nacional de Ganadería y Colonización was founded in 1903, later becoming known as the Compañía Explotadora del Baker. Families were settled in the area and deployed to fell the cypress forests and clear the land for grazing cattle. They established a base to the north of the river mouth, the opposite side to where modern Tortel is now located.

Tragedy struck in 1906 when 120 *chilote*[36] workers died of scurvy. Their remains were interred on the Isla de los Muertos, one of a scattering of mudflats in the estuary. Critics have raised doubts about the scurvy account, alleging instead that workers were poisoned when the Sociedad could no longer afford to pay wages. Whichever is true, the company dissolved shortly afterwards and work ceased.

The next group to accept the concession was the Sociedad Colectiva de Estancias in 1916, who retained the north bank as their centre of activities. However, a large fire in the early 1940s drove many away, and according to census records the area was virtually uninhabited by 1943.

Construction of the town at its present location south of the river mouth began in 1955. Before tourism, Tortel's main economic activity was timber production, with *ciprés* most important of all. All trade and visitors moved in and out by sea until the *aeródromo* was completed in 1980. Another quarter century passed before there was any road. The spur linking Caleta Tortel to the Carretera Austral opened in 2003.

*

Detaching myself from the outstanding view, I began my descent towards the village. The path became less distinct, and a succession of orange arrows nailed to tall stakes lured me into a wide, flat, squelchy depression.

When I was a child, our family holidays usually involved camping in rain-drenched Welsh valleys or tortuous walks over fog-bound mountains in the English Lake District. I always wanted to go to Butlin's, having become entranced by the weekly advert on the back cover of the Radio Times, but my parents' idea of fun was to drag us

---

[36] *Chilote* is an adjective meaning 'from the region or island of Chiloé'.

up mountains in brutal tempests of icy rain. A typical summit scene would have us sheltering from the gale behind a stone cairn, and dividing a single Penguin chocolate biscuit between the four of us. My brother and I knew that there were more Penguins and a big slab of Kendal Mint Cake hidden in my father's pack, but it was forbidden to consume our 'emergency rations'. With condensed cloud dripping from faces and ice crystals forming on boyish fringes, we were cajoled into imagining what the view might have looked like on rare cloudless days. My older brother, much to his shame, pretended to enjoy these trips.

Leaving the protection of the cairn, and at risk of being blown from gigantic cliffs, it was not unknown to misjudge the compass bearing and descend into the wrong valley. Callously, walking down mountains hurts even more than climbing up. Sometimes, though, a mercifully flat area appeared into view through the mist. What joyful anticipation; a stretch on which to walk with less discomfort. But misplaced hope is especially vindictive; of course, the flat patch was a soggy, boggy, mushy sponge intent on deepening our misery by soaking socks and freezing feet. Sometimes we backtracked and found a long, very long, alternative route. Other times we picked a course across the bog, leaping between clumps of grass and swamp plant tussocks. That was a cheerful diversion, the drunken stagger of a chessboard knight, until an ill-chosen clump would dump me up to my knees in frigid peaty water. Other kids got to spend their holidays on the beach.

There in Patagonia, I squelched forward to attempt the tussock method of crossing the wetland. I had a degree of success, but only a degree. I did avoid wetting my boots but that was because they were still back in my room; my choice of footwear that morning had been leather sandals. These were quite appropriate during the first part of the day but latterly had become less than ideal. On the positive side I was surrounded by beautiful bog vegetation, all kinds of mosses and delicate curly-leafed plants in a limitless range of colours. Spindly trees were erratically distributed, amongst them some *taique*, commonly known as Chilean holly due to its dark, prickly leaves. It has beautiful bell-shaped flowers not unlike those of foxgloves but red on the outside and with a yellow interior.

All evidence of any path disappeared. The orange signposts decreased in frequency until they vanished altogether. The previously flat ground began to incline downwards, first becoming a hillside and next a creek, channelling a stream fed by the moisture above. I had two options: return the way I'd come or press ahead. Surely descending couldn't be too difficult? The village had to be somewhere below, drawing closer with every step, so I continued forward. The forest thickened. Interwoven branches that impeded progress also helpfully supported my weight, enabling uncertain steps over the steep, greasy ground.

My flimsy sandals lost grip on the moist surface, and I slipped. Tumbling to the bottom, I rolled into a narrow channel, my face against a broad black pipe. That had to be for water, I reasoned through my festering exasperation, and most likely led to a house.

A *fío-fío* chirped encouragingly, followed by the mechanical song of a *rayadito*.

The plastic tube led through dense foliage. Bent double beneath the branches, I tracked its course, committed now to a pipe that had become my lifeline, my only hope of tasting Renata's home cooking that evening.

It proved its worth as a lifeline; a lifepipe. After repeated skirmishes with the scimitar branches, and bearing trophy scratches on arms and legs, a tall radio antenna appeared above the trees. A few minutes of painful crawling later, I emerged into an overgrown garden. In the centre was a two-roomed bungalow. There was a blue door at the back, and a metal chimney protruded through the corrugate roof. Someone had begun painting one of the aluminium-sheet walls but had either given up or had run out of paint. I wondered momentarily how to explain to the residents why I was prowling across their land, but there was fortunately no sign of anyone home. I crept stealthily to the front gate and stepped through it onto a boardwalk *pasarela*. Residencial Hielo Sur was within reach.

Image 09: One of the pasarelas at Caleta Tortel

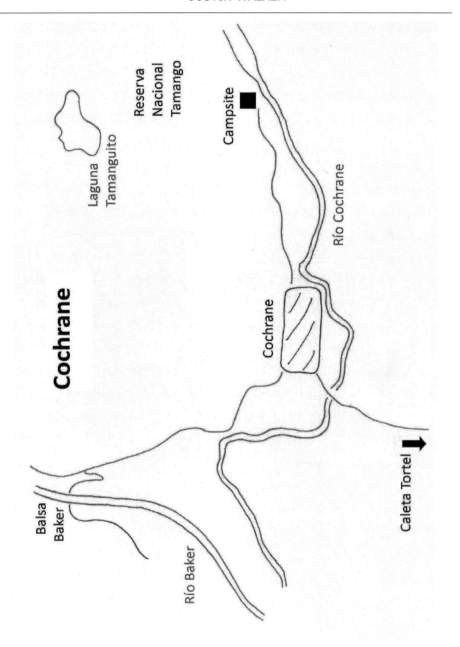

Map 05: Cochrane and Tamango

Nine: Tamango

In the parking area above the town, a 20-seater bus was attended by a pair of drivers that, by chance, I'd already met. The previous evening, we had dined together on Renata's fried fish, and had shared a carton of wine. Our unexpected meeting was a bonus. Not being wholly confident of the handwritten reservations book, an allegiance with the drivers might yet prove valuable. Their 450-kilometre journey to Coyhaique would take the whole day, but the ticket I clutched was for Cochrane, only one-third that distance away and the first settlement of any size after Tortel.

Bags for Coyhaique were stacked in the rear compartment and covered with a huge dust sheet. Those travelling to intermediate towns took their luggage inside. Too bulky for the overhead rack, my *mochila* stayed on the floor beside me, where it blocked the aisle.

The cosy bedroom at Hielo Sur had certainly been the right decision. Camping on the beach would have been less than ideal. It was far preferable to start the day with bread rolls and a shower than to board the bus hungry and smelling of sleeping bag. Nonetheless, nights under canvas were something I generally enjoyed, and I hadn't carried a tent all this way just to look impressive with it strapped to my backpack. There were several opportunities ahead where camping might be possible: Cerro Castillo, Queulat and Pumalín were just three from a long list of suitable parks. Indeed, outside the town of Cochrane there was another outdoor area within reach: Reserva Nacional Tamango. If I wanted, I could be unpacking the tent there this very same day.

Dreamily staring through the window with these thoughts tumbling around my head, it was a while before I became alert to a group of passengers who were embroiled in a surprisingly intense discussion. Three seat numbers had been allocated twice including, it transpired, my own. With trepidation, I recalled how my name had been recorded on a blank page. Unlike some, I was not particular about where I sat, but what we all had in common was a preference not to be de-bussed. The vendor arrived and consulted her list, flicking between pages with a vexed look. She reclaimed the disputed tickets and took them to the secret inner sanctum of her booth. A nervous hush descended. Glancing around, I covertly tallied passengers against seats; the prognosis was reassuring.

On her return, the lady handed back our tickets. Three had been amended with a new seat number.

'You should be in 18,' she said to one man in a tone of voice that implied the confusion had been his fault all along, 'and yours are 12 and 13,' she told a backpacking couple. Mine was unchanged, giving me a quite unmerited sense of justification.

In spite of these several minutes dedicated to seating negotiations, we departed on schedule. With the tension defused, we sat back to enjoy the ride, and a hum of friendly banter ran through the cabin as the bus rumbled along the dusty road. Before long we creaked to a halt beside a woman and her son, who were waiting on the verge. After assisting his mother up the steps, the boy jumped into a boat and rowed towards a house on the opposite bank of the river. A short time later we dropped a man and his stack of boxes at a curve in the road. There was neither any settlement, nor a vehicle waiting, nor any obvious destination across the Baker, just forest, the river and the winding track. Was he planning to construct a raft out of those boxes?

We stopped again later for road repairs. Maintaining the surface of gravel roads is an interminable task. Frequently along the Carretera Austral there were crews using machines for grading, smoothing and rolling the road. There being no alternative route around, vehicles simply had to stop and wait.

*

The town of Cochrane was founded in 1954 with the name Pueblo Nuevo but was later renamed to honour Thomas Cochrane's contributions to Chilean independence. Following a career in the British Royal Navy during the Napoleonic Wars, Cochrane was elected to the House of Commons at Westminster in 1806. He served in Parliament until being convicted in 1814 of offences relating to a Stock Market fraud. In short, the scam involved price fixing in response to rumours (later confirmed as untrue) of Napoleon's death. Cochrane abandoned his homeland to become Vice Admiral of the Chilean *Armada* during the fight for independence. Despite many successes, he left Chile complaining of plots against him. Displaying a taste for this kind of campaign, he went on to lead the Brazilian Navy against Portugal and fought with the Greeks for independence from the Ottoman Empire. He was later pardoned and restored to the British Navy, eventually rising to the rank of Admiral. Thomas Cochrane's grave is in the nave of Westminster Abbey.

Despite being the second-largest town in the region, Cochrane's population is not much over 2000, and the town barely extends beyond a handful of blocks. The central zone is arranged in a rectangular grid centred, of course, on the *plaza de armas*. A bust of Bernardo O'Higgins Riquelme is on display in the square, *Héroe Nacional, Padre de la Patria*. A second statue honours Hernán Merino Correa, the officer mentioned earlier who lost his life in an exchange of fire with an Argentine border patrol in 1965. Notable by his absence is Lord Cochrane. Instead, a third statue depicts Arturo Prat Chacón, *Nuestro Máximo Héroe Naval*.

Arturo Prat was a captain in the Chilean *Armada* during the War of the Pacific. During that conflict, fought between 1879 and 1884, Chile seized the coastal zones of Bolivia and the southern regions of Peru. A part was later returned to Peru but the majority still remains within the present-day boundaries of Chile, including the cities of Iquique and Arica and immense areas of the Atacama Desert.

This nineteenth-century land grab had enduring economic implications for all three countries. It is difficult to quantify the impact on Bolivian trade of losing direct access to the coast. Rubbing mineral salts into the wound, the northern deserts subsequently contributed much to the Chilean economy. For almost a century, nitrate deposits, known as Chilean saltpetre, were mined for export. Nitrates were a key component in the production of fertiliser and explosives, and so lucrative was this trade that it attracted investment from Great Britain and North America to accelerate the construction of railways.

Two World Wars created a heavy demand for explosives. However, with the rapid expansion of synthetic nitrate production in the mid-twentieth century, the export value of saltpetre plummeted. Mines closed and their towns were abandoned. Many have since been looted or otherwise destroyed, but some have been preserved. Near Iquique, for example, is the ghost town of Humberstone where the industrial site and the adjacent settlement, which once housed workers and their families, are both open to visitors. On view are shops, houses, a school, a large theatre, a cast-iron swimming pool and tennis courts equipped with overhead lighting. Due to the absence of atmospheric moisture, the buildings survive intact. Ambling through the deserted streets, it's not difficult to imagine them bustling with activity in the saltpetre-mining heyday.

The collapse of the nitrate industry could have produced a crisis for Chile but for the timely discovery of an alternative source of wealth. With vast and numerous mines in the Atacama Desert and the Andes, Chile became the world's largest producer of copper, a commodity accounting for around half the country's total exports. Demand from rapidly developing China has kept the global price elevated, but in depending so heavily on one product, Chile is vulnerable to the shifting sands of international trade and at risk that the value of the metal might one day fall.

When the Battle of Iquique was fought, they didn't know much about Andes copper but capitalising on the emerging nitrate trade was high amongst Chilean priorities. On 21 May 1879, the *Esmeralda*, under the command of Arturo Prat, was engaged in battle by the Peruvian ship *Huáscar*, seeking to end the Chilean blockade of Iquique, which was still in Peru at that time. Chilean accounts of the four-hour skirmish emphasise the ill-matched nature of the contest between their 850-ton wooden corvette and the 1130-ton Peruvian turret ship armoured with iron cladding. Once the *Esmeralda* had been crippled by cannon fire, the *Huáscar* repeatedly rammed the defenceless smaller vessel. The third time, she sank.

The incident that has entered Chilean folklore occurred when the *Huáscar* butted the *Esmeralda* for the first time. With the two ships locked together, Arturo Prat gave the order to board the *Huáscar* and fight. Valiantly leading his men, *Comandante* Arturo Prat was killed. He was just 31 years old. The heroic manner of his death is said to have motivated and inspired the Chilean *Armada* throughout the five-year War of the Pacific, from which they eventually emerged victorious.

Arturo Prat is considered one of Chile's finest heroes. His name is given to numerous streets and his portrait is on the $10,000 banknote. Four ships of the Chilean Navy have also carried his name, as do a university in Iquique and a research station in Antarctica. The day of his death, 21 May, is commemorated as a national holiday, *El Día de las Glorias Navales*.[37]

*

The hot sun of midday was blazing as I strode out of Cochrane in the direction of Reserva Nacional Tamango, having delayed briefly to restock with provisions. To my great delight, I'd also happened upon a shop in the town centre with a suitable canister of camping gas. Marching beside the narrow road, I had to cover my nose and mouth each time a vehicle passed to avoid breathing clouds of dust. None of them responded to my outstretched thumb, and the four-kilometre hike to the *reserva* felt longer. Ironically, on reaching the gate, a park vehicle did stop, and I rode the last few hundred metres with the warden.

Around the perimeter of the gently sloping camping field, families were enjoying summer *asados*: barbecues. All these groups, bar one, had left by evening, having stacked deckchairs, picnic hampers, rugs, gazebos, bicycles and children's toys into the back of cars and pickups. I pitched my tent at the foot of the slope, where the ground was separated from the river by a rocky ledge. The grass was lush in that low part of the field and the pegs slipped into the ground without difficulty. It crossed my mind that the greenness might indicate a plot prone to saturation, but it was a gamble worth taking with no sign of imminent rain.

With the whole afternoon still ahead, I took a hike along Sendero Los Carpinteros. The footpath followed a wide river channel that was cut through an extensive platform of rock. The water reflected a rich Lapis Lazuli blue and was so wide in places that it might have more fittingly been described as a lake and not a river. At the mercy of the uneven rock strata, the path failed to conserve altitude well. My feet

---

[37] This celebration is not the Day of Glorious Navels, but the Day of Naval Glories, since the adjective generally follows the noun. Glorious Belly-Button Day would be *El Día de los Ombligos Gloriosos*, but this is not celebrated in Chile.

and legs complained furiously at the uphill sections and even more on the steep descents. Cliff tops offered good views of surrounding landscapes but were hot and exposed, and I was glad of the lower parts where tree cover provided shade.

The *sendero* dropped to the riverside at a place called Las Correntadas, where a half-submerged rowing boat was tied to a partially collapsed jetty. I stripped off and plunged in for the coldest of baths, refreshing my aching muscles and feeling deliciously cool on a patch of carelessly obtained sunburn. Glinting like foil bottle tops, a shoal of tiny darting fish approached to inspect the great white intruder that had splashed into their world. I didn't stay long – my sensitive bits were screaming in protest against the torturously cold water.

By good fortune, I'd just covered up when voices could be heard approaching. Not feeling sociable, I snuck off in the opposite direction and located another trail. It climbed steeply to a peaceful *mirador* with views across Lago Cochrane. Submerged rocks were visible through the crystal water, even to several metres' depth. Resting on a bench, I rewarded myself with Fox's Glacier Fruits, another gift kept in reserve especially for the trip. Only then did it occur to me how aptly named were those particular sweets for a journey through Patagonia.

*

Lapis Lazuli

Lapis Lazuli is a semi-precious stone of deep blue colour. The major source of this mineral is northeast Afghanistan where it has been mined for 6000 years. It is also found in smaller quantities in Siberia and the Chilean Andes. There are specialist shops in Santiago exclusively selling jewellery and ornaments of Lapis Lazuli.

---

*

By the time I emerged the next morning, the sole other overnight tent had already disappeared. I packed for a day of hiking, slipped a map of the *reserva* into the deep leg-pocket of my walking trousers and set out along Sendero Las Águilas. It was a short trail up and down over a ridge into a parallel valley, but the path wasn't easy to decipher amongst bracken and bushes. Brushing through undergrowth dripping with moisture after heavy overnight rain, my clothing was soon sodden; I should have worn waterproof trousers. Reaching what I hoped was the ridge, it disappointingly proved to be an illusion, a false summit. Resting there in any case gave views down the valley towards Cochrane. Beyond the town an elongated cloud was draped over the hills, resembling a discarded scarf. More cloud congregated further west over the ice field. In fact, there were so many clouds right across the scene that I feared the rain might return.

Some of the trees were strewn with yellow-green clumps of parasitic mistletoe and round balls of *cyttaira*, sometimes known as Indian bread. A sac-fungus related to truffles, it grows on beech tree twigs and was eaten by native Yaghans, according to Darwin. The path eventually crested the ridge and descended towards a lonely building in the next valley: a shingle-faced timber construction on short stilts. From a distance, it had the appearance of an Alpine chalet.

Having refilled my bottle at an outside tap, I began up the next trail, labelled Sendero Las Lengas. It crossed a meadow set in motion by the breeze. Gentle slow waves washed through the tall dry grasses, transforming into shades of brown, yellow and even violet. At the side, a stunted bush had produced pink berries: unripe *calafate*. A hairy caterpillar crawled along one of the stems, arching and straightening its body, bending almost double with each forward motion. The spikes on its back were arranged with geometric precision. All twelve segments of its body were ringed by several star-like outbursts of tiny green spines.

Across a stream, the route began to ascend through a forest of *nothofagus*. Chile has ten varieties of *nothofagus* or southern beech. The seven deciduous species are *hualo, huala, lenga, ñirre, raulí, roble* and *ruil*. Informally, these are collectively termed *roble*, the Spanish for oak. Though scientifically inaccurate, *roble* was the word used by early Spanish explorers who, needing trees for boat repairs, found the timber similar to European oaks. The three evergreen species are known as *coihue, coihue de Chiloé* and *coihue de Magallanes*. Adding to the confusion, this name can also be spelt *coigüe*.

The composition of Patagonian forest depends on latitude, elevation, soil type and climate (both temperature and precipitation). In the far southwest, for example, the weather is so hostile and the topsoil so thin that only small bushes and stunted trees survive on land that is essentially tundra. In the Patagonian Andes, the dominant species is the *lenga*, after which this particular *sendero* was named. The *gigantesco tronco* from my first hitchhiking day, whose rings were labelled with events from Chilean history, was also *lenga*.

I remember, as a child, choosing a brown crayon for drawing tree trunks. Here in the forest, it dawned on me that the trunks and branches, especially but not exclusively those that had fallen, were generally of a silver-grey colour. Since that day, I've continued to notice that weathered wood, be it fence or bench or gate, is almost always grey, not brown. I've had to unlearn and correct 40 years of mistaken assumptions about wood.

With no interference from commercial forestry, fallen trees followed a natural pattern of decay. Large silver trunks had split open, revealing a fanfare of rich hues within: red, orange and gold. These toppled giants had become a feeding ground for fungi and insects, and the prostrate trunks were home to rodents and mammals that nested in the soft decaying fibres.

The wind intensified, causing slow ripples across the canopy as if each individual were leaning over in turn to whisper a message to its neighbour. The tall trees continued to sway after each gust, like the masts of yachts moored together. The ascent eased and the hill flattened into an exposed plateau. I searched my rucksack for some warmer clothes, adding a woolly hat and a sweatshirt.

The *sendero* ducked back into woodland of a different complexion, not as tall as the swaying masts on the lower slopes. The forest floor changed too, adding an undergrowth of green shrubs, clover and grasses to what had previously been bare earth. Alongside the trail were a marshy depression and then a small lake. The path crossed a clearing where the ground was soft from overnight rain, and finally, beyond another area of trees, it emerged into long grass surrounding the lake, Laguna Tamanguito.

CONAF, the Corporación Nacional Forestal, produces maps for its various parks and reserves. The map of Reserva Nacional Tamango was clear and detailed, with helpful information for hikers. Conversely, many of their other maps had limited effectiveness as navigational aids. Some were barely more than an arrangement of computer-generated blobs, bearing little resemblance to the ground they were supposed to represent. The map of *Tamango* was by far the best, having been based on a genuine survey of the land and helpfully marking noteworthy features such as streams, paths and even contours. Unfortunately I'd kept it in my pocket through the damp undergrowth in the early part of the day. When I came to unfold the sheet, the wind tore it vigorously along each of the soggy folds.

I pondered whether to continue. The tempting summits ahead were out of reach for a day trip, and the flat lake surrounds were exposed to a cold wind that blew the water into impatient choppy waves. In a comically translated paragraph, the notes on my shredded map described the plain as 'high-moisture grassland', probably a polite way of describing a bog. I decided to go no further. The lake was as good a place as any to stop.

Sheltering behind a rock, I removed my shoes and socks. They dried rapidly in the breeze and sun. Lunch was a pair of *hallulla* bread rolls. One of multiple types of bread in Chile, *hallulla* is thin and round with a fork-pricked hard crust. It has a name which, if you say it clumsily, makes you want to raise your arms and Praise the Lord. *Hallulla* often appears on the breakfast table, either alone or with *jamón*, (ham, not jam) or *queso* (cheese). Another popular type of bread is *marraqueta*, a crusty roll divided into easily separated quarters. As a friend of mine described, this is the one that looks like a bottom; she must have four buttocks. In rural areas you can find *pan amasado*, dense artisanal rolls baked in a clay oven, delicious when eaten warm but like rocks otherwise. Standard supermarket bread, though relatively uncommon, is known as *pan de molde*, not because it goes mouldy but because it takes the shape of its mould.

After the *hallulla*, I munched through a bag of dried fruits and nuts before idly reading the dietary information on the empty packet. Imagine my horror on discovering that just a few handfuls of hamster feed amounted to 500 calories. It was a lamentable oversight following a previously unblemished record of moderate lunches, plenty of fruit and a fastidiously rationed allocation of the fearsome threesome: meat, chocolate and beer. Backpacking in Patagonia was providing a perfect opportunity to reverse the unwelcome swelling of my expanding midriff. Aside from the setback of these energy-laden nuts, my early achievements had been commendable, evidenced at least by having progressed from the third to the fourth hole on my belt.

To recover from the calorific shock, I stretched out for a postprandial snooze and slept well, despite the attentions of nibbling ants. I woke to witness a throng of billowing clouds, dark beneath but dazzling white on top, accumulating over Cerro Tamango on the far side of the lake. It was manifestly time to start descending. I hastily retraced my steps through the woods, across the clearing and past the smaller lake. Although sunshine continued to blaze, the wind was sufficiently cold to merit another sweatshirt... and a fleece... and gloves. A few drops of light rain fell but not enough to dampen my spirits. I hadn't seen another soul all day and I felt wonderful.

I might have missed Reserva Nacional Tamango altogether, given its location off my principal Carretera Austral route. But as I descended from Laguna Tamanguito, I was glad to have made the effort and also to have slept under canvas again. Consecutive lengthy hikes added to a gratifying sense of achievement, and I was looking forward to spoiling myself with some town comforts the following day.

I passed the shingle-faced building without pausing. Only the final ridge separated me from the campsite. A pair of Chilean hawks struggled against the fury of the wind, each bird momentarily holding position before soaring in a huge arc to a new spot. As the trail crossed the crest, I was buffeted by unrelenting gusts and took shelter below the ridge. Weary from the long hike, I scanned the valley for the campsite. The entrance gate and shower block were easy to pick out, and a large bus was parked outside the wardens' office. But something was amiss: the lush green spot adjacent to the river was empty.

With a knot twisting horribly in my stomach, I looked again, desperate for any sign. I traversed along the ridge to check from an alternative angle, searching to left and right and amongst the trees. I systematically scoured the terrain in case it was somehow camouflaged against the grass. But my eyes had not deceived me; it wasn't there. Someone had taken my tent.

Image 10: Río Cochrane at Tamango

Ten: Huemules

I stumbled out of breath to the foot of the hill in desperate hope, but a closer look at the camping field only confirmed the troubling turn of events. All that remained on the lush grass where the tent had stood was a pair of leather sandals, one solitary aluminium peg driven into the ground, a bottle of water and a single sock. My mind raced, searching for explanations. What kind of beast would make off with a tent? Had a buzzard eagle snatched it away to an eyrie high on a cliff? Doubtful. Could it have been trampled by a marauding herd of lunatic cattle? Probably not. Had the *guardaparques* cleared it away to make room for a previous reservation? If that was the case, why hadn't they mentioned it in advance? But a more disturbing fear repeatedly surfaced: might someone really steal a tent?

Attempting to control my rising anxiety, I searched out a warden.

'Um... I've lost my tent.'

'Oh... can you show me where it was?'

I took him to the spot.

'You're right,' he said. 'There was a tent here when I came on duty – a green one. Do you think it might have blown away? We've had strong winds today.'

'Impossible!' I retorted.

Confidence can be a good thing, but this might have been an occasion in which to exhibit slightly less self-assurance. Failing to foresee the wind, I'd lazily omitted to secure the storm guys, and had pegged down only the four corners of the groundsheet. I'd then compounded that oversight by taking half my stuff on the hike, leaving insufficient weight inside to act as anchor when the storm blew its worst. My poor tent had billowed like a sail, wrenching out its pegs, and had departed on a journey of its own. It had ballooned up the rock ledge and tumbled halfway to the riverbank. Much further and I might have lost it altogether: tent, sleeping bag and all. Though it didn't feel that way at the time, I'd been lucky. Through gritted teeth I thanked the warden for his help and set to inspecting the damage. The groundsheet had shredded on the sharp rocks but the gashes were fortunately restricted to one corner. There was no sign of any other problem, and crucially the poles were sound.

I glanced sheepishly over the top of the rock. Why is it when we take a tumble that our first reaction is to wonder whether anyone else has noticed?

'This is so embarrassing,' I realised, gathering the sheets of green nylon into both arms. 'If I carry all this back to the field, everyone will see. I should pack up and leave. I could sleep tonight in a warm bed in Cochrane.'

'Are you really going to quit at the first hint of difficulty?' retorted an impatient voice inside my mind. 'What kind of adventurer are you? This is hardly a major setback. Get a grip!'

Chastised, I returned the tent to its original position and replaced my kit inside. Grassy tips poked accusingly through the damaged corner. I had to scavenge around to find the pegs. What kind of wind rips tent pegs out of the ground but leaves behind a sock?

Some of the *guardaparques* were student volunteers fulfilling university placements. One, a trainee vet from Talca, had a particular interest in *huemules*. The *huemul*[38] is the South Andean deer, found only in restricted areas of Patagonia. It is one of two living creatures on Chile's coat of arms, the other being a condor. Following their decline to critical levels, the species now enjoys legal protection. With a shoulder height of around 90 centimetres, adult *huemules* are amongst the smallest ungulate species. Even shorter, however, is another Patagonian deer known as the *southern pudú*. These usually measure less than 40 centimetres to the shoulder, similar in stature to a Cocker Spaniel but without the fluffy coat and floppy ears. Her cousin, the

---

[38] *Huemul* is pronounced weh-MOOL. In Appendix 1 see Pronunciation Note Three: HUA, HUE and HUI sounds.

northern pudú, found in the mountains of Peru, Ecuador and Colombia, is the smallest deer in the world.

'I've not seen any *huemules* yet,' I remarked to the volunteer.

'But they've probably seen you,' she replied. 'They can be so well camouflaged in the undergrowth that you might have walked right past one. They tend to freeze like a statue rather than running away.'

'How many are there in the *reserva*?'

'Fewer than there used to be. According to our census, the number is steadily dropping in this sector.'

'Why is that? Are there puma here?'

'Yes, of course, there are puma throughout the Andes, but they don't take many *huemul*. The main problem is the feral dogs that come up from Cochrane. They more commonly attack sheep, but a pack would have no difficulty overpowering a *huemul* or even an alpaca.'

'It seems there are street dogs all over Chile,' I commented.

'They've spread everywhere now,' she agreed. 'You have them in the UK, too, but they get picked up and sterilised by the RSPCA. And in your country, if a home isn't found within three months, the animal will be sacrificed.'

'Sacrificed?'

'That's the word we use. But you could say… terminated, you know… injected. That wouldn't be popular in Chile. Stray dogs are a nuisance but there would be an outcry if people knew they were being rounded up and destroyed. The government has authorised some sacrifices, but they've kept it very quiet.'

During the evening, the campsite was colonised by a group from the National Outdoor Leadership School. Animated groups of teenagers laid claim to all corners of the field. Each team had a sophisticated mountain tent, grey with orange trim, supplemented by a separate navy blue awning under which they stacked their bags and equipment. One of the supervisors explained that these were 34 'young leaders', mostly from the United States, on a training exercise. The following morning, half were to travel to Tortel to begin a month of sea-kayaking, with the others heading to the mountains. They would swap activities for a second month. It sounded like an uncompromising kind of trip. Amongst their ranks was Daniela, a lone Chilean attendee whose participation had been made possible through a scholarship she had won.

Large splats of rain began thudding onto the tents and awnings, dotting them like Dalmatians. I gathered the various trappings necessary for preparing dinner and retreated into a shelter at the side of the campsite. Eager voices drifted across the field, the young leaders establishing credentials on the eve of their adventures.

'Have you done anything like this before?'

'Sure thing. We had an outdoor bound program when I was in Junior High. We had the same activities as this out in Washington State, with climbing and orienteering, as well. What about you, man? Have you spent any time outdoors?'

'Oh, yeah. My scout troop won medals for raft-building at the county jamboree last Thanksgiving.'

'When I was in the Black Bear Protection Patrol...' and so on.

Dining on lentils and sauce, I secretly yearned for *lomo a lo pobre* to heal my wounded pride. A pair of bright yellow siskins kept me company as I ate, and a *carpintero chico*, the striped woodpecker, unperturbed by the rain which by now was falling steadily, gave a display of precise drilling on a nearby low branch. One by one, the young leaders peeled off from the group and headed to their tents. I did, too, hoping that the damaged groundsheet would resist the moisture of the ground.

*

Sometime before dawn, I made a barefoot dash to the toilet block. Although the rain had ceased, the grass and tents were still drenched. That was enough encouragement to burrow back into my sleeping bag. When I surfaced a second time, the Leadership School had already struck camp and were boarding their bus.

The young volunteer who answered the door of the wardens' cabin was robed in only a t-shirt and boxer shorts. Another looked sleepily out of an upstairs window. I was after their electricity supply. Having located a socket in the lobby, the green diode illuminated reassuringly on my camera but my phone stubbornly refused to recharge. I had a spare adaptor, left over from a previous handset that I'd carelessly left behind in a taxi, but it was safely in a drawer in Santiago. As a result,

I'd have to continue the journey without a phone. Patagonia had once again found a way to challenge the preferences of my regular pattern.

I packed at a lazy pace, allowing time for the tent to dry and the charger to do its work, until an unexpected event sped me along. With an engine's roar and the clatter of stones peppering its undercarriage, a white pickup careered into the campsite and came to a halt at the upper end of the gently sloping field. Three young men piled out of the cab and unloaded a slab of beer cans onto a picnic table. Although their chosen spot was secluded amongst trees, the persistent drum and bass that boomed from the vehicle foiled any intention they might have had of being discreet.

After briefly conferring, one of them ambled towards the spot where I was still optimising my *mochila*. This was all I needed. My young protectors had departed in their bus, leaving me to face this genial clutch of country dwellers alone. Making a swift analysis of the assorted kit around me, I stuffed binoculars and sunglasses deep into the bag.

The man swaggered to a stop and regarded me for a moment. He was not tall but had the strong build of someone who habitually worked on the land. His boots were untied, with one pale leather tongue curling forward over slack laces. His grubby jeans were too long with quoits of ruffled denim at his ankles, and a torn, open-necked shirt, which might once have been white, hung loosely from his shoulders.

'Where are you from, *amigo*?'

How can the word 'friend' be so intimidating? I had moments to decide between London and Santiago. I chose foreign.

'Ah, we have an Englishman,' he said, displaying knowledge that mightn't necessarily be taken for granted. 'We invite you. We are having *parrilla*. You know *parrilla*?'

I recognised the Argentine word for barbecue. '*Sí*.'

'We always like to invite you foreign people,' he continued, flicking strands of unkempt hair from his eyes with a pronounced jerk of the head.

'*Tengo que irme*,' I told him: I have to go.

He offered a cigarette.

'No, *gracias*.' I didn't want to upset him by seeming ungrateful but with this he gave up, shook my hand roughly, and returned to his mates.

I was torn between the urge to leave, thus reducing the risk of becoming an object of fun for a group of well-lubricated *campesinos*, and wanting to give my tent more time to dry. To my relief, the revellers left me unmolested as I resumed packing, hurriedly now. In my anxious state I nearly forgot to recover the camera battery from the office of the *guardaparques*.

Departing the field, I waved a cheery farewell and the beer drinkers chorused a rowdy acknowledgement. Further motivated by a gloomy sky awash with menacing grey clouds, I strode out down the road to Cochrane. Midway along came the sound of a vehicle approaching from behind so I leapt over a fence and ducked into the scrub as a disturbingly familiar white pickup raced by.

Looking back, I'm not sure why these three country gentlemen intimidated me quite so much. Nothing they did could be described as threatening. In fact, our only contact was a generous offer to share in their *parrilla*. In fear, probably an irrational and judgemental brand of fear, I passed up the chance to spend an hour with new *amigos*, genuine Patagonians, and missed the chance to learn a thing or two about them and their lives. Rather than open myself to discovery, I closed my mind and ran away. Did I really think they were going to steal my stuff and dump me in the lake with concrete boots? It was hardly likely. Was it the early morning alcohol consumption, clashing with my culturally conditioned beliefs regarding the hours when beer should be drunk? I guess I was feeling sensitive, especially following the disquieting affair of the missing tent with its consequent knocks to my pride. Was it their sudden brash arrival: the revved engine, squealing brakes and overloud stereo, all contaminating a peaceful setting in which I had unilaterally determined they did not belong? Or was the intrusion I found unsettling not so much about any defilement of the countryside but more an assault on my personal tranquillity? With hindsight, the whole encounter may have been a missed opportunity. Nonetheless, as I crouched in the long grass at that precise moment, I had no desire to be offered a ride into town.

Arriving in Cochrane after an hour, I headed for the shops on the plaza. Casa Melero was described in the one of my guidebooks as 'Patagonia's greatest general store'. Maybe, but they didn't have strong waterproof duct tape suitable for groundsheet repairs. I bought brown parcel tape instead, conforming to the same three-stage operation as when buying the camping gas in Puerto Montt: select the item, pay at the *caja* and collect from the *empaque*.

I took a single room at Hostal Paola. The only furniture in my room, other than a small bed, was one of those hospital-style tables with a single adjustable leg at one side, suitable for a person sitting up in bed. It was a design that also proved perfect for tent surgery. With the upper fabrics tucked out of the way, the table top slid through the open zip to permit unencumbered access to the injured area. I swabbed the cuts, washed away foreign debris and closed the wound with the best sutures I had to hand: parcel tape. Although the temporary repair was unlikely to last very long, it was better than leaving the lesions untreated. A more permanent graft would have to wait.

Two Chilean travellers in the room opposite had also checked in that morning. One of the pair was a fellow of generous proportions, and my bedroom floor creaked and shook as he paced the corridor outside. I took a shower, upsetting the woman who'd only just cleaned the bathroom, and spread my tent over the bed to finish drying. This endeavour had a fair chance of success because the shiny chrome chimney from the stove downstairs passed through a corner of my bedroom from floor to ceiling, comfortably warming the air.

Stopping a day or two in Cochrane supplied the opportunity to restart with a clean wardrobe. I emptied a heap of clothes onto the floor to pick out those that would benefit from a wash: nearly all of them – it was a simpler task to separate those that were clean. A card in the window of the tourist information booth in the *plaza de armas* advertised a *lavandería*. I wandered through the town to find the place, a plastic sack of fermenting t-shirts slung over my shoulder. Along the streets, most dwellings were of the same familiar design: wooden-framed bungalows faced in aluminium sheeting. Older properties could be differentiated by their alternative veneer of shingles or planks. Precious few had a second storey.

Lavandería Juanita was a ramshackle house in a street of similar properties, truly a cottage industry. I quite like supporting small independent businesses and prefer to deal with local and community traders. I was therefore content to hand my laundry to Juanita, who advised me to collect it at eight that evening. As a result, I spent the day in my only remaining garments: a bright orange long-sleeved t-shirt, swimming shorts, sandals and a fleece. It was a combination that looked odd on a blustery day, but with a desire to wash as many clothes as possible, I lacked the luxury of choice. Moreover, whereas back in the city the outfit might have merited surprised stares from passers-by, backpackers routinely wear garish and unusual clothing, and no-one gave me a second glance.

Cochrane was quiet that Saturday morning; perhaps it always is. At the focal point of the *plaza de armas* was an artwork that had been unveiled by the previous President of the Republic, Michelle Bachelet. The piece depicted a *huemul* in profile, cut from a thick rusted sheet and fixed atop a rock. An attractive octagonal church stood at one corner of the plaza. Nearby, four wet touring bicycles loaded with heavy panniers were propped against the wall of a coffee shop. Another café was doing business on the next block, this one inside a decommissioned red bus on a vacant plot of land.

Across a narrow stream was a park that had recently re-opened following refurbishment, according to an explanatory notice carved onto a huge slab of rock. In addition to having a tall pagoda and a children's playground, it was dotted with unusual sculptures: a large *mate* pot complete with protruding *bombilla*, an oversized cart and a regal eagle with a broken wing. Nearby, two *queltehue*[39] began harassing another pair on the stream bank, driving them away; I had no idea that lapwings could be territorial in this way. As the violence was subsiding, a fifth bird flew in from across the park to enter the scrap. It reminded me of those footballers who run the length of the pitch to join a tussle that doesn't concern them and are accordingly sent off.

*

A restaurant dinner that evening provided reward for my northward progress and consolation from the trauma of a wandering tent. My previous experiences of eating tongue had been confined to

---

[39] *Queltehue* is the local name for the southern lapwing, common throughout Chile.

cold cuts served at a buffet tea, Christmas Eve at my grandfather's home being a typical example. But when I chose a starter of *Lengua*[40] *Mayo* in Cochrane, it was an altogether different experience. This slab of tongue was loose, floppy and disturbingly tongue-like. A smothering of mayonnaise did little to disguise its true identity. The main course was *lomo* and *papas fritas*, steak and chips, with lots of *ají chileno*, strong chilli sauce. A novice diner guessing the contents of the three squeezie bottles commonly found on a restaurant table might mistakenly assume the red one to be ketchup, the yellow mustard, and have doubts about the green. To avoid mouth-burn, it's handy to learn that the green pot probably contains ketchup and the yellow one mayonnaise, and to beware of overdosing from the red bottle, which is usually full of hot *ají*.

A family occupied a nearby table, a young couple with a girl toddler and two *abuelas*: Grandma Glasses and Grandma Hat. The child was in no mood for a peaceful family meal and demanded constant entertainment. Grandma Glasses walked her up and down between the rows of tables. Grandma Hat invented a game that involved repeatedly stepping out the front door to make faces through the glass, letting in a blast of cold air each time. The exasperated father also took his turn. For a while he held his daughter and showed her the various pieces on display along the walls: ceramic pots, painted plates and a long line of fabric dolls. He appeared to be doing just fine and the girl, for once, was giggling happily. I was mystified, therefore, when the mother abruptly stood, marched across to them, grabbed the child and gave the father a stern 'you are doing it all wrong' kind of stare.

Lavandería Juanita was not far from the restaurant. Having retrieved a fresh pile of lavender-scented[41] washing, I took a circuitous route home. High on a rocky hillock, a large crucifix had been erected: a carved statue sheltered by a cement arch. Two rosaries hung around Jesus' neck, and at the base stood a vase of garish plastic flowers. A board was inscribed with the prayer of Padre Pablo Venezian, another locally cherished priest whose remains rest in the crypt of Coyhaique Cathedral. The prayer began:

---

[40] The word *lengua* can mean either 'tongue' or 'language'. Both 'language' and '*lengua*' are derived from the Latin word *lingua*, meaning 'tongue'.

[41] Somewhat disappointingly, lavender clothing conditioner is not the reason a laundry is called a *lavandería*. The verb *lavar* means 'to wash'.

Señor Jesús tú eres camino, verdad y vida para mí.
Lord Jesus you are road, truth and life for me.

Expressed in a different language, the familiar phrase conveyed fresh meaning. 'I am the road' was somehow more concrete and tangible than 'I am the way'. How apt to have mounted this inscription alongside the Carretera Austral, a highway whose construction has palpably transformed the daily lives of people in local communities.

*

The prayer of Padre Pablo Venezian

Señor Jesús, tú eres camino, verdad y vida para mí.

Lámpara es tu palabra para mis pasos y luz en mi sendero; tu que has dejado rumor de tus sandalias por los polvorientos caminos de la Palestina.

Haz Señor Jesús que pueda recorrer con mi maquina los caminos de mi Chile en búsqueda de un pan para volver con un alegría a mi querido hogar donde me esperan mi esposa e hijos con cariño y amor.

Amen

A loose translation might be as follows:

Lord Jesus you are road, truth and life for me.

Your word is a lamp for my steps and light along my path; you who left the imprints of your sandals through the dusty roads of Palestine.

Help me Lord Jesus as I travel the roads of my Chile in search of bread, to return with joy to my cherished home where my wife and children fondly await me with love.

Amen

Image 11: Distant cyclist near Cochrane

Eleven: Agua

Showers quarrelled against the window. Higher ground had taken a dusting of snow. The weather had already spoiled the plans of a visitor from Santiago, who sat opposite me at the breakfast table.

'Yesterday I wanted to get to Caleta Tortel,' he told me, 'but the Río Baker overflowed its banks and washed away the *carretera*. I'm going to try again this morning. I've never visited Tortel.'

Seeking out a climate prognosis, I received a mixed set of forecasts. The hostel owner was confident the day would turn out fine. My breakfast companion thought the rain would probably continue throughout the week, but generally at night. A third opinion came from the attendant at the bus office where, after breakfast, I called to enquire about departures to Chile Chico, a hundred kilometres away and therefore possibly distant enough to escape the rain. A sign in the window listed the Sunday opening times:

Abierto los domingos 9h – 12h, 16h – 20h.

Though the hour was beyond ten, the office showed no signs of life. Pressing my face against the glass, I noticed a list of bus times on the far wall. I tried to capture the information using my camera zoom, but as I did so, a door opened behind the counter. The man who materialised seemed taken aback that I was after a photograph of his desk, but I adeptly moved the conversation along to the pressing matter of bus departures. My not-so-reliable guidebook listed one service per week to Chile Chico, on Sundays at 13:45.

'No,' corrected the man, 'the weekly bus goes on a Wednesday. But they go more frequently from Río Tranquilo, if you can get there.'

The bus office was also the Post Office, except for Sundays. It was run by the same man, whose box of stamps and cabinet of forms were right there on the counter but those facilities were unavailable *los domingos*. Mind you, the same used to be true of rural post offices housed within general stores in the days when British villages were permitted to have such things. As for the weather, not only would the damp period continue for three more days, he asserted, but it was futile to attempt an escape to Chile Chico since similar conditions were affecting the whole region.

I briefly considered hiring a bicycle for the day but found the shop closed. In any case, the rain was rather dissuasive. A day of walking appeared to be the best option so I began to hope that the optimistic weather forecast of the hostel owner would prove correct. If conditions improved, I could possibly reach the Balsa Baker, a vehicle-carrying raft across the Río Baker that seemed worth a peek.

The persistent rain could hardly have been described as a surprise. A lot of water[42] falls on the South American continent, though the pattern is one of extreme variation between west and east. Pacific Santiago (373mm per year) is relatively dry in comparison with Buenos Aires (1066mm) on the Atlantic side, despite their similar latitudes. Some parts of the Amazon basin record over 3000mm annually, whereas the Atacama Desert on the western side of the Andes rarely witnesses precipitation at all. The east-west contrast reverses at the southern end of the continent. Weather stations in Chilean Patagonia regularly record a metre of rain in a year, but much of the Argentine side is arid.

*

The unpaved road leading north from Cochrane was, of course, the Carretera Austral. Two men were hitchhiking at the petrol station, but

---

[42] Although water is abundant on our planet, only a tiny proportion is available for human use. Most water used by human populations is drawn from rivers. This is a restricted source, accounting for a tiny proportion of the Earth's surface freshwater (approximately 0.5 per cent). Surface water is only a miniscule amount of the total fresh water (marginally over 1 per cent), and this in turn is only a small fraction of all the water on the planet (about 2.5 per cent). There is more water on Earth than almost anything else, but not much of it is readily accessible for human use. One location with a water crisis looming is the capital of Chile's northerly neighbour, Peru. With nine million inhabitants, its capital, Lima, is said to be the second-largest desert city in the world, after Cairo. The major river, the Rimac, is fed by glacial meltwater but the glaciers are shrinking. Numerous projects have been proposed to supply Lima in the future, including diverting water from the Amazon and seawater desalination.

Sunday traffic was virtually non-existent. An adjacent timber yard advertised sales of *ciprés, lenga, coihue* and *mañío*. Further on, willows trailed their dreadlocks in the green water of the Río Cochrane. Small birds flew fitfully between the branches under the watchful eye of another *carpintero chico*.

Ahead, a helmeted figure was pedalling up a long incline, making barely any headway. He wore an orange cape against the squalls and his striking yellow bike was laden with black panniers, front and back on both sides. This is why I'm not attracted to long distance cycling: weighed down with luggage on an uphill stretch of gravel road, with a strong headwind driving rain into my face. Even at a moderate walking pace, I easily caught the forlorn figure and introduced myself to Lorenzo.

'I work for a technology company in Bologna,' he said. 'You know, computers. When I was 50 a few years ago, I realised that I no longer loved my work so much, so I asked them to give me additional leave every year. It's unpaid, of course, and they took away my company car. But it's better this way. Every year I have two extra months for travelling.'

'Good decision,' I agreed.

'I usually go somewhere that I can cycle. You can use a bike wherever there's a road, in almost any place you can think of. You don't even need fuel stations.'

We walked together for several minutes towards the crest of the hill, Lorenzo pushing his bike and me offering no help – I didn't want to spoil the authentic experience for him. When I asked where else he'd toured, he listed places all over North and South America.

'This is my third visit to Patagonia. But I'm not going to cycle the Carretera Austral this time. I've done that twice already.'

Twice?! I wasn't sure whether to be impressed or horrified; one trip along this unforgiving road would surely be enough punishment for most mortals.

'This time I'm going to explore the side valleys. You miss so much when you ride only the main highway. I'm going to turn up the Chacabuco Valley and into the mountains. I can cross into Argentina and return south on Ruta 40. Then I'll drop back into Villa O'Higgins via the Sheep Bridge.'

In the vicinity of the Sheep Bridge was a section with no road at all, which was largely a tract of 'high-moisture grassland'. Perhaps he will be unearthed by thirty-first century archaeologists and will become known as Bog Cycle Man.

'I presume the bike is yours?' I guessed. 'You haven't hired it here?'

'That's right,' he confirmed, patting the handlebars affectionately. 'I built this machine and brought it with me on the flight from Italy. In fact, I have two of these, one for North America and one for South.'

'What's the difference between them?' I asked, expecting details of some obscure technical adaptation for the distinct conditions of terrain or climate.

'None at all,' he replied. 'They are identical!'

I can still hear him say this final word in his lilting voice, leaning on the second syllable in a way that split it in two: 'Aye-dayun-ti-kul'. His soft Italian accent seemed to caress the words in place of simply speaking them.

'When I am maintaining one bicycle, I can ride the other. These journeys are my life. But there is a cost,' he admitted. 'I have no family.'

Something akin to empathy resonated in my soul.

Lorenzo cycled away but soon stopped to adjust the straps of his paniers, and I caught him again.

'I'm happy to see the Baker one final time,' he remarked. 'Soon it will be changed forever.'

It took a moment to realise he was referring to the controversial HidroAysén project, a massive hydroelectric scheme. In addition to its uses for drinking and cleaning, manufacturing and Chile's rapidly-expanding fruit-growing industry, a significant quantity of water is needed for the generation of electricity. Scattered throughout the Andes are concrete turbine houses fed by way of gigantic pipes from the higher slopes, with tell-tale pylon chains strung towards the cities. Around one-third of national electricity generation comes from hydroelectric turbines, a smart move for a country that depends heavily on imported fossil fuels. In the search for new energy sources, a number of sites in Patagonia have been evaluated as suitable for hydroelectric generation, including the HidroAysén[43] proposal to build dams on the Rivers Baker and Pascua. Measured by flow, these are the largest and third-largest rivers in Chile.

'Dams are not good news for rivers,' Lorenzo told me. 'Making the water stand still disrupts the flow of sediment. That makes riverbanks downstream erode more rapidly. It also has a negative effect on agricultural land. The river needs to flood periodically.'

'Why is that; for irrigation?'

'Not so much. It's about nutrients. Organic particles in the water are good for the soil. Land becomes less productive if the river is not allowed to flood. It's usually poor people who suffer from these large dams,' he went on, 'even though they are least likely to use the electricity. When the dam is built, it will be peasant farmers who lose their homes and livelihoods. No-one ever floods a valley where bankers and lawyers live.'

Vociferous protests and militant demonstrations were raging the length of the country. The campaign was led by Patagonia Sin Represas, a movement that provided a focal point for critics to raise both environmental and economic concerns. The name means 'Patagonia Without Dams'. Their campaign emphasised the damage to wildlife that would result from flooding the Pascua and Baker Valleys. Almost 6000 hectares were set to disappear underwater,[44] including forests inhabited by the endangered *huemul*. Wetlands, on which numerous bird species depend for feeding and nesting, were at risk, and there were threats to fish, amphibians and the southern river otter, the *huillín*.

A second environmental concern pertained to the proposed installation of high-voltage transmission lines that would link the turbines in Patagonia to the main distribution grid, the *Sistema Interconectado Central*. The dam sites were a long, long way from the central regions accounting for the bulk of demand. Measuring over 2000 kilometres in length, these lines were set to match two lines in China and one in Brazil as the longest pylon chains in the world: one built every 400 metres would make 5000 towers in all. According to

---

[43] HidroAysén comprised two energy companies already established in Chile: Endesa Chile (51%) and Colbún SA (49%).

[44] HidroAysén stated that the total area of the five dams would be 5910 hectares, equal to 59.1 km^2. The largest reservoir in the UK, Rutland Water, has an area of 12.6 km^2. These areas are small compared to some of the natural lakes in Patagonia. The largest, Lago General Carrera (1850 km^2), covers 30 times the total area of the proposed dams.

Patagonia Sin Represas, transmission lines endanger birds of prey and formation flyers such as geese and swans. Beneath the lines, a strip of land was to be cleared 70 metres wide, totalling 2400 hectares, some of it native forest and wildlife habitat protected under law.

Associated with these environmental arguments were worries about the impact on visitor numbers. Unsightly towers and cables would mar the national parks and scenic valleys on which Patagonian tourism so depends. Proprietors of fishing lodges and guest houses were understandably concerned about potential losses.

As for the economic dimension, the estimated cost of the project was over three billion dollars. Campaigners argued that the scheme was too expensive and that alternative ways of generating power would be more efficient. Chile could better exploit renewable sources such as solar, wind, geothermal and tidal energies, they claimed, and update elderly turbines in existing hydroelectric plants.

A third strand of concern surrounded the social impact of a lengthy construction project. Workers would outnumber the permanent population in the locality around the dams, with unpredictable consequences for those delicate communities.

In contrast, supporters of HidroAysén emphasised the importance of increasing national electricity capacity,[45] currently registering at around 17,000 Megawatts. The projected medium-term requirement is an additional 8000 Megawatts, and the five dams could together supply one-third of that amount. Both domestic and industrial energy demand are growing rapidly. Chile's vast mining operation is amongst the culprits, running up the kind of electricity bill you would never want to receive. Nevertheless, given copper's virtually unassailable position at the top of the export economy, it's no surprise that mining companies are prioritised when it comes to infrastructure planning.

President Sebastián Piñera warned of an impending energy crisis. Citing a regular annual increase of six or seven per cent in the demand for energy and the rising costs of imported fossil fuels, he strongly

---

[45] Electricity consumption in Chile has increased significantly in recent decades. The figures below give electricity consumption in KWh per capita taken at ten-year intervals between 1981 and 2011. UK and USA figures are also given, for comparison.
Chile: 937, 1318, 2608, 3568 KWh/capita (in 1981, 1991, 2001, 2011)
UK: 4573, 5452, 6143, 5516 KWh/capita
USA: 9977, 12134, 13047, 13246 KWh/capita

backed the HidroAysén project, stating that the further development of generating capacity from renewable sources was essential.

Supporters pointed out the relatively small area of Patagonia that would be affected. The inundated portion would amount to just one twentieth of one per cent of the overall Aysén region. A large publicity hoarding outside Santiago Airport illustrated this point, showing a tiny blue square representing the total area to be flooded, against a huge empty background.

The stewardship of natural features such as forests and rivers can be regarded in various ways. An anthropocentric viewpoint regards them instrumentally: they are resources that we as humans may exploit in order to benefit and enrich ourselves. Others urge a responsible use of the planet and its resources, taking into consideration the needs of diverse people around the world, and not forgetting future generations. A third, more radical viewpoint argues that animals, plants, forests, rivers and even natural objects such as waterfalls or valleys have an inherent value regardless of their instrumental value to humans. Adopting this position calls into question our assumed right to harness, change, damage or consume these things, living or otherwise.

Environmental campaigners have a difficult task when it comes to sources of energy. That we must learn to depend less on fossil fuels is increasingly understood (although heeded pitifully). However, each of the renewable alternatives has its opponents, who complain that tidal energy production damages estuary life, that wind farms are ugly and that solar schemes consume too much land. Biofuels are criticised for displacing food production, nuclear fission for its legacy of hazardous waste and hydroelectric dams come with the problems already discussed.

Whilst proper investment and thorough research into renewable technologies would be a huge step forward, it is increasingly clear that the world's over-consumers of energy must learn to use less. Heating, lighting, air-conditioning, cars and new roads, air travel and airport expansions, technological gadgets designed to become obsolete, oversized televisions, disposable items of boundless variety, excessive packaging,[46] and the list goes on. Endless 'conveniences' in modern

---

[46] Let's not even start on the scandalous waste associated with gratuitous items like patio heaters. What will future generations make of our wantonness, burning precious fossil fuels to

society represent a consumption of energy and resource far beyond that which merits justification. Consumers are quick to complain about fuel costs but there are good reasons to raise prices yet further. The current generation of UK political leaders were happy to introduce green taxes when they won support but soon demonstrated a shocking deficiency in leadership by ditching those policies when they became unpopular with prices spiralling. The deeper costs of energy overuse do not appear on domestic gas bills. They are tragically borne by the poor who are excluded from the benefits of this cherished 'progress' and by our planet, which some coming day will have no more left to give.

Environmental responsibility is a discipline full of complex debates but one thing is obvious: nature can only continue to provide good and beautiful things as long as we stop damaging and destroying her.

*

A flat-back low loader rattled by, carrying a mechanical excavator. The six-axle truck eased into low gear and descended cautiously through a set of hairpin bends. Lorenzo mounted his yellow steed and was gone with a wave. He remained in view as I walked, becoming no more than an orange dot on the distant road. Beyond the bends, a narrow turning to the left descended into the valley, giving access to a number of *estancias*, ranches, on the opposite side of the river. But there was no bridge; the only way across was by raft: the Balsa Baker.

The flimsy *balsa* did little to inspire confidence. It looked barely strong enough to carry pedestrians, let alone vehicles. The flat raft had a steel hull supporting a tatty deck of planks. A crude ramp at either end was lowered for vehicles to drive on or off. At one side was a small booth for the pilot. On the other, three heavy chains secured the raft to a cable strung across the wide river.

The boatman, Victor, was eating his lunch but he seemed pleased to welcome unexpected company. He drove there each day from Cochrane but raft pilots of the past had lived in a house which still stood on the bank. A blue van appeared and inched aboard. Then a *gaucho* arrived on horseback with a second beast tethered behind. He dismounted and led the animals onto the *balsa*. One followed without hesitation but the second took fright at her first step on the unstable platform and reared away violently. The *gaucho* calmed her down, whispering in her ear. At the second attempt, she followed obediently onto the ferry, but only by leaping over the offending section of boards.

Victor lifted the ramp and adjusted the chains. With the water pushing against the flat-sided hull, the craft began to glide silently across the fast-flowing, silver-green milky water, guided along the cable by squeaking pulleys.

'The *balsa* is an environmentally friendly form of transport,' he announced. 'It uses the power of the current to move across the river.'

'Is it stable?' I asked. 'Has anything ever fallen off?'

'Yes, twice,' Victor confirmed. 'Both times they'd forgotten to set their handbrake.'

'And the cars rolled off the raft?'

'That's right. They floated down the river with only the top of the roofs showing.'

'How far did they go?'

'One was found later on a beach downstream. The other one – who knows?'

With Lorenzo's complaints about HidroAysén still fresh in my mind, I decided to ask the boatman's opinion. It seemed likely he would have something to say. After all, he worked on the river that was under threat.

As soon as I mentioned the project, Victor smiled and shook his head. 'It's complicated,' he said, before busying himself with the raft. I had the impression that the delay was more about contemplation and not so much any genuine need to pilot the boat. He pulled one of the chains tighter to adjust our angle against the current, fastening it within a heavy clasp on the deck. Then he fiddled with a pair of levers but it wasn't clear what difference they made. We were setting an impressive pace over the water.

At length, he spoke again. 'Like many people around here, I'm a member of Patagonia Sin Represas. They talk a lot of sense, but their most important policies are hardly ever broadcast.'

'What do you mean?'

'When you watch the news, most times you'd think that the campaign is all about protecting wildlife and saving our valleys from flooding.'

For a moment he seemed lost in thought, staring upstream into the distance.

'And the pylons?' I suggested.

'Yes, all those things. But really the countryside is not the central issue. It goes much deeper than that.'

'How do you mean?' We were approaching the midpoint of the river and I was impatient to keep Victor's explanation moving. However, in Patagonia, he who hurries the conversation... may find that all he achieves is to slow the other person down.

'Everyone wants energy,' he acknowledged at last. 'The politicians, they tell us we must have this energy because the country must grow and compete. That's what they think everyone wants: modernisation, mechanisation, globalisation... They say that Chile needs energy so we can build bigger and go faster and achieve more, but why? Who decided that the way we are today is not good enough?'

I waited, unsure whether he was expecting me to answer that question and reluctant to interrupt him again.

'It's like this,' he went on. 'We have to decide what kind of society we want. If you believe that today's economic model is working, then you have to support HidroAysén. If we want to expand, then we need the energy. That way, we can develop our export industries. But we need to decide whether the creation of wealth should outweigh all other goals. Perhaps modern society has it wrong. It seems that everyone everywhere wants more money, but it's a false religion. Everyone knows that being richer doesn't make you happy, but that's still what the politicians keep promising. They must think we are stupid.'

'What's the alternative?' I asked. 'What are you suggesting? If Chile was richer, wouldn't that benefit everyone? Look at the education system – the schools could certainly use some extra funds. And the hospitals.'

Another long pause; the far bank was drawing closer.

'Even if we manage to grow, people will never be happy. What about the UK? Are people satisfied there, or do they want more?'

It was my turn to stop and think. 'In general, salaries there are much higher than in Chile, even for the same job. I would say that people here work longer hours and are paid far less. But you're right; people want more, even those who already earn a lot. Politicians in the UK are always promising to strengthen the economy; you're right about that, too. We get told we must compete with Asia, or we'll be left behind.'

'That's crazy,' interrupted the gaucho, who'd been listening all along. 'In your country are some of the richest people on earth, and yet they still want more. It cannot be. How can people be like that?'

'So what are you saying about HidroAysén?' I asked Victor. He glanced at the *gaucho*, who gestured at him to continue.

'Maybe it's time to reconsider our goals. Modern society has an addiction to economic growth. But here's the point: policies written in Santiago don't suit a place like Patagonia, and even less so the policies that are designed in London or Brussels or New York. The people of South America need a chance to choose whether to submit to the global economic regime or to opt for something else. Rather than have Patagonia and the Amazon destroyed by a globalisation that suits the rich countries, why can't we choose a more sensitive kind of development that would be appropriate for our people, for our culture and for our land? Let us at least have a chance to talk about it so our views can be heard? What if we don't need massive, rapid growth? Maybe we need gentle growth or even no growth at all. Perhaps we should aim for equilibrium and sustainability instead. If we change our goals, if we aim for economic sustainability and social cohesion, then we could design micro-policies appropriate to Patagonia. That would be a lot better for poor people in rural places. That's the way to save the Baker and the Pascua.'

'That sounds like a good dream. Do you think it's possible?'

'Of course not,' said the *gaucho*, angrily. 'It's ridiculous. They will never listen to us. Our leaders know nothing about Chile. Half of them have never been outside Santiago.'

Victor disagreed. 'Yes it is possible,' he said, with an exaggerated calmness. 'Financial systems are designed by humans. Let us have a chance to discuss whether the model is working before places like Patagonia are lost forever. We need leaders with vision, not people who only care about keeping their rich friends happy. Quality of life and the diversity of culture are more important than increasing our exports.'

Victor skilfully brought the raft to nestle up at the bank and lowered the ramp. The *gaucho* bade us both farewell and disembarked with his horses. I followed them onto the bank and turned to thank the boatman.

'You asked me about HidroAysén,' he began before I had a chance to speak. 'I disagree with the proposal, of course. We all do. But it's not because I don't like hydroelectricity. No, if we produce electricity at all then hydro is quite a good way of doing it. The important question is not how to generate power but what sort of society we want to live in. And what our basic aims should be. It's not about opposing dams. It's about challenging the whole system that makes them necessary.'

Those were Victor's final words to me. He stepped down from the *balsa* and grasped my hand warmly.

'*Gracias*, Victor,' I said, and turned away to take a look around the land beyond the Baker. An hour later we saw each other again for my return crossing, but this time neither of us said a word.

Image 12: The Balsa Baker

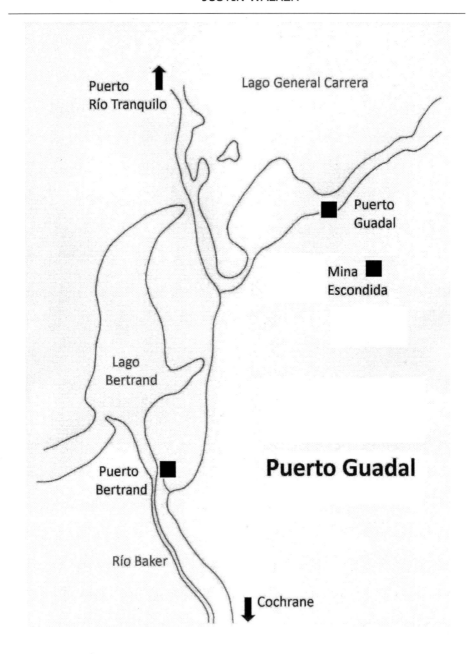

Map 06: Puerto Guadal and Puerto Bertrand

Twelve: Trucha

Since my earliest years, I've loved those cheese spreads that come in squeezie tubes. The food itself is relatively unappetizing, particularly given its greater resemblance to silicone bathroom sealant than any identifiable genre of cheese. All the same, at a profound level there is great satisfaction to be derived from twisting and twirling the tube over a slice of bread to create artistic swirly patterns of the creamy substance, like worm casts.

Silicone cheese in a toothpaste tube was one surprise highlight of the excellent Hostal Paola breakfast. Better still, there was a basket of *calzones rotos*, a deep-fried batter speciality, sugar-coated like a doughnut. The name translates as 'torn knickers', which refers to their twisted appearance, but it seems rather brutal for something presented at breakfast time. So heartening were these offerings that dipping into my limited supply of Fortnum & Mason teabags was not required, and I made do instead with standard issue Lipton Yellow Label from a tub on the table.

The man from Santiago had succeeded in his quest to Caleta Tortel, there and back via the newly repaired road. He seemed content with his reward: a two-hour visit in the rain.

'Didn't you say you were taking the bus?' queried Isidora, another *Santiaguina*, as she stepped out of the front door. 'You'd better hurry. It leaves in ten minutes.'

I glanced at the clock on the wall. Oops.

With frantic fingers, I fastened my sleeping bag and tent to the *mochila*. This was not how I'd imagined the morning, jogging several blocks with a heavy rucksack to catch the only bus of the day. The driver was Francisco, one of the pair who'd been lodging at Hielo Sur in Tortel. He showed no sign of recognising me but agreed nonetheless to drop me at the *confluencia* of the Río Baker and Río Neff. This spot had a glowing write-up in my local guidebook, recommending both the confluence and an impressive waterfall nearby. That part of the river was a vivid and unlikely turquoise, a colour apparently caused by green waters from the Río Neff mixing with the blue Río Baker.

Isidora had saved me a seat. I wasn't the only one running late. As we departed, two Scandinavian backpackers emerged from a side street and trotted beside the bus, beckoning enthusiastically. Francisco pulled over to the kerb, pushed open his window for a brief chat, and let them on. As they settled, one in the front of the bus and the other at the rear, we were on the move again, turning around three sides of the plaza and creeping out of Cochrane along the Carretera Austral.

Isidora was full of questions. 'Do you like living in Santiago?' she asked.

'Yes; usually. People are friendly. It's generally safe. The metro works well. The climate is much more enjoyable than back home.'

'Isn't it difficult being a foreigner in Chile? Don't you feel like an outsider?'

'Of course I do; I *am* a foreigner. Some things are hard to get used to, but there are many good things about living here. I like it that everyone greets each other. Back home, someone might walk into a room and not even acknowledge the others who are there. That wouldn't happen in Chile.'

'But what's it like living here?' she insisted. 'How do people treat you?'

I thought for a moment. 'People treat me well. Not everyone, of course, but there's always someone to help me when I need it. Chilean people seem very proud of their country, but they also take time to ask me about mine. It's never easy to arrive somewhere new, but I would say I've been made to feel welcome in Chile.

'Chileans are quite conservative,' she stated. 'We tend to be suspicious of anything new.'

'Yes, I suppose that's true. It can seem like the only way of doing things is the way we already know, the way we did it last year. That can be a bit frustrating. But that's not just a Chilean problem – it's common everywhere.'

Snatched sightings of features from the previous day's walk appeared through the rain-smeared windows: the petrol station, the timber yard and the willows beside the river. Crawling up Lorenzo's hill, we were barely moving. The bus seemed almost as slow as he had been when pedalling.

'Here's another thing I like,' I said to Isidora after a while. 'On the bus and the metro, young people always give up their seats for adults. You never see an older person standing. I once saw schoolchildren sitting on each other's lap to free up seats for others.'

Before she had a chance to reply, we were interrupted by a sickening bang beneath our feet. A thumping series of vibrations shook the floor as we clattered to a halt in the centre of the carriageway. Francisco climbed out and inspected under the chassis. There was a long and worrying wait as he lay in the road to peer from one side and then the other, and poked underneath with a long stick. At length, he fished a telephone out of his jacket pocket and made a long call, accompanied by some rather redundant pointing and repeated shrugs of resignation.

'Sorry folks,' he announced at last, climbing back aboard, 'we're going back to Cochrane.'

The bus began making a several-point turn. Seizing the opportunity, I asked to get out, a moment of spontaneity that left me miles from anywhere, abandoned in the morning drizzle.

I took a swig of water and strode onto a narrow bridge across a deep gorge. The bus rattled and clunked away, limping home. It disappeared into the mist, and I was alone in the Patagonian wilds. Not entirely alone, of course. No doubt vehicles would pass that way and surely someone would take pity on me, wouldn't they?

Wouldn't they?

Across the bridge, the road continued up a twisted cutting, climbing steeply from the river. It was a long slog, hemmed in either side by ochre walls. A petrol tanker crawled by, struggling against the incline and pumping out fumes. The driver showed no interest in my outstretched thumb.

How about the next one? No. They ignored me, too; a couple in a small white van.

Third time lucky? Ah, two women in a pickup. Yes? Maybe? No. They made a gesture to indicate their lack of a rear seat, gallingly ignorant that I would happily have ridden in the cargo well.

Who would be fourth? A workman's red van. This driver's hand signal appeared to show that he wasn't going far.

Fifth? A gleaming black four-wheel-drive. No chance; flashy cars never stop. A natural law of the universe appears to be that people's generosity is inversely proportional to their resources. 'Sorry my car is full', said the man's dramatic hand signal, even though he only had a small box riding beside him. Poor fellow; he'd clearly never noticed that his car had another seat in the back.

Was no-one going to offer a ride?

It was still early. Even allowing for a short stop to admire the colourful *confluencia*, there would still be plenty of time to continue to Puerto Bertrand, a small *pueblo* where the Río Baker emerged from Lago Bertrand. It looked an attractive location on the map. I was torn between pausing in Puerto Bertrand and continuing to Puerto Guadal where there was another eco hostel, but I wasn't going to make it to either place without a benevolent driver.

By the time the road flattened at the top of the climb, I had begun to wonder whether the replacement bus might cruise by. The thick mist was breaking into cotton wool clouds, allowing fleeting glimpses of the surrounding hills. A jacket was quite unnecessary when the sun found a way to penetrate the murk, but only moments would pass before the cold and blustery conditions resumed. By good fortune, waterproof trousers over zipped-off shorts turned out to suit the changeable climate perfectly.

At the sudden sound of rubber on gravel, I turned to see not one but two oncoming cars. The first sped by. Through the windscreen of the second, the driver appeared to be in two minds. The dark green pickup eventually stopped some distance later in the centre of the *carretera*. I ran there, placed my *mochila* in the back complete with its rain cover, and climbed into the passenger seat where I spent the journey cradling a holdall for the driver, Magdalena.

'I have a beauty salon in Cochrane,' she told me. 'I moved there from Chile Chico last year.'

'I haven't been to Chile Chico,' I remarked. 'Which do you prefer?'

'Business is much better in Cochrane. We only have three hairdressers there. Chile Chico had seventeen, and not enough hair to go around.'

'I'm not going far,' I explained. 'Please can you drop me at the *confluencia* of the two rivers?'

'Yes, yes,' she agreed, appearing to know exactly where I meant.

Magdalena was an exceedingly cautious driver, but that wasn't a problem. I was happy just to be moving, however sedate the pace. She chatted cheerfully with hardly a pause, pointing out her brother's house in El Manzano. The river had turned a spectacular colour which, with hindsight, was a clue to our location. Shortly afterwards, we passed a number of riverside fishing lodges.

'Where are we now?' I asked Magdalena.

'This is Puerto Bertrand.'

I hastily looked at the map. We'd passed the *confluencia* already.

'Can we stop here, please? This is as far as I need. *Muchas gracias.*'

It wasn't a disaster. It was a shame to miss the river confluence but in Patagonia, he who agonises over past mistakes will fail to enjoy the present... or some such thing. Magdalena pulled away from the junction leaving a young hitchhiker disappointed. He had simply reacted too slowly. In Patagonia, he who is dozy loses the ride.

After sharing the shelter of the hitchhiker's tree for a few minutes, I entered Puerto Bertrand down a short side road. Rapidly quenching my prior optimism, the tiny lakeside village looked soulless and grim in the falling rain. The first building was a hostel with a shop on the ground floor, but both appeared to be closed down. Beyond this, a line of houses, some of them quite substantial, overlooked Lago Bertrand. Raindrops danced across the surface of the bright blue water. There was no other person in sight. Why had I stopped here at all? Even the Adventure Centre, which had a card in the window advertising rafting trips, had evidently decided that this was no day for adventuring.

A perpendicular road climbed away from the lake to an upper part of the town. Simple houses were collected around a large green along with a church painted yellow, a community centre and a covered sports arena with an all-weather court. A path led towards a huge red-

and-white mobile phone mast. On arriving there, a man emerged from the trees.

'Have you found any *senderos*?' he asked.

'No. I've only just arrived.'

He must have been about my age and was of athletic build. Not an ounce of fat clung to his wiry frame. He introduced himself as Philippe, a Frenchman, and described his several months of travelling in South America. 'I arrived in Puerto Bertrand yesterday,' he said. 'Last night I slept in an abandoned house.'

'I'm not sure if I'll stay here,' I replied. 'It seems very quiet.'

Back at the lake, a family of six had taken occupation of the jetty.

'The blue colour is due to the depth,' the father confidently asserted.

He was mistaken. The distinctive colour of glacial lakes is caused by the refraction of sunlight through suspended sediment. Tiny particles known as rock flour are produced when glaciers erode quartz and feldspar. The silt gives the water an opaque milky appearance and is attractively coloured under sunlight.

I told him about the blue-green *confluencia*.

'Is it worth seeing?' he asked.

'Oh yes, I recommend it.'

He seemed very excited about that. His wife offered some *pan amasado*, handmade oven-baked bread, from a paper sack. Then the father spoke to a fisherman who was preparing a boat and appeared to negotiate a trip. In the end they exchanged telephone numbers, and the family piled into their plush Renault Espace and drove away.

I followed a track that ran through trees at the edge of the Puerto Bertrand, hoping to discover a route around the lake. Among the dwellings was the boarded-up house where Philippe was staying. He had company: there was a camper van and a tent in the yard. The track petered out at a fishing lodge in a stunning setting with enviable views of the lake's vivid waters, but there was no evidence of any onward path.

*

In the village centre, I met Antonia, a teenager who had a summer job at one of the lodges. Her work as a room maid followed a routine of eleven days on and three off. Today was the start of her three-day weekend.

'I can't believe how quiet everything is,' she told me. 'Nobody warned me it would be like this. I'm not used to being alone. Back home in Puerto Montt, there's always something happening. I like having other people around me, but I'm not allowed to talk to the guests at the lodge, not even during my time off. There's nothing to do.'

We sat on a bench together.

'Do you enjoy walking?' I asked.

'Not really.'

'Kayaking?'

'I've never tried. I can't swim.'

'Writing? Drawing?'

'No. That sounds too much like school. Anyway, I'm no good at drawing. My sister draws, but I can't do it.'

'You could get the bus to Cochrane. At least you could buy a burger there.'

The look on Antonia's face indicated that this was as sensible as suggesting she spend the afternoon in Miami.

'How about a Fanta? There must be a place we can buy a drink.'

She brightened up at that idea, but the shops along the front were all closed, lending support to her disparaging opinion of the village. The only one that was open sold artisanal craft products: candles, knitted clothes, hats of alpaca wool, ornaments, wooden bowls... but no drinks.

We located a tiny shop in the upper part of the village, little more than a shed in the front yard of a home. This, too, appeared to be closed, but the lady came when we rang the bell. She had no Fanta, but I bought two bottles of Coke. It was the only time I saw Antonia smile.

Returning to the lakeside bench, we were promptly joined by Philippe, who asked if I had a book to swap. I dug one out of my *mochila* and turned to the closing chapters while he sauntered back to the unoccupied house to fetch his. Behind our bench, a child rode his bicycle back and forth whilst his toddler brother gleefully pushed a plastic truck repeatedly through a deep puddle. Philippe returned with two novels, one printed in English and the other in French.[47] I

---

[47] The books Philippe offered were George Orwell's *Animal Farm* and *L'insoutenable légèreté de l'être* by Milan Kundera. I had once attempted Kundera's book in English some years earlier (*The Unbearable Lightness of Being*) but didn't get far. I fared no better with a

inexplicably chose the latter; what was I thinking of? As I finished mine, he lay on the grass and slept. That was too much for Antonia, who had already lost interest in her two sedentary companions. She disappeared shortly afterwards and did not return.

A puppy bounced over and licked Philippe's face, waking him. He kept it amused for a while until it nipped his hand. Abandoning the unrepentant dog, Philippe began fishing from the jetty. These rivers teem with brown trout and rainbow trout, all eager to be plucked from the waters with a hook in their mouths. *Trucha* are native to Patagonia. Their salmon cousins are also present, partly the consequence of hatchlings escaping from breeding nets. Several lodges around Puerto Bertrand specialise in fly-fishing tourism. Some even arrange helicopters to transport anglers to otherwise inaccessible spots. In contrast, Philippe had no special equipment, just a line wrapped around a tin, but he soon made a catch. His face was a picture of pride; on what appeared to be his maiden fishing exploit, he'd already snared his dinner. Just to clarify, it was Philippe who had the proud face. The *trucha* had the expression of someone whose day was not going well.

*

Crossing paths with Philippe and Antonia had made for an entertaining afternoon in Puerto Bertrand, but with the sun still high in the sky, I had both time and desire to reach the eco hostel in Puerto Guadal, the uninvitingly named Un Destino No Turístico. Rather than wait under the hitchhiker's tree, I followed the Carretera Austral up its gentle incline. Two distant figures, built like Lowry characters, loped towards me in the centre of the road, pulling what appeared to be golf trailers. As the gap between us gradually closed, I puzzled over what those carts could be. Eventually we came face to face. It was indeed two people on foot, each hauling a long-handled two-wheeled trailer rather like a narrow rickshaw.

The couple in question, in their late fifties or thereabouts, turned out to be from the Netherlands.

French copy. The tale was simply too obscure to read in either language. I believe it was first written in Czech; perhaps the original makes greater sense. I don't read Czech, as it happens. The novel I gave Philippe in exchange was *East of the Sun* by Julia Gregson, set in 1928 India. The first twenty pages were missing, but he didn't seem to mind.

'*¡Qué buena forma de viajar!*' I commented; what an interesting way to travel.

'What, walking?' the man retorted defensively. 'Don't you think it is natural?'

Perhaps they had already endured enough ridicule along the road but I hadn't intended to be disrespectful. Their chariots looked highly practical, an ingenious manner to portage their kit in sophisticated canvas compartments. There had been, nonetheless, plenty of opportunity for quips and jokes in the time since commencing their walk 4000 kilometres north in Visviri, the point where Chile, Peru and Bolivia all meet.

'We've travelled for seven months,' the Dutchman said, 'but it's nearly over now. We're going to see how far we can go down the Brunswick Peninsula. I'm not sure we'll make it to the very end of the continent but we'll go as far as the road will take us. So long as we can roll these trailers, we'll keep walking.'

Trudging up the hill, I periodically stopped to admire the view unfolding at my back: lakes, mountains and a distant view of the Campo de Hielo Norte. Ongoing maintenance had pushed the sandy mixture into loose ridges, and my feet sunk in with each step. It was like marching through a sandpit. The motor grader responsible for all this mess soon passed in the opposite direction, flattening and smoothing the surface with its wide blade.

A red pickup stopped for me later, the double cabin already packed with three adults and three children. I climbed in behind and made a nest amongst their luggage, a spare wheel and a quivering Labrador, and we hammered along the road, sending up a cloud of dust. The children turned on their seat and pulled faces through the rear window. At length, we came to a junction at the corner of a huge lake, Lago General Carrera. The Carretera Austral continued north but my chosen route this time was the turning to the east, along the southern shore of the lake. Everyone piled out, abandoning the car in the centre of the road, with all four doors yawning open. The adults stretched weary limbs whilst the children chased each other around the stationary vehicle.

'How far have you come?' I asked.

'From Villa O'Higgins. That's where we live, but we're visiting Coyhaique for a week's holiday.'

A motorcycle touring party roared up to the junction, complete with support van. We became an island as the stream of bikes divided to flow around us on either side.

'I'll leave you here, then. I'm going to Puerto Guadal. That's this road, I think?' I checked, pointing the way the bikers had taken.

'That's right, up there. It's not far. Good luck.'

One of the kids handed me a long-stemmed blue flower plucked from the verge and looked shyly up at me. '*Adiós, tío.*'

'Thanks for your help,' I called out as they climbed into the pickup. '*Buen viaje.*'

The Puerto Guadal road looked out over Lago General Carrera. Close by, a fishing boat was tied to a jetty at the tip of an elongated bulbous limb of the lake, its swollen outline the shape of a gourd. Ranks of sizeable waves lapped the near shore. Mountains hemmed the vast lake, some forested and others bare rock the colour of sand. The far slopes were darker, their snowy summits merging indistinctly into cloud.

Heavy machines were digging and moving and flattening the rocky soil on the route of a new road higher up the hillside, all to avoid a series of tight hairpin bends on the existing route. Exhausted by the arduous slog back and forth to the top, I set down my pack against a rock and hung my saturated shirt on a gate. After resting a while to refuel on bread and bananas, just a short walk remained to reach the lakeside village of Puerto Guadal.

Image 13: Lago Bertrand

Thirteen: Don Vicente

Half-waking at daybreak, my body thought better of it. Given the long and eventful journey from Cochrane, it was no great surprise to be weary.

Next time I woke, there was a voice outside. 'I've brought you something to read.'

Rocio handed me a book and a periodical. The former was the Bruce Chatwin travelogue *In Patagonia*. Setting it aside, I turned instead to the magazine, a recent edition of the *Patagon Journal*, and read an account of a group of mountaineers making the first recorded ascent of the Cordillera Sarmiento range (located to the south of the Campo de Hielo Sur). They, too, permitted a tent to blow away in a storm, news I found immensely reassuring.

Eventually I surfaced and washed in the solar shower. The water was cold. Once I'd dried off, Rocio was waiting for me again.

I hadn't begun the expedition intending to frequent eco hostels, but Un Destino No Turístico had been particularly recommended. Indeed, if I'd understood Mauricio correctly, it was at this site that he'd first had the inspiration to start a camp of his own. I was the sole guest. My hostess showed me around, expounding upon a multiplicity of regulations and procedures: conserving water, waste management, use of facilities and so on. She spoke passionately and with great detail, but after a while in my bleary-eyed state, her detailed discourse began to wash over me without penetrating. Having exhausted her supply of words, Rocio left me and I set about preparing breakfast.

Un Destino No Turístico had a smart central cabin with a spectacular view of snow-capped peaks across the glistening waters of Lago General Carrera, for which Rocio tended to use the indigenous name Chelenko. The hut had been constructed with care and skill, and was attractively finished. Inside, where patrons were instructed to remove shoes, were a small kitchen, showers and dry toilets. A separate entrance gave access to the lounge and dormitories. Solar lighting was installed throughout. The whole facility was plainly the product of meticulous planning and considerable industry.

Displayed around the walls, a number of posters gave advice for environmentally friendly living. One notice listed seven guidelines known as the 'Leave No Trace Principles'. There was also a chart describing the benefits of compost and a catalogue of animals that frequented the site: mink, hare, fox and skunk, for example. Written on a whiteboard were details of various workshops on offer, with topics such as sustainable living, organic agriculture and renewable energies.

Instructions were displayed in the kitchen on how to use the haybox, an insulated container for cooking. A pan of potatoes or vegetables could be boiled for two minutes and then placed in the box where it would continue to simmer on account of the insulation, in this case hay. Pulses required two minutes boiling plus two hours in the haybox, and rice needed an hour in the box after ten minutes on the stove. In this way, conventional fuels such as gas and firewood were conserved.

Finally, so as not to disappoint, there was an explanation of the environmental advantages of the composting toilet, which arise from the fact that it uses no water. The notes described that a family of five can contaminate 150,000 litres of water per year, simply by using the toilet. If the whole world had flushing toilets, the notice claimed, there would be no fresh water left for drinking. The dry toilet also saves the energy that is otherwise required to pump all that water around our cities. If the idea of installing a composting toilet in the family home is unappealing, an alternative is to flush with rainwater or grey water, which is the waste from the shower, bath, sink and laundry. The plumbing wouldn't be complicated, but the adjustment in human habits and our sense of standards and propriety might be more significant obstacles.

*

> **The Leave No Trace Seven Principles**
>
> Plan Ahead and Prepare
> Travel and Camp on Durable Surfaces
> Dispose of Waste Properly
> Leave What You Find
> Minimize Campfire Impacts
> Respect Wildlife
> Be Considerate of Other Visitors
>
> The member-driven Leave No Trace Center for Outdoor Ethics teaches people how to enjoy the outdoors responsibly. This copyrighted information has been reprinted with permission from the Leave No Trace Center for Outdoor Ethics: www.LNT.org (US spelling as per original statement).

*

In accordance with the Seven Principles, walking routes around the site were precisely defined and straying from the path was frowned upon. Sticking carefully to the worn track, I located Rocio and her husband Marcelo using second-hand timber to build a *bodega*, a store, at the back of their house. She broke off from hammering and beamed a smile in my direction.

'If you like, we can present a workshop on eco-matters,' she offered.

The idea didn't rank strongly amongst my priorities.

'Most visitors come here for a reason,' she insisted, 'not just as somewhere to sleep. We can do a session on why we live like this and how we are reducing our impact on the environment.'

I suspect the hesitant silence that hung between us gave away my limited enthusiasm for the suggestion. Nonetheless, they appeared glad to have a break and we chatted at length about the local area.

'The people around here are the children of the original pioneers,' they said. 'There's quite a difference between those who live in the town and their cousins in the mountains. The town is becoming more modern, and people there have attitudes influenced by what they see on television. The mountain dwellers are still like the original *gauchos*. Their dialect is hard to understand. Some live six months every year on the high slopes and only come to a lower house for winter. They are very self-sufficient and know how to survive on limited means.'

Rocio was obviously impressed with the *gauchos'* ability to adapt to the harsh local conditions. She described a recent programme for connecting a supply of electricity to rural homes. When it came to the turn of those living in the mountains, many had declined.

'Why would I want *luz*?' some had said. 'They connect it for free but afterwards I will have to pay every time I use it!'

*

Puerto Guadal had a welcoming atmosphere. Revived by a diet-disregarding lunch of *salchipapas*, sausage and chips, I visited the library, set out in two rooms of what had once been a family home. In one room were three elderly computers providing free internet connection, a service available in libraries nationwide. I took the opportunity to compose some emails, including one for Louise whose birthday was approaching and who has threatened unspeakable consequences if not named in these pages. The other terminals were occupied by a brother and sister, around eight and twelve years old. Only twenty minutes in, the librarian requested I gave way to a waiting customer. Glancing at the screens of the two children, I surmised that my emails must have been less important to Patagonia than their games.

The second room was furnished with tall, varnished bookshelves and included a section on local history. I selected a pamphlet with tales of the early settlers who colonised areas around the lake. One account caught my attention. The story described an indigenous man, Saturnino Inayo Treuque, who moved with his family to the north side of Lago General Carrera, where they lived undisturbed for some years since this was land that nobody else wanted. They built a house and cut timber to sell to the expanding communities on the opposite shore, transporting it by boat. One day, the daughter Guillermina found a stone embedded with shiny particles. They subsequently found more similar rocks, which Saturnino gave to his friend, Antolin Silva Ormeño, asking him to have them analysed. Silva promptly disappeared and time passed. When these shiny stones continued surfacing, the family thought little of them until one day, a long period later, Silva turned up with a group of officials and ordered them off the land. Having registered the mineral deposits in his own name, he'd secured the rights to mine them.

Thus was born the Mina Silva, where lead and zinc were extracted. The associated settlement of Puerto Cristal housed 850 people at its peak but is now deserted. The mine and port are accessible only from the lake, being isolated on the landward side by rough mountainous terrain. The mine closed amid the collapse of mineral prices at the end of the 1950s. Entry is generally prohibited, but Puerto Cristal families return annually for a commemorative celebration.

That evening, I marvelled at an extraordinary display of lenticular clouds painted on the sky, illuminated sequentially with the yellows, golds, pinks and reds of sunset. After a bowl of tasty noodles in the impressive camp building, I discovered an insect conference taking place inside my tent, bossed by several large earwigs. Braving their threatening hook-shaped pincers, I drifted off to sleep, giggling to a chapter of Chatwin's book.

*

> **Lenticular Clouds**
>
> Lenticular means 'shaped like a lens'.
>
> When moist air flows over mountains, it is lifted and then falls, setting up a wave. At the peak, vapour may condense into droplets, forming a stationary cloud. A cloud constituted in this way is typically saucer-shaped or lens-shaped. These are known as lenticular clouds.
>
> Lenticular clouds can help glider pilots locate rising air currents. In contrast, powered aircraft tend to avoid them due to their association with turbulence. Due to their shape, such clouds are commonly implicated in reported UFO sightings.

*

The night that January gave way to February, I woke to a tent already bright with mid-morning daylight. Flicking through the *Patagon Journal* a second time, a folded sheet of paper slipped out. It was a hand-drawn map of the local area. In addition to marking the location of shops and restaurants, a walk was indicated to the nearby Laguna Escondida, the Hidden Lake, and an adjacent disused mine. With no prior plan for the day and a receptive attitude to such obvious guidance, I gathered my things together, packed some lunch and set out.

The narrow vehicle track towards Puerto Guadal followed a circuitous route around some fields. Hoping to cut the corner, I hopped over a stile and plotted a more direct course. It began on a reassuringly well-worn path, and there was no cause for alarm until arriving at the top of a steep bank. Outside a house below, partially secluded in a thicket, a horse was in attendance, its reins looped around a fencepost. Preferring not to discuss the local trespass bylaws with a *gaucho*, I slipped away in a different direction, scrambling over fences and vaulting ditches on the way to recovering the *camino*. It would have been simpler never to have strayed.

The map depicted a second track, almost parallel, doubling back up the hill. It twisted around a series of bends, swiftly gaining altitude. Above a poorly hidden rubbish dump, three hawks rode on the breeze. There were excellent views over the wide open waters of the lake, surrounded on every side by tall mountains, and a clearing sky confirmed that the worst of the rain was over.

Lago General Carrera is by far the largest lake in Chile. It is another that straddles the border with Argentina, where it takes the name Lago Buenos Aires. With a surface area of 1850 square kilometres, it is almost double the size of Lago O'Higgins and 30 times bigger than Loch Ness in Scotland.

In the days before the Carretera Austral, pioneers established their communities close to the lake and travelled between them by boat. Today, many of those small towns still carry the word 'Port' in their name, such as Puerto Guadal, Puerto Río Tranquilo, Puerto Murta and Puerto Ingeniero Ibáñez. Through these ports, timber was exported from forested Chile to the treeless steppe of Argentina. The other local industry, attracting migrant workers from far away, was mining.

In its operational years, Mina Escondida principally mined lead. Taking advantage of gravity, the many steps of the refining process were arranged in sequence below the mine tunnel, which still yawned open high on the mountainside. Walking uphill, I therefore encountered the various stages in reverse order and the mine itself last of all. Thus, the first feature was a basin where sludge and residue would have drained. It was full of pallid, granular waste. Even though decades had passed since closure, there were no green signs of life in the contaminated soil. Over the years a poisonous cocktail must have washed from the rudimentary basin into the adjacent Laguna Escondida. Modern mining and refining facilities have stringent controls against pollution, but informal, unregulated mining continues without such measures in many parts of this continent, discharging waste into water courses and defiling forests, plains and valleys with septic wounds.

The narrow conduit that formerly fed the basin followed a course beside the road. Some distance uphill it passed the rubble of some brick buildings: offices and accommodation, possibly. At its peak, the mine employed 500, including many from Argentina. When it closed in 1986 following a sudden collapse in the global trading price of lead, jobless hoards returned despondently across the border, a three-day voyage on the lake.

The open channel continued upwards to the main processing compound, a treasure trove of industrial artefacts. It would have been fascinating to explore the site with a knowledgeable expert. There were discarded engine parts, mammoth flywheels leaning on their short axles like enormous gyroscopes, and a barrel of mysterious rusty spheres the size of billiard balls. A stack of oversized lead batteries leaked acid onto the ground. Technical apparatus stood inside the derelict buildings. One large machine was from Manchester, according to its manufacturer's plate, and another was stamped with 'Turner Bros. Asbestos, Rochdale'.[48]

There is something compelling about abandoned industrial units, despite the obvious risks they pose. I braved a flight of treacherous stairs to the second level and cautiously clambered about on the beams, nervously eying absent sections of floor. Up here were row upon row of machines with impressive brass pistons. Rocio had explained that the site had several times been looted, with miscellaneous mine implements fulfilling transformed purposes in the homes of local

---

[48] This caught my eye because Rochdale is a town I know, having worked there in the early part of my teaching career. Turner Bros. was one of numerous nineteenth-century Lancashire cotton companies. They diversified into asbestos cloth and subsequently manufactured a range of other asbestos products.

residents. A great quantity remained all the same, rusting and deteriorating in Patagonia's inhospitable climate.

With its entrance on a high ledge, the tunnel had been excavated level with the roof of the main building. Or rather, the reverse is more precisely correct: the tunnel was no doubt dug where the ore was accessible and the processing facility was presumably constructed in a corresponding position, with its upper level aligned to the mine entrance. To make this possible, a wide bowl had been quarried from the rock, and the refinery constructed within. Extracted ore was tipped into a chute in the roof to commence the process of crushing the rock and purifying the minerals. It continued step by step through machines on each floor, then through the stages arranged down the hill, leading ultimately to the basin at the lower end.

The mine tunnel stretched interminably into the mountain. Shining into the shadowy void, my *linterna* illuminated the regular inverted-U of strong timber props repeating far down the passageway. I stepped cautiously from rock to rock, moving inside and attempting to keep off the wet floor. Occasional fallen props provided a firm, dry footing although the presence of collapsed supports in a disused mine isn't necessarily a welcome sight. The puddles merged into a continuous linear pond, at which point avoiding the water became a near-impossible pursuit. Next was a section with no props at all, where my *linterna* failed to pick out any features in the blackness ahead. That was as much underground prospecting as I could stomach. Rapidly losing my nerve, I fled back to the light.

A man arrived with two huge bulls, their thick coats a patchwork of white and brown, hauling a cart of logs. Whatever the beasts had done to build up their strength, the man had apparently been subjected to a similar regime; he was of comparable dimensions and rippled with enormous muscles. Uncertain whether he might object to my snooping around, I offered a friendly wave, and he saluted in reply. Once I'd scrambled down the bank, he introduced himself as Pablo.

'I'm selling a lorry load to a man in Chile Chico,' he explained.

'How many carts fill a lorry?' I asked.

'My *carro* holds two metres.' The word 'cubic' was left unspoken. 'The *camión* is about twenty metres.'

This one appeared to be the first load.

'How long will it take?'

'I can chop and carry three *carros* in one day. Then another day to load the *camión*, as long as there's two of us.'

'So that's four days in all, maybe five. How much will you make?'

'The dealer pays 8000 *pesos* each metre.' About US$16.

With their thick, curved horns and angry glare, the huge animals were more than a little intimidating.

'They never cause me a problem,' Pablo stated proudly. 'They are steers, not bulls.'

A steer is an ex-bull with streamlined reproductive equipment.

'They are calmer and less impulsive like that,' he continued. 'They make better workers this way.'

It made me wonder whether the same technique could be adopted with other feisty or troublesome individuals.

We unloaded the *carro* together and stacked the wood. Each log was a metre long and about twenty centimetres thick. They were not only heavy but also awkward to handle, and my inexperienced fingers paid the price.

With the final logs thrown on top of the pile, Pablo offered me a ride up the hill on his *carro*. The makeshift chassis was constructed around a sturdy A-frame, narrowing towards the front. Where the two lateral poles met, they were lashed to a heavy yoke resting across the necks of the steers. The cart had no restraining edge other than three thin upright poles either side. A home-made vehicle, the only parts that were not wood were a rusty steel axle and metal wheels with pneumatic tyres. It was on this contraption that I perched unsteadily as we pitched, swayed and wobbled our way up the road, sharing the ride with a fat black beetle. As the track condition deteriorated, the eight-legged tractor climbed without difficulty over terrain that would have troubled even the most versatile of off-road motor vehicles.

Many of the trees were strangely stripped of their foliage.

'*Orugas*,' Pablo explained: caterpillars. 'Millions of them. They've eaten all the leaves everywhere. I've never seen it like this.'

The branches were not completely denuded. Great quantities of *usnea*, a lichen more commonly known as old man's beard, were draped over the trees as if the branches had been decorated with fraying strands of pale green wool. Our slow, lurching journey ended at a flat clearing. To one side, the forest spread over the valley like a scene from a postcard. From above, it was easy to tell which trees still had leaves and to identify patches amongst them that had been decimated, producing the appearance of a winter forest.

Pablo guided his animals up one final slope into some woodland behind the clearing. He unhitched the cart and tied the two steers loosely to a tree, still coupled by the massive yoke. He rolled the cart to a stable position on level ground, and we began filling the next load. The logs were crawling with *orugas*, which gave a painful bite if given a chance. Even the floor was carpeted with the nasty creatures.

We made a fundamental loading error. The maestro might have done better without the help of his apprentice, but we stacked the rear of the cart first. That was fine for a while, until the *carro* tipped up on its single axle with a loud creak, spilling our hard work onto the floor. Pablo appeared to find this hilarious. Once reloaded, he hitched the *carro* to the yoke of steers and set off down the hill. Two loads done; just eight more to go.

At one side of the grassy clearing was a small cottage. This, according to the map, was the home of Don Vicente, an old man who greeted me with a generous smile. I guess he was in his seventies although, being subject to constant weathering, *gauchos* can appear older than they really are. On his head was a navy blue *boina*, the characteristic Patagonian beret.

Don Vicente was keen to show me his chickens and ducks, inviting me to pay homage at each of their pens. Following a protracted session with the birds, he sent his dog to collect a ram and two ewes. I made appreciative comments and nodded vigorously as he rattled on in a thick Patagonian accent that was tricky to grasp. He also had an impressively verdant plot of potatoes and swede which had inexplicably avoided the attentions of the *orugas*; perhaps teenaged caterpillars don't like vegetables.

Then I had the chance to admire another *carro*, this time one that Don Vicente was constructing. It was smaller but more stylish than Pablo's wagon, and he seemed very proud of his handiwork. My attention was drawn to the small metal wheels; what did they remind me of? They had a flange, rather like the wheels on a railway carriage. It was suddenly obvious: Mina Escondida.

Last, Don Vicente proudly showed me his two chestnut horses which all the while had been waiting patiently beside the cottage. To my untrained eye, they appeared strong and in good health. Each had a beautiful dark mane and tail and white feet.

'What are their names?' I asked.

Don Vicente looked surprised. 'They are animals. They don't have names.'

'What about the dogs? Do they have names?'

This, too, was obviously a peculiar question.

'Of course they do! The dogs need names because you call to them and give them instructions, but not the horses; they are just horses. This one is called *caballo*,' he said, patting the haunches of the nearer horse with an open palm. 'And that one,' he pointed at the other, 'he is called *caballo*.'

We laughed out loud at the joke, although I imagine that Don Vicente was also amused by the ridiculous notion that you might give a name to a horse.

He invited me inside.

'This is my lower house,' he said. 'I used to live higher up when I was younger, but I moved down and built this one twenty years ago.'

Only twenty? It looked about a hundred years old. We had entered a room of about three by four metres, which was half the house. I suppose the other half was a bedroom. This room had a small square table, two chairs and a bench, and two small cupboards. Some laundry hung from a rack on the ceiling. Plants on the window sills were potted in the cut-off halves of plastic bottles. Arranged on a set of shelves were a bowl of sugar, a small radio, a jug, an empty mug tree and some plastic ornaments. The floor was covered in blue lino and the walls were lined with hardboard. As in Pancho's house, there was a scattering of calendars on the walls. As in every house, the room included a white enamel log-burning *estufa*.

Don Vicente rekindled the fire to warm the kettle. A handful of *orugas* had penetrated the meagre defences of the house and were slinking around the floor, up the walls and across the windows. They were of the same green-spiked variety as those at Reserva Nacional Tamango. Those that crawled within reach of Don Vicente met their destiny in the fire, the elderly *gaucho* showing no mercy to the pests that had blighted the season.

When the water was ready, he invited me to share *mate* with him. I was glad of the tuition I'd received from Maricio in Villa O'Higgins, enabling me to drink in accordance with the customs and not as a novice. Don Vicente checked the temperature by tipping water directly onto his thumb. Once satisfied, he poured from the kettle down the inside of the *mate* (the pot) to moisten the green *yerba* from beneath. Preferring to take it *amargo*, bitter, he added no sugar. He sucked through the long metal *bombilla* and spat the first mouthful outside the door. As we passed the *mate* between us, I remembered to incline the *bombilla* towards him and to avoid saying '*gracias*'.

'Do they drink *mate* in your country?' he asked.

'No, we drink tea. Black tea, and coffee, and beer.'

'Does tea grow in England?'

'No, our weather is too cold. We import it from Sri Lanka and India... and East Africa, I think. But everyone drinks tea. It's very important to drink tea if you are English.'

'It's very important to drink *mate* if you are Patagonian. And you,' he extended a knobbly-knuckled finger in my direction, 'you are Patagonian now!'

At this, he clapped his hands together and laughed heartily. As we drank, Don Vicente told me about himself. 'I was born here in Puerto Guadal,' he said. 'We were many in my family. My parents had twenty-two children.'

'Twenty-two? You could make two whole football teams!'

He laughed again. 'Not any longer,' he acknowledged with a sigh. 'Some are gone now. But fourteen are still alive. We're all in Patagonia.'

'Have you been anywhere else?' I asked. 'Have you ever travelled away?'

'Not far. I used to travel when I was younger but I didn't like it much. I've been to Coyhaique but never to the north. I once had to go south as far as Punta Arenas. That's a long way. I won't be going that far again. This is my valley. This is where I belong.'

'What are winters like?' I asked.

'We have to work through winter,' he told me. 'Sometimes the snow is a metre deep, but we still work. There is no choice; the animals must eat.'

Pablo joined us in the small room, having returned from hauling the second load of logs to the mine. I shared my bread, cheese and tomatoes, and Don Vicente poured us some wine.

He asked me to take a photograph of his cart and then wanted me to sit upon his horse. He fetched the nameless beast, saddled up and brought over a log so that I could mount.

'Have you ever ridden a horse?' he asked, but I misunderstood. His words were '¿Ha andado a caballo, alguna vez?' but I mistook *andado*, 'ridden', for *ha dado*, 'has given'. Has anyone given me a horse? I panicked. Surely he wasn't going to give me his horse?

Then he asked me to take a photo. I withdrew the camera from my pocket and offered it to him, but he waved it away dismissively. 'No, you do it,' he insisted.

'It doesn't work like that,' I explained. 'Someone else has to hold the camera.'

I handed it to Pablo. He, too, had limited experience of photography and it took several attempts before either I or the horse actually appeared in any of the shots. I should have anticipated that, perhaps.

I should also have been prepared with a gift for Don Vicente. Both he and Pablo had been wholly welcoming and I'd brought nothing with which to thank them. I left Don Vicente with a packet of biscuits, but it was a pitiful offering.

'Next time you come we will roast a *cordero*,' he said; a truly generous offer.

*

Don Vicente

A note about the prefix *Don* in a person's name:

Don Vicente was not a Scottish clansman 'Donald Vicente'. *Don* is a title, as in Don Quixote and Don Juan.

The term originates from the Latin honorific title *Dominus*. Some branches of the Catholic Church (the Benedictine order, for example) retain the prefix Dom for certain clergy. The expression 'Dons' used at Oxbridge universities is derived from the same root.

In the Hispanosphere (the Spanish-speaking world) the term Don used to be applied to royalty and noblemen. Over time it came to be used more broadly as a mark of respect for someone with social standing or who was in some way distinguished.

In *América Latina*, the term is also given as a title of respect for elderly persons. This is why I met Don Vicente, and not just Vicente. But the younger gentleman was plain Pablo, not Don Pablo.

The female equivalent is Doña. To celebrate Chile's annual Teachers' Day, I used to arrange a staff celebration at a restaurant in Santiago named for its lady proprietor, *La Doña Tina*.

One of the senior television presenters in Chile is an evergreen figure known as Don Francisco. If Brits used this title, we might watch Don David present *Question Time*, whereas Don Bruce recently retired from his role on *Strictly Come Dancing*.

*

Arriving back at Un Destino No Turístico, I frightened a pheasant in the long grass. It fussed away making a racket, like the clacking of the wooden rattle that my grandfather carried to football matches. The bizarre association caused me to wonder what he and Don Vicente, old men from such distinct worlds, neither of whom travelled far from their locality, would have made of each other. They might have had more in common than at first seemed obvious. My grandfather did what he could to support his family: he ran a grocery shop. If there were other options he could have considered, they were probably few in number. He did the work that was available to him with loyalty to customers and dedication to the business, year after year, without dreams or aspirations.

The livelihoods of the Patagonian people were not so dissimilar to that. People were doing what they could: Pablo chopped logs, Don Vicente had his animals and vegetables, the early settlers in Tortel had sold timber and raised cattle, Pancho's small farm produced wool, and Mauricio was attempting to make a living through tourism. In whichever ways they could, these people were doing their best to carve out a living. If the logs or the wool no longer sold, they would do something else, like the mineworkers returning to Argentina when Mina Escondida closed. There was no time to sit around feeling nostalgic or hard-done by. In order to survive, changing and adapting was the only choice.

Image 14: Derelict buildings at Mina Escondida

Map 07: Puerto Río Tranquilo & Lago General Carrera

Fourteen: Valle Leones

A family of beetles made a timely bid for freedom as I collapsed the tent. After paying Rocio for the three nights, I filled a water bottle and set off. The 60 kilometres from Puerto Guadal to Puerto Río Tranquilo passed without incident as I crept around the southwest corner of Lago General Carrera by way of several short rides. The short hop was a mere fraction of a 500-kilometre full circuit. Viewing the segment later on a map, it appeared that I'd hardly moved.

Outside the village of Puerto Río Tranquilo, a crooked signboard protruded from a tall hedge. 'Camping Pudú,' it read.

'I'll stop here, please,' I yelled over the engine noise, in an exceptional episode of conviction.

The campsite was equipped with a beautiful location on a narrow, grassy strip between the cliff and a pebbly beach. Each pitch had a lattice windbreak to defend against gusts from the open water. Taking the hint, I tethered my sleeping accommodation securely using all available guy ropes, before liberating four stowaway earwigs that had ventured from Puerto Guadal within the nylon folds.

Deceived by its enchanting name, I'd anticipated that Puerto Río Tranquilo would be an idyllic spot. In fact, I'd even looked forward to this particular *pueblo* as a potential highlight of the trip, imagining there might be comfortable bars, restaurants with exotic menus, and opportunities to spoil myself. I was considerably disappointed. It was a small and very ordinary place with a handful of general stores and a couple of scruffy cafés. Two caravans, one yellow and the other a greeny-blue hue that my childhood art teacher would have called aquamarine, were parked in a layby overlooking the lake, offering tourist trips. Confusingly, many of the shops were also labelled *Casa de*

Turista or something similar, whether or not they actually provided services for travellers. As a consequence, the official tourist information booth in the central *plaza de armas* had closed, thwarted by its distance from the natural focal point of the lakeside promenade.

The bandwagon onto which all these merchants were leaping was a pair of destinations for which Puerto Río Tranquilo was springboard. One was an attraction on Lago General Carrera known as the Cavernas de Mármol: the Marble Caverns. The other was Glaciar Exploradores, a mighty river of ice descending from the Campo de Hielo Norte. By first enduring a long drive on a punishing road, day trippers could hike to view the glacier from a high *mirador*. The final portion of the road through the Exploradores Valley was still under construction, intended one day to provide a land route to the spectacular Laguna San Rafael, which is presently accessible only by sea or in chartered planes.

*

> **The Campo de Hielo Norte and Laguna San Rafael**
>
> Despite extending for only one-quarter the area of its southern sister, the Campo de Hielo Norte would still cover the entire English county of Hampshire with plenty to spare. Her 28 glaciers include Glaciar Exploradores and a trio at the head of a valley I was about to visit, Valle Leones. On the opposite rim of the ice field, Glaciar San Rafael descends west into Laguna San Rafael. This sea lagoon, formed as the glacier retreated, is popularly included on cruise ship itineraries. Passengers watch ice calving from the snout and drink their whisky with glacial lumps fished from the lagoon. I had a chance to join an outing to Laguna San Rafael at the start of this trip, aboard a vessel from Puerto Chacabuco. However, given that flights to the moon are a similar price, I opted to do without.

*

An engaging incident unfolded that afternoon in the river mouth at the far end of the village, where a sandy beach dropped sharply into the river over a low bank. A family was spectacularly failing to extricate their motor boat and its trailer from the water. Three brothers, aged about 12, 15 and 17, had been out fishing in the small craft. Rods and equipment were strewn across the deck. Their huge four-wheel-drive Chevrolet coped proficiently with the sand, and the father confidently reversed the trailer off the ledge and into the river. Once the vessel was loaded on, however, they found it impossible to haul the apparatus back out, no matter how loudly the engine squealed.

They tried different approaches: first straight on and then from increasingly unlikely angles. They made attempts with the trolley fully in the river or only partly submerged. They tried various positions along the sandy bank, but the trailer and its load stubbornly refused to climb the ledge. All they succeeded in doing was to bury its wheels deeper and deeper into the sand, a predicament from which it was periodically rescued through the energetic digging of the three boys. And when they spun the vehicle around to use its winch, the only thing that slid forward was the Chevrolet and not the boat.

Away from the river mouth, the beach sloped gently into the lake in the way that sandy beaches do. The family might have done better to consider backing the trailer into the lake there, but the father could possibly foresee his expensive status symbol sinking into the wet sand. In contrast, attempting to recover the boat from the river rather than the beach had the advantage of a deep-water approach, enabling the vehicle to stay on dry land. This is why yacht clubs have a concrete ramp for launching and landing, I now understood.

Observing all this from the road bridge, I was joined by a group of four men who, like me, were gripped by the entertainment. All five of us had opinions about what they were doing wrong but it was easy to be an expert at a distance. So led by the boldest of the quartet, we traipsed together to the riverbank to stir our ingredients into the mix.

There was some risk of too many chiefs, but after some initial exchanges to establish a pecking order, one of the four assumed command. By a combination of winching, levering with long pieces of timber found handily nearby, and adjusting the boat's position fore and aft, slowly we enticed the trailer and its burden up onto the beach. The father's relief was evident, but their success had come at the cost of family unity. The youngest brother had given up helping well before the drama reached its conclusion and had resumed fishing in the river, and the father had snapped at the middle one for getting in the way. One trailer wheel had also taken a battering. Piling into the Chevrolet, the family drove off to seek out a mechanic somewhere in the small town.

The five of us repaired to a café and ordered homemade burgers. It turned out that my companions were a pair of crustal motion geodesists from Ohio State University, Michael and Dana, who were working in the Valle Leones alongside the two Chilean colleagues, Tito and Carlos.

'What on earth is a geodesist?' I plucked up the courage to enquire, slightly ashamed of exposing my ignorance.

'*On earth* is the correct expression,' quipped Dana. 'Geodesy, or geodetics if you prefer, is one discipline within geodynamics. It is part mathematics, part Earth science and part geophysics.'

I was none the wiser. 'But what do you do?'

'We measure adjustments in the Earth's surface,' clarified Michael. 'We use very precise GPS measurements to track the motion and deformation of the Earth's outer crust.'

'Are you here to study earthquakes?' I asked.

'No. Some geodesists take an interest in plate motion and seismic activity, but this project in Patagonia is about climate change and the melting ice. Our main objective is to measure the solid Earth's response to changes in the weight of the ice fields. As the ice melts, it reduces the load, so the ground lifts as subsurface rocks relax. We want to track the lifting of the crust over time...'

'But the plates also shift for other reasons,' interrupted Dana. 'The tectonic movements in this region of the globe are quite unpredictable, so that complicates the measurements.'

'...and in fact, the movement due to melting ice is already tricky,' added Michael. 'The Earth's crust appears to respond in both a rapid elastic way when the load is reduced, and then in a much slower viscous way over an extended period. The changes we measure in a given time-frame are usually a mixture of both.'

'So all the GPS gear gives us very accurate data,' Dana again, 'but unscrambling these overlapping crustal motion signals is pretty challenging.'

When it came to my turn to describe my work, I mumbled a description of my school in Santiago. Dana was kind enough to say that my job was 'a great gig', but it seemed rather lacklustre compared to theirs, installing GPS systems in beautiful spots all over the world.

We sloped off to their rented accommodation and emptied some bottles of wine, illuminated by diverting and colourful anecdotes from far-flung places.

Some hours later, when Dana threatened to subject us to an all-night *Lord of the Rings* marathon from his DVD box set, I absconded to my tent, a languid half-hour walk away under a rising moon. Making my way into Camping Pudú late that evening, I stumbled across an extraordinary sight. As I descended the cliff path, admiring the evening views it offered over the huge lake, I was startled by an unexpected apparition. Quietly at rest in the centre of the field was a Behemoth.

*

Throughout the early weeks of the expedition, landscapes denuded by forest clearances were a recurrent feature. In what was supposed to be one of the world's great temperate rainforests, vast areas were marked by an alarming absence of trees. Many of the hillsides were stark, bare and littered with toppled grey trunks. Widespread burning of the forest had been effected for one reason: to produce land on which to rear cattle; razing for grazing. The devastation of the Patagonian rainforest mirrors an extensive global problem associated with commercial meat production. Along with logging, energy development and mineral extraction, the clearing of land for agriculture and grazing is one of four key threats to the world's remaining forest.

Satisfying the demand for meat has a surprisingly large environmental impact. 70 per cent of the world's farmland is used for rearing stock, and 30 per cent of the remainder produces crops for their feed. Industrially produced meat is an inefficient way to feed human populations, with seven kilogrammes of grain required to produce each kilogramme of beef, and four kilos of grain for one of pork. Whilst destitute millions go hungry, mountains of cereal are shovelled into animal troughs. It doesn't end with arable crops; one-third of the world's fish catch is also fed directly to livestock. Moreover, it takes more fossil fuel and vastly more water to produce meat than it does to supply an equivalent quantity of vegetable protein. Returning to the issue of forests, if meat consumption were lower, large areas of agricultural land could be released to grow crops for human stomachs.

That would ease the never-ending pressure to clear even more forest for grazing estates. Every year, 20,000 square kilometres of Latin American rainforest are felled to create cattle pasture.

Wild herbivores tend to roam grassland habitats in low-density herds. Conversely, it is common on cattle and sheep farms to see large numbers in a restricted area. Where pastures are stocked above their carrying capacity, they become stripped to a minimal level of vegetation. If grazing is allowed to continue, damage can be irrevocable. Overgrazing leads to deterioration of the pasture. Since depleted grassland retains less moisture, the soil dries and breaks up. The return of perennial plants would help recovery since they absorb carbon dioxide and enrich the soil, but with the ground reduced to dust, native flora cannot take hold. Loose soil with sparse vegetation is vulnerable to wind erosion, and pastures become barren within a few years.

The environmental campaign group Conservación Patagónica[49] estimates that 90 per cent of Patagonian land (taking the Chilean and Argentine sides together) suffers from degraded soils and 30 per cent from severe desertification. Conservación Patagónica is experimenting with ecosystem restoration practices in the Chacabuco Valley (not far from the place where my bus broke down). As grasslands have recovered, the native herbivores (the *vicuña* and *guanaco*, for example) have reportedly begun returning.

*

The following morning, heavy clouds drifted over Lago General Carrera but not sufficient to disrupt my plans for a day of hiking. The Behemoth was still there, a mammoth red-orange articulated vehicle operated by a German tour company. The front part was a burly truck resembling those used on overland safari tours, but larger and with seats for about 40. It towed a trailer with sleeping cabins on three levels, like a capsule hotel on wheels, and customers took their meals at folding tables under a canvas shelter.

Whoever first conceived of bringing such a vehicle on Patagonia's spindly roads was either very courageous or utterly foolhardy. A well-

---

[49] Conservación Patagónica is a sister organisation of the Conservation Land Trust mentioned in Chapter 22, sharing similar aims.

equipped tour of this kind enables people to visit wilderness locations whilst retaining a measure of comfort. Although they were hardly roughing it, the experience was certainly more adventurous than two weeks on a sun lounger. On the other hand, I doubt the rigid programme would suit the independent travellers who were a more typical sight along the Carretera Austral. As for me, given how much I enjoy inventing my own schedule, I suspect that not long would pass before the irresistible urge to slip away through the bars of the cage would overtake me.

Programmed for a horrifyingly early start, the driver showed little consideration for other campers as he manoeuvred the vehicle out of the field. Not surprisingly, it was proving quite a challenge to turn the 23-metre lorry-and-trailer in a constricted campsite. The Behemoth edged forward and back, its reversing siren intermittently wailing. One man was beckoned out of a tent to move his car. Could they not have turned the absurd contraption on arrival rather than waiting until morning? When they made their exit at last, crawling up the impossibly narrow and tight access ramp, their parting gift was a criss-cross pattern of ugly scars on the soft ground.

*

The GPS scientists collected me later that morning from the campsite gate. I threw my *mochila* in the back of their pickup, noticing too late an intriguing assortment of delicate technical equipment, and squeezed into the rear seat between two burly scientists. As Tito drove, Michael played an eclectic selection of music on the car stereo. Heading south, and consequently tracking back the way I'd already come, we stopped for several minutes at a spot where a yellow motor grader was recrowning the road. I hadn't realised that 'recrowning' was the precise expression for this work, but much can be learned when spending time with scientists and engineers.

Once we turned off the Carretera Austral, what had initially been an episode of unwelcome but tolerable discomfort became a violent, cramp-inducing and deeply unpleasant experience. The valley road tilted one way then the other, and we bounced through divots and over tree roots. In the front passenger seat, Michael clutched the grab handle as if his life depended on it. We three who were rear seat ballast became better and better acquainted with every jolt of the car. I would have liked to rub circulation back into my numb legs, but my arms were pinned helplessly to my sides by two large men.

The equipment we had on board was to be installed at the home of a man who owned a good portion of the Valle Leones. It was a considerable relief when his house came into view and we stopped at a fork in the track. With pins and needles in every part of my body, I disentangled myself from the car and retrieved my *mochila*. The Ohio team continued along the left fork, and after recovering sufficient use of my limbs, I took the road to the right. My track headed due west towards the Campo de Hielo Norte, where the Leones Glaciers were shrouded in gloomy cloud.

The right fork appeared to be seldom used so it came as quite a surprise a few minutes later to meet a vehicle coming the other way.

'*Buenos días*,' greeted the driver. 'Are you walking to Lago León?'

'I doubt that I'll get there. I'm only here for one day so I won't go far.'

'I see. You are welcome.'

The identity of the man suddenly dawned on me. 'Oh… are you the guy who owns the house?' With hindsight I could have phrased the question more respectfully, but in the moment that's what came out.

He laughed. 'Yes. I'm John.' He extended a hand.

'*Buenos días*, John. Is it alright if I walk in the valley?'

'Yes, of course.' He laughed again.

'I took a ride with the GPS team from Ohio. I'm going to meet up with them later at the house. I mean… your house… if that's okay?'

'Ah, have they arrived? Good. Yes, no problem, see you later. Enjoy the walk. It's a beautiful valley.'

The track passed through a plantation of beech saplings. The mountains on both sides were thickly wooded lower down but bare and rocky closer to the peaks. The cliffs had been smoothed into graceful forms, relentlessly polished over eons under the enormous weight of the slow-moving ice. A glacier snout peeped from a high hanging valley. As the plantation ended, there began an extensive boulder field. The debris was the result of a glacial lake outburst flood or GLOF from the winter of 2000. Some of the rocks were immense, the size of houses, yet they'd been propelled to this spot by the force of water (with a little help from gravity, no doubt). A cold breeze blew across the dry grasses of the meadow. I started towards a waterfall that cascaded down far cliffs, but before long the route was cut off by the river, so I moved into the shelter of a boulder to eat lunch. The mountain scenery transformed continuously, virtually minute to minute, as clouds lifted one by one from the Campo de Hielo Norte. One peak remained cloaked throughout: Monte San Valentín.

*

Measuring the elevation of Monte San Valentín

The highest peak in the ice field, Monte San Valentín is also the tallest mountain in Patagonia. The elevation of the peak is generally stated as 4058m, but some doubt hangs over the accuracy of that figure.

Global Positioning Systems (GPS) use data from multiple satellites to determine the location of a receiver on the Earth's surface. GPS satellites continuously transmit their coordinates in space, together with the time of each transmission. The signal takes around 70 milliseconds to travel 20,000 kilometres to Earth. Each GPS receiver calculates its own position using those satellite coordinates and the time lapse before the transmission arrives, which is an indication of distance. However, GPS readings for location and elevation are not infallible. Various confounding factors introduce tiny inaccuracies to the incoming data. Though miniscule, these discrepancies are significant because the orbiting transmitters speed through space at four kilometres every second. Even an error of a single one-thousandth of a second makes a difference.

GPS readings for elevation above sea level are further complicated by an additional factor: the problem of determining where sea level actually is. What is taken to be mean sea level varies around the planet. The sea level model used by GPS technologies is a smooth ellipsoid around the surface of the Earth. This ellipsoid (a sphere squashed at the poles, like a satsuma) is a good approximation of the shape of the planet, but not a perfectly accurate representation. More specifically, the model (known as a geoid) does not precisely correspond to sea level in every part of the world. In fact, mean sea level is actually as much as 70 metres higher or lower than the geoid, depending on where you are. This obviously makes a difference when estimating the elevation of a mountain.

> Throughout history, diverse methods have been used to determine mountain heights. In the past they involved geometric techniques such as levelling and triangulation, or judging the distance from which the mountain is visible at sea. An estimate can also be obtained by measuring the temperature at which water boils at the summit, since boiling point varies with air pressure, which itself depends on altitude, at least in part.
>
> Returning to the uncertainty of San Valentín, on-peak GPS data is in short supply as this mountain is rarely climbed. French surveyors estimated an elevation of 'somewhere near 4080m' (plus or minus 20m) in 1993. Eight years later, Chilean climbers reported a GPS-measured elevation of approximately 4070m (or 40m either way). It is now generally accepted that Monte San Valentín is over 4000 metres high, and is certainly taller than the 3876m cited in 1921 by the Scandinavian explorer Otto Nordenskiöld.

*

High above in a tributary valley was another hanging glacier, which Michael had suggested could be reached on foot. I began the climb, carefully picking a route along the rocky bed of a meltwater stream. Initially it was easy to step from boulder to boulder, until the turbulent water forced me up the moraine bank. Slippery conditions underfoot made the steep ground hazardous, my shoes filling uncomfortably with grit and sand. Even some of the larger rocks, despite appearing deceptively stable, could wobble dangerously when stepped upon.

Higher up, the ravine became steeper. Abundant water had encouraged a proliferation of plant life including the broad-leaved *nalca*, a giant cross-breed of rhubarb and triffid.[50] The strong, thick stalks were as resistant as steel bars, and the huge leaves concealed shin-high rocks and menacing rabbit holes. Shortly afterwards, the bank became a near-vertical wall and I was forced back into the stream. With the glacier still distant and climbing perilous, I quit and carefully followed the stream back down, wondering exactly how Michael had made the ascent some years earlier.

---

[50] Triffids are fictitious plants that first appeared in John Wyndham's 1951 novel 'The Day of the Triffids'. In the book, the plants are venomous, carnivorous and able to move, organise collectively and hunt. As far as I know, *nalca* has none of these qualities.

*

> **Nalca**
>
> *Nalca* [*Gunnera tinctoria*], also known as Chilean rhubarb, is a perennial plant native to Patagonia. Stems can stand two metres tall and leaves can exceed two metres in diameter. As with rhubarb the stalks are edible; *nalca* jam is popular, for example.
>
> *Nalca* has been widely introduced outside Chile as an ornamental plant and has escaped to grow wild in places, including beside some British waterways. It is considered an invasive species in New Zealand, where both propagation and sales are illegal.

*

Back at John's house, I found the scientists hard at work bolting a stanchion to a rock. Their box of sensors was to be fixed upon the pole, and the necessary cables had already been sunk into a trench. This location would take advantage of the internet connection already installed at the house, for the transmission of data to the university.

John showed me his hydroelectric turbine in an outhouse, along with a wall full of dials, switches and electronic equipment with an impressive array of flashing LEDs. It was like walking onto the bridge of the *USS Enterprise*.

'Fancy another walk?' he asked.

I didn't, but was interested to see the small dam, and Michael the geodesist joined us. The reservoir, if it deserved that name, was much smaller than I'd anticipated. Located high on the slopes above the house, it was tiny: only a metre in diameter. John explained that power generation had more to do with vertical drop than pond dimensions, but nevertheless it was surprisingly small.

'What about drinking water?' I asked. 'Where do you get that?'

'That's from here as well,' he said. 'This reservoir provides the house with all its water, and is used to generate all the electricity.'

I asked about the plantation in the valley.

'We are reforesting all our land with southern beech,' said John. 'On your travels you must have seen all the bare land set aside for grazing, and the fallen tree trunks. That's not how this area should be; it's supposed to be a forest. Between the 1920s and 1940s, hundreds of thousands of acres were burned in order to clear land for cattle. When I bought Valle Leones, the first thing I did was to remove the cattle and sheep. We are down to just twenty animals belonging to our workman. Now we're attempting to reforest this part of the valley.'

'I guess that's difficult,' said Michael. 'Have you encountered any problems with soil erosion?'

'Replanting on the valley floor isn't difficult,' John replied, 'but it's more problematic to reforest the higher slopes. That's where wind and rain have eroded much of the soil. Mountain forests tiptoe a delicate balance, and soils can be surprisingly thin. Once the trees have gone, it's very hard to put them back.'

*

The following morning, I woke to the sound of raindrops. By the time I'd finished in the shower block, the weather was truly grim: persistent drizzle with poor visibility across the lake. Short on ideas for amusement, I spoke to the agent in the yellow caravan about the Exploradores trip. The hikers in her publicity photograph were viewing the glacier from a distant balustrade. It didn't appear to be an experience that would be close up and personal, and it was hardly a day for admiring landscapes, in any case. Glaciar Exploradores could be given a miss. I retreated to the warmth of a café and lunched on *carbonada*. Not carbonara, but *carbonada*, a flimsy goulash containing lumps of meat, onion, a boiled potato and some vegetables.

Soon after midday, the rain became less convinced of itself, first thinning into a fine drizzle and ultimately giving up altogether. After a quick map consultation, I decided that a walk to nearby Puerto Mármol would be a good use of the afternoon. The five-kilometre route was all hill, first a steep climb and then an even steeper road downhill. The twisting descent gave a clear though distant view of the Cavernas de Mármol. Small motor boats were zipping across the water and poking into the caves like mice nosing at a lump of cheese. The central feature of the attraction is a solitary dome of rock in the lake, known as the Catedral de Marmól: the Marble Cathedral. Centuries of erosion have undercut the base, creating long caverns. The interior has formed into low arches and smooth rounded walls, curvaceous shapes further emphasised by sweeping patterns of colour, handsome enough to make even Michelangelo take a second look. On sunny days, a bluish tint washes onto the cave walls.

On this occasion the open water varied from bright turquoise under the glare of the sun to a deep indigo under shadow. Rain was visible on the lake's southern banks, angled strokes beneath the clouds. At the foot of the long descent, I ambled along the beach and lay on a rock tablet. Some of the surrounding pebbles were the same marble as the caves, infused with intricate veins of rich colour. A boat arrived at the jetty, returning from the *cavernas*. Had there been a group assembled, I might have been tempted to join an excursion. In Patagonia, however, he who mopes around indecisively… misses the chance to see the marble caves.

Map 08: Carretera Austral – Centre

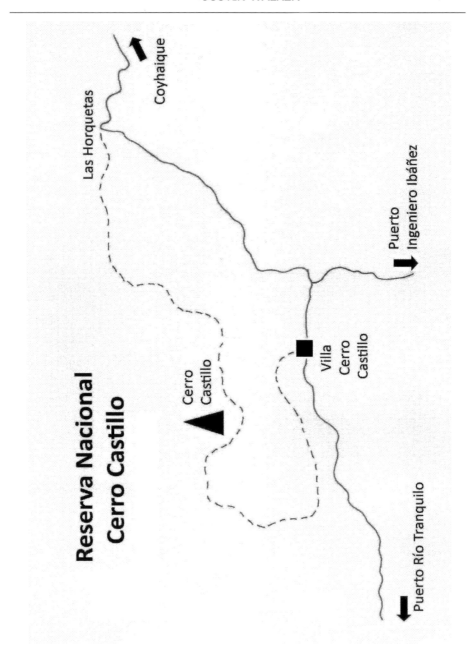

Map 09: Reserva Nacional Cerro Castillo

Fifteen: Cerro Castillo

A momentous day had come. One of the most striking mountains in Patagonia was finally within reach: Cerro Castillo. Capitalising on an early start, I chose a bridge at the north side of Puerto Río Tranquilo as a suitable hitchhiking site. At the opposite end of the promenade, a number of backpackers were competing for lifts in the other direction, but I was fortunately the only one hitchhiking north. Later that morning, a bus was due to pass through, so if my thumb let me down then public transport was a secure second bet. It hadn't been possible to book a seat, but the lady from the yellow caravan had given every assurance that there would not be any problem.

Waiting at the bridge that Sunday morning became a teeny bit disheartening. Occasional vehicles arrived from the south but none continued to my end of the lakeside *costanera*. Some, making brief visits to the waterfront businesses, parked along the shore, and others disappeared into the village. Nobody was leaving Puerto Río Tranquilo in the direction I wanted to go.

Behind the tall windows of a comfortable hotel, family groups were enjoying Sunday breakfast. Surely one of these would be heading towards Coyhaique? I tried to catch the eye of likely candidates, but they were all too focused on their granola and grapefruit to notice the hitchhiking voyeur pulling hopeful faces outside.

Eons passed.

Eventually, the minibus from Puerto Guadal rolled across the southern bridge; this would have to do.

'*Buenos días, señor.* Are you going to Coyhaique?'

'Yes, but we're full.'

He was not a man given to demonstrations of sympathy. To be fair, his van lacked the spare capacity to accommodate standing passengers in the way that a larger bus might have. Nonetheless, this unwelcome development left me in a bit of a pickle.

A family was packing a gargantuan automobile in the hotel car park but they adeptly closed ranks. Another couple shrugged, explaining that they were travelling south. I asked another man as he left the hotel, but he appeared to lack both his helpfulness gene and his compassion gene. In fact, his politeness gene was stunted, too. As I contemplated my next move, a young backpacking couple appeared at my shoulder. They were direct competitors for any ride but I did my best to be friendly.

Unexpectedly, a second bus arrived. It was unexpected to me, at least, because I'd not seen it publicised. It's not easy to tell how many buses will pass through these small towns on a given day. There's never any comprehensive timetable encompassing the various operators. If an independent company runs a service between Cochrane and Coyhaique, for example, it won't necessarily be advertised in the intermediate towns. Local people may know but it won't be obvious to outsiders. Even in the tourist information offices, it pays not only to ask, 'Is there a bus from here to Coyhaique on a Sunday?' but also something like, 'Is there a bus that starts in some other place and passes through here on the way to Coyhaique?' assuming you can manage that in *castellano*.

In the event, this service did indeed originate in Cochrane. The blue 50-seater came to a halt alongside the yellow and turquoise tourist-trip caravans. Materialising from nowhere, a clutch of Río Tranquilians converged on the door. What made this especially worrying was the fact that all the seats appeared to be occupied. Would it be best in this situation to be patient or pushy, I wondered? I chose patience, adopting an assured posture and a facial expression of unruffled calm. I'd been practising the same all morning for the non-existent drivers. The backpacking couple and I had responded smartly and were closest to the door. Desperate voices called out as the driver came down the steps. He conducted an extended conversation with a talkative, white-haired lady and sauntered away to smoke a cigarette. The bus stood for twenty minutes: the breakfast stop.

There was nothing to be gained by stepping away; mine was potentially a profitable spot. A false move now could jeopardise the whole day's plans. In spite of learning Patagonian serenity for three weeks, I was fretting inside and my jaw was beginning to ache. When at length the driver returned, he invited the chosen senior citizen to fill the final seat on his bus. I tried to tune in to several conversations being spoken simultaneously in rapid *castellano*, whilst maintaining my composed appearance. It worked. The driver asked the couple where they were headed, then me, and in no time we were climbing the steps. *¡Estupendo!* The couple sat together on a raised section of floor next to the driver's seat, and I rested on a cushioned pillar near the front steps. Anyway, our seating arrangement was hardly relevant; all that mattered was that we were aboard.

The road was rough and ridged. When rain began to fall, the surface became muddy and slushy. Our driver slalomed around potholes, and progress was slow. We prowled past an accident: a yellow van with a canoe on the roof had come to rest at an impossible angle down the bank. The young occupants had climbed up to the road and were overlooking the catastrophe with humiliated smirks on their faces. No-one appeared to be hurt and another vehicle had stopped to tow them out.

Leaving the lake behind, we started into the mountains, following the course of another river valley. The engine whined in low gear up steep gradients and around tight bends. In contrast to the grazing land further south, this area was densely forested. The tree canopy above and the jungle-thick undergrowth beneath all dripped with moisture after so much rain. Passing a Catholic shrine, the driver crossed himself. He had a *San Cristóbal* emblem hanging from the windscreen displaying the exhortation *Ilumina mi camino*, Light my path. The Catholic faith is widespread and strong throughout Chile, and such religious tokens are common. At last we began a long, slow, winding descent towards the town of Villa Cerro Castillo. Pockets of mist billowed dramatically over the river, and the mountain stood prominently like a hilltop castle, in accordance with her name.

I set myself an impossible task on arrival in the village. About to commence a two-day hike, I needed somewhere to store my excess kit. If the driver waited a while, a repeat of the twenty-minute stop in Puerto Río Tranquilo for example, I had a slim chance of returning in time to continue to the trailhead on the same bus. There was a *residencial* adjacent to the bus stop. I tried the handle, and the front door eased open. After a rapid explanation of what I needed, the proprietor indicated a place under the stairs where I could leave my things. In a hastily executed flurry of bag sorting, I emptied my surplus possessions into a bin liner and closed it with a strip of tent-fixing brown parcel tape. Hoping that no-one would mistake it for rubbish, I concealed the package where I'd been shown and raced back into the street with a hasty '*muchas gracias*'. The layby was empty.

The road through Villa Cerro Castillo divided into a dual carriageway. It was also dead straight and surprisingly, even disconcertingly, was paved. It later became clear that this marked the furthest extent of a continuous tarmac stretch all the way to Coyhaique. There was not a soul about and no cars on the road. A loose panel on the bus shelter roof flapped noisily in the unrelenting brisk wind. Two grocery shops on the main road were closed, but only a short search was necessary to find a small store on a back street and a bakery nearby. It was a good thing the bus had gone. It would have been senseless to set out into the mountains with limited supplies.

Cerro Castillo was a fantastic sight. Slender, jagged basalt needles encircled the summit, fully 2000 metres above the surrounding plain. By far the tallest mountain in the immediate area, Cerro Castillo was both majestic and daunting. Although an ascent to the crest was not an option, a challenging trail had been established through the area following its designation as a Reserva Nacional in 1970.

*

> **Ultra-prominent peaks and the topological prominence of Cerro Castillo**
>
> One physical characteristic of mountains, of interest to climbers and geologists, is their topological prominence. Cerro Castillo is one of a select few that are described as ultra-prominent peaks, a title given to a summit that is very prominent compared to its neighbours.
>
> Many of the world's mountains are connected to others within a chain, group or range. As a result, it is often possible to ascend one peak after another without the need to descend a great distance between them.

Even though a peak might be high above sea level, it may not be very prominent. In crude terms, prominence is a measure of how much a mountain peak is elevated above the pass that connects to its taller neighbours.

To consider the definition more precisely, imagine two connected mountains known as Taller Peak and Shorter Peak. Imagine descending from Shorter Peak into the pass that forms the lowest point between the two. This vertical drop between the summit and the pass might be 150m, for example. Across the pass the land begins rising again, climbing towards Taller Peak. In this scenario, the topological prominence of Shorter Peak is 150m. However, the topological prominence of Taller Peak is not measured to that same pass but to the shoulder of an even taller neighbour, if there is one.

Describing it another way, imagine a contour line encircling a mountain. Drop that contour to the lowest position that avoids including any part of any taller peak. Consider the vertical distance between the summit and the contour line just described. This vertical height is the topological prominence of the mountain. If that's too confusing, a helpful way to picture the position of this contour line is as follows. Imagine the valleys were full of water. Flood the whole range, raising sea level until the mountains become separate islands. When the level of the water is just enough to cut off a peak, making its summit the highest point on its island (no longer connected to any higher peaks) then the new imaginary sea level reveals the level of the contour line described above. The topological prominence of that peak would be the elevation above the hypothetical sea level of this imaginary island.

By this definition, the tallest peak on any island or continental landmass is equal to its full elevation, because it is not connected to any higher peak. Aconcagua, being the tallest peak in the Americas, has both height and prominence of 6692m. Mount Everest has a height of 8848m and an equal prominence. However, although the elevation of the South Summit of Everest is 8749m, its prominence is only about 10m, because it rises from the shoulder of the main peak. The South Summit is higher than K2, but K2 (8611m) is considered to be the second-highest mountain in the world. Since the South Summit has

> such low prominence, climbers do not regard it as a separate mountain.
>
> Mountains with a topological prominence greater than 1500m are known as ultra-prominent peaks, or just 'ultras'. There are more than 1500 ultras in the world, including 209 in South America. Of these, 29 are located in this part of Patagonia, the tallest being Monte San Valentín (height 4058m, prominence 3696m) in the Campo de Hielo Norte. Cerro Castillo is rather smaller, reaching an elevation of just 2675m. Its topological prominence is nonetheless significant, at 2088m. Cerro Castillo, therefore, is an ultra-prominent peak.

*

Beside the main road, a man was maintaining a sombre vigil, holding a handwritten cardboard sign:
C o y h a i q u e
The lettering was far too small to see from any distance.

'I've been climbing in Cerro Castillo,' he told me, 'but I fly back to Santiago tomorrow.'

Not wishing to hijack his position, I retreated to the bus shelter with its roof still flapping loudly, and took bites from a fresh bread roll. A bout of activity further down the road caught my attention. A group were loading a pickup and appeared to be equipped for a long journey. I ran to speak to the driver.

'Are you going north?' I asked. 'I need to get to Las Horquetas.'

'I'm driving to Coyhaique,' he confirmed. 'I don't know Las Horquetas, but tell me when we pass there and I'll drop you.'

'*Muchas gracias; sería perfecto.*'

'There's no room in the cabin,' he apologised. 'You'll have to sit in the back.'

The rear of a pickup easily beat a wind-blown bus shelter. By the time we departed, three of us were sat side by side on the open luggage bed, leaning back against the cabin rear window and facing aft. I commandeered the sheltered centre, sandwiched between the climber and another backpacking *Chileno*.

Climbing steadily through a succession of hairpin bends, it was a gentle relief to travel on tarmac. My map of Reserva Nacional Cerro

Castillo extended far enough to depict this part of the road, a twisted orange strand of spaghetti at the foot of the sheet.

'That map sucks,' said a voice next to me, the first English the climber had spoken.

Las Horquetas was easy to identify, being situated on a pronounced 180-degree switchback. Having thanked the driver, I waved farewell to my cargo box companions as they disappeared around the next turn.

A sign on the gate advised of an entrance fee but there was no-one to collect it. I started down the trail, crossing a gurgling brook on a dilapidated timber bridge. Spots of rain began to fall. Ahead was a long walk through beautiful mountains, and the prospect of two days off the road boosted my spirits.

Traversing a hillside, the trail passed a row of derelict shacks and descended into woodland. The terrain was friendly, and only a series of wide streams posed any difficulty on that first afternoon. Other national park authorities might have constructed bridges but apparently not this one. On the first occasion, I managed to keep my feet dry by stepping between prominent stones onto a central bank of pebbles and then shuffling over a fallen tree. But for three subsequent streams there was no such assistance, and I resorted to removing shoes and socks in order to wade through. The icy water urged haste but the stony stream bed and the burden of a heavy pack both prevented it. After each crossing, I sat on the bank to massage my shivering, numb feet before re-shoeing for the onward hike.

The rocky pinnacles of Cerro Castillo were far ahead, seen through a haze of falling rain. The woods were eerily quiet with a peculiar absence of birdsong. Green foliage showed no sign of the caterpillar infestation that had decimated the forest around Puerto Guadal. A group of brown-and-white cows reacted as if this was the first time they'd ever seen a human; they bounded off in a startled manner to a safe distance where they turned and stared as if transfixed. The tree cover grew dense, and the gently ascending trail became increasingly muddy. After a creek, a marsh and a dark pond, it led at last to a warden's hut.

The *guardaparque* welcomed me to his lair and collected the park fee. We drank *mate* together, enjoying the fire burning in his *estufa*.

'Why are there no bridges?' I asked.

'This is hiking,' he said. 'It needs to be a genuine outdoor experience. If we built bridges over the rivers, it would be too easy.'

I wasn't convinced. Hiking can be sufficiently exerting without the obligation to catch foot pneumonia.

'How much food are you carrying?' he checked, before going on to advise taking supplies for the expected duration of the hike plus an extra day. 'You can drink any running water,' he added, 'but avoid the standing water.'

I asked about the weather.

'You'll have plenty of rain in the coming days, but only showers, mixed in with dry spells. The most important thing is to cross the high passes early in the day. The wind gets pretty strong in the afternoon.'

Sufficient daylight remained to reach the next camping area, another three or four kilometres ahead on a low, flat island in the river. There, the water ran fast and deep on one side, but the nearer channels were shallow and easy to jump. The location didn't appear to be prone to flooding, so I pitched my tent on the bank and ate. After soup and lentils, I spoiled myself with a few squares of chocolate and some fresh apricots that had turned to mush in my bag. At 900 metres of elevation, it was cold in the tent, but exhausted from a full day of travelling, the music of the running river soon lulled me to sleep.

*

The following day began with delicious conditions. Across the milky river, the mountain slopes were bathed attractively in morning sunlight. The shaded end of the tent was moist with dew, but on lifting it into the cold breeze, the material filled like a parachute and dried in moments. Rolling the fabric, I noticed a stowaway caterpillar just in time and persuaded him onto a tasty leaf.

A path led up the backbone of the narrow island, the river dancing to the right and the rocky channel on the left. After a minute or two, I discovered a camping area. Mistakenly, I'd pitched my tent short of the main site. The camp proper, about 200 metres on, had picnic tables and circles of stones for fires.

The footpath alternated indecisively between opposite sides of the elongated island. Forest birds filled the branches with their morning songs. A *vista* of sunlit mountains appeared through the trees. The first high pass was visible far ahead, at this distance no more than a tiny notch cut into the ridge. The river was dotted with smooth, rounded rocks resembling a herd of fat animals taking a bath. Across the water, forested mountain slopes scrambled towards exposed peaks of craggy rock. Avalanches had cut vertical scars through the trees. Above it all, a pair of condors circled amongst the peaks against a backdrop of intense blue sky.

The island concluded at a narrow point, and the trail crossed the drier branch of the river bed. It disappeared into woodland and began climbing towards the pass, fording another stream some way up. Crystal water poured across a wide, sloping rock face on which attractive mosses grew: another palette of impossibly varied greens, vibrant in the sunlight. I drank deeply, cupping my hands under the flow, and decided to pause there for breakfast, taking the opportunity to dry my two clammy shirts on a branch. The bread had turned chewy and rubbery, rather like morning-after naan bread. A hummingbird hovered into view and alighted momentarily on a bush, displaying the full splendour of his beautiful colours. He was a green-backed firecrown, the only hummer that ventures this far south.

Across the stream, the trail rose above the tree line and entered an open gully strewn with loose rocks. Turning to look back gave awesome views of the route already travelled. The river ran along the flat base of the valley, dividing some distance away around the island with its campsite. It was also possible to trace the path of the previous day's walk, disappearing over the shoulder of an impressive red-flanked mountain. High above, another condor circled in the azure sky, appearing to gleam brilliant white like a cruising airliner, the sun glinting off her feathers.

At intervals along the gully, stripes of red and white paint on trailside rocks provided reassurance, hardly necessary in the sunshine but presumably essential when cloud descended. The pass came closer, a narrow fissure in the ridge. There was hardly any sign of vegetation, just a solitary stunted shrub in the shelter of a cliff. Under the cloudless sky, the pale rocks reflected a dazzling glare. As I stopped to reapply sunblock to my flaking face, a lone climber trudged by in the opposite direction.

'You'll need to be careful,' he warned. 'Yesterday we had gusts at over a hundred kilometres per hour. It was hard work hanging on, even with ropes.'

Snow lay in the highest parts of the pass. Cautious steps were required on the descent, stamping heels into the slippery surface. The valley ahead opened wide, dominated at first by a golden mountain that wore a neat skirt of green forest, its barren rounded summit warm against the open sky. Moments later, this attractive hill was shown to be no more than the support act. As the gully came to an end, Cerro Castillo magnificently appeared. Dozens of basalt pinnacles pointed to the sky. The sharp needles protruded above a thick covering of blue ice that sprawled over the mountain like a colossal fungus. The ice was as creased and cracked as the rock itself, each fracture accentuated by a trapped accumulation of eroded fragments. At its snout, the south-facing glacier peeked over a tall cliff and waterfalls tumbled down the red rock.

Descending from the pass, I caught up with a pair on a rocky plain. With specialist boots and bags, it appeared that they took their trekking seriously. We entered a stand of beech and promptly lost the path. All three of us scouted round in the thicket trying to relocate the trail. After a fruitless search, it became clear that we should have crossed the river. Continuing ahead, I came to a clearing with another superb view of Cerro Castillo. A second glacier was the centre piece again, overlooked by dark frost-shattered peaks.

I paused at another camping area and ate more rubbery bread. The two trekkers passed me, but it wasn't long before I overtook them again; perhaps they didn't realise it was a race. The next river crossing thankfully had a bridge, a pair of narrow planks that bowed alarmingly in the centre and a flimsy handrail fashioned from a thin branch. The instability hardly mattered – it was a mercy to have any kind of crossing, and it would have been foolhardy to wade through the raging glacial meltwater. After meandering between trees, the path emerged into a flat, swampy area. Beyond the bog was the southeast face of Cerro Castillo, capped by slender rock turrets and with another *cascada* crashing from the ice above. Across the resultant stream was a moraine slope at the front edge of a large glacial corrie. Climbing over the lip, I caught a breathtaking first sight of the turquoise corrie lake. The right hand bank was a lofty cliff with a third pale blue glacier on top and more slender spires above. Cloud swirled threateningly amongst the auburn needles. It was a stunning sight.

From a closer inspection of its leading edge, it was clear that the glacier was structured with successive strata of compressed ice. It looked like a slice of a popular cake known as *mil hojas*, thousand leaves, composed of multiple pastry sheets. Dirt and debris trapped between the layers revealed how the glacier was curved over the uneven surface of the rock platform, like the deformations in sedimentary rock.

To the left of the corrie, across the water from the vertical wall of rock, the lake was confined by a high moraine slope of stones and boulders, enclosed behind by the ridge of another mountain spur. The route taken by the *sendero* was unclear, so I crossed the river near its lake outlet and continued diagonally up the slope. Though not technically difficult, the ascent was tiring all the same. It was rather like climbing an endless staircase, with steps that were prone to wobble or slide. It paid to go steadily, taking particular care on the loose boulders. I stopped frequently to catch my breath, drinking in the exquisite *vista* of lake and mountain. The trekkers had arrived below the lake and were resting beside the river, tiny figures dwarfed by the vast mountain-scape.

A hiker in a yellow jacket appeared over the ridge, moving swiftly. She carried only a small *mochila* and no tent. Risa was the second person that day to report strong winds on the other side. With a sense of foreboding, I remembered the advice of the *guardaparque* to cross passes in the early part of the day.

'Are you with Karsten?' asked Risa.

'No. Who is Karsten?'

'I met a *chico* called Karsten earlier,' she explained. 'He said he'd become separated from his two friends. I wondered if you were in his group.'

'No, I'm alone, but there are two guys there.' I pointed out the trekkers.

Risa sprang down the slope, making impressive progress over the loose scree. I climbed to the ridge, which afforded a spectacular view of a valley to the south. A thousand metres below, the Río Ibáñez wound towards Lago General Carrera. Overlooking the immense lake was the distinctive and aptly named Cerro Pirámide. In the distance, another cone also broke the horizon: Cerro de la Subida, located a hundred kilometres away on the Argentinean steppe.

Closer by, threatening clouds were accumulating on the mountains to the west, and nearer still, thin white wisps unfurled around the turrets of Cerro Castillo right above me. I took a compass bearing and checked the ridge for an emergency camping spot, just in case. Far below, the trekkers had pitched their tent near the lake. Risa's yellow jacket was already well beyond them. With plenty of hours of daylight still in the sky, I pressed ahead. It was a decision I would regret during the tortuous descent that followed.

The wind strengthened. The painted waymarkers became infrequent. In their place, occasional stone cairns had been constructed, but they were small and easy to miss. Although the footpath appeared to stay on the ridge, the climber's prophetic words troubled me: 'That map sucks!'

The trail continued ascending, surprisingly high, until it looked down on the glaciers which had once been so far above. The air temperature dropped a degree or two, and gusts of wind tore at my clothes. A sudden crash startled me. A chunk of ice had detached, smashing and splintering on the rocks below and raining fragments into the lake. A terrifying, steep drop fell away on either side of the ridge. The highest point was a plateau of flat stones. Amongst them, tiny plants somehow survived in pockets of soil. A low wall of stones offered shelter from the wind – evidently someone had once had reason to pitch a tent there, but it was not a spot in which I would want to spend the night. I checked my compass and pressed on.

Beyond the plateau, the descent began at last. The path dropped into the steep cutting of a mountain stream, where grit repeatedly filled my shoes. My legs complained at the effort to stand upright on such a punishing gradient, but overnighting on the rocky mountainside was not a good option. According to the map, there was a campsite ahead. Even if I couldn't find it, there would surely be a patch of earth flat enough for a tent, somewhere in the woods. I had to keep going.

The direction pursued by the path became increasingly puzzling. The map indicated quite distinctly how the trail curved away to the south, heading towards a disused mine. In contrast, the route I was slithering down didn't diverge at all; it continued belligerently west, making ominously towards a deep gully. Each time I doubted, however, a reassuring cairn appeared, or an arrow of red paint on a rock. Loose gravel gave way to larger, secure boulders, but my progress was hopelessly slow. In the hour since leaving the top, I'd advanced only a single kilometre. All the same, I dared not hurry; the consequences of breaking an ankle in this exposed and lonely place did not bear contemplation.

In pursuit of firm terrain, I zigzagged between alternate sides of the stream. At one point, I quit the river and searched for the curving path shown on the map but in no distance at all was beaten back by thorny bushes, whose long spines slid deep beneath the skin of my palms. And then: calamity. As I'd feared it might, the stream fell away over a waterfall.

¡Pucha!

I peered over the lip, but there was no obvious route down. Steep walls rose forbiddingly on either side, confining the river in its chasm. In my determination to descend, and failing to pay attention to the deepening gorge, I'd marched right into a dead end.

'This is madness,' I screamed out loud, crouching to hold my head in my hands, taken aback by the anxiety in my own voice.

Scrambling a short way up the bank, there was a narrow channel that seemed just possible to climb. Trampled vegetation nearby indicated that previous walkers might have escaped that way before. I wedged myself into the narrow crevice and slowly hauled myself upwards. My breaths came in anguished gasps, and my fingers turned white as they gripped whatever protrusions might serve as handholds. I shuffled upwards, my knees wedged between boulders. Loose fragments fell away, but I dared not look down. What was I doing here, alone, halfway up a cliff?

¡Pucha!

I stopped to draw breath, one arm looped over a helpfully positioned tree branch. Aware of a tightening in my shoulders, I turned my head slowly one way then the other, gently easing the muscles in my neck. This was crazy. I was utterly unprepared and ill-equipped for this kind of climb. One slip, and…

'No, I mustn't think like that,' I scolded myself. 'Don't even consider failing. Believe, and climb.'

Wheezing and fretting, after several more minutes grappling with the cliff, my head popped out the top of the cleft. I scrambled onto a platform and examined the way ahead. The subsequent descent to the base of the waterfall was a treacherous, slimy slope. I slid down, aiming intentionally for the wayward shrubs that might slow my plunging progress. I reached the riverbed with genuine relief and sat to rest, but the respite was temporary; the first waterfall was quickly followed by another. There was no way back; up and over was the only real option. Scaling the bank a second time, I was grateful for the bendy saplings to which I tightly clutched, my heavy pack doing nothing to improve stability or balance as it swung from my shoulders.

The worst had passed. No further life-threatening obstacles followed that moment of crisis. For a while it became possible to walk in the woods. What a joy to set foot on an earth path rather than stepping from rock to rock. A short-lived joy, it turned out; a boggy ditch forced me back into the river bed. Later, cutting into the forest a second time, I followed a path that diverged from the river. I'd lost my exact position on the map, but with the friendlier terrain, my racing pulse rate calmed. Suddenly, unexpectedly, of all the reassuring sights I could have hoped to see, there was one I shall always remember: a toilet shed. It was followed by a footbridge over a shallow channel. These were signs of human habitation. Simmering despair turned to bubbling joy.

'*¿Estoy dónde?*' I asked three young adventurers sat at a table. Faced by blank expressions, I switched to English. 'Where am I?'

'Camping Los Porteadores,' one of them said. 'At least, we hope it is.'

It was Karsten and his two friends. Separated from the other pair, Karsten had taken a different route to the rest of us. From the high stony plateau, he'd followed a series of red poles that neither I nor the other two had noticed; this was the curving path shown on the map. It was also the exposed windy section where Karsten had met Risa. Neither route was very appealing; it had been a choice between a lethal ravine and a merciless gale.

Having pitched my tent, I bathed my weary feet in the icy river. Whilst the three friends played an unintelligible card game, I read pages from their trekking book. The notes recommended tackling the two passes on separate days; no wonder I felt exhausted. By the time I'd prepared my meal, night had fallen and the game was continuing by the light of head torches. As I lay down for the night, everything hurt: my arms, my legs, my feet and toes, my neck and shoulders; all parts of me ached. But I was safe. Listening to the slow breaths of the night from the darkness of my tent, I drew comfort from the irregular gurgle of the river and the swish of wind in the trees, and from the slumber-inducing toasty warmth of my sleeping bag.

*

Next morning, both shoes were inhabited by caterpillars, whose appetite had taken a toll on the campsite trees. Fragments of sky visible through the canopy were cloudy with only rare patches of blue. Rain fell in squalls. I had a decision to make: hike up to a higher camp or descend to Villa Cerro Castillo? After breakfast, a sachet of oats generously described as chocolate flavoured and a mug of tea that tasted strangely of stock cube, a lone hiker strode into the campsite. His face was familiar. It was Philippe, the trout-fishing Frenchman from Puerto Bertrand.

'*Bonjour*. Have you finished reading that book?'

'Not exactly finished,' I confessed. 'Did you cross the pass this morning?'

'No, I came over a couple of days ago. I've been staying further up the mountain, but the weather this morning was so bad that I decided to come down. In any case, I have no money left, so I need to get to the bank in Coyhaique.'

'Which way did you descend from the pass?' I pressed. 'Did you come down the ravine or past the mine?'

'I didn't see any mine. I followed some arrows down a narrow stream.'

'What did you think of the path? I found it difficult.'

'It was ridiculous; very dangerous. This is a national park. You'd think they could make some better arrangement.'

With a rapid '*Au revoir*,' he was gone.

With rain persisting, I abandoned any idea of climbing higher and packed to leave. A wet tent is bad news in many respects. It is heavier, can damage the fabric, and tends to make everything else wet, too. On this occasion I had pitched on bare earth so the groundsheet was muddy when I rolled it. I bade farewell to my three neighbours. Their response in the face of the rain was to hole up in their tent playing cards.

The descent began across the river, on an easy path through the forest. The air was very still. The only sounds came from the water running in its deep cutting, the methodical thud of footsteps and the rhythmic friction of waterproofs and backpack. There was no hum of traffic, no human voices calling, no radio blaring or text message alert chirping and not even any birds.

A stile marked the exit from Reserva Nacional Cerro Castillo. Standing on the step, I turned to salute the mountain but her peaks were enclosed by murky cloud. I felt grateful that the previous day had stayed dry, and not at all envious of the trekking pair who'd camped at the lake, quite possibly preparing to tackle the second pass in troublesome conditions. An extra day's food was valuable advice.

Moving at pace, I stumbled over a stone and turned my foot. After all the difficult ground of the previous day, it would have been ironic to twist an ankle on a virtually flat path, but the sharp pain was short-lived. All the arrows pointed against me now, directing hikers making the ascent. In spite of the horrible weather, a group of four went by, and later another pair, plodding upwards.

The final kilometres back to the town of Villa Cerro Castillo crossed the Río Ibáñez plain. Ironically, where they were hardly necessary, the stone cairns were plentiful.

A young *gaucho* rode towards me. 'Have you seen a horse?' he asked.

I resisted the temptation to suggest he check what he was sitting on. 'No, sorry,' I said instead. 'Good luck'.

'*Buen viaje,*' he wished me and rode on.

The track towards the village was part of the *Sendero de Chile*. This project, inaugurated in celebration of the bicentenary of Chile's independence, aims to construct a footpath the full length of the country. Once completed, it will be one of the longest walking trails in the world.

After I'd walked in the base of the valley for what seemed like hours, the trail eventually reached the Carretera Austral. As I waited to cross the road, a truck came to a halt at the bus shelter with the noisy flapping roof. It was the front cab of an articulated lorry. Two pairs of hitchhikers spoke to the driver and climbed aboard. I raced across.

'*Señor*, do you have room for one more, *por favor*?'

'No,' said the driver. 'Look!'

But the four kindly squeezed onto the rear bench together, leaving the front passenger seat free.

'Wait, please,' I begged. 'I have to go and get my stuff.'

The driver rolled his eyes. I hurried back to the *residencial* to retrieve the bin liner with my belongings from under the stairs. I apologised to the lady; I wouldn't need a room after all, very sorry. But hooray, hooray, hooray, I would get to Coyhaique today. A warm bed and a hot shower. Pizza. All things were possible in Coyhaique. Even *lomo a lo pobre*.

Image 15: Glacier on Cerro Castillo

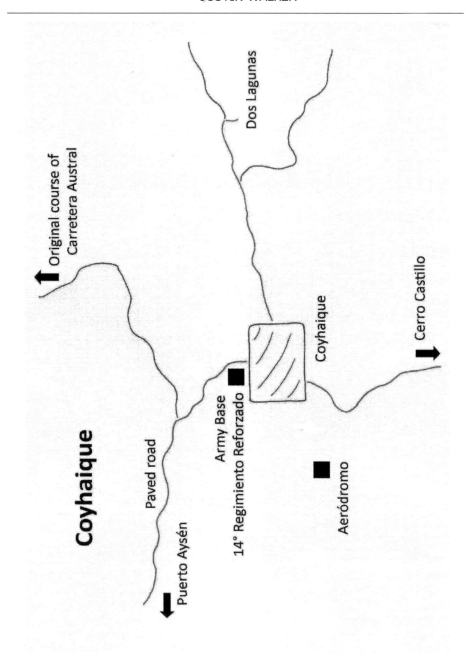

Map 10: Coyhaique

Sixteen: Claudia

Three enormous windscreen wipers sloshed away the heavy rain. With six of us inside, the truck windows soon misted up, but it might nonetheless have been preferable if the driver, tackling repeated tight bends on the climb towards Las Horquetas, had concentrated more on steering and less on adjusting the ventilation. The four cradling backpacks on the rear bench were an English couple and a Scottish-French duo. Each told their account of battling wind and terrain on Cerro Castillo. The French woman had been blown off her feet on the exposed path and her head was clumsily bandaged.

Nearing the principal town of Chilean Patagonia, changes in land use were apparent. In contrast to the rock-strewn valleys, the open pastures and the forests and ex-forests further south, the scenery here bore more obvious signs of human influence. Potato crops were interspersed amongst hayfields and the land was dotted with barns and farmhouses. The traffic, although still light, had become denser than anywhere since the start.

On arrival in Coyhaique, the truck driver took the injured French hiker to the hospital, accompanied by her Scottish companion. I headed straight for Hospedaje Marluz only to find that Nomi had no rooms available.

'Why didn't you call me?' she sighed.

'My phone is out of battery,' I replied. 'In any case, I didn't know I was coming until a couple of hours ago.'

Instead I took a room with bunk beds at Hospedaje Natti, arriving with three distinct sets of belongings: my rucksack, the bin liner from Villa Cerro Castillo and the items retrieved from storage at Marluz. Emptying everything onto the top bunk, I began to sort through piles of stuff. There was too much to carry. What had I been thinking when I'd originally packed in Santiago? What could I get rid of now? Was there any way of shipping some of it home or would I have to abandon the surplus here? I managed to offload some camping gas, the two bottles I'd been unable to take on the Villa O'Higgins flight, by offering around amongst the tents crammed together on a square of grass in the yard. One camper quite bizarrely kept her bike inside her tiny tent; she didn't need any gas, she said. Another couple also declined; they were booked on a bus to the island of Chiloé and had dismantled their bicycles into classy canvas travel bags. Eventually I found grateful recipients: a loud and lively group of *chicos* heading south.

A notice in the bathroom prohibited washing clothes in the shower, but it didn't mention tents. It took half an hour throwing water around the cubicle to rinse off the mud, and then the sunny, blustery afternoon gave perfect conditions in which to dry the nylon sheeting. There was a *lavandería* next door, so I spent another afternoon scantily attired, reduced to an airy and liberating outfit comprising no more than a fleece, hiking trousers and sandals. In celebration of conquering Cerro Castillo, I found a restaurant with an excellent *lomo a lo pobre*. Lubricated with a litre of *schop*, draft beer, I took advantage of my partially stupefied state to pick splinters out of my palms with the aid of toothpicks from a tub on the table.

The mid-journey luxuries available in Coyhaique helped to reinvigorate me for the northern portion of my trip. I was not alone in refuelling. Amongst the others resting at Hospedaje Natti was a couple from Dortmund. Devoted cyclists, they'd been on the road several months and could frequently be found attending to their upturned bicycles clutching spanners, screwdrivers and a small canister of oil.

'When we finish the Carretera Austral, we're going to ride in the Bolivian *altiplano*,' they explained.

Their other primary activity was conjuring elaborate salads from lacy leaves, colourful pulses, Andean grains and odd-shaped capsicums. They complemented this by smoking a range of herbs: a balanced diet. In light of the efforts they invested preparing intricate healthy meals, I was rather ashamed of the mediocre selection in my basket as I joined the checkout line: my standard fare of bread, cheese and fruit. Ahead in the queue, a foreigner hadn't weighed his bread at the *panadería* nor his oranges at the *frutería*. I felt smug, having lived in

Chile long enough to be familiar with this supermarket requirement. The tourist was struggling to understand why the cashier was sending him back, so I explained. Lamentably my self-assured poise quickly evaporated when it was my turn. I had forgotten to weigh my *duraznos*.[51]

*

In addition to a desire for rest and recuperation, another factor required that I stayed a few extra days in Coyhaique. The reason was disappointingly dull. I would like to pretend it was because I'd joined a team traversing the Patagonian Ice Sheet or had decided to kayak into Argentina, but sadly this was not so. It was down to an essay I had to write. I'm aware that not everyone takes their study books on holiday, but this was just the way it worked out with an Open University course onto which I had enrolled. Naturally, I had no control over the assignment submission date.

The course had the rather dry title of *Institutional Development: Theory, Policy and Practice*. 'Institutions' in this context refers to the accepted norms in a community or society. For example, universal schooling and local government are institutions (accepted norms) in the UK. The five-day working week might be an institution in one society, Friday prayers in another and the rights enjoyed by or withheld from women in yet another, illustrating how norms vary from place to place. The module was concerned with how such institutional practices form and take shape in different types of society, with a particular focus on 'developing countries'. Many of these norms emerge progressively through history, but could they be encouraged to develop through intentional interventions? If so, under what circumstances would that be desirable? The essay brief was to discuss strategies for developing new institutions that might be considered

---

[51] A *durazno* is a peach, but in Spain the word is *melocotón*. Food words commonly vary between Latin America and Spain. In many cases a word from one of the indigenous languages has been adopted rather than the Castilian translation. Evening class students who have diligently learned that apricot and avocado are *albaricoque* and *aguacate* will need to ditch those in favour of the Chilean words *damasco* and *palta*. Similarly, sweetcorn is *choclo*, not *maíz*, and strawberry is *frutilla*, not *fresa*. I used to get *durazno* and *damasco* terribly mixed up. When I bought a jar of *mermelada* (jam, not marmalade) or a carton of juice (*jugo*, not *zumo*), I was never sure if it was apricot or peach and the picture of a generic golden-coloured soft fruit on the label rarely gave much clue either way.

beneficial, in terms of equality, rights, social cohesion or growth, for example, all concepts that needed careful definition and elaboration.

With the deadline looming, the pragmatic choice was to complete the assignment before leaving the town, taking advantage of internet connectivity. It also occurred to me that I might find someone travelling by car who could return my books to Santiago. For all this, I allotted four days; an imminent deadline can help focus the mind. I began drafting text the following morning. At midday, I went out in search of a *menú del día*, a set three course lunch, and found an excellent offer priced at only 3000 *pesos*. I was slightly taken aback to receive a dish of chewy pieces that resembled strips of llama hide. Having a tendency to gravitate to the cheapest place in town exposed me, I realised, to the risk of being served a bowl of canine treats. Doubtless I'd already learned the folly of overenthusiastic economising in multiple previous contexts, but I have a habit of wilfully forgetting the lessons that life has tried her best to teach me.

Having worked in education for two decades in a variety of roles, it was somehow fitting to revert to the student end of the chain. I was reminded of the delights of essay deadlines, the frustrations of losing hours of work on fickle computers and the disappointment of grades that were lower than anticipated. Whereas distance learning has long existed, internet applications have greatly enhanced this kind of tuition, facilitating access to study materials in diverse forms and speeding interactions with both tutor and fellow students. We had real-time discussion forums involving peers on several continents, some of whom had stayed awake into the early hours to participate. It was easy to lose sight of the overarching goals beneath a tide of mundane tasks, but it goes without saying that quality education is a valuable gift.

However, good education is far more nuanced than at first seems obvious. In addition to learning the material in their curriculum subjects, students also receive implicit messages along the way. If girls and boys are treated differently, they will learn that one gender is superior. Through the manner that adults choose to wield authority, they will learn to face difficulties and opponents through diplomacy and patience or through anger and violence. They will learn about inclusion and fairness or about discrimination and favouritism. They will learn that they as individuals, or their religion, or their ethnic group, are either lovely and cherished or revolting and hated. Through repeated exposure to success or failure, they will either learn that they meet the standard or that they are not good enough. Where children are placed differentially in separate schools or separate classes, they may start to believe that they are valued more, or less, than the others. These are the things that children really learn in schools, much more than any lesson about spelling difficult words, speaking a few sentences in French, categorising Caribbean islands by their colonial oppressor or calculating the spare angle in a diagram.

Education is commonly held to be a key component in development and in solving society's ills. And indeed it could be, but it's important not to confuse education with schooling. The education of children has always existed, throughout history, in every society around the world, but it has not always taken place in schools. The education of children in much of the world today has become fixated on a traditional model of classrooms, instructional materials, teachers spouting information and students memorising it (with a greater or lesser degree of understanding) for the purposes of formal assessment. Without wishing to question the undoubted benefits that a healthy and supportive school community can offer a child, this pedagogical paradigm was devised so long ago and has so many known flaws that it is quite a surprise it still exists. How would it be if news media, communications, travel and trade, to pick just four examples, had remained more-or-less unchanged since the nineteenth century?

If schools are to be involved in the broader task of educating, then it may be advantageous to stop designing them, architecturally and organisationally, around an inappropriate blueprint. On what basis do we assume that the traditional European conceptualisation of how a good school should look and behave must be imposed on communities with dissimilar cultures, different rhythms to the year and varied sets of beliefs, expectations and needs? It is a matter for debate and analysis whether schools are an effective vehicle for the delivery of education, but even if they were, then why should they all look the same? Do we really want a monochrome world where variety and difference are viewed with suspicion, and even worse, required to be eliminated?

The traditional model often includes a standard and unsurprising set of subjects, a curriculum that came into being generations ago. The Chilean National Curriculum at secondary school level emphasises four subjects: *Castellano*, *Matemáticas*, *Ciencias* and *Ciencias Sociales*

(Spanish, Maths, Science and Social Science). Irrespective of the chosen degree pathway, university admission depends on passing multiple-choice exams in two or more of these disciplines (frequently just *Castellano* and *Matemáticas*) combined with a component carried forward from the school's continuous internal assessment. In my school, as students entered the crucial final years, families who had previously been enthusiastic about a holistic and broad education became obsessed only with *notas*, student grades. *Notas* dominated every planning meeting, every parent-teacher liaison and every review of student progress or conduct. Elements such as student wellbeing, personal growth, respect for teachers and fairness were pushed aside. The only thing that mattered was the *nota*. Grades became more important than learning. These observations are not designed to take a swipe at the Chilean system – the situation is not so very different in my home land.

My Chilean colleagues talked about *formación*, which is usually translated as 'training' but implies so much more. The goal of education is to contribute to the formation of the person. Whether that *formación* is achieved by formal schooling or via some other route doesn't matter very much. It is also difficult to see why the ultimate evaluation of that *formación* should be condensed into a particular set of numbers or letters on a certificate. In taking my arduous journey along the Carretera Austral, the things that contributed most to my *formación* were the experiences and incidents and encounters along the way and hardly at all the date of my arrival in Puerto Montt, the total distance travelled or the speed that I got there.

*

That afternoon, I discovered the town library. I pushed bravely through the melee of youths in hooded tops that had hijacked the internet facilities in the lobby and entered the impressive modern building beyond. With lots of natural light and a large collection of resources, it was a more satisfactory place to study than the wobbly table in my bunk-bedded room. I worked the whole afternoon. Unfortunately for those of us intent on study, silence was not well observed. A girl at a nearby table conducted a lengthy conversation on her mobile phone, disregarding a conspicuous sign forbidding it, and this in full view of the librarian's desk. There were also a number of children attending a holiday reading club in one of the side rooms. Each time they had a break, the double doors burst open, and the delightful brood was puked into the library atrium where they ran up and down the stairs screeching, yelling and throwing paper aeroplanes.

In the evening, I typed and printed a first draft at an internet café located just off the plaza in a pedestrianised sector with restaurants, bars and tour agencies. The environment was not conducive to good concentration. The terminals on either side were occupied by backpacking North Americans, both embroiled in boisterous Skype conversations with the folks back home. On eventually finishing, I faced the uncomfortable question of an evening meal. Having misguidedly consumed tasty dog chews in sauce earlier that day, my nutritional regime dictated that the evening meal be something light.

The *empanada* is an iconic food of Chile. A pastry envelope with a cooked filling served hot or cold, it is not dissimilar to an Indian samosa or Cornish pasty. The word comes from *empanar*, meaning to wrap in *pan*, bread. Traditional Chilean *empanadas* are filled with *pino*, a minced mix of meat and onion with cumin and chilli, a slice of hard-boiled egg, a single black olive complete with its stone and possibly some raisins. *Empanada* variants can be filled with vegetables, fish, seafood, or the popular *napolitana* (ham, cheese, tomato and oregano). Judging that it wouldn't count as a cooked meal, I bought bread and an *empanada* and sat morosely in the square feeling hungry.

That evening, I took a walk to a thickly wooded river gorge on the edge of Coyhaique. At the base of the ravine, a road bridge crossed the river, from where there was a view of a protruding section of cliff known locally as the *Piedra del Indio*, the Indian's Rock. It bore a passing resemblance to a face. Actually most rocks do if you look at them for long enough, and squint, and incline your head… and hold your nose. I detected the facial profile but quite why it was supposed to be an Indian[52] was not clear.

---

[52] The word 'Indian' in this context may appear to be contentious. Controversy surrounds the choice of term most suitable to name the indigenous people of the American continent. 'American' is an outsider's word. The continent was named America after Italian explorer Amerigo Vespucci so these peoples cannot have been known as 'Native Americans' prior to his arrival. Neither are they Indians, the choice of another outsider. Cristoforo Colombo, reportedly believing that he'd discovered a western route into Asia, insisted on using this term even though it soon became plain that they were far from India. Moreover, the indigenous people of the time

A half-blind kitten approached nervously and mewed. She was reasonably cute, despite the gammy eye.

'There isn't much I can do for you,' I told her. 'You'll have to learn to survive out here as best you can.'

Unless... a car was descending into the gorge. It stopped at the bridge and the occupants climbed out to view the *piedra*. I struck up an innocent conversation about the Indian face and then attempted to sell them the one-eyed kitten. Sadly it seems that my vocational skills do not lie in the area of livestock sales.

*

The deadline arrived. Fortified by Fortnum & Mason tea, I completed a final draft in the morning. It took the whole afternoon to type the amendments at the internet café, alone by request on a mezzanine where the isolation suited me well, surrounded by piles of dusty circuit boards and twisted cables. Eventually, with a sigh of relief and an aching mouse arm, I clicked 'Send' on the university's essay-submission website.

The next priority was to find someone willing to spirit away a stack of books, bar one that I kept in preparation for another assignment. The following morning, I sidled up to a family packing their car at Hospedaje Natti.

'Are you from Santiago?' I asked.

'Yes we are. We start our journey back there today.'

'Please can you do me a favour?'

They seemed delighted to help, surprisingly unconcerned about carrying a stranger's belongings through both Argentine and Chilean customs checkpoints on their route back to the capital. I hurriedly packed a small bag, and the eldest daughter, Claudia, persuaded it into a small space amongst their luggage.

'You have no idea what this journey is going to be like for me,' she said. 'I have to sit between my brother and sister all the way, otherwise they fight.'

---

had no generic term meaning 'the peoples of this continent'. Distances were far, communications slow, languages many, and the need to have such a word had never arisen. Whatever term is chosen can be disputed from one position or another. According to surveys, two of the expressions favoured by modern indigenous peoples are 'American Indian' (or just 'Indian') and 'Native American'. Interestingly, as explained above, both are outsiders' words.

The pair beamed innocent smiles in my direction.

'Why do you live in Santiago?' asked Claudia.

I confessed to being a headteacher.

'My school was *en toma* this year,' she said. 'Now I have to repeat the whole grade.'

En toma means 'taken'. The sites of numerous schools and universities had been occupied during months of protests. Classes had been abandoned and students were demanding increased funding for public schools and an end to profit-making in private education.

'I don't mind retaking the year,' she said. 'It's a sacrifice. As long as we can bring a change, it's worth protesting now. The system is not fair. Children in public schools need better opportunities.'

*

At the level of primary and secondary education, Chile has three main categories of school (at the time of writing). *Colegios públicos* are free schools maintained by municipal authorities. *Colegios subvencionados* (subsidised or voucher schools) are partially private and charge fees in some form in addition to receiving public money. Third, there are fully private *colegios particulares* with no state funding. Due to this tiered system, nearly 40 per cent of spending on schools comes not from state coffers but through fees, making the education system in Chile amongst the most privatised in the world.

Not surprisingly, choice of school divides up broadly in accordance with socioeconomic demographics. Further deepening the divide, state funding is the responsibility of local boroughs, not central government. The tax-raising potential of distinct municipalities varies widely across the city and country. Therefore, a school in a wealthy borough can expect higher funding than schools in a poorer district.

State funding for universities is even lower, at only 16 per cent of costs compared to an average for OECD[53] countries of 70 per cent.

---

[53] The OECD (Organisation of Economic Co-operation and Development) was formed in 1961 with the intention of overseeing global economic issues. The 20 founding members were a group of Western European countries plus Canada and the USA. Membership enlarged over subsequent years with Japan, Australia and New Zealand being amongst the early additions. A number of Eastern European nations joined in the 1990s along with Mexico. Chile was accepted into membership in 2010, the first representative of South America. Attaining membership is a convoluted process, and members must meet stringent conditions. Amongst the stated aims of

Private universities outnumber their traditional counterparts by three to one. Although universities are forbidden by law to generate profit, there are ways in which loopholes can be exploited. For example, the owners might let the building to the university management authorities at premium rates, enabling the university to charge higher fees without registering a profit.

The 2011 student protests began in May. Their specific pleas were numerous and complicated but included demands for greater funding of public universities, efforts to improve both quality and equality, a repeal of laws forbidding student participation in university governance and for the government to tighten and more effective enforcement of the law against profit-making. They also wanted to see greater equality by having public schools administered centrally rather than by municipalities, a national plan to attract the best talent into the teaching profession and modifications to the voucher funding system.

Protests spread to universities throughout Chile. In some, students stopped attending lectures. In others, university buildings were taken over and occupied by students. By the first week of June, a handful of schools were also *en toma*, and the numbers rose rapidly. Students locked themselves inside, barricading entrances with chairs and tables. In some schools this lasted for months, during which time countless young people received no formal education at all.

As the months rolled by, a succession of marches and protests took place in Santiago and elsewhere. In regular public *manifestaciones*, protestors waved banners and chanted their demands. One event came to be known as the *marcha de los paraguas*, the march of the umbrellas, when thousands turned out in persistent heavy rain. Opinion polls suggested high public approval for the students, who were often joined at their demonstrations by teachers, lecturers and other sympathisers. What did not impress the public was the violence that flared around these marches. Shops were looted, bus shelters wrecked and vehicles burned. Police responded with water cannon[54] and tear gas.

---

the OECD is to 'to help governments foster prosperity and fight poverty through economic growth and financial stability', but the organisation has been criticised for concentrating principally on a small number of wealthier nations. The OECD collects and publishes data related to multiple facets of economic life, in order to drive discussions and decisions on policy and strategy. One such area is educational achievement. Statistics are available on the OECD website: www.oecd.org.

[54] The local slang expression for the vehicle-mounted water cannon is a *guanaco*.

The government announced successive reforms, but each one was rejected by student leaders, who declared that they failed to address their chief concerns. A major sticking point was the issue of profit. Students maintained that private universities should not make profits but should reinvest their income in educational improvements. '¡No al lucro!' became a regular cry: 'No profit!' In early September, student leaders attended talks with the government. The Education Minister set out an agenda for a 'month of dialogue'. Protestors cited various minimum requirements before they would negotiate, but the minister rejected the pre-conditions. Negotiations broke down altogether, each side blaming the other.

School students in Chile must perform satisfactorily in order to progress to the subsequent level. Since classes had been heavily disrupted, many schools had no assessment data on which to base these decisions. MINEDUC, the Ministerio de Educación de Chile, designed a programme in order to help students recover the lost ground, making it possible for them to advance. All affected students were invited to inscribe to a programme known as *Salvemos el Año Escolar*: Let's Save the School Year. Thousands failed to register, condemning themselves to retaking their entire year of studies. This, it would seem, is what had happened to Claudia.

*

Discrimination in education provision is common throughout the world, chiefly on the basis of wealth. The opportunities that a child is deemed to deserve – in the form of schooling at least – depend on her family's ability to pay. The outcome is that significant advantages are preferentially bestowed upon children from wealthier families in almost every country around the globe. The privileged minority benefit from smaller class sizes and better-resourced environments with the latest technologies, equipment and pedagogies. Budgetary restrictions apply so commonly in life that it becomes easy to accept their existence without so much as a shrug. When it comes to your house, your holiday or your haircut, you can only have what you can afford. But shouldn't basic education be made free of such favouritism? Can any

---

Guanacos (mentioned in Chapter 1, the wild ancestor of the domesticated llama) have the ability to spit, accurately and with force.

society tarnished by such partiality consider itself genuinely fair and wholly just?

Wealth is just one factor amongst several in which the world's schoolchildren are treated unequally. City schools may have advantages over those in rural areas. Teachers may gravitate to successful schools or might even migrate across borders to command a superior wage. Some families send sons to school but not daughters. A disabled child may be denied a place in the classroom due to lack of expertise or facilities, or through the family's fear of public shame. Some children are denied access to formal education by impossible journeys or war, or because they are trapped in refugee camps. Others, having defied the odds in order to reach a school, encounter a teacher workforce decimated by AIDS, or classes conducted in a language that they do not understand.

Access to quality education has the potential to bring tremendous benefits. As yet, these treasures are not yet offered equally to all the world's children. Neither here, nor there.

Image 16: Piedra del Indio

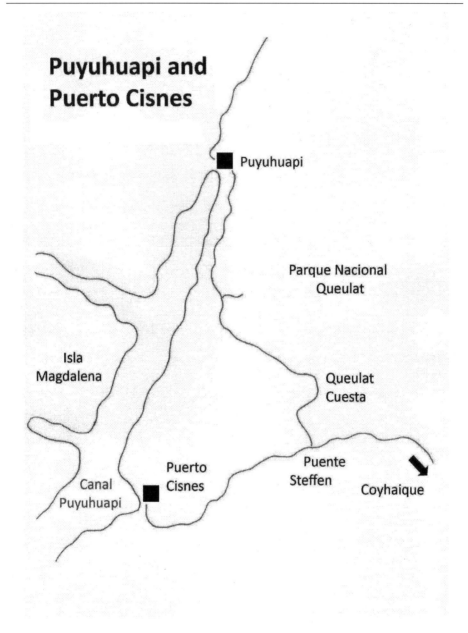

Map 11: Puyuhuapi and Puerto Cisnes

Seventeen: Merluza

In de-regulated Chile, multiple bus companies compete along interurban routes. A few large carriers cover comprehensive networks, and hundreds of smaller operators run a handful of services each, including individuals with a single bus. Consequently, principal bus stations have rank upon rank of ticket windows. For the uninitiated traveller, it can sometimes be necessary to trawl round any number of kiosks to identify those serving a particular destination.

Calling at Coyhaique's small bus terminal one evening to investigate suitable onward routes, I found a packed ticket hall. Enormous queues snaked away from each of the half-dozen counters. Panicking, I rapidly decided upon a bus to Puerto Cisnes and joined the back of the line, eventually securing a ticket for a departure a couple of days later. Puerto Cisnes, literally meaning Port Swans, was some way north. I'd seen a poster in Coyhaique library advertising their *Fiesta del Pescado Frito*; any town that had a Fried Fish Festival was certainly worth a visit. The photograph appeared to show a house being floated across the sea, supported on a raft of fishing boats. What could that be about?

With a spare day to fill and a nagging yearning for open spaces, I found my way to the eastern fringe of Coyhaique and spent a forlorn morning attempting to catch a ride to a small park known as Dos Lagunas, Two Lakes. After an age, I tried another spot; still no luck. I felt invisible. Grumbling to myself, I walked on again, now some distance out of the town. After a few minutes of grinning expectantly at the oncoming traffic, I began to lose interest in the whole outing. I was about to give up completely when a car stopped and the electric window was lowered.

'I'm trying to get to a *reserva* called Dos Lagunas. Do you know it?' I asked.

'Yes, *ningún problema*. Get in.'

He was a young driver, and I had the impression it was his parents' car. 'I'm going to my girlfriend's house,' he told me. 'She's been looking after my dog, but now we're going on holiday together.'

'That sounds nice. Where are you taking her?'

'Him, not her. She's a boy.'

'Oh, I'm sorry. I thought you said girlfriend.'

'I did. I'm not going on holiday with my girlfriend. Her father wouldn't allow that. No, I'm going away with my dog. He always comes with me. He's my best friend.'

'And your girlfriend, she lives near Dos Lagunas?'

'No; not especially.'

The house was only a few minutes away, leaving me well short of the park. I'd made hardly any ground, but the short ride had nonetheless carried me beyond the critical quitting threshold, out of range of a straightforward return to Coyhaique. The sun was high and hot. It must have been approaching midday and there was no shade to be found. It was a fast downhill stretch, hardly suitable for hitchhiking, and several cars whizzed by. I sat for a while on the black-and-white crash barrier and constructed a sandwich of sweaty cheese.

When a vehicle approached with Argentine licence plates, I performed star jumps and cartwheels on the white line.

'*Buenos días*,' I said, as charmingly as I could manage. 'Are you driving into Argentina?'

'Yes. We have an *estancia* over the border.'

'Will you pass Dos Lagunas?'

'I know the place,' the man replied, 'but no, we take a different road. Sorry.'

'Okay, never mind. Thank you for stopping.'

'Wait!' interrupted the woman in the passenger seat. 'Why don't we take you to the junction? You'll be a lot closer than here.'

Their young son wailed when he realised I was about to get in beside him, so he shared the front seat with his mother.

'Don't worry,' the father told me. 'It's not you. He's just a boy!'

The paved road ended and we climbed into hills on gravel. The couple eagerly struck up conversation, speaking good English.

'Have you ever been to Argentina?' they asked.

They seemed pleased when I listed my visits to their country: to Calafate and El Chaltén in the south, to the vineyard-surrounded town of Mendoza just over the Andes from Santiago, to the magnificent waterfalls at Iguazú and on several occasions to their home city of Buenos Aires. The Argentine capital is sometimes described as 'the Paris of South America', characterised by elegant architecture and sophisticated inhabitants. This couple fitted the stereotype. Even their choice of casual clothing bore witness to an awareness of colour complementarity and tasteful style, whereas my leisure outfit that day bore tell-tale signs of the 'whichever tatty garment comes to hand' school of wardrobe selection.

After the junction, they continued towards their *estancia*. The remote spot to which I'd been delivered was beautiful, high amongst magnificent mountains and with great views down the valley towards Coyhaique. The yellow road meandered in graceful curves through green grazing land. Imposing cliffs formed the abrupt end of a short range of hills close to the town. In the far distance, the western horizon was a row of snow-capped peaks.

The map was surprisingly vague regarding the precise location of the park entrance, so I took a chance and continued on foot. Making half-hearted attempts to flag down the occasional vehicles, I was taken by surprise when one rattled to a halt. So battered was the machine, it must have been subjected to this brutal journey a thousand previous times. Inside was a local family. Yes, they knew Dos Lagunas and could drop me at the gate. They were dressed for outdoor work: father in overalls, mother's hair covered by a traditional headscarf, and two cheerful boys wearing stained, scruffy sweatshirts. They were a lovely family, and I felt immediately at ease. Their affection was clear in kind remarks, fondly exchanged glances and frequent infectious laughter.

'Where are you from?' they asked.

'London,' I said – not quite true but often the most straightforward response.

'I'd love to go there,' said the father. 'I've seen London in films.'

Arriving at Dos Lagunas, my new friends dropped me at the entrance. Cars were gathered in the shade of tall trees. Their owners congregated at picnic tables, preparing *asados*: barbecues. Recognising some as those who'd passed me on the road, I may have entertained some mildly resentful thoughts, but only momentarily. A signpost pointed to a *sendero interpretivo*, a nature trail with labels and descriptions of many of the plant species. There was not another soul on the path. Midway around was a bank overlooking one of the two lakes, Laguna El Toro, a pretty spot to stop and read. Within moments I was mercilessly attacked by a gang of *tábanos*. In spite of my polished proficiency in *tábano* slaughter, their malicious hovering and kamikaze assaults became too distracting to allow even a single sentence to be read. The most judicious course of action was to keep moving. No longer interested in the explanatory notices, I hurried around the trail and completed the loop back to the *asado* site. There, at a picnic table under trees, the vile insects relented somewhat. Glancing around, it was somehow reassuring to see the other visitors flapping arms, hats and scarves in attempts to deter the vicious assailants.

One of the passers-by suddenly stopped, stared at me for a moment, and then approached and sat on the bench opposite me. It was Steve, the hiker who'd accompanied the injured French woman on Cerro Castillo. He told me about what had happened. There had been three of them, he explained, travelling separately but walking together that day, the third an Israeli man. When the girl had fallen in a sudden gust and cracked her head, Steve had stayed with her while the Israeli hurried to summon assistance. He'd returned with men and mules and they'd managed to descend before dusk. She'd been patched up in Villa Cerro Castillo, but staff in the small clinic had advised returning to Coyhaique for an x-ray. With her wound stitched, she had set off alone once again. A tough *chica*. Or more correctly I suppose, a tough *jeune fille*.

*

Two separate companies operated buses to Puerto Cisnes, both leaving on Saturday at 4pm. After first approaching the wrong vehicle, I joined the queue for the larger *Terraustral* bus. For once, seat numbers were not stated on the ticket. Instead, the efficient lady had collected passenger names with each booking and had subsequently assigned seats. Protectively guarding a beautifully prepared handwritten list, she unashamedly exulted in the authority it bestowed upon her to direct each passenger as they reported to the door.

The drizzly afternoon was unable to dampen my rising excitement about travelling to a town which held a *Fiesta del Pescado Frito*. With a salute of appreciation as we passed the *14° Regimiento Reforzado*, we departed Coyhaique and climbed the hill towards the rotating blades of three wind turbines. A turning to the right was the former route of the Carretera Austral. On this one day, to my great shame, I failed to follow the precise original course of the highway. Instead of the gravel road through a village called Villa Ortega, the bus took a longer paved road. As a result, there were 76 kilometres of genuine Carretera Austral on which I did not travel. I should go back and do it all again.

Clouds nestled in hanging valleys. Most of the way, settlement was restricted to a few isolated farmhouses, but in the small *pueblo* of Villa Mañihuales, we stopped for refreshments at a café painted a mesmerising lime green. The two buses arrived simultaneously and both sets of passengers crowded into one small hostelry. Local children boarded the bus selling jam and packets of *maquis*, a wild purple berry. Health food devotees may have heard of *maquis*. Their beneficial properties have long been known to indigenous Mapuche people who use both berries and leaves.

The forest grew thicker beyond Villa Mañihuales, a taste of how the whole area must once have been. Jungle extended way up the steep valley sides. Plants clung tenaciously to the ledges and cracks of towering cliffs, all drenched by the heavy rain. In the midst of it all there was suddenly a lake. It's interesting how people are drawn to stare out across open water. There is something hypnotic about the sight of lakes and the sea. Is it the tranquillity? Is it the rare openness in an otherwise cluttered world? Or is there something primordial within us yearning for our aquatic origins?

At the next village, we paused in a layby and the driver shouted out the name: Villa Amerigual. One man woke up, stumbled along the gangway and disembarked. It was a lonely spot: a small collection of houses and a church, dwarfed by a pair of mighty red-and-white antennae. From there, the road descended along the valley of the Río Cisnes, deep green in colour and cascading over turbulent rapids. Frequent tributaries added to the flow. Some of them crashed over tall waterfalls that would have warranted greater attention in a more accessible spot. The bus window offered occasional snatches, but so far from any population, these beautiful sights must rarely be admired.

How much more stunning scenery must there also have been out of sight and away from the road, never viewed by a human being from one decade to the next? The deep forest remains the preserve of wild creatures.

Nearing our destination, we crossed a bridge known as Puente Steffen. A pile of abandoned backpacks gave away the presence, somewhere, of hitchhikers. As we turned along a lateral road to Puerto Cisnes, the driver's assistant checked where each passenger wished to be dropped. Uncertain where to head for, I stayed aboard all the way to the *costanera*, where the bus paused outside Hospedaje Río Anita. A family got off there and entered through the gate, so I followed. This was their home, and I became their guest. The building was in two distinct parts: a traditional shingle-covered house complemented by a large modern extension. An enormous television hung on the living room, and they also had internet access. In spite of the isolated location, it was the fastest connection of the whole trip.

Puerto Cisnes was spread around a wide and gently curving bay, encircled by forested hills. The *hospedaje* was one of the final buildings at the northern end of the town. With the tide low, fishing boats lay drunkenly on the mud and stones. Others were tied to orange-and-white buoys in the water. Across the channel, the cliffs of Isla Magdalena rose from the waters. Padre Antonio Ronchi had undertaken some of his later work on that island, but it was here in Puerto Cisnes that his Patagonian ministry had begun.

A small river flowed out across the beach, dividing the town neatly in two. Beyond the road bridge was a refurbished promenade. The inner face of the new sea wall had attracted some street art: the words P U E R T O   C I S N E S were colourfully sprayed, each letter containing an emblem or image of some kind. The C was a puma and the S a butterfly. A whale's tail was designed into the N and a penguin in the T. There were other birds: kingfisher, *chucao*, and of course, a black-necked swan or *cisne de cuello negro*, this being Puerto Cisnes after all. There was also a *maqui* fruit, a church, and one letter E was home to a sneering stag beetle. As the road curved round with the bay, there were three shrines set back on the cliff, dedicated to Santa Teresa,[55] to Mary and to Jesus. Each shrine had a statue of the relevant figure enclosed in a shelter up a short flight of steps, decorated with candles and vivid plastic flowers. Discarded candle wrappers littered the ground beneath.

Beyond the shrines, the narrow road had been carved from the side of a cliff. An ongoing campaign was evidently failing to prevent it slipping into the sea. At the furthest point of the bay, a second beach faced back over the water towards the town. Fishing boats were under repair. Others rotted in the mud, one hull no more than a skeleton of ribs, resembling fish bones. Nets had been strung across one of the tidal channels, an ingenious method of catching fish when the tide flowed out, but one which had trapped an unsightly mess of reeds and flotsam.

The predominant fish-related business in Patagonia is no longer concerned with catching fish but breeding them. A flat-bottomed boat loaded with sacks of feed was moored against a landing stage. Out in the bay was an enormous grid of jetties and platforms supported on huge orange floats and anchored to the sea floor. Slung beneath the sprawling network of aluminium structures with their rubber-matted walkways was a *salmonera*, a fish farm, with acres of salmon nets.

*

Salmon Farming

Salmon farming has been criticised for its environmental impact. Hatchlings that escape cages compete with wild fish for food and habitat. If they interbreed with native salmon, genetic strains become compromised. In farm sites with weak currents, metal deposits build up on the sea floor. Another concern is the apparent inefficiency of production: it requires three kilogrammes of wild fish in the form of feed to produce one kilogramme of farmed salmon. These

---

[55] Santa Teresa de Los Andes was Chile's first Saint and is remembered in the Catholic Church on 13 July. Born in 1900 in a small town known as Los Andes, not far north of Santiago, she became a nun of the Discalced Carmelite order. Santa Teresa is particularly known for her writings on the spiritual life, even though she died of typhus at the age of just 19 years. She was canonised in 1993 by Pope John Paul II. Her astoundingly long birth name was Juana Enriqueta Josefina de los Sagrados Corazones Fernández Solar. 'Josefina de los Sagrados Corazones' is a single forename meaning 'Josephine of the Sacred Hearts'.

environmental impacts are likely to increase, of course, as global salmon consumption rises.

Rapid expansion in the 1990s turned Chile into the world's second-largest producer of Atlantic salmon, behind Norway. However, an outbreak of Infectious Salmon Anemia Virus (ISAV) in 2007, compounded by global financial instability, resulted in Chilean salmon exports falling by three-quarters. Infected salmon develop blood-related problems including poor circulation and damage to liver and spleen. The virus is considered so serious that the European Commission requires the total eradication of fish stocks in farms where an outbreak is confirmed. Nevertheless, the disease is not likely to spread to humans; the virus depends on low temperatures and ceases to be active in the warmer blood of mammals and birds.

When ISAV was found to have spread to wild fish, public pressure for changes in farming procedures escalated. Some farmers use pens in artificial lakes rather than sea nets, eliminating the problem of escapes and reducing the probability of contaminating open water.

Marea Roja – Red Tide

Marea roja is a harmful algal bloom. It has no connection with the tide but is actually a dense accumulation of aquatic phytoplankton. Shellfish such as oysters absorb the microorganisms whilst filtering affected water, becoming toxic to humans as a result. In large concentrations, phytoplankton blooms turn the sea red or brown.

Why they become concentrated in certain areas isn't fully understood. The depletion of filter-feeding shellfish may increase the likelihood of microorganism proliferation. Human activities may also play a role, possibly through agricultural nitrate run-off and increased sea temperatures at the coasts. Seasonal ocean currents may also be a factor, especially the circulation of water known as coastal upwelling.

*

Over lunch, back at Hospedaje Río Anita, I spoke with the father, Maximo.

'I was born here,' he told me. 'My parents were amongst the first colonisers who founded Puerto Cisnes. I've lived here all my life.'

The early settlers had lived from the sea, eating molluscs.

'We cannot eat our local shellfish anymore,' Maximo said. 'Not since the *marea roja* began. We have to send samples to Santiago for testing. There's only one local bay with molluscs that are safe to eat, and everyone knows that one day we will lose that bay as well.'

'When did the road first arrive in Puerto Cisnes?' I asked.

'It's actually older than the Carretera Austral,' he replied. 'The road from here to Villa Mañihuales opened in 1979. But during my childhood the only connection to the interior was a path cut by machete. The *campesinos* brought their animals down that way so they could be shipped to the market in Puerto Montt.'

'Is there a school here?'

'There is now; we even have a secondary school. Children come to Puerto Cisnes from the surrounding villages.'

'Where do they stay?' I asked, recalling my conversation with Paloma from Villa O'Higgins.

'The school has boarding accommodation for older students, and the younger ones are settled with local families. But when I was young, the secondary school was in Rancagua.'

That was a surprise. Rancagua was very far north, only 90 kilometres from Santiago.

'We used to take a boat from Puerto Cisnes to Puerto Aysén,' Maximo continued, 'and then we flew to Rancagua in a military plane. We spent the whole year away from home. There was a two-week winter break between the first and second semester but that wasn't enough to travel back here. It's different now. My children go to school in their home town. I never dreamed that would happen.'

'I enjoyed seeing the forest from the bus,' I commented. 'It's much more attractive than the bare grazing land.'

'You're right,' he agreed. 'It makes me sad to see the dead tree trunks and the land that has been cleared. It was a mistake to ever light the fires. Some of them burned continuously for years. Even if the winter snow lay metres deep, the fires would reappear the following spring, still burning. We're improving, though. Local people have become much better at caring for the natural environment. It takes time for people to change their ways. People need education, even adults, especially adults, but it's difficult where people are poor. They have other things on their mind. Just surviving day to day is enough trouble for many families.'

I later remembered to ask about the *Fiesta del Pescado Frito*.

'It's a festival for the town,' Maximo explained. 'Have you seen the small beach on the far side of the bay?'

I mentioned my visit there that morning.

'We build a wooden house over there and float it across the sea to the main beach. It gets paraded through the town on a cart pulled by steers, and donated to a family in need.'

This was the floating house I'd seen on the poster in Coyhaique.

'The family chosen this year lives high on a hill, Maximo continued. 'It took many of us, and several cattle, to haul the house onto their land.'

'What else happens at the *fiesta*?' I asked.

'We promote our local customs and sell artisanal products. Now that we have the road, people are changing. Young people are not the same, even my children. They see too much television and are slow to learn Patagonian ways.'

'But why is it called the *Fiesta del Pescado Frito*?'

'It's obvious!' insisted Maximo. 'Everyone eats fried fish, of course! We all eat *merluza austral*'.

That afternoon, at Maximo's suggestion, I followed an overgrown path behind the port. Initially it appeared quite unpromising. A stream ran down the centre and I had to bow low under obstructing trees and bushes. After that, the narrow way was peppered with deep muddy hoofmarks and overhung on either side by huge wet ferns.

After a while, the trail opened into a small clearing with a single electricity cable passing high overhead. Sitting on the wire was a tiny bird, an Austral pygmy owl or *chuncho*. Her head swivelled in that characteristic owl-like manner, but she showed no fear of the giant biped that had emerged from the thicket. For several minutes I admired the beautiful creature, snapping her portrait on my camera. I assumed she would eventually fly away, but she seemed quite content on her perch. In the end, the one who left first was the human.

Feeling like a pioneer penetrating the jungle, I pushed through brush and thicket and stooped beneath wayward branches. Unseen, a *huet-huet* called out, but unlike the owl he didn't loiter for long. I squelched on, having given up trying to avoid becoming muddy and damp. Light filtered through thick foliage, turning the whole environment intensely green. In the midst of all this, quite incongruously, there was a five-bar gate, sturdily constructed but now covered thickly in lichen and moss. It seemed hardly believable that at some point in the past there had been a road through the impenetrable copse.

The path opened onto a hillside with a view along the coast. Across the water a succession of headlands lined up on Isla Magdelena like a row of obliquely parked buses in a festival field. At that point, a sudden, strange noise came from high in a tree. It sounded as if someone was banging a plastic gutter with a stick. I searched through binoculars for the bird that was responsible. It was like something had stuck in his throat. He called again, and then once more, and I spotted him. The raptor was perched on a moss-covered branch. A creamy face and neck contrasted with his grey back and wings: a *carancho*. I crept closer, but he flew off to join his mate in a more distant tree.

Keeping my eyes fixed in the treetops, I set off in pursuit, paying scant attention to the terrain. When my gaze returned to ground level, three furry faces were staring at me. Bulls. Or steers, possibly, but in that precise second I was not inclined to check whether or not they still had possession of their *pelotas*. They looked displeased. Taking hasty evasive action, I skirted around them onto higher ground.

The path soon became overgrown again, thick with bamboo. I slipped in the mud and reached out to steady myself, clasping a tree trunk covered in long thorns. That was motivation enough to end the walk, so after picking needles out of my fingers, I started back.

A father and son appeared through the undergrowth and initially mistook me for the landowner, a pretence I was unable to maintain for long.

'I don't suppose you're heading towards Puyuhuapi tomorrow?' I asked. 'I'd like to get to Queulat National Park.'

'I'm going to Coyhaique first thing in the morning,' José replied. 'I'll be glad to take you to Puente Steffen if that would help.'

Perfecto. An early ride to the Carretera Austral junction would be a great start.

'I'm leaving at nine o'clock,' José confirmed. 'If I see you by the road, I'll pick you up.'

Image 17: Austral pygmy owl

Eighteen: Queulat

Save for a circuitous route around the bay, driving out of Puerto Cisnes usually meant crossing one particular bridge. Reporting there at half past eight, I found two travellers already in position. Although it was a fair bet that they were after a ride, it was an assumption that was tricky to verify. They were mummified in their sleeping bags and comatose. Hitchhiking is usually a first-come, first-served kind of activity but sleeping by the road is cheating; so instead of going beyond them as dictated by protocol, I snuck back towards the town and stood out of sight. My skulduggery must have upset the hitchhiking gods.

Nine o'clock came and went. José, who had virtually promised me a ride the previous afternoon, failed to show up; turncoat. Spots of rain began to fall. Another hiker arrived and placed his bag next to mine. Five minutes later, a couple appeared. That made four of us waiting already, plus the two sleepers. It was difficult to remain optimistic. The lone traveller began to tell me about his season guiding in the Torres del Paine National Park. He suddenly broke off mid-sentence and leapt into the road, boldly hauling to a halt a car that hadn't shown any sign of stopping, thus securing a ride for both of us. So that's how to hitchhike around here!

At Puente Steffen, a group of three already occupied the best position; they had been at the bridge overnight, they said. Several others were collapsing tents nearby. We were as many as a dozen altogether, and all of us were heading north. Hanging around there would have been hopeless, so I consoled myself with a snack and started to walk. Maybe a demonstration of determination might nudge drivers towards benevolence.

The road climbed steeply through the thick forest of Parque Nacional Queulat. Of the many parks and reserves throughout Patagonia, Queulat was a relatively straightforward one to visit. Not far off the Carretera Austral, the visitor centre was an obvious calling point for anyone passing that way. The park encloses 1500 square kilometres of Valdivian temperate rainforest. Mountains at the centre reach elevations of around 2000 metres, and an ice field of 80 square kilometres feeds several glaciers. One of these is a photogenic hanging glacier known as Ventisquero Colgante. It would be an idyllic spot in which to spend the night, and anyone driving to Puyuhuapi would be able to drop me right outside.

The forest was thick on both sides of the road, winding around multiple tight bends towards the Queulat pass or *cuesta*. How many unseen pygmy owls and *caranchos* might there have been, making their home in those branches? Or did the rainforest conceal those rare Andean deer, the *huemul* and *pudú*. More intriguing still, was there even a pair of stealthy puma eyes silently watching at that very moment from the camouflage of the tree cover?

It was a full hour before any car stopped. I gratefully greeted Marco and Verónica through the open window and was pleased when their two young sons raised no objection to sharing the back seat with a foreign stranger. We drove over the *cuesta*, chatting about our lives in the other world outside Patagonia. Verónica worked in shipping, managing trade routes between China and Chile, she said, and Marco designed helicopter motors.

Having descended the northern side of the pass, we approached the park entrance at last, where my heart sank to see a teeming mass of hitchhiking hopefuls gathered around the gate. Competition for rides was much fiercer than it had been further south. Given the number of people waiting, it seemed foolish to stop, especially given that I already had a seat in a car. I would continue to Puyuhuapi instead and return to Queulat the following day. In fact, my not-to-be-trusted guidebook mentioned a daily bus.

We called at the Termas Ventisqueros de Puyuhuapi, a spa resort with natural hot springs. The fjord rippled where warm water bubbled to the surface. Whilst we three indulged ourselves with slices of orange meringue pie, the two boys scampered off to soak in the hot and cold pools.

Leaving the generous family at the *termas* a while later, I returned to Puyuhuapi on foot. An ambulance raced in the opposite direction, a reminder of the isolation that these communities still face, even with the Carretera Austral. The fjord shore teasingly twisted the road into long, slow curves, and a lonely house stood at the water's edge. Rounding the final corner, Puyuhuapi came into view. Blue smoke rose from hundreds of chimneys, venting the log-burning stove at the heart of every home.

*

Puyuhuapi was founded in the 1930s by four young Germans[56] who'd deserted Europe after the First World War. They visited Patagonia with the explorer Augusto Grosse and identified the tip of the Puyuhuapi Channel as a suitable place to settle. Once permission was granted by the Ministerio de Tierras y Colonización in Santiago, they founded Puyuhuapi in 1935. The name means 'nest of *puyes*', *puye* being a common local fish whose juveniles are one of the many species served as whitebait. From the outset, the four pioneers planned for their families to join them, but the Second World War had other ideas, and their arrival was delayed until 1947. Having begun in tents on the beach, the settlers later constructed permanent houses in a distinctive Bavarian style. One of the four, Walter Hopperdietzel, was an expert in textiles. He opened a factory and taught weaving techniques to women migrants from Chiloé. Wool carpets are still woven by hand in the Puyuhuapi factory, using the same traditional techniques.

At the entrance to the village, I called in at Casa Ludwig, recommended by Marco and Verónica. The huge house had been built

---

[56] The presence of German immigrants in Chile should not come as a surprise. It is a fallacy to believe that Chile was colonised solely by the Spanish. Immigrants of diverse nationalities have been attracted by Chilean government incentives. Others came to escape war or other difficult conditions in their homeland, or were otherwise seeking the promise of a better life in a new place. In the nineteenth and early twentieth centuries, there were arrivals from Germany, France, Italy, Britain, Croatia and Montenegro, whilst those from Spain mainly represented the Basque region and Andalucía. As for the well-known Welsh communities, these can be found in Argentine Patagonia, not Chile. Welsh immigrants began to arrive in 1865 and settled close to the Atlantic along the Chubut River. Intermarriage and cross-cultural influences have diluted the Welsh flavour of those communities, but certain traditions survive. Supported by a Welsh Office project sending teachers to the region, the language continues to be learned and spoken.

in 1953 by Ernesto Ludwig, one of the four original settlers. Once inside, it was obvious that I was punching above my weight. I suspect it was pretty clear to the helpful owner as well. She showed me a very sweet attic room, their smallest, but even this was well out of my price range. I didn't wait long at Residencial Belen either; the room had someone else's shirt and boots on the bed. I was nearly enticed into Camping La Sirena by a pleasingly proportioned mermaid on the signboard, but in a village with a spectacular setting, the campsite had contrived to offer the least attractive situation possible. Instead of a grassy meadow overlooking the fjord, I was offered a patch of dirt cheek-by-jowl with other tents under a stretched-out tarpaulin canopy. The arrangement combined all the worst aspects of camping with none of the good bits. They were proud of their tarpaulin all the same; covered camping sites were specifically mentioned on the mermaid sign. I've not checked all other varieties of tent, but mine already has a roof.

Four weeks on the road had made me tetchy and I'd already had my fill of Puyuhuapi. Back along the main road, I spied what appeared to be a godsend. Another house advertised camping… on grass. I knocked at the door but my joy was short-lived. The ground was not only lumpy but was adjacent to a public footpath where I wasn't keen to leave all my stuff. They also had a yappy dog.

I sulked to the river and sat on the railings of a bridge. 'I should have stayed at Queulat,' I thought, regretfully. Faced with a fork in the paths, I'd chosen the easier option and was now paying for my lack of courage. 'I suppose I don't have to stay in Puyuhuapi at all,' I realised, a light switching on in my brain. 'I could continue north.'

Then I heard another voice, the one that had spoken in Tamango when I'd been tempted to pack up my wind-wandering tent and retreat to Cochrane. 'Get a grip,' it rebuked. 'This town is full of accommodation. Forget camping and go find a bed.'

I resolved to look again with fresh eyes. Pretending I'd just arrived, I walked a third time into the town. I found lodging at Hospedaje Juanita, a clean and charming two-storey home. Happily, the owner had not felt the need to paste notices all over the walls instructing guests not to wash clothes in the sink, not to sing in the shower and not to leave boots on the breakfast table. Even better, the bed had ladybird sheets.

*

'Are there any *senderos* around here?' I asked the assistant at the tourist office.

'There are trails in the Parque Nacional Queulat.'

'Ah, good. I'm going there tomorrow. Can you tell me about the bus?'

'There is no bus. You need a car.'

'I see. Is there somewhere else I can go for a walk this afternoon?'

'Yes. There is a popular walk to a lake.'

'Where's that?'

'Keep driving north towards La Junta. You will find the trail at kilometre 17.'

'I don't have a car,' I explained. 'Is there anything closer?'

'There's a *sendero interpretivo* around the town.' She showed me the instructions in a folder.

'Can you spare a copy?'

'Of course… ah, no I cannot. This is the last one.'

I photographed the map and used the digital image to navigate, and corresponding information was also posted on boards around the route. I felt middle-aged, taking the elementary town tour rather than some rugged mountain path. Fruitless personal insecurity aside, the *sendero interpretivo* made for a very interesting afternoon. I learned that the Carretera Austral was not originally designed to pass through this town but on a course through Lago Verde, further east. The plan was changed because the people of Puyuhuapi had already built a road to the north, a stretch that was then incorporated into the new highway.

There was a disused water mill and a boat-building yard, and the walk also included sights related to Padre Antonio Ronchi, notably the church and the radio station. Disappointingly, the carpet factory was closed for repairs, but giant looms were visible through the tall windows. At the head of the fjord were the remains of the settlers' first house beside an oak they grew from a European acorn. Further on was a tiny marina. Ignoring the unfriendly notice forbidding entry, I snuck inside to admire a row of yachts. Particularly jaundice-inducing was an eye-catching, plush catamaran. Maybe next time?

Around the village were examples of houses quite dissimilar to the boxy Patagonian standard. Some were impressive Germanic buildings whose history could be traced to the original families, all remarkably constructed with no powered machinery. The largest of these, on a raised bank overlooking the fjord, had an impressive four storeys. In contrast were the smaller but equally attractive 'Puyuhuapi-style' houses, a fusion of German and *Chilote*[57] architecture. The roofs of these quaint fairy-tale cottages wrapped around the upper level as if each house were wearing a bonnet.

There was also a more recent housing development slightly separated from the original village. Widespread programmes of home construction have taken place throughout Chile over recent years in both urban and rural settings. These houses stood on thick stilts and were non-rectangular, each one having a projecting angle at the front like the bow of a ship. As a result, the estate had more character than the new build in Villa O'Higgins. One resident had stained his shingled walls with preservative and the building gleamed bright like an orange beacon amongst the faded, weathered wood of the other properties. I didn't venture too close, conscious of being monitored throughout by a muscular dog, which attentively shepherded me to the perimeter of the estate.

As the tourist information lady had described, the final section of the *sendero* climbed to a *mirador*. I'd imagined a small hill with a lame view, but my pre-judgement did it a grave disservice. At the top of the lengthy climb was a bench painted sky-blue. I circled widely to avoid a stubborn cow and sat to rest. The valley was a green bowl. Reflections of the mountains opposite inked the surface of the fjord. A single road wound through the scene, bisecting the waterfront congregation of aluminium roofs. A bee was plundering thistles around the blue bench, her furry fragile body the fiery colour of copper. Her work done, she rose from the lilac bloom, caught a breath of breeze and was gone. As for me, I sat a while more, drinking deeply of the silence.

*

Un Techo Para Chile

This nation's need for housing is such that one of the best-known charitable organisations is *Un Techo Para Chile*, which means 'A Roof

---

[57] Reminder: *Chilote* is an adjective meaning 'from the island or region of Chiloé'.

For Chile'. Techo was founded in 1997 by Jesuit priest Felipe Berríos, working with students from the Universidad Católica. One of their activities is to assist poor people in the construction of basic wooden homes known as *mediaguas*. Although this aspect is their most visible and best known, the full scope of Techo covers a lot more than emergency housing. Striving for a just society free from poverty, their programmes help people in precarious situations find ways of overcoming the obstacles they face. Building a *mediagua* is not so much an end in itself but is part of an integrated commitment to communities, working with them to identify needs and formulate ways to address them. Programmes include micro credit, education and training, community organisation and the development of libraries. They also promote social conscience and activism amongst young people, with many of their programmes depending on young volunteers. Having launched a first international mission in 2001 in response to earthquakes in El Salvador and Peru, Techo now delivers programmes throughout Latin America and the Caribbean.

*

At breakfast I met Juan and his two apprentices, in the area to install some mechanised feeding apparatus at a *salmonera* on the fjord. Juan offered a ride towards Queulat in the back of his pickup. In the square at the centre of Puyuhuapi, we also collected Ignacio and María Fernanda, fourth year university students who were backpacking through their final holiday. A second ride took us from the fish farm to the park entrance. Predictably, a crowd of hopeful overnighters had already gathered on the road, but Ignacio wasn't perturbed.

'Look how far we've come in one hour,' he smiled. 'It's going to be a good day; I know it already.'

It had been a promising start for me, too. Twenty-four hours later than I'd originally intended, at last I was about to see Parque Nacional Queulat and its hanging glacier. At the office, up a lengthy access road, the *guardaparque* pointed out a diagram of the park painted on a large board. On the left side, flickering red flames showed the location of ten permanent *asado* stations. Each one had a space for vehicles, a picnic table and of course, a barbecue grill. This part of the diagram was out of scale with the rest of the map, no doubt reflecting the priorities of a good many visitors. The other half depicted the park itself with its lake, river and the popular Ventisquero Colgante. Thin yellow lines on the map were walking trails, one of which the warden particularly recommended.

'What about that one?' I asked, pointing to a path he hadn't mentioned.

'No, that one is closed. It needs maintenance.'

I needed no further encouragement. The forbidden trail was fairly overgrown but not impassable. Scaling a steep bank, it pushed through bamboo and overhanging branches. The surrounding woods were lush green; Queulat had a reputation for the quality of its virgin forest. In the stream bed beneath a slippery bridge, an incredible range of mosses and tiny plants huddled together on the damp rocks. Delicate ferns uncurled on the banks. The most astonishing symphony of life was gathered there, zealously competing for moisture, nutrition and light. Tree trunks were carpeted with mosses and with thousands of tiny plants that had taken root in niches in the bark. Something grew in every available spot, with no space left vacant. It was a quite exceptional setting. Even the light that penetrated the forest canopy seemed to be infused with green. After a sublime walk through this incredible scenery, there was a pronounced knoll beside the path. A slither of daylight slipped through a small aperture between the branches. Standing on the knoll to peer through the opening, I stole a first secret glimpse of the distant blue ice of the iconic hanging glacier.

*

The warden's recommended trail began on a curious suspended bridge, its parabolic form dipping low over a set of foaming rapids. Moments later, the Angel of Chocolate favoured me with a spontaneous blessing. As I turned a corner, bristling with sweet goodness in the centre of the path was a *Super 8*, a tasty wafer bar, one of my favourites, still in pristine condition in its wrapper. Pocketing the bar for a later time of need, I whispered a prayer of gratitude to the Angel.

Not surprisingly, the *sendero* was much clearer than the one that had supposedly been closed, and I made brisk progress against the incline. Again, the forest was verdant and beautiful. A number of those making the climb wore clothing, footwear and dispirited expressions suggestive that lengthy walks were not their usual pastime. The reward at the top was a *mirador* with a view of Ventisquero Colgante, high above the green waters of Laguna Témpanos. A patch of cloud initially obscured the glacier but it gradually cleared to reveal a spectacular sight. The face of the ice was a pale blue triangle atop dark cliffs. A thin cascade of meltwater issued from the lower vertex whilst a larger fall spouted from one side, crashing energetically onto rocks in a perpetual drifting cloud of spray. The hikers that had conquered the ascent, a large number, shared the restricted space of the *mirador* with a hungry rat and a cheerfully chirping *chucao*. Leaning on the crooked fence, I gratefully partook of the Angel's *Super 8*, marvelling at the spectacular sight.

*

The following morning was the start of the day that I would have returned to work. In Santiago, my ex-colleagues were gathering to prepare for the new school year. It gave me particular pleasure to wake a thousand kilometres distant from my ex-desk, my ex-office, my ex-computer, my ex-in-tray and all those ex-responsibilities. This day of all days, nothing was going to spoil my enjoyment of the open air, the open landscape and the open recipe of possibilities flavouring the journey. Neither rain, nor delays, nor even dietary restrictions would be able to sour that day's cherished liberty.

Just two days had passed since I'd walked around Puyuhuapi under a gloomy cloud, struggling to find somewhere suitable to lodge. The difficulty had doubtless been in my head, not in any genuine shortage of accommodation. Forty-eight rewarding hours on, and boosted by an enjoyable visit to Queulat, I marched along the main street with a purposeful and contented stride, refreshed and invigorated for the next adventure. The road ahead led to a town called La Junta. There were various possible onward choices from there, but that decision could wait. Four weeks in Patagonia had taught me to take one step at a time.

On the edge of Puyuhuapi was a colourful *cementario*. Many of the graves were decorated with artificial flowers, as is common in cemeteries throughout the country. Some were surrounded by ornate railings or a line of dressed stones. The tombs of certain families were arranged together within private shelters. At the enormous Cementario General in Recoleta, Santiago, ostentatious marble mausoleums with domed roofs and gothic pillars are watched over by beautifully carved cherubim. By contrast, the equivalent structures in Puyuhuapi could have been mistaken for greenhouses, with clear plastic sheeting stretched over a wooden frame. Each one was bedecked with ornaments and mementos: shiny streamers, toy windmills, photographs, teddy bears and all manner of adornments. It made me wonder what special memorabilia also accompanied the deceased inside their coffin.

The chapel in the centre of the grassy graveyard was shaped like a Toblerone, or more geometrically a triangular prism. The sides were all roof and no walls, extending from the pointed ridge down to the grass. The gloomy interior was lit only by patches of daylight penetrating the tatty shingled roof. On the inside, the walls were lined with bamboo canes, arranged in herringbone fashion on the triangular gable end. There were no pews or chairs on the uneven earth floor. A narrow altar, crudely nailed together, stood on a raised platform supporting a small plaster statue of Mary. Several crosses were propped up against the end wall, and bright plastic flowers were fastened to the bamboo strips above them.

I pulled the gate closed as I left, much to the annoyance of a cow that gazed forlornly at the lush grass within. Hearing a vehicle, I hurried to the road, arriving just in time. My new companions were a German couple in a motor caravan. I'm not sure if standing by a cemetery would always be successful for hitchhikers. It might be interesting to try it dressed as a vampire or trailing an unwinding shroud. The rear of the vehicle was dominated by the bed, which had not been folded away. When I sat on the front edge, my neck was awkwardly twisted with one ear pressed to the ceiling. Instead I tried crouching on the floor between the two front seats, squashing my legs rather uncomfortably. I shuffled and fidgeted, becoming increasingly numb.

Somewhere along the bumpy, potholed road, we passed a group of backpackers. At least, I assume they were a group. In reality, the five were strung out over a distance of several hundred metres, each one walking alone, a chain of cagouled souls who had the look of folk who were regretting their choice of holiday. And not long after the last of these had disappeared behind us, the road divided into another stretch of seemingly unnecessary dual carriageway. This was La Junta.

Image 18: Ventisquero Colgante

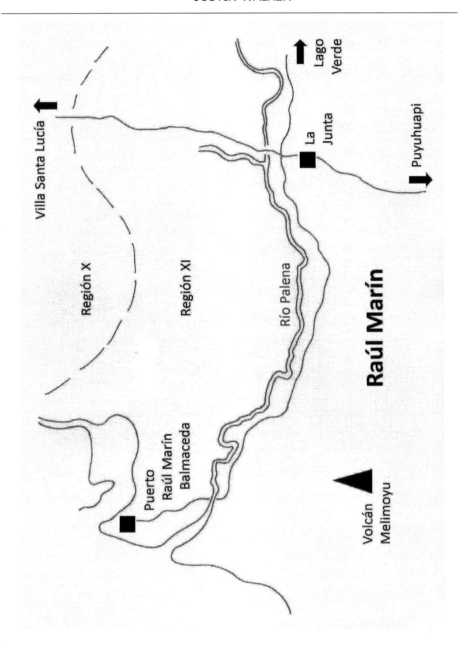

Map 12: La Junta and Raúl Marín

Nineteen: Huelga

One summer night towards the end of February 2010, one of the largest earthquakes ever recorded tore into the central regions of Chile. Hundreds were killed in the 8.8 magnitude quake and its tsunami. Thousands of homes collapsed and infrastructure was devastated over a vast area. The following month, Sebastián Piñera was sworn in as the thirty-fifth President of the Republic. During his inauguration ceremony another tremor hit (measured at 6.9), causing some of the invited foreign dignitaries to flee the building.

As the first right-leaning president since the return to democracy, Piñera was always likely to face close scrutiny, not to mention a generous serving of public opposition. In the event, protest after protest blighted his four-year term as one group after another took to the streets. Change can be hard to achieve, especially in a nation that, it's probably fair to say, is home to one of the more conservative cultures in Latin America.

Sebastián Piñera was thrust (quite willingly, it appeared) onto the global media stage later that first year through the plight of the 33 miners trapped underground in the northern desert. From the start, even when the prospects for *Los 33* appeared bleak, the president very publically threw his support behind the rescue efforts at the San José mine. The worldwide media event that surrounded their miraculous release 69 days later contributed greatly to his public acclaim.

President Piñera's approval ratings began to slide during 2011, which became a year of *manifestaciones*, public demonstrations. In January, roads in the southernmost Magallanes Region were barricaded by residents protesting over sharp rises in the price of domestic gas, paralysing the region's transport network. In May, the president's annual State of the Nation address was interrupted by opponents of the HidroAysén project. Copper miners began industrial action in July in response to the threatened privatisation of the national copper company, Codelco. Furthermore, throughout that year, university and school students demonstrated in Santiago and other cities, occupying school and college buildings. Riot police were regularly deployed. Water cannon and tear gas became common sights along the wide boulevards of central Santiago.

The capital tends to become a quieter place over the summer. Many who are able prefer to escape the stifling heat and head to the coast. City traffic eases and the street cafés become much less crowded. For those not afraid of roasting, February can be a pleasant time to visit Santiago. After the frequent disturbances of 2011, the summer lull at the start of 2012 was a time of nervous waiting, like a clear day between two storms. How would the authorities take hold of public order? Would Piñera's government push ahead with their planned reforms? Would protestors return to the streets?

*

From its humble beginnings as an *estancia* at the intersection of *gaucho* trading paths, La Junta has grown into a town of over a thousand inhabitants. The name means 'The Meeting Point'.

On arrival, the German couple headed straight for a café, and I set to investigating transport options.

'Is it possible to travel from here to Puerto Raúl Marín Balmaceda?' I asked the assistant at the office of the municipality. Raúl Marín was a small port on the Pacific Coast, lying beyond the wide Río Palena.

'There's a bus to Raúl Marín twice each week,' she replied. 'One goes this afternoon at three.'

'How about Lago Verde?' This village was in the opposite direction, up in the mountains.

'That's more difficult,' she replied. 'There's no bus to Lago Verde. You would need your own car to get there.'

'What about hitchhiking? Would I get a ride?'

'You could be waiting a long time. There won't be much traffic up either road.'

That seemed fairly conclusive. 'So where do I find the bus to Raúl Marín?'

'Right outside the office. Get here fifteen minutes early, just to be sure.'

Decision made.

A local woman on a bicycle directed me to Mi Casita de Té, My Little Tea House. In the conspicuously chic restaurant, I felt out of place in my scruffy backpacker apparel. The *menú del día* was unrivalled as the finest of the trip: a steaming *sopa de porotos*, bean soup, a thick pink chunk of salmon topped with melted cheese, followed by banana tart and a mug of *manzanilla*, camomile tea.

Teacup drained, I took a brief look around in the few minutes that remained before I had to get my bus. Many of the avenues were recently paved. A new library stood on a prominent corner and refurbishments were in progress at the school. The attractive *plaza de armas* was dotted with juvenile *araucaria*, monkey puzzle trees, and a plaque listed the names of residents who'd contributed to the remodelling efforts.

On the advice of both guidebooks, I also took a look at La Junta's other noteworthy (or notorious) feature: a monument to General Augusto Pinochet. For some reason I'd expected a statue, but it was simply a commemorative plaque on a low plinth, beneath a wide signboard bearing the name of the dictator.

*

Contextualising the Coup:
Locating Augusto Pinochet in a brief timeline of Chilean political history.[58]

In the first half of the twentieth century, wealthy landowners in Chile had control of large *haciendas* that were worked by tenant farmers. Later, the *hacienda* system came under threat, as governments began to introduce land reforms.

The 1964 election was won by the Christian Democrats, led by Eduardo Frei Montalva, at a time of complex change. Rapid urban migration

---

[58] Chilean twentieth-century history is highly complex. The economic and social development of any country is influenced by numerous internal and external factors. This is merely an overview of some of the events and is not intended to be a thorough analysis of that passage of history.

fuelled the growth of squatter camps. Policies to reform land, health and education upset conservative elites but were considered too slow by militant workers. Inflation was high and income distribution unbalanced.

Salvador Allende's Unidad Popular coalition narrowly won the 1970 election. They introduced reforms to nationalise private industries and redistribute wealth. Some factory proprietors and landowners chose to sell their assets, worried that they might be expropriated. Low production brought shortages, and black markets grew. Inflation increased and reserves of foreign currency were used to import food. Allende brought in an army commander as Interior Minister, General Carlos Prats.

As with Frei, Allende's policies were too radical for some but did not go far enough for others. Strikes brought the country to a standstill in 1972. Allende's strongly socialist programme was of concern to certain observers outside the country and to key figures within it. An unsuccessful military coup took place in June 1973 and Prats resigned. He was replaced by General Augusto Pinochet.

On 11 September 1973, a second coup overthrew the government. The presidential palace, La Moneda, was attacked and President Allende died in the siege. Whether he was killed or committed suicide is fiercely debated. With Pinochet as leader, a military junta took charge of Chile for the next 17 years.

Economic policies reversed the previous nationalisations and introduced radical free market reforms, welcoming foreign investment and private ownership. The economy of Chile quickly changed from one that was heavily managed and relatively isolated to one that was globally integrated and characterised by laissez-faire and fiscally conservative policies.

At the same time, opponents were pursued without compromise. Congress was dissolved and political parties were banned. Politicians, civil leaders, poets, musicians and sundry other undesirables all disappeared; thousands were tortured or executed, and many others fled the country.

In 1980, Pinochet presented a new constitution to the electorate, enabling him to retain power until 1989; it was approved in a plebiscite. Seeking a further extension, Pinochet lost a second plebiscite in 1988. Nonetheless, under the terms of the constitution, the military still held considerable power. Pinochet himself had a seat in the senate even after he retired from the army in 1997. Unelected senators were eventually abolished in 2005, and the president recovered the authority to dismiss armed forces commanders.

The first multiparty elections since the dictatorship were held in 1989. Patricio Aylwin won a four-year term, defeating Pinochet's nominee, Hernán Büchi. Eduardo Frei Ruiz-Tagle[59] took office in 1994, and Ricardo Lagos in 2000. Michelle Bachelet became the first woman president in 2006. Sebastián Piñera won in 2010, and Michelle Bachelet returned for a second term in 2014.

Broadly speaking, the basic economic direction established by Pinochet's neoliberal reforms has not changed a great deal. Economic policies encourage foreign investment and private ownership, and accordingly, Chile has a large number of free trade partners. Advocates of Pinochet's leadership point to the success of these policies. Chilean GDP is the highest in South America (2012 figures) and the country ranks in fortieth position in the UNDP's Human Development Index (2012 table). Whilst some commentators point out that most of this progress took place since the return to democracy, others emphasise the importance of the economic reforms that followed the 1973 coup.

Augusto Pinochet died in 2006 at the age of 91. Some mourned the loss of the leader that they believe rescued Chile from Marxism and gave the country a secure economic foundation. Others celebrated the demise of a man whose brutal regime ripped apart families, set neighbour against neighbour and ruthlessly murdered opponents. The human cost of the dictatorship remains a daily reality to bereaved families throughout the country.

Amongst the people I met during my four years in Chile, these polarised views remained.

*

---

[59] Eduardo Frei Ruiz-Tagle (president 1994 to 2000) was the son of Eduardo Frei Montalva (president 1964 to 1970). The second (maternal) surname helps to distinguish between these two.

A small minibus, metallic gold in colour, arrived promptly at three. Other than an older woman who was dropped at her house, miles from anywhere, and a man who worked at the ferry by which we later crossed the Río Palena, the others came all the way to Raúl Marín. Amongst the passengers was a pair of young Swiss backpackers. Ramond and Harriette were some months into a lengthy South American trip, having already travelled through Ecuador, Peru and now much of Chile.

The narrow lane was lined with large-leaved *nalca*. Trees grew on impossible cliffs. The stones were larger and paler than those that formed the surface of roads elsewhere, and the vehicle slid and jolted as we crawled towards the coast. It was exciting to be destined for a remote outpost via a track that the map depicted as no more than a thin dotted line. My good fortune to coincide so perfectly with the infrequent bus somehow made the adventure all the more satisfying.

After occasional sightings of the Río Palena along the way, we arrived after two hours at the *embarcadero* and boarded the ferry. The small craft had space for only three or four vehicles. Our driver, Antonio, sorted through the packages stacked around the front passenger seat to find a box of groceries for the crew, whose living accommodation was in a walled compound on the bank.

The captain's voice boomed from the ship's tannoy, 'Has he remembered my lettuce?'

The village is named after Chilean politician Raúl Marín Balmaceda, who died in office in 1957. Antonio took each passenger to their home and delivered another box of groceries. I've noticed that London's 87 bus route to Trafalgar Square offers neither of these services; someone should have a word with the mayor.

'And you; where are you staying?' Antonio's question was directed to the Swiss backpackers and me.

'Nowhere,' replied Harriette. 'We're boarding a ship to Chiloé tonight.'

'Is there anywhere to camp?' I asked.

'I have a campsite,' the driver replied. 'I'll take you all there.'

The field was opposite Antonio's home. After pitching my tent, we pooled supplies for lunch. We traded stories of Ecuador and Peru, and

I desperately tried to remember the *castellano* word for Switzerland. Of two countries, *Suecia* and *Suiza*, one was Switzerland and the other Sweden, but I always struggled to remember which was which. It's relatively obvious in written form but less so when spoken. Embarrassingly, in Santiago I lived for a while on a street called *Suecia*, but even there I could never remember to which country the name referred. When I'd offended Ramond and Harriette one time too many by calling them Swedish, they went to make enquires about their ship, scheduled to call through the port at three o'clock the following morning.

Puerto Raúl Marín Balmaceda was very small, with not many more than 300 inhabitants. It also had an unusual layout. The other villages, Tortel aside, took the form of a grid around a central plaza, a pattern typical of Chilean towns. Raúl Marín was less regular, appearing to have emerged organically as opposed to conforming to any kind of plan. The sandy roads followed the natural contour of the land, giving the place an informal or even mildly rebellious air.

There was a fire station complete with a small fire engine – just a red van parked outside a bungalow. The car and speedboat at the police station had matching green-and-white *carabineros* livery. Electricity was produced by a noisy diesel generator that belched fumes, and next to it stood a tall water tower dated 2005. At the tiny cemetery, some of the graves were as colourful and ornate as those in Puyuhuapi but most were marked by nothing more than an anonymous wooden cross on a pile of soil.

The tiny quay or *muelle* was on the estuary bank just outside the village. It had only the most basic facilities: a concrete loading ramp and an office in a temporary cabin. As I stood on the ramp, a peculiar sight caught my eye. One of the distant mountains appeared to be covered by an artificial dome. The white form was quite regular and smooth, rather like that bulbous arena in Greenwich that was once known as the Millennium Dome. Both through binoculars and with the naked eye, it was difficult to be sure what it was. A cloud formation? Ice? Why did no other mountain have anything similar? I couldn't make it out, but resolved to check my map for clues.

The tourist office was closed. Instead I called at a store for essential supplies like wine and cookies, and asked there about the local area.

'You could take a walk along Sendero Chucao,' said the man. 'It's a *sendero interpretivo* that members of the community recently constructed.'

At the campsite, Ramond and Harriette had pitched their tent, having discovered that their ship's departure was delayed. We succeeded in lighting a fire, after a few hundred attempts, and gathered around it long into the dark Patagonian night eating cookies dipped in *carmenère*, which did little to help me distinguish Suecia from Suiza.

*

Carmenère

Until recently, the *carmenère* grape was believed to be extinct. In the mid-nineteenth century, acres of French *carmenère* vineyards, along with many other grape varieties, were devastated by the sap-sucking insect phylloxera and the fungus oidium. European vines were replanted using pest-resistant North American rootstock, but *carmenère* did not graft well and was abandoned. In time, it died out altogether.

In the 1980s, Chilean *merlot* received acclaim for its quality and distinctive taste and connoisseurs began to take more than a passing interest in Chilean viticulture. When French expert Jean-Michel Boursiquot tasted a particular sample of Chilean *merlot* in 1994, he surprised the wine-producing world by declaring it to be the lost grape *carmenère*, a fact later confirmed by DNA analysis. *Carmenère* has since become a popular wine in Chile. More recently, exports have become available in UK wine stores.

---

*

A whispered conversation in French: Ramond and Harriette were packing to leave. The blast of a ship's horn echoed around the valley, but comfortable in a warm sleeping bag, I dozed a while longer in an attempt to dismiss the troublesome attentions of red-wine-head that lurked menacingly like a playground bully. When finally I found the fortitude to face it, I braved the shower, located in a concrete shed at the side of the field. The temperature alternated without warning between Atacaman and Antarctic.

The tourist office stood in what appeared to be a park, although the dry, straggly grass and sandy patches made it indistinguishable from other vacant plots. Even though the mid-morning hour was well within the displayed opening hours, a notice on the door of the octagonal building stated *Cerrado*: Closed. Peering through a window into the gloomy room, a girl in a stripy t-shirt could be seen using Facebook on the office computer. Noticing a face pressed against the glass, she rose at once to unlock the door. I understand that operating such a facility in a place that no-one ever visits must be a fairly low-adrenaline profession, but at least you might turn the sign round to say '*Abierto*'.

Stripy t-shirt girl confirmed the existence of Sendero Chucao.

'In fact, at this moment it's the only *sendero*,' she told me, twisting a long ponytail around her fingers, 'but we are constructing another.' She beamed with pride at this prospect.

'Will it be ready this afternoon?' I asked eagerly.

It rarely pays to risk humour in a second language unless you know the people well. Such attempts tend to result in awkward silences while your counterpart tries to decide if you really were too stupid to understand what they just said.

'What else could I do around here today?' I asked, attempting to rescue myself from the linguistic mire.

The other possibility was canoeing on the estuary. That might have been fun, had there been two of me, but I settled for the walk instead.

The trail was much longer than I'd anticipated. Along the *sendero interpretivo*, exemplars of particular trees were labelled: *coihue* and *canelo*, for example. Trunks in deeper shade were thick with moss. One dead giant was covered with any number of piggy-back plants. Ferns, a huge vine and countless others had taken root on the mammoth host.

Resounding through the woodland cathedral, the anthems of a birdsong choir were bewilderingly various.

The *rayadito* trilled her clockwork soprano.

'*Fío-fío, fío-fío,*' sounded a familiar alto whistle, the olive-grey flycatcher delighting in a feast of forest insects.

'*Chuuu, chu-chu-chu-caaow*' called a tenor, another who sung his own name.

Distant percussion was provided by a headbanging *carpintero*.

'*Huet-huet, huet-huet,*' completed the set. There she was, on a surprisingly high branch for a ground dwelling bird.

'*Huet-huet, huet-huet.*' It was a duet, the two bass voices responding alternately to one another.

A ferocious species roamed the forest. Camouflaged amongst the foliage were some enormous Chilean stag beetles, otherwise known also as Darwin's Beetle. They had oily purple backs, long legs with ghastly hooks at the end and oversized bottle-green serrated mandibles, the extended antler-like jaws that give the species its common name and with which the males fight. As I braved a closer look, one of them stood on his hind legs, all ten centimetres of him, and shook his mandibles threateningly in my face.

The woods ultimately thinned, and Sendero Chucao led out onto white dunes. Mud flats cluttered the estuary, and waves broke over a crescent sand bar at the river mouth. The open ocean beyond was the Golfo Corcovado, across which I'd sailed some weeks earlier aboard the *Amadeo*. Grasses and small bushes had taken root, along with more of the giant rhubarbesque *nalca*. Meandering through openings in the vegetation, like negotiating a garden maze at a stately home, I found a way to the water's edge. Hundreds of jellyfish were stranded on the sand. Around them, a set of bird footprints resembled fighter jets in formation. Also in peril, a huge stag beetle was flat on his back, legs pedalling desperately. Demonstrating compassion and courage in equal measure, I turned him over.

Tree trunks had washed up on the beach, each one perished by the water, full of holes like a sponge. I sat on a trunk and watched two men fishing from a yellow rowing boat. They took turns to dive from the prow into the water, collecting shellfish from submerged rocks. Dressed only in shorts, they must have been terribly cold. A plane approached low over the estuary. It looked initially as if it were preparing to touch down on the water but it turned behind trees and towards an *aeródromo*. I skimmed stones and felt lonesome. I'd been glad of Swiss company the previous evening and was looking forward to Futaleufú, by all accounts a lively place.

I saw Antonio outside his house later that evening.

'Is the bus going to La Junta tomorrow?' I checked. 'Can I reserve a place, *por favor?*'

'*Ningún problema.* I leave at seven.'

'My alarm is broken. If I'm not there, will you please come and wake me?'

'*No te preocupes,*' don't worry, he said. 'I won't leave without you.'

I returned to the *muelle* to look again at the odd white dome, reflected now in the glassy estuary under evening light. The map confirmed the strange sight as a volcano, 2400-metre Volcán Melimoyu. Its perfect form still looked strangely artificial. Melimoyu is a stratovolcano,[60] the type formed by repeated eruptions laying down successive strata, which accounts for its regular conical shape. The white dome was a veneer of snow and ice covering the cone. With the sun setting, the clouds and snow began to throb with yellow and orange light, until the entire skyline was gloriously ablaze with molten metal. Then, as if ashamed of its splendour, the spectacle began to dim, the colour seeping away, diminishing steadily until the shallow cone became a dusky silhouette against the darkening sky.

*

I didn't need waking. By 5:30, heavy rain had already seen to that. I packed my bag and ran it across to the shelter of the shower block. A fortuitous lull in the storm provided some measure of comfort as I collapsed the tent. The sole other camper was also preparing to depart. Over the sandy road, the minibus was waiting, engine running. As passengers were collected from their homes, a damp stack of rucksacks and bags grew high on one of the seats. Each new customer boarded rapidly on account of the rain, abandoning luggage on the disorganised mound and squeezing together on the benches.

The petrol station at La Junta looked to be a promising spot for hitchhiking. It had shelter under the canopy and a convenient shop with snacks, and was positioned right on the main road. The minor drawback was the fifteen others already waiting there. The idea of spending the whole day on the forecourt didn't appeal much.

Not far out of town was the crossroads, left for Raúl Marín and right to Lago Verde, and then another striking orange suspension bridge. There, amongst the puddles, I handed my camera to a passer-by. By

---

[60] The classic cone of Mount Fuji is also a stratovolcano. So is Chile's tallest mountain, Nevado Ojos del Salado, near Copiapó in the Atacama Desert. At 6879m, this is the highest active volcano in the world.

virtue of travelling alone, I had plenty of photos of sights along the Carretera Austral but not many of me. This gentleman appeared to consider the orange bridge far more interesting than the wet backpacker. In his relatively artistic picture of the magnificent structure, I featured as an obscure dot.

As I reached the safety of the far bank, a car clattered onto the deck behind me. The occupants had the appearance of stylish upper-end travellers, the kind who never in a hundred years would open their doors to a scruffy hiker. How wrong my hasty judgement was. The two women were enthusiastic to help, even excited.

Further along the valley, one of the pair persuaded a traditionally dressed (and commendably patient) *gaucho* on horseback to pose for a photograph. More rain fell. The road was a soggy strip through the forest and our tyres squelched through slush and mud. It was not a day to be walking.

'Have you heard about the *huelga*?' they asked: industrial action.

'No. What's happening?'

'Aysén is on strike. We have to go north to get into the next region. You'll be stuck if you stay here.'

Even before the summer break was over, protests had returned to Patagonia. Residents were obstructing the delivery of fuel and strategic road junctions had been blockaded. A few kilometres ahead we would cross into Region X, Los Lagos, leaving behind the affected Region XI, Aysén.[61] It sounded like we were escaping just in time.

*

The Aysén protests began in early February when fishermen seized the orange suspension bridge; not the one I'd just crossed at La Junta, but Puente Presidente Ibañez at Puerto Aysén. This action effectively severed the region from its principal port, Puerto Chacabuco. The nearby *aeródromo* was also seized, and roads were barricaded around Puerto Aysén and Coyhaique.

---

[61] In 1974, Chile was organised into 13 administrative regions, from Region I (Antofagasta) in the north to Region XII (Magallanes) furthest south. The thirteenth was the *Región Metropolitana* around Santiago. A reorganisation in 2007 created a new Region XIV in the far north, and added Region XV between Regions IX and X in the south. The Carretera Austral passes only through Regions X and XI, Los Lagos and Aysén.

The cost of living tends to be higher in Aysén than elsewhere in Chile. Large distances and disobliging geography make it difficult to transport supplies. With limited agriculture in the region, basic foodstuffs and vegetables are usually imported, driving up prices. Against this background, the Aysén protestors demanded preferential salaries relative to the cost of living and rebates on fuels: petrol, diesel, paraffin, gas and wood. Amongst a range of other concerns, they also wanted fishing quotas protected, improvements in health infrastructure, a programme of road construction and a greater say in infrastructure projects affecting the region, such as the HidroAysén proposals to dam the Rivers Baker and Pascua.

The *manifestaciones* began in Puerto Aysén and Coyhaique. A thousand attended one march and police reinforcements were called up from other regions. The disruption spread. The road between Puerto Aysén and Villa Mañihuales was barricaded, then the junction of the Chile Chico road with the Carretera Austral, and next the Coyhaique to Argentina road. The *aeródromo* was taken in Villa O'Higgins. The regional airport at Balmaceda continued operating, but passengers had to walk from terminal to plane as airport buses had no fuel. When the airport road from Coyhaique was blocked, tourists missed their flights. A sympathetic bishop held a cathedral mass for the demonstrators. Imagine the surprise of government officials when the same clergyman offered to act as mediator in the negotiations, a suggestion that was promptly declined.

In the latter part of February, the dispute grew more violent. There was damage to commercial property and an increase in arrests. Police and protestors sustained injuries. Authorities deployed water cannon in attempts to remove activists from the orange bridge, but they held firm. Amnesty International called for an investigation into allegations of excessive force, arbitrary detentions and reckless use of metal pellet shot and tear gas. The Minister of Energy travelled to the region but refused to open discussions until road blockades were dismantled. When this demand was ignored, he returned to Santiago. Shops ran low on provisions and fuel supplies were scarce. Petrol was rationed and supplies of bottled gas ran short. Bus companies ceased operations and travellers were trapped. My not being amongst them was pure good fortune.

*

It wasn't far to Villa Santa Lucía, an uninspiring row of low buildings set back from the road. Under heavy skies, the dreary, damp village had little to recommend it. There wasn't a soul about. For the fiftieth time in the day, it began to rain heavily. I took refuge in a bus shelter, a tin shed with a roof so low I had to crouch. Opposite was the turning towards Futaleufú and Palena. Ideally I wanted a look at the white water of Futa, but in those conditions I would have accepted a ride to either destination. Whenever a vehicle approached, I hurried through the rain, negotiating puddles and mud, to stand in a likely spot at the junction.

Rivers ran from my waterproof gear. The eager smile I beamed did nothing to prevent me looking a sodden wreck. I was not the kind of being you would want to invite to sit on your sheepskin seat covers. The thought of how far I'd already come was some consolation: all the way from Raúl Marín to La Junta by bus and then to Villa Santa Lucía with an easy ride. I was a lot better off than the legion of hitchhikers sheltering at the petrol station. Be patient, I urged myself; enjoy the solitude. I'm not sure that I would have stopped in any case, had I been at the wheel.

Miraculously, as I was musing over all this, a pickup stopped. I ran to retrieve my *mochila* from the bus shelter, stacked it on top of their camping gear and gratefully climbed in. This young couple were also escaping the *huelga*.

'We're on our way to Argentina,' they said. 'It's the only place to get fuel.'

Nearly 80 kilometres off the Carretera Austral, Futaleufú occupies a mountain location on the road towards the international *frontera*. Its 2000 residents are engaged in similar trades to many in the region: forestry, cattle farming and tourism. However, the thing that sets Futa apart is its river. Descending a brutal course through the Andes, the Río Futaleufú surges through dozens of churning rapids. A top white water destination, the Fu attracts rafters and kayakers from around the world.

The couple dropped me at the tourist office, where I was given a street map indicating various *hospedajes*. The first two were full, but I took a room at Hospedaje Cañete and enjoyed a warm (but this time not scalding) shower. The owner kindly offered me the chance to go online, so I spent two hours using the slowest-ever computer. Listening to the rain drumming heavily on the roof, the owner's daughter (sitting opposite me using a smart new laptop) said it was set to continue for at least two more days. Coincidentally, that was also the length of time required to send one email, availing me the opportunity to demonstrate what I'd been learning about patience. The machine had two preferred operating modes: frozen and crashed. In Patagonia, he who touches the keyboard when the computer is working on something else… wastes his time.

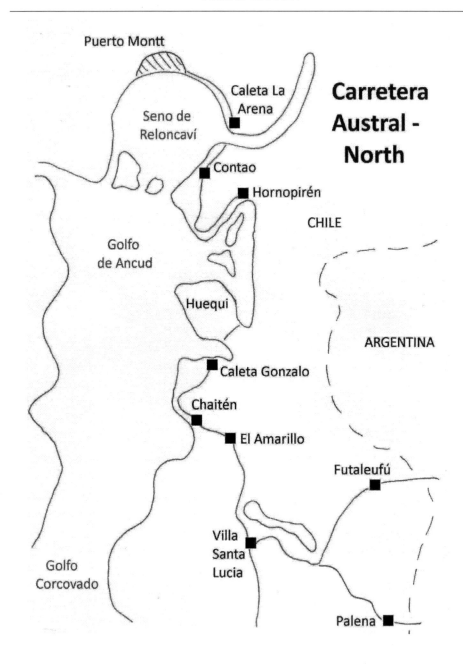

Map 13: Carretera Austral – North

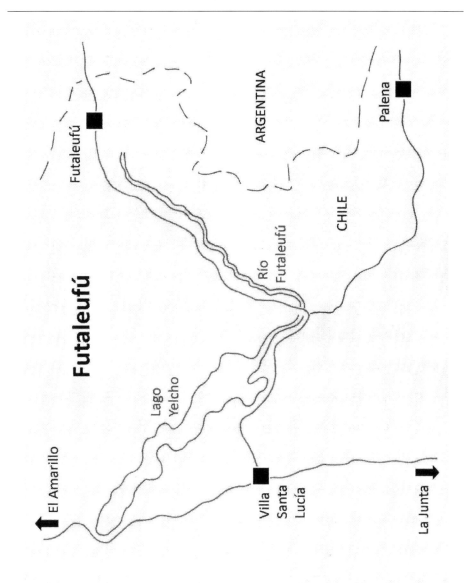

Map 14: Futaleufú

Twenty: Zeta

When the downpour eased from tempestuous to merely ludicrous, I ventured out for something to eat. A couple of blocks away, there was a very fine restaurant. Set in a comfortable room with exposed beams and heavy, panelled doors, it was attractively finished with tasteful furnishings. Dark, polished tables, principally for twos, were set with chunky cutlery and gleaming glasses. It would have been perfect if I'd wished to impress someone.

Trying a second place further along the same street, I was invited no further than the doormat.

'What do you have in the kitchen this evening?' I enquired.

'Salmon.'

'Okay. Salmon with…?'

'Potatoes… and bread.'

'Is there room for me?' I surveyed the scene of empty tables, all set out in sixes like a school dining room.

'Is it just you? I'm not sure. Let me check.'

'Actually, I guess I won't bother,' I conceded, and backpedalled into the monsoon.

In the front yard of one property, a several members of the household were building a UFO (or *OVNI*, as they are termed here, *Objeto Volador No Identificado*). The spaceship was apparently being readied for some kind of parade. A black cloth had been spread over a frame to produce a convincing flying-saucer shape. There was a bulging red dome on top complete with bug-eyed alien inside. Reflective CDs encircled the base of the *OVNI*, convincingly resembling a ring of lights. Buried beneath all this was the family car, its head and tail lights wrapped in orange cellophane. The result was a plausible extra-terrestrial craft, although the driver wasn't left with much of a forward view.

A neighbour along the same street was building a tall ship on a trailer, a square-rigger with twin masts, each one carrying three white sails. The hull was surrounded by blue fabric waves. Written on her prow was *El Caleuche*, the name of a ghostly vessel from Chilean mythology whose luminous form is said to appear on the seas around Chiloé, crewed by the souls of drowned sailors.

A few blocks further on, a bar-restaurant on a corner was opening for the evening at a few minutes past eight. I was glad I'd persisted; a generous glass of frothy *pisco sour* and a juicy homemade burger were worth the extra walk. The paper place mats featured a Río Futaleufú sketch map, labelled with the names of the various rapids: Infierno Canyon; Himalayas; Terminator; Chaos.

'Would the river be safe for a beginner?' I wondered.

*

Sleep, sleep, sleep.

Several consecutive journeys had taken their toll, compounded by numerous nights under canvas. Next morning, concerned that the table would be cleared if I waited any longer, I stumbled into breakfast as late as I dared. Served with slices of cold meat, the breads were soft and delicious.

The amenable assistants in the tourist office were wearing matching green t-shirts. 'Are there good places to hike around here?' I asked one of them.

'Many,' she confirmed, unfolding a map. 'One of the best walks is a climb to the Piedra del Águila,' Eagle's Rock.

This was also an opportune moment to enquire about the Hornopirén ferry. The five-hour crossing from Caleta Gonzalo to Hornopirén was the longest sea connection of the expedition. Ferries sailed twice daily during the summer months, and given their limited capacity, booking ahead was important for anyone in a vehicle.

'Do foot passengers just pay on board?' I asked the assistant, 'or will I need a reservation?' It seemed unlikely that all the backpackers and cyclists would manage to purchase tickets for specific ferries days in advance.

'I'm not sure,' she admitted. 'Maybe you could ask at the Naviera Austral office here in Futa, or there's another branch in Chaitén.'

'Are you not here to go on the river?' the other woman enquired.

'Um… maybe. Do you recommend it?'

'Absolutely! The rapids are *estupendo*,' wonderful, she assured me. 'That's why people come to Futaleufú. Everyone is either rafting or kayaking. We have the best white water in the world.'

It cannot be straightforward to compare one river with another, but the Fu has a formidable reputation for its sustained stretches of strong rapids. What a place to taste a white water experience for the first time. The Río Futaleufú is rated among the top ten rafting locations in the National Geographic book *Journeys of a Lifetime*, along with rivers in Ecuador, Nepal, North America, Australia, Turkey, Italy, and at number ten, the Zambezi in southern Africa.

Disregarding my non-committal response, she circled the offices of some of the rafting agencies on my town map.

It's difficult to identify exactly why I was so reticent. It can be intimidating to be placed as a beginner amongst experts, I suppose. Whether they are rafters or snowboarders, rock climbers or scuba divers, cool types one and all, it's easy to believe that the others are confident and self-assured. It's awkward to arrive as a stranger into a cohesive group, nervous about fitting in or failing to find a friend. Furthermore, on this occasion, I was also keen not to drown. If the white water of the Fu was so overwhelming, then wasn't it best left to experienced crews? Nonetheless, finding out more couldn't do any harm. Indeed, what a waste to have travelled so far without experiencing the river. Those two voices again, the adversarial duet of my courage and my fear. An arbiter in my mind proposed a compromise: I could start with an easy, restful day, possibly a short hike, and maybe I would find a trip for another day in a robust, stable boat on a placid stretch of river.

How dramatically plans can change. How easy it is, especially with a wavering, uncertain mind, to lose footing and slip into the relentless current. How quickly a moment of calm can become a turbulent rapid.

Locating the agency was simple, given away by the large blue raft on a trailer outside and a row of colourful canoes in a rack at the entrance.

'*Buenos días*,' greeted Martina, the owner. 'Are you hoping to go rafting?'

I glanced around. A group occupied some low wooden benches, ordinary-looking people, not intimidating at all. 'I might be. What are the options?'

'There's one raft going this morning; we could find a space for you. It's a long trip: today and tomorrow, with delicious lunches included.'

She went on to describe the route and some of the rapids. I'd imagined signing up for the standard half-day 'bridge to bridge' experience, about two hours on the river, not two days.

'I've never rafted before.'

'That's even better. You can learn as you go, and we'll give some instruction at the start. Our guide is the most experienced man on the river.'

'Are you sure it's safe for a novice?'

Martina laughed. 'We take beginners out all the time,' she said. 'One family in the boat, they were beginners yesterday so they're only one day ahead of you.'

Contrasting with my fear of looking incompetent, I tend to be quite good at jumping into opportunities that unexpectedly present themselves. I also like bargains, and two full days of rafting for only double the cost of two hours sounded like a good deal.

'How long do I have to make up my mind?' I asked Martina.

'We're leaving in ten minutes.'

Moments later, the man who was rushing back to Hospedaje Cañete for a change of clothes was no longer a footloose and carefree backpacker, but had been conscripted as the newest member of the Río Futaleufú Adventure Association Elite Rafting Division. At least, with my heart pumping and a feeling of doom oozing through my veins, that was how it felt.

*

The entry point, known as Las Escalas, was a wide beach on a slow bend where the green river slipped into an innocuous pool. Nothing here was suggestive of the terrifying white water for which the Fu was acclaimed.

Martina explained why Las Escalas had been chosen for our launch. 'We're just below the Infierno Canyon. You can't see it from here, but there's a fantastic rapid around that corner, a short paddle upstream. It's not recommended for beginners.'

Infierno means 'hell', of course. Knowing there were deadly parts of the river in such close quarters did nothing to calm my nerves. By this stage, I'd become convinced that I was about to embark on my final trip in this world. Next I would be joining the crew of *El Caleuche*.

Clad in wetsuit, neoprene shoes, jacket and helmet, I paid careful attention to the briefing on rafting techniques and safety: hold the paddle with both hands; keep it down when not in use to avoid clobbering others; always obey the guide's instructions.

'How likely is it that I will fall out?'

'Well, some people do,' was the reply. 'If it happens, the worst thing to do is to panic. Just remember what we said: lie on your back, face forward, feet downriver to help you bounce off the rocks, and you can get back in the boat at the end of the rapid.'

Martina had unpacked an impressive picnic during the briefing. I've often wondered what condemned men and women choose for their final meal. Ours was to be a healthy spread of *quinoa*, salad, bread, exquisite local honey and soft cheese.

*

> **Quinoa**
>
> Quinoa is an ancient cereal crop from the Andes, where it was bred selectively from wild grasses. There are terraces where Quinoa has grown without interruption for thousands of years. The pale round seeds are highly nutritious and a good source of both fibre and protein. It contains amino acids and vitamins but is gluten-free. Quinoa can be eaten as grain or ground into flour for making pasta or bread, and is also used to produce fermented drinks. In the UK, it is increasingly available in health food stores and supermarkets.
>
> The United Nations declared 2013 the 'International Year of Quinoa' to promote awareness of the role that this cereal could play in eradicating hunger and malnutrition. Quinoa has proved to be highly versatile, growing at altitudes of up to 4000 metres and withstanding temperatures below freezing point and as high as 38 degrees Celsius. It is resistant to drought and produces good yields even in poor or saline

> soils. From its origins in Peru and Bolivia, quinoa has been successfully cultivated as far afield as India, Kenya and the Himalayas.

*

We pushed our blue raft into the pool for some preliminary practice. Sitting on the sides of the boat, three each side, we wedged our legs between the thwarts, inflated struts across the raft, as a way to hold fast during the bumpy ride. Our veteran guide, Luis, leaned back against an upright board at the stern and used two long oars to steer. Instructed by Luis, we practiced paddling forward, reversing, and nimbly spinning the raft by the crew on either side paddling in opposite directions.

One of our team was Natalya from Russia.

'*¿Cuánto tiempo has estado en Sudamérica?*' I asked her.

'Я не говорю по испански,' she replied.

'How long have you been in South America?' I tried instead.

'Я не говорю по английски,' she added.

The obstacles this presented to team communications were not the slightest concern, naturally. The ability to understand one another can't be all that important in averting drowning-type scenarios. What did become apparent was that, despite being a proficient kayaker, she was as nervous as me about this particular trip. I was hoping not to learn the Russian for 'abandon ship' that afternoon.

Natalya was taking a break whilst her husband competed in the Patagonia Expedition Race, contested by teams of four through Patagonia's rarely-explored wilderness. Competitors trek, climb, kayak and mountain bike between checkpoints. A new route is prepared every year, and is made known the night before the start. That year, the winning team completed the course in six days and four hours. Natalya's husband and his team adventured for almost eight days, finishing in eighth place.

Half our crew was a family of three from England. Their grown-up daughter, Flora, was living in Buenos Aires, hence the choice of South America for the family vacation. The modus operandi of their holiday was at the opposite end of the organisational spectrum to mine. Their itinerary was completely planned with all hotel reservations and activities pre-booked. Following the rafting, they were set to continue with pony trekking and fly fishing. It was difficult to imagine Flora in a pair of waders; that final activity must have been included for someone else's benefit. The fifth and sixth members of our crew were Martina and me.

My prior fears quickly dissipated as I was carried along in the drama and excitement of white water rafting. The rubber raft leapt and lurched, slid over the surface of the bubbling cauldron and raced headlong into mountainous waves. Luis kept a forward vigil, straining on the oars to steer, usually down the centre of the channel but sometimes tight up against the bank.

'Forward!' he'd shout, and we dug in hard, all except Flora's father who cradled the plastic paddle in his lap and allowed the rest of us to benefit from the exercise.

'Only the left side!' Luis would yell, veering away from a dark rock the size of a car.

'Stop paddling!' was sometimes the cry, when the force of the water was enough on its own, our guide using the oars as a rudder.

In case of need, we were accompanied by two kayaks and a cataraft, a raft of catamaran design that was rowed, not paddled. Twice that afternoon Luis steered us to the riverbank where we disembarked to avoid a section of river considered too dangerous for novice paddlers. These two rapids, Zeta and the Throne Room, were both category V-plus.

Class VI rapids: Nearly impossible and very dangerous; a definite hazard to life.

Class V rapids: Long rapids with wild turbulence, extremely congested, requiring complex manoeuvring.

Zeta was a Z-shaped canyon. Climbing onto steep rocks permitted a view from above. Luis and the kayakers tethered the raft to a long nylon line in order to guide it through. With helpers atop the rocks on both sides, the first of the boats was released into the narrow cleft. The current pushed the raft into one corner of the Z where it spun in a dizzying vortex. That was where the line was needed, to yank it away from the foaming ferment of that dead end.

'If you fell in there,' Martina remarked coolly, 'your body would never be found.'

At the Throne Room we clambered around the bank again. Spending an age on the opposite side, the kayakers checked and examined the rapids from multiple angles before eventually deciding it was safe to canoe through. Both of them capsized repeatedly, each time rolling upright, until one was finally dumped out.

'The paddle was ripped out of my hands,' he complained later. 'I had no way to roll upright. I had to eject.'

The two rafts were sent through the Throne Room untethered and collected below. One was thrown upside-down by the waves, tearing away an oar that had been lashed to the side and which we later found some distance downstream. Swapping crew positions, I took the front row with Flora, a seat that came with the special honour of taking spray and splash full in our faces. We tackled some Class III and Class IV rapids with three-metre waves during the final part of the day, with names such as Roller Coaster and the Wild Mile. Those were plenty exciting enough; we hadn't missed out by omitting the Throne Room and Zeta. Having moored that evening at a gorge called El Azul, we climbed through brambles to the road, exhausted and buzzing with exhilaration.

Class IV Rapids: Difficult rapids, abrupt bends, narrow passages, scouting often necessary, precise manoeuvring required.

Class III Rapids: Numerous waves, narrow passages, manoeuvring required, may require scouting.

---

*

As I cooked, that evening, on the log stove at Cañete, an elderly *abuela*, the grandmother, shared her *mate* with me. She explained that the previous night's *OVNI* and tall ship must have been part of a parade for the annual Futaleufú week. At least, I think she did, but it was hard to understand much of her tooth-free rural accent. Furthermore, as celebrations continued, she quite possibly said, there would be a show in the gymnasium that night. Having missed the *Fiesta del Pescado Frito* in Puerto Cisnes, I was keen this time to sample the local festival.

After a lively band began proceedings, a pair of slapstick comedians had everyone around me in stitches. It had similar qualities to a genre of comedy shown frequently on television, with subtlety not amongst its more conspicuous traits. Both on the screen and live, the approach appeared rather in-your-face and direct, readily resorting to custard pies, silly voices and ill-fitting trousers. But who was I to judge? To appreciate the humour of a foreign place, it's not sufficient to be fluent in the language, you also need a good grasp of culture and history. It's a matter of knowing the local story, the heroes and villains, their successes and failures, and being familiar with how that community perceives its place in the wider world.

*

Arriving at the rafting office after a breakfast featuring apple cake and Fortnum & Mason tea, I deduced that the kayakers, still asleep in an upstairs room, had participated wholeheartedly in the night's celebrations. Soothed by fresh air and invigorated with black coffee, we set off to the river, arriving only fifteen minutes beyond our agreed ten o'clock.

The road bridge across the narrow gorge at El Azul was ominously labelled Puente La Difficultad. The name was a reference to an earlier crossing, a *gauchos'* footbridge, which had collapsed on more than one occasion, dropping batches of surprised animals into the river below.

Having wriggled into wetsuits, we descended to the water. Natalya was nowhere to be seen, and we were joined instead by Catalina and Esteban, both experienced crew. The rapids on this second day were immense. Surging waves tossed our raft around as if it was a toy, lifting us high to be momentarily suspended in both time and space before crashing unceremoniously back onto the seething surface of the water with a loud smack. Before there was time to catch a breath or regain composure, we would pitch one way and then the other, or bounce over rolling waves, or plummet into the cavernous hollows behind them. At times, the raft reared up to what felt like a vertical position, and we gawked helplessly into the hideously swirling waters, clutching onto paddle and raft in desperate horror.

In another location, appropriately named the Magic Carpet, a counter-current beside the bank swept the raft back upstream, curiously enabling us to repeat the ride through the rapid. In calmer sections, there was time to enjoy the stunning beauty of the natural environment: the rich blue river; the energetic, frothy, bubbly white water; billowing clouds in mountain chasms; kingfishers and cormorants patrolling their territories. When not fending off chaotic torrents with our paddles, we drifted in serene silence as if hypnotised by the extraordinary surroundings.

The English family was staying at a luxury riverside lodge. We stopped there on the second day for a hot lunch of soup, *paella* and a delicious baked-apple dessert. With agreeable timing, rain fell heavily during the break but ceased when we returned to the river. The remaining rapids were fantastic, although we had to miss the Class V-plus Terminator through which our guide piloted the raft alone. At another, we stopped to scout the conditions before Luis allowed us to paddle through. My first experience of white water rafting was so intensely enjoyable, I found myself wondering why I'd waited so many years before trying it.

In our final rapid, within sight of the minibus waiting at our destination beach, we pitched into a big hole. The raft rocked forward and Captain Luis cartwheeled through the air. In flight he collided with Esteban, and they both slipped over the side of the raft leaving us mid-rapid without a guide. With many years' experience on the river, Luis appeared utterly unfazed and swam to the safety of the cataraft. Keeping a cool head, Catalina stepped into the helm and took the oars. Eventually, someone remembered to haul Esteban back on board.

Our excursion concluded with a second visit to the lunchtime lodge, devouring crepes with honey around a roaring log fire, made all the sweeter for having conquered the Fu.

*

The Naviera Austral office was closed, thus eliminating the chance to purchase a ferry ticket in advance. As I read a notice in the window, a man appeared beside me.

'I believe there are no places available until the twenty-eighth; *ninguna*,' none at all.

Something about his condescending manner was difficult to tolerate. 'That won't be a problem for me, *señor*,' I haughtily replied. 'I don't have a car.'

A young couple at Hospedaje Cañete had arrived from the north. They assured me that foot passengers could purchase tickets aboard the Hornopirén ferry.

'It's no longer one ferry,' they added. 'It's a bit more complicated now. First you take a boat from Caleta Gonzalo; that's a short passage. Then you cross the peninsula by road, and there's a second ferry to Hornopirén.'

'How did you get along that road between the two ferries?' I asked.

'There's a free bus for foot passengers. It's easy, *no te preocupes*,' don't worry.

A day of lazy recuperation in Fualeufú was recompense for my white water courage. I took a bag of laundry to a *lavandería* where the price was set by weighing the clothes on a set of scales in the porch. In a well-established routine, I wore what remained, this time swimming shorts and the long-sleeved orange t-shirt.[62] That afternoon, I fell asleep in a sheltered spot on a stony riverside beach. It was a mild surprise on waking to find myself in the midst of a flock of sheep munching at grassy tussocks in the warm sunshine. Taking fright as I sat upright, they bleated off into the bushes.

Futaleufú had been worth the lengthy diversion. The show, the resting, the rafting and the people I'd met had all made this particular dogleg worthwhile. The lengthy ferry crossing to Hornopirén was coming, marking the beginning of the end for my Patagonian exploits. But it wasn't over yet; a great deal more lay between here and Puerto Montt. For one thing, I was about to enter volcano territory.

---

[62] Looking back, I wonder whether I ever washed that orange shirt. Possibly not, but in my defence I didn't wear it often.

Image 19: Río Futaleufú

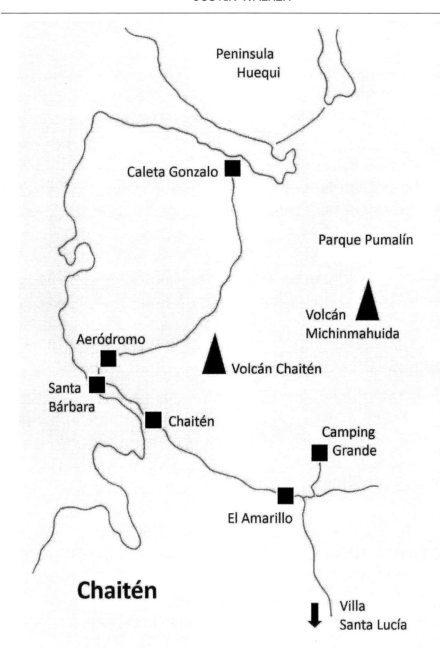

Map 15: Chaitén

Twenty-One: Colilargo

One summer Sunday in Santiago, I attended a christening celebration lunch at the home of a family from school. Succulent steak was served from the *asado* accompanied by chilled Sauvignon Blanc from a local vineyard, and later in the afternoon there was a chance to cool off in the swimming pool. On this occasion, green and yellow balloons had been tied in clumps around the courtyard, matching the serviettes and tablecloth. As we filled our paper plates at the buffet table, the convivial atmosphere was interrupted by a loud bang. Moments later, a child's wail pierced the anxious silence. Then another bang. As the day became hotter and the afternoon air stifled, the colourful balloons popped one by one. Diners looked around nervously, wondering where the next assault might come from. Of course, it was impossible to tell which one would burst next or how long would pass before it happened. But you could be sure that, in time, there would be another.

Anticipating volcanic eruptions is similarly unpredictable. From the desert north to the glacial south, Chile is well accustomed to volcanoes. Villarrica and Lascar erupted in 2013, Copahue in 2012, Puyhue-Cordón Caulle rather dramatically in 2011, Planchón-Peteroa in 2010 and Llaima in 2009. Whereas this activity can warrant the temporary displacement of human populations and livestock, the majority of eruptions are minor, amounting only to the short-term venting of gas and steam with some hot cinders spat out from time to time. Once in a while, though, something much, much bigger goes bang.

*

Volcanic Explosivity Index

The Volcanic Explosivity Index was devised at the University of Hawaii in 1982 as a way to classify volcanic explosions. Eruptions are matched to a scale from 0 to 8, according to the volume of material ejected and the height of the plume.

The more explosive end of the scale is shown in this table.

Volcanic Explosivity Index	Name	Minimum volume of material ejected (km^3)	Height of plume (km)	Approximate frequency (one expected per N years)
VEI 4	Cataclysmic	0.1	10-25	1+
VEI 5	Super	1	20-35	10+
VEI 6	Huge	10	>30	100+
VEI 7	Colossal	100	>40	1,000+
VEI 8	Catastrophic	1000	>50	10,000+

The most recent VEI 7 event was an eruption of Mount Tambora in April 1815, which ejected 160km^3 of debris. The mountain, on the island of Sumbawa, Indonesia, was reduced in height from 4300m to 2850m in the explosion. The ash cloud is thought to have been responsible for the loss of an entire northern hemisphere summer in 1816, leading to severe famine. This is the most powerful volcanic event in recorded history. The Tambora volcano is still active.

The most recent VEI 8 eruption is believed to have occurred 26,500 years ago. This was the Oruanui eruption at Lake Taupo in New Zealand, which covered North Island in debris to a depth of up to 200 metres. According to the scale, another VEI 8 eruption is long overdue.

*

Back between Puerto Río Tranquilo and Villa Cerro Castillo on the occasion of the serendipitous bus ride, the road we took through the dense rainforest skirted the south side of Volcán Hudson. This volcano might have put an end to my trip even before it began. Hudson's 500-

metre wide crater is thick with ice, and one of the dangers of glacier-covered volcanoes is that rapid melting can cause flooding and deadly rivers of mud. With activity exceeding critical levels, an alert was issued and the 130 nearby residents were ordered to evacuate. A plume of smoke rose from the vent... but having spat and fizzed for some days, the eruption subsided. By the time that we passed in our bus, speaking in reverent tones so as not to upset the volcano gods, Hudson was dozing peacefully again, and the only rumbling came from a straining engine and six heavy wheels gripping the rutted road.

Authorities had reason to be cautious. A violent eruption there in 1991 had registered at Volcanic Explosivity Index Five (VEI 5), a phenomenon seen globally only once per decade or thereabouts. On that occasion, Hudson ejected more than four cubic kilometres of material and clouds of sulphur dioxide gas. An eruption of VEI 6 is believed to have occurred there in approximately 4750BC. Such energetic activity would explain Hudson's huge caldera, ten kilometres across, and it probably put an end to human settlement in central Patagonia for quite some time. Eruptions of this magnitude are rare, occurring approximately once per century. The 1991 eruption was Chile's largest in decades, but Volcán Hudson lost that title just two decades later when another of the balloons unexpectedly burst: Volcán Chaitén.

*

Without the borrowed alarm, I would never have woken at half past five. The timber house creaked as I crept down the narrow stairs with my bulky bag. My hostess at Hospedaje Cañete had risen early to prepare breakfast, bless her. With three hurriedly-constructed cheese-and-salami sandwiches, I bade farewell to the kindly woman, repeating my gratitude.

It was a short walk in the silent darkness of the sleepy town to an anonymous corner where the bus was due. Gradually, a loose assembly of somnolent backpackers gathered, togged up in jackets, hoods and hats. Couples hibernated together in each other's warmth, and sparse conversation was murmured in the hushed voices usually reserved for cathedrals. The bus came punctually at six, and we began our journey, rattling and squeaking down the uneven road in the gloom.

The seats were already set in the reclined position and many passengers were soon asleep. Folding my long legs into the restricted space was uncomfortable but somewhere beyond Puente Futaleufú, I eventually drifted off and dreamed of cascading through white water torrents in an inflatable boat, clutching only a plastic paddle. In reality, of course, no-one would contemplate anything so imprudent. When I woke, a pale light had begun to wash night from the valley. With tight bends and a disintegrating road surface, the short descent to Villa Santa Lucía had taken two hours.

From there, the bus turned north up the Carretera Austral. We halted a considerable while at a set of roadworks, but it was worth the wait. Beyond the repairs, the rattling abruptly stilled as the surface turned to tarmac. What a relief to the ears. I had forgotten how it was to travel on a paved road. The absence of shaking and noise were like a soothing ointment on an angry wound.

*

Parque Pumalín

Parque Pumalín is a privately owned park associated with the philanthropist Doug Tompkins. The Conservation Land Trust[63] in the United States bought 700,000 acres of Patagonian land from various landowners, combining them to form the park. Some locals have expressed their opposition to the project, unhappy to see a large area of Patagonia pass into foreign hands. Nevertheless, the land is now owned by the Pumalín Foundation, which is registered in Chile.

Tompkins' goal is to protect the area from development and provide a place for visitors to enjoy pristine nature, including virgin rainforest. He also aims to foster understanding of the need to protect Chile's wild lands and biodiversity and set an example to other philanthropists of what can be achieved in environmental protection. The centres where the park wardens work double as rural businesses, and therefore they employ local people and contribute to the Patagonian economy. These businesses focus on eco-tourism, farms for livestock and fruit, and the production of cheese and wool products.

---

[63] The Conservation Land Trust is a sister organisation of Conservación Patagónica mentioned in Chapter 14, sharing similar aims.

*

At the village of El Amarillo, I made enquiries at the Puma Verde store. The *guardaparque* gave me a map of Parque Pumalín and described the hiking trails and various overnight options. I chose to stay at Camping Grande, a few kilometres inside the park, and there greeted four *chicos*[64] who had pitched their tents under a wooden shelter known as a *quincho*.[65] These were four new *chicos*, of course, not the group from Villa O'Higgins. Attached to a battered noticeboard were dog-eared posters warning of the risk of the nasty rat-borne *hantavirus*. As I read it, one of the campers wandered over.

'Are you sleeping here?' she asked. 'You have to be careful of *hanta*.'

Following widespread news coverage, I was aware that hantavirus pulmonary syndrome was a dangerous virus. The human disease typically starts with symptoms similar to flu, but can be fatal if it spreads to lungs or kidneys. Some in Chile had developed a fear of *hanta* that bordered on the hysterical, even in urban areas where contact with the disease was unlikely. Usually spread through rat excrement or saliva, human infection is usually traced back to outdoor areas such as national parks, and especially to camping in forests. Risk is higher during dry weather when infected dust becomes airborne.

'Wash your hands and your cooking utensils thoroughly,' she advised me, 'and always keep your food carefully wrapped.'

No antivirus was yet available. Humans had been known to recover, but only with intensive hospital care including mechanical respiration. Hantavirus sounded worth avoiding.

A trail meandered through the woods. Volcanic ash was everywhere, resembling deep sand. In the 2008 eruption of Volcán Chaitén, large quantities of ash were deposited on fields and forests. This southern sector of the park was closed to visitors during a lengthy clean-up operation. Many tons of ash had been shifted and buried but in other places, a smooth grey-white blanket remained. The sandy

---

[64] Reminder: *chicos* refers to young people, especially teenagers. Whereas *chicas* applies exclusively to girls, *chicos* can either be boys, or a mixed group.

[65] A *quincho* is a shelter or outdoor space set aside for the preparation and consumption of food, often cooked on the *asado*, the barbecue.

layer had penetrated even beneath the trees and clung, rather strangely, to the underside of branches. In contrast to the crystal waters elsewhere, the river ran the colour of chocolate milk. Denuded trees stood in dejected clumps, and siskin chicks played in the branches, never settling.

Seven or eight kilometres on, the trail reached an open plain. Far ahead, the snout of Glaciar Michinmahuida[66] extended into the valley. The wide expanse of deep ash was a peculiar sight, like a moonscape or a salt flat or even like snow. Although I left a trail of lightly indented footprints on the crisp, brittle surface, the compacted material was plenty substantial enough to support my weight. Here and there feeble, stunted plants made half-hearted attempts to grow in the alien soil. Flowing from the distant glacier, the river had re-established a course through the ash, criss-crossing in multiple experimental channels.

With the wind strengthening, the glacier disappeared into a haze. Rain was imminent so I retreated briskly to the nearby Ventisquero campsite. Long, unflattened grass suggested that recent visitors had been few. Sitting on a sturdy picnic bench in the shelter of another *quincho*, I tucked into my lunch and watched the rain. Lost to the surroundings, I was obliviously mid-song when the four *chicos* arrived. I hastily busied myself with something in my bag. Had they heard my sonata? With luck, the drumming rain and the rustling of coat hoods might have spared me. I shared some squares of chocolate, a popular way to build Anglo-Chilean relations, and then lay back on the bench, and dozed off.

When the rain paused, we commenced the long walk back to Camping Grande. It didn't hold off for long, and I was glad of my waterproofs. Disappointingly, my leather shoes had adopted the water-retardant qualities of sponge. As the rain persisted late into the evening, I prepared to cook, sharing the *quincho* with the *chicos*. Although they had colonised the whole shelter, I found a corner in which to hang my jacket to dry. It was to be my final camp dinner so I treated myself to both remaining packets of noodles. I was nearly out of gas: shaking the canister afterwards, a tinny rattle could just about be heard.

---

[66] *Michinmahuida* is pronounced 'mee-chin-ma-WEE-dah'.

The *chicos* had a didgeridoo and a drum. Generously, they invited me to join the band, my instrument being a spoon and a tin cup. Nico played the didgeridoo well; what an odd instrument. The others were making an appetising lentil-and-vegetable dish for their dinner, with *cebolla, zapallo, zanahoria* and *ají*: onion, pumpkin, carrot and chilli. I ached with vegetable longings, but on the positive side was glad not to be hitchhiking with a didgeridoo and a drum. They concluded their banquet with crepes and *manjar*, a sickly sweet spread of caramelised sweetened milk, known outside Chile as *dulce de leche*. My earlier chocolate generosity was rewarded with a tasty crepe. It was a charming evening in genial company.

The night was cold, the coldest so far. The short southern summer was ending. My sleeping mat was no more sophisticated than a roll of thin compacted foam, but it gave adequate insulation from the frigid ground. The first good news of the morning was the absence of raindrop percussion on the fabric roof. Warily, I unzipped the tent... blue sky! Sunlight illuminated the far side of the valley. The tent would dry rapidly once the sun moved around, except... I realised with a pinch of regret that I'd pitched on the shady side of some tall bushes, forsaking the early rays. That was something to remember another time.

I had a week left. My flight left for Santiago in just seven more days, but there was no need to hurry. I could afford a slow morning in the park before the short journey to Chaitén. I rinsed my sodden socks and hung them in the sun, and raised the heels of my shoes on a stone to help the sun peer inside. Then the final drops of gas sufficed for two lazy cups of Countess Grey.

The two *chicas* found a ride to the park entrance. The *chicos* followed on foot, and it was not long before I left too. A short way along was a *sendero interpretivo* called Sendero Ranita de Darwin: Darwin's Frog, native to Patagonia. After hatching, these tadpoles spend the first part of their lives inside the vocal sac of the male parent. I'm glad I'm not one of those. The *guardaparque* had given me a laminated instruction sheet for the trail. As the route climbed and descended, crossing both dry and swampy ground, the notes described the species that thrived in the different conditions, emphasising the interdependence of particular trees and birds. There was a disused sawmill and an overgrown track along which oxen once hauled the massive trunks.

Finally, there was a description of the cycle of forest life that restarts when an old tree falls, allowing individuals to compete for the newly opened pool of light and for the nutrients released by the decomposing material.

The previous day's rain had polished the air, and the hills and forests stood out in sharp relief; it was like walking through a painted scene. The greens of grass and foliage contrasted with a rich blue sky. Turning to look back, snow covered Volcán Michinmahuida raised her head above the surrounding mountains, poking out her white glacier tongue.

*

All four *chicos* were lazing on the ground at the park entrance, in no apparent hurry. At the edge of the village, another young man sat on the kerb, hoping to hitch a ride to the hot springs, Termas El Amarillo. His girlfriend was purchasing food nearby in an incredibly sparse *almacén*. There were a few packets of pasta and rice, some dried soups and tinned fruit, sugar and salt, cartons of milk, matches, toothpaste and batteries. A suburban family stocking up would have emptied the whole shop. The vegetable stand contained only a small cabbage, a pepper, three tomatoes, a handful of carrots and half a pumpkin. There was an unwrapped block of cheese on the counter so I said a prayer against lurking bacteria and asked the young assistant, around ten years old, to carve a chunk for me. Adding bread and a tomato, my purchases totalled 920 *pesos*. When I gave a $1000 note to the girl along with two $10 coins, she punched the numbers into a calculator, bit her lip nervously, and handed over the correct change.

Along the main road, a man in a hard hat was painting property identification numbers on the fence. All over Chile, even in the most out-of-the-way places, you can find these numbers by the side of the road. Where there are no houses, these figures, generally black characters on a yellow background, are painted every twenty metres onto fences and walls, on small boards pinned to trees or even on roadside boulders. In Santiago, all streets are numbered outwards from Plaza Italia in the city centre. Consequently, properties on the periphery of the city have numbers in the many thousands; mine was 9644.

A bus appeared. Only after flagging it down did I realise that it was a private contract vehicle, full of workmen in orange boiler suits. They welcomed me aboard all the same, and took me to Chaitén, just a short distance away on a wonderfully smooth road.

The name Chaitén had become infamous throughout Chile in the years leading up to my trip, and this was one of the places I'd most looked forward to visiting. Whenever I'd mentioned plans to travel this way, Chilean friends had made sure I knew about the tiny town demolished in a violent volcanic eruption. Despite their graphic descriptions of homes overwhelmed by ash and acres of forest swept away, it was difficult to imagine what it might actually be like. I'd heard it was even possible to climb the volcano, a long dusty hike to the rim of the crater, but of the devastated town itself I had no real idea what to expect.

In just twenty minutes we'd become best of friends. As I stepped from the bus in the centre of Chaitén, the workmen chorused a cheery farewell and waved a forest of grubby-gloved hands. Accommodation was in short supply. The few *hospedajes* that hadn't closed down were occupied by gangs of builders working on the numerous reconstruction projects. At Hospedaje Don Carlos the owner (Don Carlos, I presume) suggested I pitched my tent in his *bodega*, his store, adding a reassuring word that other campers had done so before. The solidly constructed outhouse was dry and secure, with showers and internet facilities both on offer in the adjoining main building. My British sense of propriety was mildly taken aback by the extended duration of Don Carlos' tender handshake, and by what seemed to be a quite unnecessary arm draped around my shoulder, but without doubt, the accommodation itself was an excellent option.

This was no garden shed. The *bodega* was fully twenty paces long and eight wide, not that striding across it was a realistic proposition since it was piled high with hotel supplies. Next to a catering-sized cooking range were racks holding bottles of wine, whisky and *pisco*. Another cabinet held teetering stacks of plates and bowls. There were shelves of mugs and glasses and a set of super-large saucepans. At the opposite end of the store were building materials: timber, chipboard and a pallet piled high with sacks of cement.

Pitching a tent on the concrete floor required a certain amount of ingenuity. Whilst dome tents can stand unaided, mine is a tunnel with three hooped ribs, a design that collapses unless secured at both ends. One peg at each of the four corners is the minimum requirement, but that was impossible on a solid floor. I strung out the four corner guy ropes instead and tied them to whatever I could find. The rear pair knotted around a shelving unit holding towels and linen. In front was one of the central pillars of the *bodega*, so I looped a third cord around that. And the last one… well, there was nothing available at that corner so three would have to do.

*

The story of Chaitén is both dramatic and tragic. Were it not for the events of 2008, Chaitén might have been just another stop along the Carretera Austral, one of the larger towns but otherwise unremarkable. In April that year, some faint seismic murmurings were detected emanating from the mountains to the north. Local geologists knew where to point the finger of suspicion: at 2404-metre Volcán Michinmahuida, which had erupted for Charles Darwin passing that way in 1834 during his Galapagos Islands voyage. Confusingly, when readings were taken on Michinmahuida in 2008, there was nothing to confirm any activity. Yet, deep underground, the rumbling continued.

Early one morning in May 2008, the townspeople of Chaitén met a catastrophe. Suddenly and spectacularly, the volcano exploded. Not Michinmahuida, but *their* volcano. Until that day, little Volcán Chaitén had always seemed a modest and unassuming hill, rather pretty but not particularly special. Previously active an estimated 9400 years ago, this smaller cone had never been considered a threat, even though it stands just ten kilometres from the town. But that late-autumn morning, it produced a ferocious eruption measured at VEI 5, one of the strongest in decades anywhere in the world.

The column of ash reached an altitude of 17 kilometres. It fell thickly on Chaitén, on a large area of Chile and Argentina, and further afield over parts of the South Atlantic. When ash blocked the Chaitén River, it produced lahars. These are mudflows of volcanic debris mixed with water, and can be as destructive as fast-flowing liquid concrete. The lethal mix washed through the streets, poured through doors and windows and wrecked everything in its path. Residents had no time to gather their belongings, no chance to search for the quivering cat or collect any treasured memento. For many there was not even time to find a pair of shoes or turn back to lock the door. The only thing to do when a volcano erupts in your back yard is to flee. Four thousand people, virtually everyone in the town, took to the sea.

The ash cloud played havoc with passenger planes and hundreds of flights were cancelled. Roads were closed within a 50-kilometre radius and access forbidden. Farm animals and pets were abandoned. With no clean water left to drink and pastures blanketed in choking dust, farm animals perished, and so did the fish in poisoned rivers. Miraculously, the only recorded human fatality was a woman of 92 years who died during the evacuation, en route to Puerto Montt by ship.

Eruptions have continued, emitting gas, ash and steam. Periodic collapses in the lava dome have triggered pyroclastic flows: scorching avalanches of lava and gas racing down the mountain slopes at speeds approaching 700 kilometres per hour. In the largest of these, in February 2009, a crack appeared in the side of the dome, and a torrent of material at 500 degrees Celsius emptied towards the town, stopping mercifully short in the valley.

*

The Liquiñe-Ofqui fault

The three recent volcanic eruptions in this part of Chile had a common cause. The Hudson, Chaitén and Cordon de Caule volcanoes lie in a straight line above the Liquiñe-Ofqui geological fault, all within a range of 800 kilometres. The same activity also warms the spa water at the various hot springs in the region, such as the Termas El Amarillo and the Termas Ventisqueros de Puyuhuapi.

This fault represents one act of a broader geological drama: the tectonic activity of the Peru-Chile subduction zone where the South American and Nazca plates meet. In elementary terms, the Nazca plate (beneath the Southeast Pacific) is pushing under the South American plate. This subduction activity has two notable impacts. First, Chile has more active volcanoes than any other country on Earth. As Nazca crust melts, magma rises to erupt through volcanic fissures. Secondly, it also explains the frequent earthquakes experienced in Chile. The devastatingly powerful 9.5 magnitude quake in Valdivia in 1960 is still

> the strongest earthquake ever recorded, with the 2010 Maule quake of magnitude 8.8 not far behind.

*

Exploring Chaitén that afternoon was a shocking experience. The whole town had been laid waste. Homes had been overcome by a deep layer of filthy, solidified debris. Unlike El Amarillo, gently blanketed by a snowfall of airborne deposits, this material had been delivered by a swell of powerfully surging lahars, unstoppable and irresistible. Reaching halfway up the walls inside many homes, it had set like concrete. The end of the school building beside the river channel had sheared off and washed away. Entire houses had been picked up, swept along and dumped haphazardly at peculiar angles, half submerged in the granular dirt. Where the gritty mess had seeped into a minibus on the seafront, a huge *nalca* plant had somehow germinated within, filling the van as if it were a greenhouse. There was no way to tell where the former beach ended and the ash deposits began – the sandy material simply merged into a seamless expanse, littered with crates and doors and rafters and furniture and tree trunks and all manner of detritus that had been caught in the formidable currents of the lahars.

Official notices pinned to houses prohibited entry. On another wall someone had painted:

Amo a Chaitén; Volveré.

I love Chaitén; I will return.

Some had returned, but probably fewer than half. Businesses were closed and countless homes were abandoned. Inside one dwelling, family possessions were scattered in the dust: a television, cassette tapes, shoes, clothes and a cracked pair of spectacles. There was a pile of dinner plates in the sink. In a child's bedroom were text books, a school report, posters on the wall and a box of toys. For this family, for many, it would be too harrowing to return to the place where on that terrible May morning, their former lives were blown away. All the while, as I meandered through these devastating scenes of loss, somewhat overwhelmed, Volcán Chaitén continued to mark her position at the rear of the townscape with a fat column of steam, an ominous reminder of the searing furnace sizzling below.

*

Having figured out the cooking range, I sat that evening with a bowl of pasta beside the log-burning stove, which the disconcertingly charming Don Carlos had prepared and lit. Hoping for company, I was pleased when two other campers were shown into the *bodega*, Carlos and Maijito. They spent a few minutes weighing up the unique selling points of the luxurious suite and discussed it by telephone with friends who were searching elsewhere. An agreement was struck. There would be three tents in the *bodega* that night.

The second pair turned out to be the couple who'd been in El Amarillo that morning, namely Tomás who'd wanted to visit the *termas* and Gabriela from the shop. The five of us sat drinking wine from a box, enjoying the warmth of the *estufa*. We compared Patagonian experiences and ventured occasional details about our lives in the other world. Like so many others I'd encountered, they were students on summer breaks from universities in Santiago.

The cheery relaxed atmosphere was rudely shattered when Gabriela shrieked, '¡*Ratón!*'

Of course a *bodega* like this would always have a mouse, but this was no ordinary case of rodent phobia. What she actually feared was *hantavirus*. The beast usually implicated when *hanta* strikes in Chile is the *ratón de cola larga*, literally 'rat of long tail', also called the *colilargo común*. The English name is the long-tailed colilargo, a bizarre translation since it means the 'long-tailed longtail'. A more descriptive English alternative, hinting at its preferred diet of seeds, is the long-tailed pygmy rice rat; great name, but a nasty disease.

The proprietor was summoned. Gabriela described the *ratón* with repeated references to its long tail. Don Carlos said it was probably a mouse. Gabriela wasn't convinced. After all, it was she who'd seen it. Rounding on Tomás, she made clear her feelings about his choice of hotel. Then the monster made a second appearance and we all saw it that time. The rat was huge – stood on his hind legs he would have towered over Gabriela. There was no telling whether he was carrying *hanta* as he neither foamed at the mouth nor brandished a little placard, but he was a fat rat and no ordinary house mouse.

In truth he was unlikely to have been a *colilargo*. Not only was he far too large, but the relatively small *colilargos* also tend to prefer the outdoors. That's why *hanta* warnings are displayed at camping and barbecue sites. They nest in trees, even using abandoned bird nests, and can travel swiftly through forest by propelling themselves between the branches like squirrels. However, this was hardly a moment for an intricate analysis of rodent ethology. The party bubble had burst and our convivial atmosphere subsided into tension and gloom. Gabriela was understandably uneasy about sleeping in the same room as a giant rat, but there was little choice. The hour was late and the half-destroyed town of Chaitén lay in darkness. We sombrely prepared for bed and zipped our doors firmly closed, and I fell asleep to a tuneless ballad of pitiful whimpering from the tent next door.

Image 20: Chaitén

Map 16 : Peninsula Huequi

Twenty-Two: Pudú

When I woke, Gabriela and Tomás had collapsed their tent and were almost ready to leave. Tomás wore a harried expression, but they were otherwise in good humour. It wasn't difficult to imagine the discussions that may have taken place inside their tent at dawn, regarding the importance of securing rat-free accommodation. That wasn't as easy as it might sound; rats can be fairly determined fellows and they do have a preference for hanging out in places where there are humans. Originally from China, the common brown rat has spread right around the world and boasts the most successful record of all when it comes to colonising new lands.

The episode with the fearless *colilargo* (or whatever the species actually was that had shown its whiskered face the previous evening) ranked as the journey's closest sighting of a wild mammal. I hadn't yet spotted any *huemul* or *pudú* or puma, and each day my northward route was creeping further from their forest habitats. I should have made more effort at Tamango – the wardens there would have been able to locate a *huemul*. It sounds obvious, but when you really desire something, it can be worth taking steps to make it happen. Was I expecting these timorous creatures to reveal themselves voluntarily?

A perfect sky through the *bodega* window lifted my spirits. Having witnessed the effects of her destructive power, it was a promising day to climb the culprit volcano herself. I soon had a ride out of Chaitén as far as the Santa Bárbara turning, a village built along a beach of dark volcanic sand. Santa Bárbara was initially identified as a safe site for the reconstruction of Chaitén. Returning residents, wanting to resurrect their original homes rather than rebuild in a different place, disputed the decision. They were eventually granted their wish. Why? Was it because new geological data had come to light or improved lahar defences were installed? Not according to one man I met; the concession was promised to the townspeople during campaigns for the 2010 presidential election. Volcán Chaitén remains active all the same and could certainly erupt again.

A narrow vehicle track led away from the ebony beach. Assuming it would loop back to the Carretera Austral, I followed it confidently, heading in what initially appeared to be the right direction. It was disappointing, therefore, to find that it led only to the gate of a depot painted in the green and white horizontal halves of the *carabineros*. The road I wished to reach passed the property along its opposite site, where another entrance stood open. It is usually considered unwise to enter police premises uninvited, especially in a foreign country. On the other hand, I had no desire to retrace the path I'd already taken, so I snuck inside, stood beside the wall and kept watch. Nothing happened. I delayed there for several empty, silent minutes; was anybody home? I waited still longer; after all, he who hurries… At length, seeing no sign of life within, I tiptoed through the yard.

Once out through the gate at the other end, it wasn't long before a vehicle arrived. The driver looked at me in apparent disbelief.

'Is this the Carretera Austral?' I asked.

'No,' said the man, seemingly flustered. 'This road doesn't go anywhere. How did you get here?'

It seemed wise not to answer that. 'How can I get to the Carretera Austral? Is it that way?' I pointed down the road the way he'd come.

'No. Down there is the sea. Come with me.'

We arrived at a curious junction where the long arm of a yellow barrier was lowered across the road and a uniformed sentry stood in attendance. What kind of place had I just trespassed within? No wonder the man had looked surprised. Lifting the barrier, the sentry waved us through and the driver dropped me beyond. It became clear that the barrier was not there to protect the depot I'd left behind but the territory we'd just entered. It was an *aeródromo*. At this point, the Carretera Austral ran straight and wide for a thousand metres. Vehicles had to drive along the edge, leaving the central *pista* for planes. Road barriers on three sides were lowered whenever the runway became operational. Two light aircraft were parked beside a small white prefabricated terminal building, one of which was being readied for departure.

I walked up the wide strip, along the edge where the road supposedly ran, until I reached the yellow barrier-arm at its northern end. A sign there announced:

¡Precaución! Pista aérea en el camino.

Caution! Airstrip in the road.

That's a warning you don't see every day on the A12. Another board offered more detailed advice: 'Check for planes. Keep to the vehicular track. Do not drive on the runway.'

A uniformed official drove up and lowered the barrier. One of the aircraft departed the terminal and rolled towards us, jolting along the bumpy surface. With several rows of seats, it was larger than the Villa O'Higgins plane. A single propeller spun at the front, and in a slightly ungainly design, the wings were mounted over the roof of the cabin. The plane completed a turn in front of us, paused, and then accelerated down the runway before soaring up and banking out over the sea.

Once the barriers were raised, a short procession of cars started slowly towards me. I rehearsed a wide, friendly smile, attempting to look like the kind of hitchhiker you couldn't possibly turn down.

I need to work on that smile.

Fifteen minutes later there was another car. I held out my thumb but it was the barrier man again. An incoming aircraft was about to land.

'Is it usual to have so many planes here?' I asked.

'At least six per day,' he replied. 'A scheduled service from Puerto Montt and various chartered flights depending on the season.'

The craft approached noisily over our heads, its undercarriage silhouetted against the pale sky, and made a perfect landing at Aeródromo Santa Bárbara.

Another convoy was released onto the airstrip. I prepared my thumb and fixed a grin. A four-wheel-drive Toyota halted and the window wound down.

'I'm sorry; we're full,' explained the man.

The back was crammed with bags and boxes, but I spied a small space on the seat, approximately wide enough for a *colilargo*.

'I could fit there,' I offered, hopefully.

'Are you sure?' asked the woman. 'It seems quite small.'

'Let me try.'

With some gentle persuasion, they graciously rearranged their belongings, and I contorted myself onto the seat. My rucksack and a cool-box were balanced on my lap. An unidentified object on the floor prevented me setting my feet down.

'Will you be alright like that?' asked the woman.

'Yes thank you; it's very comfortable.'

The *sendero* for Volcán Chaitén started beside the road. Although it had become a popular climb since the eruption, it was still an informal route and the trailhead was not clearly marked. Eventually we stopped to ask two workmen, who pointed back the way we'd come. The woman helped to extricate me from my den, and for a few moments I stumbled around like a drunk, easing circulation into my lifeless limbs.

The trail weaved across terrain littered with broken branches and thick with boulders, grit and ash. Swarms of *tábanos* attacked, and maintaining momentum provided the best hope of keeping them at bay. A forest of grey spikes spread up the slope ahead: bare trunks with the treetops ripped off. From a distance it looked like a film star's designer stubble. The trees on Volcán Chaitén itself had all perished, but on neighbouring slopes, strips of forest that had escaped the calamity defiantly fanned their green branches to the sky. Far above, the crest of the lava dome vented gas and steam.

On closer inspection, it wasn't that the branches had been broken off, but the trees themselves had been snapped in two. Many of the trunks remained rooted in the ground, but the upper parts had been torn away by a torrent of volcanic debris; what terrifying power. The scene was thirsty and lifeless, but amongst the devastation were signs of new life: modest green bushes and bracken had begun to sprout, brave pioneers triumphing over the arid, poisonous earth.

It was a punishing climb. The steps cut roughly into the path were tall, straining even my long legs. The rim of the volcano neared, little by little. On the steep upper slopes, it was a tough job to make progress up the loose ash surface. Assaults by the *tábanos* became less common, reward for attaining loftier elevations, but clouds of flying ants came instead, equally irritating and nasty. My feet were sore, the sun hot, and the insects a persistent nuisance. Then finally, within the distance of just a few slipping, sliding paces, the gaping crater opened in front of me. The ground fell away steeply into a deep void, its base full of ashy slurry. A tall volcanic cone had formed in the centre, standing even higher than the outer rim. Clouds of steamy gas rose from the crest against a spotless sky.

A local guide appeared, introducing himself as Nicolás from the Chaitur agency. His German patrons had climbed with smart carbon fibre trekking poles.

'Is it possible to get any closer than this?' I asked.

'It may be,' he said, 'but you'd be a fool to try. It's still erupting. You have no idea what is venting from that cone even now.' He pointed to fissures in the crimson rock, where white vapours were being emitted. 'The gas is hot and poisonous. It can shoot out of any crack or crevice at any time. When people work on volcanoes, they stay for a minimal length of time and wear protective equipment like a spacesuit. So I'm not going to stop you,' he laughed, 'but it's not something I would do.'

Nicolás told me more about the volcano as I swatted the ants around my face. He stood there impassively as though they didn't bother him at all.

'It is a rhyolite magma dome,' he said, 'the youngest one in the world. In fact, it was the first large eruption of its kind for nearly a century, anywhere on the planet.'

The colours were extraordinarily vivid: the dome a rich raspberry red, the crater inner wall formed of purple rock, pale green sludge at the base, and the whole scene set against a stunning blue sky. I'd been fortunate with my choice of day for the trek. A narrow path started around the rim, until steep banks made it impassable, both ways, so I sat for a while and watched, and wondered, and marvelled.

The descent began with a long slide in the ash, shoes filling with grit. Inspired by the German squad's ostentatious poles, I used a stick for a while. It was a good support for the larger downward steps, until it snapped. Once down, Nicolás and his clients gave me a ride back to Chaitén.

'We're from *München*,' said one with a chiselled face like Arnold Schwarzenegger's.

I asked about the Oktoberfest.

'Munich people never go to that. It's just an event for tourists.'

'You can tell which visitors are English,' croaked another, gesturing accusingly in my direction; 'they are the ones lying drunk in the street. They are not used to drinking beer.'

*

Back at Hospedaje Don Carlos, I showered the dust out of my hair and washed a thick coating of volcanic grime from my feet. My young friends had been replaced by another four hikers. They soon disappeared into their tents, so I ate my ravioli alone and went to join a group in the lounge. They were watching an act from the international music festival of Viña del Mar. Viña is a popular coastal resort within reach of the millions living in Santiago. Since it started in 1960, the annual music festival has gained a noteworthy reputation. In addition to Latin American performers such as Ricky Martin, Soda Stereo and Shakira, the show has included international acts over the years including Sting, Franz Ferdinand, Bryan Adams and Tom Jones. The first performers that evening were a Mexican trio known as Camila, whose leader is the talented pianist and singer, Mario Domm. Mark Anthony was the headline act that night, and sandwiched between the music was comedy from a duo calling themselves *Dinamita Show*. 'Dynamite' was another act of silly voices and ill-fitting trousers, but those in the lounge that evening roared their approval. Perhaps with better language skills I might have understood the jokes.

Sitting in that comfortable room, I tried to imagine what it must have been like when the volcano erupted. You live in a place all your life. It's a seismic area, you know that, but there's been no real activity for generations. You have a home, a business, a family, a regular life. So what is it like when one day, without warning, a neighbouring mountain explodes? Before you've had a chance to think, you find yourself in the middle of a terrified crowd: people you know, people you grew up around, people you love; all of you sprinting away from a surge of liquid concrete flooding the streets, racing to the docks and piling onto boats. Everything you own will be lost to the deadly deluge.

'What would that be like?' I wondered.

*

Next morning, I untied my tent from its unconventional anchors, packed up promptly and set out. The moment had arrived to make the long voyage to Hornopirén. Though it would almost certainly be a long day, with luck it needn't be especially demanding. All I had to do was hitchhike to Caleta Gonzao, and the ferry would do the rest.

The northern exit from Chaitén overlooked the wide, ash-covered beach. After a fruitless hour, I gave up appealing to the occasional vehicles and walked instead to the Kémelbus office. A scrum had formed around the door and it soon became obvious that tickets had sold out. Where had all these backpackers come from? Even more baffling, where had they spent the night?

A couple had taken occupation of what I considered to be 'my' hitchhiking spot. One was Spanish and the other Argentine. 'We want to climb the *volcán*,' they explained, so I described how to spot the trailhead. When a bus approached a few minutes later, I held out my arm with little expectation and was rather surprised when it stopped, allowing the three of us to board the otherwise empty vehicle. So I left Chaitén in the manner I'd arrived: hitchhiking by bus. Moving at the pace of a bicycle on the rough road, the driver took us as far as the *aeródromo*, where a plane swept into the air over our heads. Leaving the other two at the barrier, I continued on, for the second time in two days on foot along the edge of the runway.

Some way down the *pista*, I flagged down a blue truck. An entire family was squashed into the cab and in the rear, seated on the floor, was the same Spanish-Argentine pair. I clambered up and sat on my *mochila*. The family appeared determined to pick up every hopeful traveller they could find. More and more grateful hikers climbed aboard at frequent stops, even a group of six on one occasion. The truck rattled and swayed on the uneven road, bumping through potholes and throwing its human cargo painfully from side to side. Dust settled thickly on our clothes and bags, but such things are somehow tolerable when there is progress towards the principal goal. We paused to let the hiking couple out, but they were quickly replaced by several others. By the time we arrived at the Caleta Gonzalo ferry ramp, we had 19 on board, and several others had been dropped at intermediate points. The driver asked for nothing in return except a picture of the survivors in a huddle.

Amongst the crowd were two familiar faces: Carlos and Maijito from the *bodega* in Chaitén. They'd spent the night in another part of Parque Pumalín after walking the Los Alerces trail. All the way up the road, most of the land around us belonged to the park. Los Alerces was a walk that led, as the name suggests, to woodlands where the towering *alerce* or Patagonian Cypress could be admired. The bark of these giants was traditionally used for roofing shingles, and the timber for building. Many acres of *alerce* have been lost, and since being designated a Natural Monument of Chile, the few surviving stands are highly protected. With the age of certain individuals exceeding 3000 years, the *alerce* is the second-longest-living tree on Earth, after the bristlecone pine.

Caleta Gonzalo had few facilities: one café, a shop with craft items at silly prices and an exhibition about Parque Pumalín. Where the gravel road ended, a concrete ramp ran into the water. There was no settlement or village, just the lonely *embarcadero*. But the setting was stunning: a small inlet at the edge of the wide fjord, where tiny fish swam in the shallows. Forested mountains plunged into the dark sea, their peaks poking through low white clouds.

An hour remained before the ferry was due. The short queue of vehicles was a clue that the ship itself was not large; in fact, many of us would not have made it without the generous family and their empty truck. Oddly, there was no sign of the Kémelbus. Then we were informed that the ferry would not be departing at 1:15 that day but at 5:30. That was confusing; I'd understood that the 5:30 was supposed to be the second sailing of the day. It was unlikely to be a problem for foot passengers, but there wouldn't be space for two sets of vehicles on one ferry, especially if it was fully booked as the man in Futaleufú had smugly declared.

With a free afternoon suddenly available, there was time for a short hike. The Pumalín map depicted a trail to what it described as a spectacular waterfall. None of the others could be persuaded of the appeal of a brisk walk, so I left my *mochila* with Carlos and Maijito, who had settled in for the long wait by digging out camping stoves and soup.

It would be important to cover the ground speedily. To be sure of catching the ferry, I needed to turn round at three o'clock whether or not I'd found the *cascada*. The *sendero* began on boardwalks reminiscent of the *pasarelas* of Caleta Tortel. Although the route initially followed the coast, any views of the fjord were denied by dense forest. Once the boards ended, the path continued along the earth floor and up crude stepladders on the steeper banks, little more than split logs nailed across long uprights.

A *chucao* hopped onto the path but she was camera shy. Next, and just as beautiful, there was a pineapple beside the track. Well, strictly speaking not a genuine pineapple, but in the undergrowth were some pretty plants of the same family: the bromeliads. They had slender green leaves like pineapple spears but much longer. These mature specimens had a small flower at the centre, and some of the leaf spikes had turned a vibrant red, giving origin to the name: fascicularia bicolor.

After a while, the path began to climb sharply up a narrow ravine. Conditions on the bank became muddy and moist underfoot and then… ¡Pucha! The trail marched straight across the river. With no bridge, it was going to mean jumping from boulder to boulder across the fast-flowing icy water. The crossing was wide and the rocks looked perilous. This was far enough. I snacked on an apple and drank fresh, clear water from the stream. There was no shame in turning back; I'd had a decent walk in any case. Then that voice came again: 'Are you going to quit now? What kind of explorer are you?'

Stepping onto the first rock was easy enough. From the safety of its stable platform, I looked ahead to determine a suitable route. The next two or three were straightforward: large flat stones separated by a comfortable stride. A wider gap followed, requiring a leap, fortunately onto a broad target. At this point, the crossing became more taxing. Surfaces were greasy with spray and many were unhelpfully slanted. After two or three more leaps there was a channel that was simply too wide, so I doubled back to select an alternative course. A partially submerged tree bridged the gap between two of the stones. Then there was a fat boulder to scramble over and, finally, a few easy rocks at the far side. Success!

The three o'clock deadline was approaching but there was no way of telling how close the *cascada* might be. The trail traversed a cliff face by way of several stepladders – could this be it? No; the *sendero* continued along a boardwalk fixed high on the side of the gorge, with the river far below. Next was another set of steps, steeply down to the mossy rocks. Surely this was it. A massive boulder loomed in the centre of the stream, several metres tall. The path continued right over the giant rock via a wooden ladder. Clutching the rails with both hands, I cautiously climbed the uneven rungs. At the top, a rope was secured around the boulder's great girth, fastened at intervals with steel bolts. How was this equipment fixed there in the first place? Tightly clutching the rope and leaning outwards, I inched around the huge rock. At the far side, the onward route was a leap of faith across a gaping drop where the turbulent torrent boiled below. With all those obstacles overcome at last, I clambered down onto solid ground, my heart pumping. The time was ten to three.

Gazing around, I saw that I'd arrived in a rounded bowl of dramatic cliff walls, like the inside of a drum. A single opening marked the place where the river had cut its exit. The moist environment had nurtured an abundance of life. All kinds of ferns and mosses carpeted the canyon floor, and even the vertical surrounds were thick with bushes and plants. The *cascada*, still out of sight, announced its whereabouts by an echoing roar. I zigzagged cautiously over the slippery rocks until it came into view on the opposite side: a tall chute of water crashing into a blue-green pool. Centuries of patient work had cut a deep cleft in the cliff, through which the cataract poured.

For just those few minutes, the waterfall was solely mine. How long it had been there was impossible to know – a mindboggling number of years, never ceasing, slowly carving out that circular chasm. But fleetingly, the whole place was mine. Lingering in that spot, alone, I was emperor of that verdant and watery domain.

I surveyed my world. The waterfall was a thousand times prettier than the Cascada de la Virgen in the Simpson Valley, from that trial day of hitchhiking, long ago now. And the extra effort of getting there, and the chance opportunity created by the late-running ferry, made it somehow seem all the more worthwhile.

*

Several weeks had passed since I'd first spotted the Huequi peninsula on a mariners' chart in Puerto Montt. It owed its rectangular shape to a pair of rather straight fjords, one either side, Fiordo Reñihue and Fiordo Leptepú. If Huequi was shaped like England's Wirral, then these two bodies of water were equivalent to the Rivers Dee and Mersey, and the *embarcadero* at Caleta Gonzalo would match the location of Flint in North Wales. There were two ferry crossings in rapid succession, hopping first over the River Dee and then trawling along the Mersey, with a bus ride across the peninsula in between. Or, switching back to local geography, we were to cross Fiordo Reñihue by ferry, take a bus across Peninsula Huequi and board a second ferry to sail northward for several hours along Fiordo Leptepú all the way to Hornopirén.

The *Tehuelche* had the profile of an aircraft carrier, albeit loosely, with the flat vehicle deck taking up most of the ship and a narrow tower of accommodation at the side. There was scant indoor space for foot passengers, so we sheltered from the rain under whatever ledges we could find. As anticipated, not all the vehicles were able to board. Ferry personnel appeared to be working down a list of license plates. Near the end of the line, a small van crept aboard, and last of all a blue family car was persuaded into a space at the back, skewed awkwardly. Sailing away, we cheekily waved to the final three left dejected on the ramp. Our blue truck was also parked there; the reason they had driven to the *embarcadero* remained a mystery. The Kémelbus was aboard, having prudently delayed its departure from Chaitén to correspond with the ferry's late running. Amongst the bus passengers were the *colilargo* couple, Tomás and Gabriela.

As the *Tehuelche* edged into Fiordo Reñihue, the isolation of Caleta Gonzalo became increasingly clear. All around, for absolutely miles, there was nothing but row upon row of Patagonian mountains rising out of the fjord like the backs of hippos. In damp air the coastal hills greyed into haze as we sailed across the channel and slipped silently past an array of salmon nets, huge circular booms on the dark water. The ferry soon nudged up against the ramp on Peninsula Huequi. None of my companions would understand, but it was privately an achievement of some satisfaction to set foot on the narrow Wirral-shaped protrusion of land.

Chaos exploded as soon as we disembarked. Foot passengers stacked their *mochilas* in a van to have them driven to the Leptepú ramp on the far side of the peninsula. There began the most insane episode of mass hitchhiking. Backpackers commandeered seats in family cars and climbed into the cargo wells of pickups, irrespective of any driver's permission or wishes. There also appeared to be a deal whereby the Kémelbus would carry foot passengers *gratis*, but of course the bus was already full; had nobody foreseen that this might present a problem? Due to the generosity of the family in the blue truck there were hikers in excessive numbers, probably many more than might usually board one single ferry, and more pressingly, one single Kémelbus.

The heaving mob piled onto the bus, crowding along the central aisle and dripping rain onto the seated paying passengers, who could have been forgiven any feelings of injustice that might have stirred within them. Virtually last to board, my lowly position on the front steps came with the benefit of a view through the windscreen, a fact that was to prove somewhat fortuitous. It was here, on a lonely road across Huequi, that one of the more unlikely boxes on my list was finally ticked. A strange, squat animal was padding about in the centre of the narrow road; at first, I thought it was an abandoned dog.

'¡*Pudú!*' shouted the driver, excitedly, causing a horde of standing passengers to lurch eagerly forward and start wiping mist from the glass.

She was short, unbelievably short for a deer. I knew these animals were small, but this was extraordinary. As described earlier, the *pudú* is about the size of a spaniel. She had stumpy legs, a dark brown coat and tiny antlers no longer than human fingers. She trotted unconcerned along the road in a lolloping spaniel-like way before disappearing into the forest.

No *huemul*. No puma. Almost certainly no *colilargo*.

A *pudú* sighting? Mission accomplished. *Pudú* successfully engaged.

In Patagonia, he who is last aboard the overcrowded bus... spies the *pudú*.

Image 21: Rhyolite magma dome – Volcán Chaitén

Twenty-Three: Corte de Luz

At the Leptepú *embarcadero*, foot-passengers had to wait in the rain whilst vehicles were loaded onto the second ferry, the *Mailen*. Reprobates who attempted to bypass the system were officiously reprimanded and sent away in disgrace. We gathered instead under overhanging branches in the mistaken belief that this would keep us dry. It could have been a photo shoot to model outdoor gear, all of us kitted out in jackets, ponchos and cagoules in reds, yellows, greens and blues, and everyone with a rain cover fitted over their *mochila*.

As we waited, each of us pretending not to be miserable, vehicles were selected from the queue and loaded onto the ferry, the bus in the centre. Each vehicle had to reverse aboard so as to face forward for unloading after the voyage. A car with a trailer proved troublesome, taking an age to manoeuvre. In the end they detached the wagon and pushed it back by hand. If the *Tehuelche* had resembled an aircraft carrier, then the *Mailen* was shaped like an oil tanker, with cars occupying the flat part, and the passenger lounge and captain's bridge at the stern.

The troop of hikers was finally invited on board, each one of us handing our *carnet*, identity card, to a member of the crew. Bags were stacked in a watertight vault. The moment that mine disappeared behind the steel door, I regretted not having taken a book for the long journey. We clunked up the metal steps to the lounge. The *Mailen* had better accommodation than the *Tehuelche* but it was still cramped. Not only the foot passengers, but all the vehicle occupants too, crammed together into a small lounge equipped with benched seating, catering hatch and a television. The backpacking horde had the misfortune of arriving last, and found the room already packed. For a while I shared a table with three motorcyclists.

'We're nine altogether,' they told me. 'Two guides and seven tourists.'

'Where are you from?' I asked.

'Canada. But the guides are German. They've ridden it several times, so they know the road.'

The ferry's late running had given them a problem. Their hotel reservations were not in Hornopirén, where we were to dock, but in Puerto Varas, a considerable ride north.

On deck later, I found shelter from the blustery wind at the stern, and dried out next to a huge metal grill through which a constant stream of cosy, warm air was blowing. Fiordo Leptepú was long and narrow, and tall mountains rose up on both sides. It was as though we were sailing through a gloomy tunnel: sea beneath, low cloud above and pressed in either side by shadowy mountain forms. The lights of tiny coastal settlements were visible to the east. As dusk fell, tailing the ferry was a pair of *toninas*, a small dolphin unique to Chilean waters, cavorting in our churning wake.

Back in the lounge, I paid for my passage at a booth alongside the catering hatch. The man handed back my *carnet* in return and was pleased to practice speaking English for a few minutes. When I squeezed onto a bench with Carlos and his friends, one of the Canadian bikers let his aggravation at the claustrophobic conditions get the better of him.

'We were here first,' he complained like a four-year old. 'Why can't you people sit still instead of coming and going the whole time?'

'Take it easy,' I told him. 'Look around you; it's full in here. Nobody is comfortable, but the only one complaining is you.'

My Chilean pals sniggered, and the rotund biker turned away with the expression of a distressed *pudú*. We probably upset him some more towards the end of our voyage when we all got up to herald the approaching lights of Hornopirén.

It was half past ten when we collected our bags from the vault. A ram that had been tied there throughout the journey had demonstrated his feelings about the arrangement by fertilising the area. The bikers thundered off to Puerto Varas, and we crystallised into a gang of seven with an urgent need for accommodation. Someone had heard of one *hospedaje* and another had been recommended a different place. But it proved rather hard to find street names in the dark, and in any case, who was likely to have seven beds free at this hour?

'Let's rent a *cabaña* together,' someone suggested. It would have been a good idea, had we been searching earlier in the evening.

By some circuitous route, we found our way to the *plaza de armas* where Carlos proposed a strategy. 'Let's all leave our *mochilas* in one place. Someone should volunteer to stay with the bags, and the rest of us will go in different directions to find what we can. See you back here in ten minutes.'

Gabriela volunteered to stay, possibly judging this a safe way to avoid unexpected encounters with any nocturnal *colilargos*. Searching as instructed, I happened upon a *residencial* on a back street nearby. A boisterous group was gathered in the dining area, but the owner, Yasmine, did indeed have vacant rooms, lots of them. I went for the others – seven had become eight in my absence – and we all piled into the *residencial* in a celebratory mood.

Trooping back out minutes later, we raided a supermarket, sneaking through the door just before it closed at half past eleven. Taking over the kitchen, we cooked an eclectic meal, drank *piscola* (a cocktail of *pisco* with cola favoured by young *Chilenos*) and chatted into the early hours. Firm friendships had formed during hours on the ferry, and everyone was bubbling with tales of their Patagonian adventures. It was as though the constrained atmosphere of the *Mailen* lounge had caused everyone to bottle up their stories, which, now uncorked, were flowing as readily as the *piscola*.

Most of us were nearing the end of several weeks on the road. As ever, my day had been packed with surprises, especially the blue van, the waterfall and the *pudú*, then the bonus of a communal midnight feast. At some unspeakable hour of the morning, I finally reclined on my bed, the room lit by the glow of an orange streetlight outside the window. What might there be to occupy a day or two in Hornopirén, I wondered? And afterwards, could I visit one of the villages along the road to Puerto Montt? But what was I doing, planning and scheming? It was time to sleep. The *ratón* couple, on the other hand, had to wake for the five o'clock bus. There were creaks and thuds as they crept downstairs, but aside from their departure, I slept deeply and for hours and hours.

*

Heavy rain beat its familiar percussion against the upstairs window. Looking out, the prospect was one of murky cloud. The last clear day must have been the volcano climb, now a distant memory. An unhurried breakfast was shared, and then in ones and twos, the *Mailen* group slipped away until my only companion was Cecilia, a medical student from Valdivia. With the storm easing, we took a midday walk, gingerly pulling on damp shoes and socks rather than risk anything dry. The house had no heating, unusually not even a log stove, and an unsightly assortment of wet clothes hung from the curtain rail in my room.

Defeated by the muddy riverside path, we headed instead through the town. A surprising number of houses doubled as grocery stores. Of course, this kind of thing can be seen all over the world, but in Hornopirén it seemed that every second household had decided to run a shop. Most had a Coca Cola signboard displaying a name such as Minimarket Rodrigo or Patty Bazar. Those with delusions of grandeur amusingly adopted the term *supermercardo* even though they, like all the others, had no greater facilities than a few grocery-stacked shelves behind a small counter.

The *Mailen* was preparing to sail. By this late stage of the season, she was less than half full, with only the returning Kémelbus and a handful of cars aboard. Boats cast sharp reflections in the glassy water. Tree-covered islands in the bay were laden with white clouds. The ferry departed with a friendly whistle, her conspicuous orange hull cheerfully bold as she slid through the mercury fjord.

A committee of ugly vultures dismembered a carcass on the beach. Further along the seafront, a flock of sanderlings scurried in unison, tiny frenetic birds darting in and out with each lapping wave to feed, their collective movement resembling a shoal of fish. A disdainful oystercatcher observed from his rocky castle, and a pair of curlew flew off screeching, tracing a broad arc low over the water and returning to land some distance away.

Marine industries were much in evidence. Numerous fishing boats were moored to colourful buoys on the placid bay, and the pebbled beach was littered with lobster pots, metre-diameter floats and acres of coiled, twisted nets. Behind tall metal fencing, premises adjacent to the beach contained a wide variety of nautical equipment and fish processing machinery. A whitewashed shrine against the wall enclosed a statue of San Pedro, patron saint of fishers, and a plaque told of one young fisherman who had failed to return from a night at sea.

*

Returning by a different route, we passed a gathering of rudimentary dwellings occupying a small plot of land, a group of shacks that would be known locally as a *campamento*. The buildings were constructed from plain boards and corrugated sheets, patched here and there with tarpaulin. Some of the houses were minimarkets, of course. The crudely cut roads lacked any kind of preparation, and the only sign that the area had been adopted by local authorities was the occasional street lamps. Living conditions in *pueblos* throughout the journey had been basic, but this *campamento* was amongst the most deprived. It was a world away from the glittering towers of central Santiago and the gated detached residences that look down on the city from Andean foothills.

Throughout South America, the polarisation of material wealth is palpable. Whilst the economy of Chile has grown impressively in recent decades, the benefits have not been served up to everyone in equal portion. Large numbers of people – children, working men and women, grandparents, whole families – have been left behind. Although Chile has been classified as a high income country by the World Bank, with Gross National Income per capita (GNI[67]) rising above US$12,616 for the first time in July 2013, extreme poverty is still pervasive and the contrast between rich and poor is alarming.

---

[67] Gross National Income (GNI) is a measure of income claimed by nationals of a particular country. It includes overseas income to nationals living abroad and excludes income to foreign residents within the country.

Chile's experiment with free market economics under Pinochet pioneered a movement that spread rapidly around the globe. Released from unwieldy restrictions and prohibitive tariffs, the unconstrained market has proved capable of invigorating trade, promoting entrepreneurship and ingenuity, and streamlining business processes. Some economists claim with steadfast certainty that there has never been a more effective vehicle for wealth creation than free market capitalism. A few go even further, adding that neither has there ever been a better system for ensuring global economic development and the reduction of poverty.

That's an attractive idea, but it doesn't appear to have worked. Arguably, in fact, the unfettered market has proved just as effective at creating poverty as prosperity. As a consequence of liberalisation, the command that each state has over its own national economy has been eroded, and the ease and speed with which capital can be transferred from one place to another has greatly increased. Wealth is increasingly concentrated in the hands of a minority. Those that profit most from this new reality are a few countries, a few transnational companies and a handful of influential individuals. Disenfranchised, disempowered and disadvantaged, the losers are the global poor.

The reality for many millions is that all they have to offer is their daily wage labour. Under a competitive system, wages (like everything else) become squeezed in drives for efficiency. Where there is surplus labour (almost everywhere), employers are free to name their price, and those who refuse to work for a reduced wage soon find they have no work at all. Effectively, human labour becomes a commodity that can be purchased or rejected at will. Employers may feel that their hands are tied by competitors able to undercut their prices. One side of this equation is a ready supply of cheap products for thirsty consumers; the other side, directly connected, spawns sweatshops, industrial accidents and child labour.

Although these inequalities are particularly apparent in parts of South America, they are actually a disturbingly prevalent feature of the modern world as a whole. Whereas some luxuriate with private housing, private healthcare, private education and yachts, others stare daily into the scornful faces of oppression, repression, hookworm and hunger. The story is all too familiar but it doesn't have to be this way. Let's not lose our fervour in the fight against injustice and greed.

Income inequalities

A range of statistical methods exist for describing the wealth distribution and income inequalities of a country or region. One measure published by the UNDP (United Nations Development Project) is the Quintile Income Ratio (sometimes referred to as the 20:20 ratio), which compares the incomes of the richest and poorest 20 per cent in each country. In the 2013 Human Development Report, the richest 20 per cent in Chile were reported to have 13.5 times the income of the poorest 20 per cent. Giving this figure some Latin American context, Argentina, Peru, Uruguay and Venezuela all had ratios between 10.3 and 11.5, Brazil scored 20.6, and the wealthiest 20 per cent in Bolivia had 27.8 times the income of the poorest.

Some development professionals consider the Quintile Income Ratio to be rather unsophisticated and prefer alternative techniques. A common measure of income inequalities is the Gini coefficient. In broad terms, Gini is a measure of dispersion away from perfect equality, with values ranging from zero (perfect equality) to one (absolute inequality). The Gini coefficient for incomes in Chile has been measured at 0.521, a high score for any OECD country. Again, the coefficients for Brazil (0.547) and Bolivia (0.563) reflect even greater inequality there.

All statistics have shortcomings, however, and it pays to be circumspect about straight comparisons between countries. These figures don't convey anything about the wealth of those people in absolute terms; we cannot tell whether the poorer Chileans have higher or lower weekly incomes than the poorer Brazilians or Bolivians. Nor do they indicate anything about the relative spending power of incomes in each country. Furthermore, a single-year snapshot like this disguises any upward or downward trend, whether inequalities are increasing or decreasing over time. It is also worth remembering that data like these can be notoriously difficult to collect and harder to verify. Understanding poverty is complex and making simplistic statements or assumptions is best avoided. What this does indicate, though, is that although prosperity has increased in some Latin American countries, the distribution of that wealth is subject to inequalities that are relatively large in global terms.

> A third technique, which is relatively new, was devised by the Chilean economist Gabriel Palma. It is a measure that specifically compares the 'wealthy few' with the 'poorer many'. Take the income share of the highest 10 per cent of earners in a country or region and divide it by that of the lowest 40 per cent; this gives a figure that some call the 'Palma ratio'. One rationale for this calculation is as follows. Across many countries, even with diverse economic circumstances, it is not unusual to find that around 50 per cent of Gross National Income (GNI) falls to around 50 per cent of the population (who could loosely be described as the 'middle classes'). Noting the stability of this pattern between countries, Palma wanted to set aside the middle portion and give more attention to the two extremes. He found that countries vary considerably in terms of the income share commanded by the richest 10 per cent and the poorest 40 per cent. Palma's work has generated a flurry of discussion on whether this new measure might come to replace the Gini coefficient in development dialogue.

*

On the river bank in Hornopirén, there was a salmon nursery. A broad yellow tube ran from transportation chambers on a flat-backed truck to the permanent tanks of the *salmonera*. Dark shapes were swimming down the tube: a delivery of baby salmon. They were going to be confused if they ever tried to swim back upstream to their place of birth.

Rival packs of feral dogs were patrolling territories in the plaza. A handwritten note in the window of the Buses Fierro office listed departure times. Three services left for Puerto Montt each morning, at 4:55am, 5:20am and 7:30am. A more comfortably attainable departure was scheduled for 1:30pm.

When the rain returned, I spent an hour or two with my one remaining study book, cooped up in my sock-perfumed room. The lack of any opening window compounded the ventilation problem, so I removed the offending items to the corridor. The spell of academic exercise must have awakened a creative area of my brain. I suddenly realised that the damp socks I'd been wearing had dried, unlike those hanging on the curtain rail. Wearing wet socks appeared to be an efficient way of drying them; I don't remember learning about that in science classes. I peeled off the dry socks and replaced them with a second damp pair. By nightfall, all were dry.

That evening, Yasmine prepared some delicious crepes with *helado* and *manjar*.[68] Energised by the sugar overdose, I headed out again: back over the bridge, past the *salmonera* and up an unlit road leading north. Amongst the properties was a holiday *cabaña* declared as vacant. Beyond this was the noisy power plant. The smells and rattles of diesel generators were somehow a disappointment after the hydroelectric installations of so many other *pueblos*.

A car stopped. 'Do you know the area?' asked the driver.

'Yes,' I replied. 'I live here.'

When will I learn not to tell such ridiculous fibs?

'I need a place to stay,' he continued. 'There are three of us, my two daughters and me. We were delayed on the road. Do you know where we might find a room?'

'Yes of course,' I said, and told him about the empty *cabaña* just down the road.

Further up the dark hill, there was a solitary house set back up a long drive. Light blazed invitingly from the windows. A morose cloud enveloped my spirit, giving rise to a sudden yearning for something more permanent than the traveller's bed. How refreshing it would be to enjoy the company of people I'd known for more than a day or two. That was far enough for a night walk, especially with thoughts turning precariously melancholic. After chatting a second time with the travelling family, by then unloading their possessions into the *cabaña*, I whispered goodnight to the salmon hatchlings tucked up in fishy beds for a first night in their new home. I was just through the *plaza de armas* when the lights went out: the street lights; the shop lights; the house lights; everything. *Corte de luz*. Someone had forgotten to fill the tank with diesel.

Just then, a group of backpackers approached, recently off the boat. Apparently my reputation as an accommodation consultant had spread.

'We need a place to camp,' they said. 'Do you know of anywhere?'

The only camping I'd seen was some distance out of town, and given that it was already late, I recommended my *residencial* instead,

---

[68] *Helado* is ice cream. We met *manjar* in Chapter 21; it is a sweet spread of caramelised milk, known outside Chile as *dulce de leche*.

and the weary hikers accompanied me there. The lack of *luz* precluded any further viewing of the Viña festival, so like the baby salmon, I was soon in bed. Sometime later I became half aware of the street lights flickering back into life, but by that stage I was almost asleep, dreaming of swimming into the dark unknown through a long yellow tube.

*

Waking unexpectedly at seven, I was tempted to hurry for the early bus; early for me, that is, but actually the third departure that day. Predictably, that inspired idea was soon lost in a couple more hours of dozy slumber. The highlight of breakfast, when at last I surfaced, was savouring a last Fortnum & Mason Countess Grey tea brewed from a stowaway bag discovered hiding in my disorganised *mochila*.

Puerto Montt, where my midweek flight departed, was now within reach of a single direct bus. Rather than go all the way at once, my plan was to visit one of the intermediate towns, so I bought a ticket as far as Contao. The bus departed punctually at one-thirty, taking the same road past the *cabaña* and the power plant, where someone had topped up the diesel. In El Manzano,[69] a large group of children with their adult leaders was lucky to squash on board. The vehicle was now packed, with the youngsters standing in the central aisle. Those waiting further along were about to find out that this bus would not stop for them.

Ninety minutes later, I escaped from the crowded capsule into the cool, fresh air of Contao village. I collected my bag from the luggage locker beneath, and sheltered in a porch because, of course, it was raining. Standing there watching the fat drops falling, it didn't take long to be persuaded of the merits of Residencial Reloncaví, right across the road. Not only had the rain washed away any motivation I might otherwise have had to compare lodging options further afield, I also reasoned that this same spot would be a likely place to join the Puerto Montt bus the following morning.

---

[69] This was a second village called El Manzano. The name means 'The Apple Tree' whereas *manzana* is an apple. Similarly, *naranja* is an orange, and *naranjo* an orange tree. The same pattern applies for various other fruits and their trees.

For the first and only time in the trip, my room had a private bathroom and cable TV. It was clean and modern, a treat for the penultimate sleep of my adventure. I tested the mattress and surfed TV channels for a few minutes to absorb the sense of luxury before heading out. With just one afternoon in this tiny town, I wanted to make the most of it.

On a corner close to the *residencial* was a very smart tourist information centre.

'What is there to do around here?' I asked.

The girl began to tell me about Hornopirén.

'But what about here?' I interrupted.

'Most people go to Hornopirén,' she admitted, glancing up nervously.

'But suppose I'd already been there,' I insisted, 'what could I do here in Contao?'

Now she looked very anxious, not to mention bewildered. It seemed that no-one had ever asked this before. She took a deep breath. 'Well, you could climb the *volcán*, but you would need a guide.'

'Is there no marked trail?' I asked.

'No,' she confirmed. So that was that.

'Is your family from Contao?' I asked the girl.

'Yes, I've always lived here,' she said. 'It's quiet, but I like it.'

A pair of backpackers were sheltering in the tourist office and running outside to hitchhike whenever a vehicle approached. This technique was not meeting with much success.

'At what time of the morning do the early buses pass here?' I asked the girl.

'Usually before half past six,' she said, 'but you may have to stand.'

'That's okay,' I said, 'as long as I arrive in Puerto Montt.'

'Oh yes, you'll get there,' she nodded. But then her concerned face reappeared and she checked her calendar. 'Ah,' she said, clearly troubled now. 'The bus will definitely be *very* full; the teachers get paid tomorrow.'

I was left to wonder what the connection might be between the teachers getting paid and the bus being full. Did they have to collect their wages in Puerto Montt? Or could it be, I speculated, that every month on payday the teachers organised a bus outing together to celebrate?

Contao had fewer homes masquerading as supermarkets than did Hornopirén, but as they had been there, the dwellings were simple and the streets were strewn with puddle-filled holes. Major renovations were underway at the school, where the yard was stacked with bricks, pipework, timber and discarded window frames. A new block was glazed and painted and looked almost ready; a good thing given that classes would restart the following week, and especially considering that the due date stated on a large noticeboard had long passed.

A narrow road down a gentle slope at the edge of the village led to a substantial dark-green building beside the *aeródromo*, suspiciously hangar-like in appearance but now in use as a sports hall. A footpath crossed the grass runway and led through undergrowth. Juicy, ripe blackberries lined the way to a pebbly beach. This sea was the Seno de Reloncaví, that huge rounded bay I'd admired six weeks previously from a hilltop in Puerto Montt. Standing now at its opposite side, the full circuit of my journey was almost complete. There were islands in the bay, and the coast of mainland Chile lay beyond. I skimmed pebbles across the water under the watchful gaze of a lone egret. A pair of oystercatchers paddled in the shallows wearing their comedy outfits: white belly, brown back, long pink sticks for legs, orange berries for eyes set into a jet black head, and an oversized beak resembling a snowman's carrot nose.

*

The tourist office girl had recommended a restaurant along the main road, beyond a pair of bridges spanning twin channels of the Río Contao. Los Braseros resembled a quiet country pub... if a country pub could be faced with yellow shingles and have a corrugated roof. Chairs inside were stacked on table tops like in a school classroom. Behind the bar, an old man balanced on a tall stool, arranging cartons of wine on high shelves.

'Are you open?' I asked.
'No.'
'Will you open later?'
'No, only tomorrow.'
'Is there anywhere I can get dinner?'
'Yes, in Puelche,' he helpfully replied.
'Is there anywhere nearer? I don't have a car.'

He smiled. 'Try the *residencial* up the road.'

Residencial Mary was a short walk away. Groups of men sat at tables in two adjoining rooms, hungrily tucking into their evening meal.

'Any chance of dinner?' I asked at the kitchen.

'Yes, we have fresh salmon,' both ladies replied, almost in unison. 'Are you hungry?' they both enquired, the duet continuing. 'Take a place at the table,' both said. 'We'll bring you some dinner.'

I sat with the smaller group who, they explained, had lodgings there at Residencial Mary whilst they worked on the school renovation. I thought it best not to mention the overdue deadline. Others were working at a *salmonera*. In the centre of the table were a basket of bread and a bowl of *ají*. My companions laughed to see my enthusiasm for the hot sauce. Next came a bowl of tasty soup and finally, as promised, salmon with potato. I'm not sure if restaurants in my homeland would have fried the tender, pink salmon in batter but when you're feeding workmen and salmon is the commonly available fish, this is what they expect. The men were welcoming and chatty. As we ate our battered salmon and washed it down with strong coffee, we watched a few minutes of an incomprehensible horror film on an ancient fuzzy-screened television that rested on a bureau in a corner of the room.

I returned to the kitchen to pay.

'You were hungry, weren't you?' both ladies agreed. 'Wasn't he hungry?' they remarked to each other. 'He was hungry,' they both said to a man at the sink.

'*Muchas gracias*,' I interjected. '*¡Muy rico!*'

'*De nada*,' they both replied. 'You were hungry, weren't you?'

Contented, I ambled along the wet road, crossed the pair of bridges and cut into the town. I bought a *Super 8*, and the assistant, who seemed excited to have an Englishman in her shop, wanted to chat for a while. In spite of the late hour, I returned to the *aeródromo* and perched on a tree stump that afforded a view across the sea. Occasional sets of village lights, sporadically arranged, punctuated the curve of the dark shore. Beyond these, on the far side of that expansive bay, Puerto Montt glimmered reassuringly, like the expiring embers of a late evening fire.

Image 22: Supermarket

THE DICTATOR'S HIGHWAY

Map 17: Hornopirén, Contao and Puerto Montt

Twenty-Four: Lomo a lo Pobre

The red digital display at the bedside flashed 01:30.
Waking a second time, 04:01.
And finally 05:59. Time to go.

I prowled through the silent house, intruder-like in the gloom, careful to avoid colliding with furniture or knocking anything with my wobbling backpack. The front door opened without difficulty – that was a relief – and I slipped out. I'd taken no more than a pace or two across the yard when a bus swept past the gate.

¡Pucha!

I shuffled dejectedly to the road. Another bus!

Flailing my arms madly, I raced into the carriageway. The huge beast shuddered by, growling away into the night.

¡Pucha! ¡Pucha! ¡Pucha! Surely that can't have been the 4:55 *and* the 5:20? The second departure couldn't have reached Contao in only 70 minutes, could it? With all the determination I could muster, I hoped not, but with a gut full of doubt, I feared that it just might have. And they'd both been full, with passengers even standing in the central aisle; bloody teachers.

Grateful for a rudimentary shelter on the verge, I rested my *mochila* against the inside wall. A black puppy materialised out of the inky night, causing me to jump. For a moment it juggled with a plastic bag before pushing through the flaps of an upended cardboard box and settling down to sleep.

Two vehicles passed, pushing a pool of light ahead of them on the wet road. I made a lame request for a ride, but they didn't stop, hardly surprising given the sudden attentions of a shadowy apparition at half past six that rainy morning.

Quite unexpectedly, I felt a peculiar and unfamiliar sense of contentment. Despite having sufficient material to agonise over, I didn't feel terribly upset. Alone in the dark and locked out of my *residencial* with its comfortable mattress and cable TV, there was nothing to be gained by fretting. The 7:30 bus would pass by nine o'clock and another, the service I'd used yesterday, left Hornopirén at half past one.

'I will get to Puerto Montt,' I resolved, 'and that is my only target for the day.' Moreover, it seemed unlikely that the 5:20 had already gone by. Perhaps a second company also had a five o'clock departure. That would explain the two buses passing in rapid succession.

All had been quiet since the pair of cars. With no bench in the shelter, I leant back on the slatted rear wall, wishing I was a puppy who could curl up in a cardboard box. Resting my eyes, I contemplated whether it was possible to sleep standing up and wondered how long it might be before I could get back into the *residencial* for some breakfast.

Travelling unaccompanied had provided frequent moments for introspection. Two incidents in Villa O'Higgins had set up an opportune state of disequilibrium. One was the demoralising day-long failure to hitchhike and the other was Luci's timely comment along the lines of 'Enjoy the road and cast aside your predetermined goals.' Her words had ruffled my feathers at the time, but she was right. In stark contrast to my life in Santiago, a defining characteristic of the whole journey had been the absence of prescriptive structures and rigid timescales. Relishing the liberty that comes with anonymity, I'd been able to respond spontaneously to impulsive whims without worrying unduly about where they led. It had been uplifting to tune in to the preferences and wishes that arise quietly from deep within, rather than having to negotiate a tangle of sensitivities at every turn. One of Patagonia's lessons seemed to be about letting go, or at least slackening the reins.

The sound of an engine returned me abruptly to the present. It came closer... a bus! I grabbed my *mochila* and danced into the centre of the road. The vehicle came to a stop and the door opened slowly with a pneumatic hiss. *¡Estupendo!* Next to the gangway in the third row, there was an empty seat. *¡Qué maravilloso!*

Many of the passengers were sleeping. I briefly dozed too, but woke at the ferry queue in Puelche. A bend in the dark road made it impossible to see how far the line extended. A woman wrapped in long skirts climbed aboard and edged down the aisle, skilfully balancing a tray piled high with film-wrapped breakfast rolls. A few minutes later we edged forward down the slope and clunked over the iron ramp onto the ship, taking our place in line behind the two earlier buses.

The Estuario Reloncaví was choppy, and the six-kilometre crossing became the roughest of the whole trip. I stood out on deck to dismiss an unwelcome queasiness. A pelican soared past on huge wings, effortlessly overtaking the boat. The sister ferry headed in the opposite direction on our starboard side. Dawn crept up virtually unnoticed, the indigo sky turning battleship grey before easing almost indiscernibly into paler shades. That was the best the new morning could muster. Eventually, Caleta La Arena came into view, a huddle of houses at the foot of colossal coastal mountains. A short row of trucks was waiting there at the *embarcadero*.

I rejoined the bus, and we bumped back onto land, still in third place behind the two five o'clock departures. One hour to Puerto Montt. The road was etched onto a rocky shelf above the waterline. With the backdrop becoming increasingly urban, this final stretch of the highway was paved.

On arrival, the densely packed tall buildings seemed quite alien after rural Patagonia, and so did the broad streets awash with traffic. And although Puerto Montt was not such a large city, there was something intimidating about the thronging, engulfing crowds.

*

Time becomes dislocated after an early start. You somehow forget that others will be following a more conventional schedule. When I reported to the aptly named Hospedaje Patagonia to request a room, it was quite a jolt to find that guests there were only sitting down to breakfast. The receptionist suggested I returned later, so I found a quiet corner in a café along the *costanera* to escape the hefty drops of rain.

A large, tatty map of Patagonia hung on the wall, depicting the course of the Carretera Austral from Puerto Montt to Villa O'Higgins or, as my case had been, the reverse route from south to north. The road looked like the straggly, fragile stem of a sickly plant, generally upright but haplessly kinked here and there. Fat berries along the stalk were labelled with newly-familiar names: Puyuhuapi, Puerto Río Tranquilo and Hornopirén. Thin twigs stuck out on either side to reach further red dots: Caleta Tortel, Puerto Cisnes and Puerto Guadal.

Until recently, all these towns and villages had belonged to the undiscovered mysteries of a far-off land. Now, each one evoked a collection of memories and stories: volcanoes and glaciers, hiking and rafting, rivers and lakes, rainforest and reforestation, mines and airstrips.

One intriguing thing about Chilean Patagonia was how recently the human story had unfolded there. So wild and unexplored was the region that even the *frontera* between Chile and Argentina was yet to be fully agreed. No significant human settlement had been established until the twentieth century,[70] and the *pueblos* count their histories only in decades. Coyhaique and Cochrane were established in 1929 and 1930, Chaitén and Puyuhuapi in 1935, Hornopirén in 1939 and Villa O'Higgins not until 1966. Given their recent arrival on the map, many of these little communities felt surprisingly old. That's not to say that they were historic, just that they appeared tired and worn. Many of them gave the unambiguous impression of being places where daily existence is a perpetual struggle.

Despite this weary veneer, signs of an unfolding transformation poked through like crocuses in spring, most visibly evident in the building work underway throughout the region. Numerous housing projects were complemented by various other construction schemes including school renovations in Contao and Cochrane, a new community library in La Junta and a refurbished sports arena in Puerto Guadal. Town centre streets were being paved, bridges strengthened and the boardwalk *costanera* replaced in Caleta Tortel. All this development was made possible, or at least had been greatly accelerated, by the region's most influential recent change: the construction of the dictator's highway.

---

[70] Although modern settlement of Chilean Patagonia is recent, archaeological evidence shows that there may have been human habitation near Coyhaique 8000 years ago, and there are sites near Puerto Montt that may even be 12,500 years old.

Another sign of Patagonia's evolution was the expansion of tourism, with fly fishing, hiking, cycling, white water rafting, glacier boat trips and excursions on the ice fields all on offer. I crossed paths with visitors from France, Belgium and Switzerland, from Israel and Italy, from Argentina and Spain, from Canada, Australia and the United States, and the list goes on. Having arrived to the region by air, land or sea, travellers were making journeys by bicycle or motorcycle, in all-terrain leisure vehicles, in a custom-built hotel trailer, on buses, and in some rare cases, even on foot… and all of them, along the Carretera Austral.

Some of my most memorable encounters were with young *Chilenos*: the Tsonek Four in Villa O'Higgins, the Pumalín Four in El Amarillo, the Colilargo Four in Chaitén and finally the Hornopirén Eight. These *chicos* were clearly proud of their country. Most were passionately committed to a vision of Chilean prosperity. Young people like these will inherit responsibility for the onward direction of the nation. What will they make of this long and narrow land, and how will they treat her people?

One question that tomorrow's leaders will face is what to do with Patagonia. The same road that opens up the region to new possibilities simultaneously poses a threat to her unspoiled nature. Chile has a growing population and a strengthening economy.[71] There are reckoned to be fewer metal ores in this region than in the higher Andes further north, but the south of Patagonia has coal, oil and gas. To some, it is self-evident that Chilean authorities should extract these reserves. But why does humanity assume the right to rake up the planet's resources irrespective of cost and consequence? As an alternative, might tomorrow herald the coming of an era in which the world's remaining wild lands, places like Chilean Patagonia, can come to enjoy robust and meaningful protection?

It was inspiring to meet people taking tangible steps to protect the natural environment. There was the volunteer *guardaparque* at Tamango with her desire to protect the *huemul*. Rocio and Marcelo at

---

[71] In the 60 years between 1950 and 2010, the population of Chile expanded from around 6 million to over 17 million. GDP per capita in 2012 ($15,245) was more than seven times greater than 30 years previously ($2,109) (GDP figures in US dollars, adjusted to 2014 values). GDP (Gross Domestic Product) is an estimate of the gross value of all the economic activities in a country. It is usually measured in one of three ways: by production, by income or by expenditure.

Un Destino No Turístico had adopted a lifestyle following the 'Leave No Trace' principles and ran workshops to motivate others to follow suit. John was seeking to reforest the Valle Leones. On an even greater scale, there was the ambitious conservation work underway at Parque Pumalín.

Inevitable calls for development will increase the pressures on the region. Decades ago, early colonisers cleared acres of forest by lighting fires that burned for years. Today, the contrast between the forested north and the denuded grazing land further south is horrifying. You could argue that razing the forests represented progress in a direction that was good and beneficial, or you might think not. As Chilean young people become leaders and discuss plans for Patagonia and her natural riches, they might do well to consider the impact of those fires in order to guard against rehashing the mistakes of the past.

Spending time with these Chilean students also prompted me to reflect on the varied prospects laid out before the world's young people. Some were studying at Chile's top universities, a solid foundation on which to build a secure career. Others, like Claudia, had been delayed in their school lives by a year of tumultuous protests. Whilst Chilean education provision is marred by arresting inequalities, how much wider is the gulf when one country is compared to another within and between the distinct continents of the world? The participants on the Leadership Camp at Tamango had received that enviable opportunity in accordance with their talent and dedication but equally as a result of their nationality and wealth. In time, will these future leaders seek to redress such imbalances or, through either action or inaction, might they reinforce them?

For my own part, I suspect I took my schooldays for granted and considered a university education to be mine by right. Wasn't it closer to the truth that those years were a priceless gift, an annually repeating series of treasures showered upon me when I was too innocent to understand their potential and too inexperienced to invest in their true worth?

Stepping back from the map to order a mug of hot chocolate, I wondered how many of my compatriots would be able to cope with living in this part of Patagonia. I thought of the simplicity of Pancho's house and the back-breaking work of Pablo and his yoke of steers. I contemplated the itinerant lives of the *gauchos*, genuine cowboys. Even moreso, what must it have been like for the earliest pioneers in a place like Puerto Cisnes, determinedly surviving under temporary shelters and dining daily on shellfish? What must it be like even now to live in the manner of Don Vicente, a gentle and generous man who had spent much of his life tending livestock high on a mountain, who once travelled a short distance away but 'didn't like it much' and who couldn't understand why some of his neighbours wanted a supply of electricity connected to their homes?

Don Vicente quite spontaneously showed me great kindness. Many others, too, without any obligation or need, were similarly thoughtful. From the shop owner in Villa O'Higgins who charged my camera battery to the two chefs in Contao who spared a battered chunk of salmon, the people of Patagonia were considerate and generous. Some of them directed me along the way or gave advice, others shared their food, and plenty offered a place to stay. Then there were those who simply gave their interest and their time, who enquired about my world and told me of theirs.

More than anything else, such people as these gave my journey its gilt edge: Mauricio the birdman, hospitable Renata in Caleta Tortel, rodent-phobic Gabriela, Lorenzo the cyclist, Nomi in Coyhaique who treated me like a member of her family, Dana and his GPS colleagues, Philippe who fished for his supper in Puerto Bertrand, and trainee doctor Cecilia in Hornopirén. There were plenty of others whose names were already slipping from my grasp or that I never knew to begin with: the climber on Cerro Castillo, stripy t-shirt girl in the Raúl Marín tourist office, the two women who rescued me from the *huelga*, a busload of workmen on the road to Chaitén and dozens of individuals with whom I shared a breakfast table or a ferry ride.

And finally, another important group helped tremendously. For all I have complained about the drivers that ignored my pleading and petitioning thumb, let me candidly record my gratitude to those who gave me a ride along the Carretera Austral, who stopped of their own volition and with nothing to gain, even when I was miserably drenched by the rain.

In the end, I didn't return to Hospedaje Patagonia but tried instead further from the town centre, towards the Navimag port: the Hospedaje Costanera had no vacant rooms; the Altamar offered me a broom cupboard with half a bed inside; but just along the road, above a parade of shops, was a bright and cheery alternative, the Hostal Bahia de Reloncaví – *perfecto*.

A haircut was my next priority. I returned to the same *peluquería*, but the clipper-wielding *señora* showed no sign of recognising me. In an internet café next door, I checked my flight time on the Lan website and emailed the kind-hearted family who had carried my books to Santiago. At the artisans' market along the promenade, I bought hand-knitted alpaca-wool gifts for nephews and nieces and Patagonian honey for *Santiaguino* friends. And as dusk fell, I celebrated my journey's end at the Cirus Bar with a jug of *schop* Torobayo and a meal. *Lomo a lo pobre,* of course.

Image 23: Weary Feet

Epilogue

In the months that followed my Carretera Austral adventure, I continued to discover new holes in my belt, finally graduating to the fifth hole by April. Further progress has proved elusive; it's too easy to graze from the fridge whilst writing.

The *huelga* in Aysén continued throughout February 2012. Though most protests remained peaceful, a few turned violent, especially at the orange bridge outside Puerto Aysén where demonstrators and *carabineros* sustained injuries. At the beginning of March, the government reiterated that they would only commence dialogue once all the roadblocks had been removed. Leaders of the protest movement passed a resolution to dismantle the barricades a week later. This move, they insisted, was to reduce the hardship suffered by local residents and not due to any pressure from the authorities.

School and university students resumed their *manifestaciones* after the summer break. Three successive Ministers of Education instigated a flurry of policy reforms before each one was harangued from the post, dejected and demoralised. Student loan interest repayments were capped at two per cent. Scholarships were announced to target students from less-wealthy backgrounds who would also be able to take up university places with lower scores in the admissions examinations. Complaining that these initiatives failed to address their central concerns, students kept marching and campuses were occupied again. This time, *carabineros* responded rapidly and with force, and ugly eviction scenes at schools and universities were broadcast on national news channels.

The Commission of Inquiry into Higher Education concluded that the law forbidding profit-making in education was ineffective, naming seven universities that had generated profits through mechanisms related to salaries, premises, outsourcing and tax avoidance. Allegations of corruption and money-laundering were published, leading to the arrest of senior university figures and the imprisonment of the official in charge of university accreditation. This was followed by the resignation of the Justice Minister, whose close links to that official and to a private university under investigation implicated him in the controversy.

The student campaign continued into 2013, during which time increasing attention fell on the education policies proposed by candidates for the approaching presidential election. Front-runner and former president Michelle Bachelet promised to eliminate profit-making in publically-financed educational institutions. She also offered free university education, first for the poorest students and ultimately for all students within a timescale of six years.

In January 2012, President Sebastián Piñera outlined an eight-point plan for meeting Chile's energy needs, including a call to expand hydroelectric generation. By that time, a Chilean government subcommittee had already given preliminary approval for the HidroAysén dams, but the companies involved were instructed not to commence construction, pending the resolution of objections raised at the Court of Appeals. When the complaint was finally rejected by the Supreme Court in April 2012, thousands of protestors marched in Santiago. In June 2012, one of the two principal HidroAysén partners, Colbún SA, suspended work on an environmental impact study relating to the high-voltage transmission lines and accused the government of lacking a clear energy policy. With this move putting in doubt Colbún's further involvement in the project, the other partner, Endesa Chile, removed HidroAysén from their list of active projects as presented to investors at the end of 2013.

The global trading price of copper continues to support a strong Chilean economy. From a peak of $4.50 per pound early in 2011, the price declined somewhat and traded at around $3.50 per pound for most of 2012 and something over $3.00 per pound since mid-2013 (US dollars and pounds weight). Despite the downward movement, copper still commands a much higher price than in the period between 1990 and 2005 when it was priced at values between $0.50 and $1.50 per pound.

Chile witnessed three *hantavirus* deaths in February 2012 and several other patients were hospitalised. One factor may have been summer wildfires that drove rat colonies closer to areas of human population.

Fish farming representatives from Chile, Norway and Scotland met during 2012 to find ways of tackling the problems associated with commercial salmon production. The Global Salmon Initiative (GSI) was launched in April that year, aiming to improve the sustainability of the industry and reduce its environmental impact. By 2050, a projected 500 million people may depend on farmed fish as a regular food supply. The World Wide Fund for Nature (WWF) stated that the GSI could significantly improve the welfare of salmon populations both farmed and in the wild.

In April 2013, Transportes Aéreos Don Carlos flew for the final time between Coyhaique and Villa O'Higgins, concluding 35 years of Patagonian service. The route is now operated by the carrier Aerocord.

The eruption of Volcán Chaitén spurred the government agency SERNAGEOMIN, *Servicio Nacional de Geologia y Mineria*, to improve the monitoring of Chile's 43 high-threat volcanoes. Two thousand people were evacuated in May 2013, when activity at Volcán Copahue on the Chile-Argentina border southeast of Los Ángeles was found to be increasing. In the event, the volcano vented only ash and gas.

Late in his presidential term, Sebastián Piñera caused mild controversy by sitting at Barack Obama's Oval Office desk on a visit to Washington. Such behaviour contravenes White House protocols and the locals were not amused.

Michelle Bachelet won the presidential election in late 2013 and commenced her second term in office the following March. The new government cancelled the HidroAysén project in June 2014, removing authorisation for construction of the dams and the transmission lines. The Bachelet administration also introduced what they termed the 'most significant education reform in 50 years'. The first emphasis was a set of proposals for the funding, support, evaluation and regulation of preschool education. A second strand of measures was designed to address the issues of profit, selection of entrants and the payments required from parents in publically-subsidised schools. The proposals were criticised for failing to address the notoriously low salaries of teachers.

Negotiations are underway between the Chilean Ministry of Works and representatives of Parque Pumalín to discuss the construction of a 60-kilometre link from Hornopirén to Caleta Gonzalo. Such a road would enhance connectivity by eliminating the twin ferries either side of Peninsula Huequi. The proposed highway, through the virgin forest of the park, has not been universally popular. Aside from those who think the plan should be abandoned completely, disagreement has centred on whether the route should follow the coast or take an inland course.

There are also proposals to extend the Carretera Austral beyond Villa O'Higgins all the way to Puerto Natales. This would complete an overland connection between the southernmost Magallanes Region and the rest of Chile. The suggested 935-kilometre route could include as many as nine ferry crossings, and when it opens in 2040 will be a good excuse for another book.

Image 24: The Carretera Austral near Fiordo Mitchell

Acknowledgements

Exploring Patagonia alone was a less solitary activity than at first I anticipated. In every stage of the journey, I was pleased to enjoy company at some point or other. Never a day passed that failed to include a conversation, a shared joke, a handshake, an idle chat with a shop assistant or a rapid greeting with a determined traveller hurrying in the opposite direction.

I have been similarly blessed with committed companions during the subsequent long trek of writing. I am indebted to a team of kindly folk from five continents (or four if you count the Americas as one) who urged me forward, held up maps, pointed out directions or suggested alternative paths. In the next few lines, I express my thanks to many of those who lent a hand, proposed contrasting viewpoints or dragged me out of the sand.

It has been fascinating to discover how little I know about grammar and the rules for writing English. Maybe you noticed. Happily, it seems to be accepted in modern writing that rules can be broken without great harm, and that most reasonable forms of expression will suffice as long as they do not confuse or mislead. For any glaring errors that remain, I apologise. There might have been many more, but for the efforts of a formidable troop of proofreading pixies. Thank you to the members of this dedicated crew, who each combed through a chapter or two: to Adrian, Alicia, Ally, Anna, Bekki, Claire, Daniel, Debbye, Duncan, Gemma, Genette, Helen, Jane, Jo, Jude, Kathi, Kirsty, Liz, Lyndsey, Martin, Michael, Michelle, Nicola, Richard, Sara, Shana, Sheila, Sue and Vicky. An additional thank you those in this list who would not be satiated, and kept asking for more.

Much, much earlier, way back, long before we got anywhere near proofreading, a core team of diplomatic and patient people read the earliest drafts and very gently explained quite how much needed to change. For your honest feedback I thank Jane, Mike, Roy, Shaz and Vicky. For going above and beyond, and beyond, and beyond, and beyond, sincere thanks to Helen, Jack and Kate. To those who helped with in-country research and with checking and correcting Spanish (or Chilean) language expressions and vocabulary, *muchas gracias* to Carolina and Maribel.

I am indebted to Caroline, who produced the artwork for the front cover. Not only for your talent in concocting this exceptional final image, but also for your generous and forgiving spirit over tortuous months of amendments and revisions.

Thank you to those who originally offered me the chance to work in Chile, and to all who made the experience so satisfying, so enjoyable and so worthwhile. My work contract included somewhere to live, which was handy. Declining further employment left me somewhat lacking in the roof-over-head department. Consequently, I owe a great deal to those who have provided bed and board. Thank you to Simon, Rachel and Jeffrey for temporary lodgings in Santiago. Enormous thanks to Stephanie and Roger in Chelmsford for allowing me to extend 'a couple of weeks' into 'a couple of years', for a desk with a very funky lamp, for giving me a writer's room with two windows, and for a rare kind of patience. Thanks also to their two daughters, for commendable tolerance and occasional cups of tea.

This book has been a long time coming. But, as we know, he who hurries…

It has been an arduous journey, and I'm deeply grateful to all who have supported me, momentarily or throughout. Many have encouraged me and exhorted me to keep going. The confidence expressed by others helped me find reserves of energy and inspiration when I stood at the base of the mountain in the rain. To all of you, dear family and friends, I thank you.

Special and particular thanks to Louise, who never gave up, who lifted my head, who listened, who believed, and who never turned her back. You may never realise how much you gave. Thank you.

About the Author

Justin Walker is a restless person who sometimes writes.

In the past, he has been a teacher in Lancashire, Yorkshire and Essex, an education consultant in West Africa, and a headteacher in Chile.

Still intent on pursuing discovery and growth, he has not yet tired of seeking unconventional pathways to interesting places.

For more of Justin's writing, visit his website.

Additional colour photographs from *The Dictator's Highway* are also available there.

---

justinwalkerwriter.wordpress.com - stories across borders

Dictating Your Own Highway

This is a work of non-ficton, based on real events. Where practical, permission has been obtained from the characters mentioned in the narrative. In some cases, names and identifying characteristics of individuals and businesses have been modified to protect their privacy.

Aside from these changes, every effort has been made to ensure accuracy, but the author and publishers accept no liability for any mistakes that may remain. This is a collection of memoires, and is not intended as a travel guide. The material contained here is not suitable for those planning any expedition or similar pursuit in the regions described. The descriptions and maps included in this work are not to be used for the purposes of navigation. Prospective travellers should seek independent, reliable and up-to-date travel advice.

Appendix 1: Pronunciation Notes

Pronunciation Note One. Double-L sounds.

'Villa O'Higgins' is tricky to pronounce. The word *villa* does not sound as it does in English.

The double-L in Spanish is takes a Y-sound as in yak or Yorkshire (although in Argentina it is pronounced more like "sh"). So Villa is said *VEE-ya* (or *VEE-sha* if you are Argentine). It's the same for all double-L words: *mantequilla*, which is butter; *Sevilla*, the city of Seville; *caballo*, horse; *cordillera*, mountain range; and *llama*, which translates as, err... llama.

Pronunciation Note Two. Emphasis and accents.

In order to sound convincingly Spanish, most words should be emphasised on the penultimate syllable. In *mochila* and *custodia*, emphasise the CHIL and the TO (which sounds like toe, not too). Place the emphasis on PUER in both *puerto* and *aeropuerto* and on TER in both *frontera* and *carretera*. (In these cases, incidentally, both PUER and TER would rhyme with the English words air and share).

The rule changes if there is an accent over a vowel. In these cases the accented syllable is emphasised. Taking an example from early in Chapter 1, the word *Reloncaví* is stressed on the concluding VÍ, and in the subsequent paragraph, *peluquería* is emphasised on the syllable RÍ.

Two words from Chapter 1 provide a convenient comparison of the case with and without the accent: *custodia* is emphasised on TO and *peluquería* is emphasised on RÍ.

> **Pronunciation Note Three. HUA, HUE and HUI sounds.**
>
> *Hua*, *Hue* and *Hui* words are pronounced as if they begin with a W, so *Huequi* would be something like WEH-kee and *huemul* is weh-MOOL. If you listen carefully to a native speaker, the W-sound is sometimes preceded with a little bit of H.

> **Pronunciation Note Four. The letter ñ.**
>
> The letter ñ is pronounced as if 'n-y' was in its place. So *Ibañez* sounds like 'Iban-yez'. The same letter makes *español* sound like espan-yol and *señor* sound like sen-yor. This creature is not just N with a tilde (nor N with a squiggle, as it is sometimes called) but is a distinct letter of the Castilian alphabet that follows M and N and is called *enye*, pronounced EN-yay.
>
> In the first chapter of the book, we met two Chilean wild animals whose name includes this letter: *vicuña*, pronounced vi-COON-YA, and *ñandú*, pronounced nyan-DOO.
>
> The President of the Republic of Chile from 2010 to 2013 was a man called Sebastian Piñera. His name was sometimes printed in the British press as 'Pinera'. This is not only lazy in a computer age in which the ñ character is easily reproduced, but is also incorrect; it changes the sound significantly. As a compromise, 'Pinyera' might be a more helpful spelling for non-native speakers. Calling him Pinera is as wayward as spelling the name of the British Prime Minister as David Cameroon. *Camarón*, incidentally, means shrimp.
>
> Also worth a brief mention is that the terminal E letters in *Puente* and *Presidente* are sounded and not silent, and count as a syllable.
>
> Therefore *Puente Presidente Ibáñez* is pronounced:
>
> PWEN-tay Pre-si-DEN-tay ee-BAN-yez.
>
> Finally, whereas in Spain the Z would require a lisping sound: ee-BAN-yeth, in Latin America it is correct to maintain a pure Z sound: ee-BAN-yez.

> **Pronunciation Note Five.**
>
> Aéreos.
>
> Say all the vowels separately:
>
> a-AIR-ay-os.

Pronunciation Note Six. J and G.

Jorge is the Castilian form of the name George. The pronunciations of both J and the G are somewhat similar to an H, so this name is something like HOR-hay. J in *castellano* is almost always pronounced like the H in 'hot', although with a bit more of a rasping throaty sound. Words like *jefe, joven* and *juvenil* (chief, young and juvenile) all commence with this sound.

The pronunciation of G varies depending on the subsequent vowel. If followed by A, O or U, it takes a hard G sound as in 'got'. For example, *gasolina, golfo* and *guanaco* (petrol, gulf and guanaco) all commence with a hard G sound. However, when the G is followed by E or I, as in *gente* and *gimnasio* (people and gymnasium), the G becomes softer and sounds more like an H.

Pronunciation Note Seven. B and V.

Students of Spanish (or rather, Castilian) quickly learn that the V sound is pronounced B. Hence:

verde (green) is pronounced [BER-day]

viaje (journey) is pronounced [be-AH-hay]

Sevilla (Seville) is pronounced [se-BEE-yah]

In my experience, when in Spain it is generally safe to use a similar B sound for both V and B. However, in some parts of Latin America I have occasionally found the two sounds to be reversed, not only with V sounding like B but with B also sounding like V.

For example, depending on who is speaking:

the word *pueblo* (town) can sound a bit like [poo-AY-vlo]

and *caballo* (horse) can sound like [cah-VAH-yo]

In the example of the shower room notice in Chapter 8, the word *deben* (must) had been incorrectly written as *deven*, presumably because that was the way the writer pronounced it when speaking.

Interestingly, the local spelling of the Cuban capital is *Habana*, pronounced with a V sound.

Appendix 2: Journey Data

Distances travelled

From:	To:	Distance (km)
Puerto Bahamondez	Villa O'Higgins	7
Villa O'Higgins	Caleta Tortel	155
Caleta Tortel	Tamango	131
Tamango	Cochrane	5
Cochrane	Puerto Guadal	72
Puerto Guadal	Puerto Río Tranquilo	59
Puerto Río Tranquilo	Villa Cerro Castillo	151
Villa Cerro Castillo	Coyhaique	93
Coyhaique	Puerto Cisnes	250
Puerto Cisnes	Puyuhuapi	91
Puyuhuapi	Raúl Marín Balmaceda	104
Raúl Marín Balmaceda	Futaleufú	203
Futaleufú	Parque Pumalín	135
Parque Pumalín	Chaitén	34
Chaitén	Hornopirén	153
Hornopirén	Contao	44
Contao	Puerto Montt	61
		1748 km

Stopping points

Location	Hospedaje Nights	Camping Nights
Tsonek, Villa O'Higgins		4
Hielo Sur, Caleta Tortel	2	
Reserva Nacional Tamango		2
Hostal Paola, Cochrane	2	
Un Destino No Turístico, Puerto Guadal		3
Camping Pudú, Puerto Río Tranquilo		3
Reserva Nacional Cerro Castillo		2
Hospedaje Natti, Coyhaique	4	
Hospedaje Río Anita, Puerto Cisnes	2	
Hospedaje Juanita, Puyuhuapi	2	
Campsite, Raúl Marín Balmaceda		2
Hospedaje Cañete, Futaleufú	4	
Parque Pumalín		1
Hospedaje Don Carlos, Chaitén		2
Residencial in Hornopirén	3	
Hospedaje Reloncaví, Contao	1	
Hostal Bahia de Reloncaví, Puerto Montt	1	
	21	19

Appendix 3: Glossary

Bird Species 349
Animal Species 351
Plant Species 352
Food and Drink 354
General Vocabulary 359
Complete Phrases Included 364
Russian 367
Abbreviations 368
Data 369

Bird Species

Chilean Name	English Name	Latin Name
águila	eagle	
águila mora, águila chilena	black-chested buzzard eagle	*Geranoaetus melanoleucus*
bandurria	black-faced ibis	*Theristicus melanopis*
cachudito	tufted tit tyrant	*Anairetes parulus*
carancho	southern caracara	*Caracara plancus*
carpintero chico	striped woodpecker	*Picoides lignarius*
carpintero negro	Magellanic woodpecker	*Campephilus magellanicus*
chucao	chucao tapaculo	*Scelorchilus rubecula*
chuncho	austral pygmy owl	*Glaucidium nanum*
churrete acanelado	buff-winged cinclodes	*Cinclodes fuscus*

cisne	swan	
cisne de cuello negro	black-necked swan	*Cygnus melancoryphus*
cóndor	Andean condor	*Vultur gryphus*
fío-fío	white-crested elaenia	*Elaenia albiceps*
flamenco chileno	Chilean flamingo	*Phoenicopterus chilensis*
garza grande	great egret	*Ardea alba*
golondrina chilena	Chilean swallow	*Tachycineta meyeni*
huet-huet del sur	black-throated huet-huet	*Pteroptochos tarnii*
jilguero	black-chinned siskin	*Carduelis barbata*
jote de cabeza negra	black vulture	*Coragyps atratus*
ñandú	lesser rhea	*Pterocnemia pennata*
pato real	Chiloé widgeon	*Anas sibilatrix*
pelícano	Peruvian brown pelican	*Pelecanus thagus*
peuquito	Chilean hawk	*Accipiter chilensis*
picaflor	hummingbird	
picaflor chico	green-backed firecrown	*Sephanoides sephanoides*
pilpilén	American oystercatcher	*Haematopus palliates*
pingüino de Magallanes	Magellanic penguin	*Spheniscus magellanicus*
playero blanco	sanderling	*Calidris alba*
queltehue	southern lapwing	*Vanellus chilensis*
quetru austral	Magellanic flightless steamer-duck	*Tachyeres pteneres*
rayadito	thorn-tailed rayadito	*Aphrastura spinicauda*
zarapito	curlew	*Numenius phaeopus*
zorzal	austral thrush	*Turdus falklandii*

Animal Species

Chilean Name	English Name	Latin Name
alpaca	alpaca	*Lama pacos*
ballena	whale	
buey	steer (castrated bull)	
caballo	horse	
chilla	South American grey fox	*Lycalopex griseus*
chingue	hog-nosed skunk	*Conepatus chinga*
escarabajo de Darwin	Chilean stag beetle, Darwin's beetle	*Chiasognathus grantii*
galgo	greyhound	*Canis lupus familiaris*
guanaco	guanaco	*Lama guanicoe*
guarén	brown rat	*Rattus norvegicus*
huemul	South Andean deer	*Hippocamelus bisulcus*
langosta	lobster	
langosta de Juan Fernández	Juan Fernandez rock lobster	*Jasus frontalis*
liebre	European hare	*Lepus europaeus*
llama	llama	*Lama glama*
pudú	pudu	
pudú del norte	northern pudu	*Pudu mephistophiles*
pudú del sur	southern pudu	*Pudu puda*
puma	Patagonian puma, cougar	*Puma concolor patagonica*
puye	common galaxias, inanga (a small fish whose juveniles are served as whitebait)	*Galaxias maculatus*
ranita de Darwin	Darwin's frog	*Rhinoderma darwinii*

ratón chileno de cola larga, or colilargo común	long-tailed pygmy rice rat, or long-tailed colilargo	*Oligoryzomys longicaudatus*
salmón del Atlántico	Atlantic salmon	*Salmo salar*
tonina	Chilean dolphin	*Cephalorhynchus eutropia*
toro	bull	
trucha	trout	
trucha común	brown trout	*Salmo trutta*
trucha arcoíris	rainbow trout	*Oncorhynchus mykiss*
vicuña	vicuña	*Vicugna vicugna*
visón	American mink	*Neovison vison*

Plant Species

Chilean Name	English Name	Latin Name
alerce patagónico, lahuán	Patagonian cypress	*Fitzroya cupressoides*
araucaria, pehuén	Chilean pine, monkey puzzle	*Araucaria araucana*
calafate	calafate	*Berberis trigona*
canelo	winter's bark	*Drimys winteri*
chilco	fuchsia	*Fuchsia magellanica*
ciprés	cypress	
ciprés de las Guaitecas	Guaitecas cypress	*Pilgerodendon uviferum*
coihue	coigüe	*Nothofagus dombeyi*
coihue de Chiloé	Chiloé coigüe	*Nothofagus nitida*
coihue de Magallanes	Magellanic coigüe	*Nothofagus betuloides*

fascicularia bicolor	fascicularia bicolour (or bicolor)	*Fascicularia bicolor*
helecho	bracken, fern	*Pteridium*
huala	three varieties of	*Nothofagus x leonii*
hualo	decidious southern	*Nothofagus glauca*
lenga	beech	*Nothofagus pumilio*
maqui	maqui, Chilean wineberry	*Aristotelia chilensis*
mañío de hojas cortas	short-leafed mañío	*Saxegothaea conspicua*
mañío de hojas punzantes	prickly-leafed mañío	*Podocarpus nubigena*
muérdago	mistletoe	*Misodendrum*
nalca	nalca	*Gunnera tinctoria*
ñirre	Antarctic beech	*Nothofagus antarctica*
pan de Indio	Darwin's fungus, Indian bread	*Cyttaria darwinii*
pino longevo	bristlecone pine	*Pinus longaeva*
raulí	three varieties of	*Nothofagus nervosa*
roble	decidious southern	*Nothofagus oblique*
ruil	beech	*Nothofagus alessandrii*
sauce chileno	Chilean willow	*Salix chilensis*
taique	Chilean holly	*Desfontainea spinosa*
trífido	triffid	
usnea	usnea, old man's beard	A lichen of the *Parmeliaceae* family
yerba mate	Paraguay tea, South American holly	*Ilex paraguariensis*

Food and Drink

Some food vocabulary in Latin America come from local indigenous languages, and therefore differs to the words used in Spain.

Castellano	English	Notes
agua	water	
agua de la llave	tap water	Argentina: agua de la canilla
ají	chilli (either whole or as sauce)	
ají cacho de cabra	goat's horn chilli pepper	capsicum annuum (lungum variety)
ají chileno	hot chilli sauce	a common accompaniment to meals, especially meat
calzones rotos	a sugar-coated, deep-fried batter speciality	the name means 'torn knickers'
camarón	shrimp, prawn	
carbonada	goulash containing meat, onion, potato and vegetables	confusable on a menu with the Italian pasta dish 'carbonara'
carmenère	carmenère	a red wine grape
cebolla	onion	
cerveza	beer	
choclo	sweetcorn	Spain: maíz
chimbombo	cheap white wine	sold in large plastic kegs
chorizo	spiced pork sausage	can be dried or fresh
cordero	Patagonian lamb	

curanto	a stew of shellfish, meat, potatoes, dumplings and vegetables	originating from the island of Chiloé, this stew is traditionally cooked over hot stones in a hole in the ground, covered with *nalca* leaves
damasco	apricot	Spain: *albaricoque*
dulce de leche	see *manjar* below	literally: 'sweet of milk'
durazno	peach	Spain: *melocotón*
empanada	a pastry envelope with a cooked filling, served hot or cold	common fillings include *pino*, vegetables, fish, seafood, and *napolitana*
frutilla	strawberry	Spain: *fresa*
hallulla	thin flat round bread rolls	
helado	ice cream	
jamón	ham	
jaiba	crab	
jugo	juice	Spain: *zumo*
lechuga	lettuce	
lengua	tongue	also means language
lomo	steak	tenderloin
lomo a lo pobre	steak served with chips, caramelised onions and fried eggs	literally: 'steak how the poor have it'
maqui	maqui, Chilean wineberry	a purple berry that grows on wild trees

manzana	apple	
manzanilla	camomile	camomile tea
manjar (known as *dulce de leche* outside Chile)	sweet spread made of caramelised milk	popular on bread or to fill pastries, cakes or crepes
marraqueta	crusty bread roll made in four detachable sections	
mate (pronounced MA-tay)	a green tea-like infusion	traditional drink of Patagonia
mil hojas (French: *mille feuille*)	a cake made of multiple thin layers	literally: 'thousand leaves'
merkén	a spice made from *ají cacho de cabra*, the goat's horn chilli pepper, which is smoked, dried, and mixed with cumin and coriander seeds	merkén has long been used by the indigenous *Mapuche* people
merluza	hake	
merluza austral	southern hake	
mermelada	jam	
napolitana	an empanada filling	ham, cheese, tomato and oregano
paella	paella	a dish of seasoned rice, vegetables and usually seafood or meat; traditional dish of Valencia
palta	avocado	Spain: *aguacate*

pan	bread	other Chilean breads include *hallulla* and *marraqueta*
pan amasado	dense handmade bread rolls prepared in a clay oven	
pan de molde	standard supermarket bread	
papas	potatoes	Spain: *patatas*
papas fritas	chips	
pastel de jaiba	crab pie	
pebre	a sauce of chilli, finely chopped tomatoes, onion, garlic and coriander in olive oil	a condiment commonly accompanying bread in restaurants
pino	the traditional filling for a Chilean *empanada*	minced meat and onion with cumin and chilli, a slice of hard-boiled egg, a black olive and raisins
pisco	pisco	a grape brandy distilled in Chile (and Peru)
pisco sour	pisco sour	a cocktail of *pisco* with lime juice, syrup and ice; there are many variations on the recipe
piscola		a combination of pisco and cola

pizza dulce	sweet pizza	
porotos	beans	
queso	cheese	
quinoa	quinoa	
rodizio de pizzas	all-you-can-eat pizza buffet	local term, not a common expression
salchicha	sausage	
salchipapas	sausage and chips	alternatively, this can be a dish of chips and chopped sausage mixed together
schop	draught beer	
sopa	soup	
sopa de porotos	bean soup	
Super 8	Super 8	the brand name of a popular chocolate wafer bar
té	tea	
yerba (alternatively spelt *hierba*)	yerba	the dried leaves used for brewing the infusion *mate*; also means grass, herb or weed
zapallo	pumpkin	
zanahoria	carrot	

General Vocabulary

abierto	open
abuela	grandmother
adiós	goodbye
aeródromo	aerodrome, airfield
alcalde	mayor
alianzas	house teams (school)
alianza blanca	white house team
alianza verde	green house team
almacén	store, grocer's shop
altiplano	high altitude plateau
amargo	bitter
amigo	friend
armada	navy
asado	barbecue
balsa	raft
bandera	flag
barco	boat
bodega	store
boina	beret
bomba	pump
(also means fire station or petrol station)	
bomberos	fire fighters
bombilla	a metal straw for drinking mate (has a filter or strainer at its lower end)
caballo	horse
cabaña	cabin (usually holiday accommodation)
caja	box, cash desk
caleta	cove, inlet
camino	road, path, way
camino turístico	tourist route
camión	lorry, truck
campesino	farmer, peasant farmer
campo	field, farm, farmland
campo de hielo	ice field
canilla	water tap
(*llave* is more common in Chile)	
carabineros	police force
carnet de identidad	identity card
carnicería	butcher, meat shop
carpintero	carpenter, woodpecker

carretera	road, highway	chilote	adjective meaning 'from the region or island of Chiloé'
Carretera Austral	Southern Highway		
carro	cart		
casa	house	chupalla	sombrero, usually of straw
casa de turista	literally: 'house of the tourist'		

(characteristic of *huasos*, cowboys)

cascada	waterfall	colegio	school
casino	dining room	colegios particulares	private fee-paying schools
castellano	Castilian		

the principal language of Chile (and Spain)

		colegios públicos	state-funded public schools
catedral	cathedral	colegios subvencionados	subsidised (or 'voucher') schools
católica, católico	catholic		

(partially private but also receive a public subsidy)

caverna	cave, cavern	colgante	hanging
cementario	cemetery	comandante	commander
centro de eventos comunitarios	community centre	común	common, ordinary
		confluencia	confluence (of rivers)
cerrado	closed		
chacra	small farm or smallholding		
chica	young woman or female youth	cordillera	mountain range
		cordonería	a shop that sells various types of cord: ie. thread, string, wool, shoe laces and so on
chico	young man or a male youth		
chilena, chileno	Chilean woman (or man)		

(also an adjective meaning Chilean)

corte	cut	*flaco*	thin, skinny
corte de luz	power cut	*formación*	training
costanera	coast road or lakeside road	*frontera*	frontier, boundary
cueca	the traditional dance of Chile	*frutería*	green grocer, fruit shop
cuesta	mountain pass	*fuego*	fire

(also used for slopes and hills more generally)

dieciocho	eighteen	*galgo*	greyhound
		gasolina	petrol

(often refers to Chile's national day, 18 September)

		gaucho	Patagonian cowboy
dinamita	dynamite	*gimnasio*	gymnasium
desierto	desert	*glaciar*	glacier
desierto florido	flowering desert	*golfo*	gulf
embarcadero	ferry ramp, landing stage, pier	*gracias*	thank you
		gratis	free, at no cost
		guanaco	guanaco
embarcar	to embark		
empaque	packing area	(a wild ancestor of the domesticated llama; also a police water cannon vehicle)	
escondida	hidden		
escuela	school	*guardaparque*	park warden
espectacular	spectacular	*hacienda*	large country property or ranch
estancia	ranch		
estufa	stove, heater, log-burning stove	*hielo*	ice
		hogar	home
		hospedaje	guest house, lodging
estupendo	wonderful		
fiesta	party, festival	*hostal*	hostel
fiordo	fjord		

huaso	cowboy	*medialuna*	half-moon
(the word *gaucho* is more common in Patagonia)		(also means a rodeo arena, a croissant or a semi-circular dance pattern in the traditional *cueca*)	
huelga	strike, industrial dispute		
infierno	hell	*mirador*	viewpoint
isla	island	*mochila*	rucksack
lago	lake	*momento*	a moment
laguna	(small) lake	*momentito*	an especially short *momento*
lana	wool		
lavandería	laundry	*muchas gracias*	thank you very much
leña	firewood logs	*muelle*	port, wharf, jetty
linterna	torch, flashlight		
llave	doorkey, tap	*naranjo*	orange tree
luz	light	*ninguna*	none
(*luz* is also used to mean electricity, as in 'we have *luz* connected to this house')		*norte*	north, northern
		ombligo	navel, belly-button
manifestaciones	protests, demonstrations	*pájaro*	bird
		El Pajarero	The Bird Man
manzano	apple tree	*panadería*	bakery
maravilloso	marvellous	*parrilla*	barbecue or grill
mármol	marble	*pasarela*	footbridge, gangway
matrimonial	double room in a hotel		
		peligroso	dangerous
media, medio	half	*pelotas*	balls
mediagua	a design of simple wooden house, easily assembled	*peluquería*	hairdressing salon, barber
		perfecto	perfect
		picante	spicy hot

pista	track, runway	*santa, san*	saint, holy
un poco	a little	*santiaguina, santiaguino*	resident of Santiago (female, male)
pueblo	town		
puente	bridge	*sendero*	footpath, hiking trail
puerta	door		
puerto	port	*sendero interpretivo*	interpretive footpath eg. nature trail or special interest trail
quincho	a shelter		
ratón	mouse, rat		
redondería (a made-up word)	a shop that sells spherical objects		
		señor	sir, mister
represa	dam	*sí*	yes
reserva	a reserve	*sociedad*	society
reserva nacional	national reserve	*submarino*	submarine
		subvencionado	subsidised
(eg. nature reserve)		*Suecia*	Sweden
residencial	guest house	*Suiza*	Switzerland
(often those offering longer-term lodging rather than tourist accommodation)		*supermercardo*	supermarket
		sur	southern, south
rico	rich, tasty, delicious	*tábano*	Patagonian horsefly
		techo	roof
río	river	*termas*	thermal pools, hot springs
rollería (a made-up word)	a shop that sells items that are rolled up		
		tía	aunt
		tío	uncle
ropa	clothes	*tierra*	earth, land
ruta	route	*tubalería* (a made-up word)	a shop that sells tubular objects
salmonera	salmon farm, fish farm		
salón	room, hall		

universidad	university	*virgen*	virgin
valle	valley	*La Virgen*	The Virgin Mary
ventisquero	glacier	*vista*	vista, view
(also means snowdrift)		*volcán*	volcano
verde	green		
viaje	journey		

Complete Phrases Included

abierto los domingos	open Sundays
Aerotaxis del Sur	Air-Taxis of the South
América Latina	Latin America
Amo a Chaitén; volveré	I love Chaitén; I will return
buen viaje	have a good journey (equivalent to *bon voyage*)
buenos días	good morning (literally: 'good days')
café con piernas	coffee with legs: a style of café prevalent in Santiago, in which waitresses wear miniskirts or revealing outfits
Campo de Hielo Norte	Northern Ice Field
Campo de Hielo Sur	Southern Ice Field
Compañía Explotadora del Baker	The Baker Exploitation Company
Confirmemos cuando vuelva	Let's decide/confirm when I return
Corporación Nacional Forestal	National Forestry Corporation

Esta máquina desarrolló su trabajo en la construcción de la Carretera Austral… colaborando… a la conquista de las fronteras interiores.	This machine worked on the construction of the Carretera Austral… collaborating… in the conquest of the internal frontiers.
¿Cuánto tiempo has estado en Sudamérica?	How long have you been in South America?
de nada	you're welcome; it's a pleasure
El Día de las Glorias Navales	The Day of Naval Glories
El Día de los Ombligos Gloriosos	The Day of Glorious Navels
En Patagonia, el que se apura pierde tiempo	In Patagonia, he who hurries wastes his time
en toma	taken, occupied
Es altamente peligroso, señor	It's highly dangerous, sir
¿Estoy dónde?	Where am I?
Fiesta del Pescado Frito	Festival of Fried Fish
fin del camino	end of the road
gigantesco tronco de mañío	gigantic mañío tree trunk
¿Ha andado a caballo, alguna vez?	Have you ever ridden a horse?
Héroe Nacional, Padre de la Patria	National Hero, Father of the Nation
Ilumina mi camino	Light my path
Los 33	The 33 (refers to the 33 miners trapped underground at the San José mine in 2010)
marcha de los paraguas	march of the umbrellas
menú del día	menu of the day; an economical lunch with restricted options
Mi Casita de Té	My Little Tea House
Ministerio de Tierras y Colonización	Ministry of Lands and Colonisation

Muchas gracias; sería perfecto	Thank you very much; that would be perfect
¡Muy amable!	How kind! How thoughtful!
¡Muy rico!	Very tasty! Delicious!
Nuestra Señora del Trabajo	Our Lady of the Work
Nuestro Máximo Héroe Naval	Our Definitive Naval Hero
Ningún problema, señor	No problem, sir
¡No al lucro!	No profit!
No te preocupes	Don't worry
Objeto Volador No Identificado, OVNI	Unidentified Flying Object, UFO
¿Para una persona, señor?	For one person, sir?
Patagonia Sin Represas	Patagonia Without Dams
Piedra del Águila	Eagle's Rock
Piedra del Indio	Indian's Rock
plaza de armas	town square
Por favor no fumar ni dejar mochilas sobre las camas	Please don't smoke nor place rucksacks on the beds
¡Precaución! Pista aérea en el camino	Caution! Airstrip in the road
¡Pucha!	Bother! Damn! Oh crap! (Although this is a mild expletive in Chile, it can be more vulgar and offensive in some parts of Latin America).
pueblo nuevo	new town
¡Qué buena forma de viajar!	What an interesting way to travel!
¡Qué lindo es su pueblo!	How beautiful your town is!
¡Qué maravilloso!	How marvellous!
¡Qué pena!	What a shame!

¡Qué rico!	How tasty!
Revisión Técnica	The certificate of vehicle roadworthiness, like the British MOT
Salvemos el año escolar	Let's save the school year
Se necesita carpintero	Carpenter required
Señor Jesús tú eres camino, verdad y vida para mí	Lord Jesus you are road, truth and life for me
Sociedad Colectiva de Estancias	Collective Society of Ranches
Sociedad Nacional de Ganadería y Colonización	National Society for Livestock and Colonisation
tengo que irme	I have to go
tirar la cuerda	to pull the rope, a tug-of-war
Tratado de Límites	Boundary Treaty
Universidad Católica	Catholic University
Un Techo Para Chile	An organisation that works through community projects, towards a society that is just and free from poverty; (literally: 'A Roof For Chile').

Russian

Я не говорю по испански	I don't speak Spanish
Я не говорю на английском языке	I don't speak English
всем покинуть судно	Abandon ship

Abbreviations

4x4	Four-wheel-drive vehicle
CD	Compact Disc
CONAF	*Corporación Nacional Forestal*
DVD	Digital Video Disc (or Digital Versatile Disc)
FM	Frequency Modulation (radio band)
GDP	Gross Domestic Product
GLOF	Glacial Lake Outburst Flood
GNI	Gross National Income
GSI	Global Salmon Initiative
GPS	Global Positioning System
ISAV	Infectious Salmon Anemia Virus
MADIPRO	*Madre de la Divina Providencia*; a network of FM antennae in Patagonia. The name means Mother of the Divine Providence
MINEDUC	*Ministerio de Educación de Chile*
MOT	Ministry of Transport vehicle test
OECD	Organisation of Economic Co-operation and Development
OVNI	*Objeto Volador No Identificado* (or UFO in English)
RSPCA	Royal Society for the Prevention of Cruelty to Animals
Sat-Nav	Navigation system taking information from GPS satellites
SERNAGEOMIN	*Servicio Nacional de Geología y Minería*
UFO	Unidentified Flying Object (or OVNI in Spanish)
UK	United Kingdom

US	United States
UNDP	United Nations Development Project
VEI	Volcanic Explosivity Index
WWF	World Wide Fund for Nature (also operates as World Wildlife Fund in some global regions)

Data

Currency equivalence; at the time of the expedition:

US $1 = 500 Chilean pesos approximately;

UK £1 = 800 Chilean pesos approximately.

Appendix 4: Sources and Further Reading

Disclaimer

Details of external websites are provided for the convenience of readers. You access these websites at your own risk. The author and publishers accept no liability for the following sites and their content. External websites are under the control of third parties.

The reference below of any external website does not indicate that the author or publishers endorse or accept any responsibility for the website. We do not give any guarantees regarding the quality, safety, suitability or reliability of material to be found there.

Users should take appropriate security measures against viruses and other potentially destructive items.

Terms used in Glossary

BBC News	UK News website
CONAF	*Corporación Nacional Forestal*
Emol	Mercurio Online; Chilean news website
GPS	Global Positioning System
IUCN	International Union for Conservation of Nature and Natural Resources
NASA	National Aeronautics and Space Administration
UNESCO	United Nations Educational, Scientific and Cultural Organization
Sernatur	*Servicio Nacional de Turismo*
UNDP	United Nations Development Project
USGS	United States Geological Survey

Author website of Justin Walker
http://justinwalkerwriter.wordpress.com/

Travel and Tourism in Chile, and Regional Information

Sernatur; Servicio Nacional de Turismo:
http://www.sernatur.cl/ Website in Spanish

Chile Travel; supported by Sernatur:
http://chile.travel/ Website in Spanish
http://chile.travel/en/ English version

Recorre Aysén; supported by Sernatur:
http://www.recorreaysen.cl/ Website in Spanish
http://eng.recorreaysen.cl/ English version

Turismo Chile; a non-profit organisation promoting tourist destinations in Chile:
http://chiletourism.travel/ Website in Spanish

Turismo Sustenable; sustainable tourism:
http://www.chilesustentable.travel/ Website in Spanish

Patagon Journal; the online version of an English-language print magazine featuring issues of relevance in Patagonia (both Argentina and Chile), based in Puerto Varas, Chile.
http://www.patagonjournal.com/

Living Atlas Chile; an online collection of videos relating to Chile:
http://www.livingatlaschile.com/

Sources and Further Reading by Chapter

Chapter One

List of volcanoes in Chile; Global Volcanism Program:
http://www.volcano.si.edu/search_volcano_results.cfm

Data on Volcán Puyehue-Cordón Caulle; Global Volcanism Program:
http://www.volcano.si.edu/volcano.cfm?vn=357150

Navimag Ferries:
http://www.navimag.com/site/en

Rainforest types:
Chester, Sharon R. (2008) **A Wildlife Guide to Chile**, Princeton University Press, Princeton NJ. pp52-60.

Torres del Paine fire, December 2011:
BBC News (2011) **Chile forest fire ravages Torres del Paine park**. Available online at: http://www.bbc.co.uk/news/world-latin-america-16366349 [Accessed 14 July 2014]

Population and area data, Europe and South America:
World Atlas (2014) **Continents**. Available online at:
http://worldatlas.com/aatlas/infopage/contnent.htm [accessed 14 July 2014]

Population density data:
World Bank (2014) **Population density (people per sq. km of land area)**. Available online at: http://data.worldbank.org/indicator/EN.POP.DNST [accessed 14 July 2014]

Chapter Two

Cuerpo Militar del Trabajo:
http://www.ejercito.cl/cmt.php Website in Spanish

Construction of the Carretera Austral:
McCarthy, C. et al. (2009) **Chile and Easter Island**, Lonely Planet, London. p345.

Construction of the Carretera Austral:
Tourism Chile (2004) **History of the Carretera Austral**. Available online at: http://www.tourismchile.com/guide/austral_north_road/articles/675 [Accessed 14 July 2014]

Beagle Channel Dispute:
Encyclopedia (2008) **Beagle Channel Dispute**. Available online at:
http://www.encyclopedia.com/article-1G2-3078900632/beagle-channel-dispute.html [Accessed 14 July 2014]

Languages of Spain:
Ethnologue (2014) **Languages of the World; Spain**. Available online at:
http://www.ethnologue.com/country/ES/default [Accessed 15 July 2014]

Languages of Chile:
Ethnologue (2014) **Languages of the World; Chile**. Available online at:
https://www.ethnologue.com/country/CL [Accessed 15 July 2014]

Languages of Spain and Europe:
European Commission (2006) **Europeans and their Languages**, Special Eurobarometer 243 / Wave 64.3 – TNS Opinion and Social. Available online at:
http://ec.europa.eu/public_opinion/archives/ebs/ebs_243_sum_en.pdf [Accessed 15 July 2014]

Chapter Three

Transportes Aéreos Don Carlos:
Transportes Aéreos Don Carlos no longer operates the route between Coyhaique and Villa O'Higgins. For information on this route, check the website of the airline Aerocord: http://www.aerocord.cl/ Website in Spanish

Bernardo O'Higgins biography:
Latin American Studies (2014) **Bernardo O'Higgins**. Available online at:
http://www.latinamericanstudies.org/chile/ohiggins-bio.htm [Accessed 15 July 2014]

Bernardo O'Higgins biography:
Minster, C. (date unknown) **Bernardo O'Higgins; liberator of Chile**, Latin American History. Available online at:
http://latinamericanhistory.about.com/od/thehistoryofchile/a/10bernardoohiggins.htm
[Accessed 15 July 2014]

Rescue of Los 33 at San José mine:
BBC News (2010) **Celebrations as last trapped Chile miner is rescued**. Available online at: http://www.bbc.co.uk/news/world-latin-america-11518015 [Accessed 15 July 2014]

Villa O'Higgins:
http://www.villaohiggins.com/

Chapter Four

Astronaut's photograph of the Southern Patagonian Ice Field:
NASA (2014) **Southern Patagonia Icefield**. Available online at:
http://www.nasa.gov/content/southern-patagonia-icefield/ [Accessed 15 July 2014]
Lago O'Higgins is the many-fingered lake to the right (north) of the photograph and below (east of) the ice field. At the tip of the bottom-right finger of the lake (north-east) is the location of Villa O'Higgins. Glaciar O'Higgins can be seen extending into the top-left (south-west) finger of the lake.

Southern Patagonian Ice Field:
USGS (2014) **Southern Patagonian Ice Field**. Available online at:
http://pubs.usgs.gov/pp/p1386i/chile-arg/wet/southpat.html [Accessed 15 July 2014]

Northern and Southern Patagonian Ice Fields:
Glasser, N.F., Hambrey, M.J. and Jansson, K. (2014) **The Patagonian Icefields: Landforms, Sediments and Glacier Fluctuations**, Aberystwyth University (School of Geography and Earth Sciences). Available online at:
https://www.aber.ac.uk/en/iges/research-groups/centre-glaciology/research-intro/patagonia/ [Accessed 18 July 2014]

Surface areas of Patagonian Ice Fields:
Lliboutry, L. (1999) **Satellite Image Atlas of Glaciers of the World; Introduction**, USGS. Available online at: http://pubs.usgs.gov/pp/p1386i/chile-arg/intro.html [Accessed 15 July 2014]

Deepest lakes in the world:
Circle of Blue (2009) **Top 10 Deepest Freshwater Lakes in the World**. Available online at: http://www.circleofblue.org/waternews/2009/world/infographic-top-ten-deepest-freshwater-lakes-in-the-world/ [Accessed 08 December 2014]

The Gherkin, London:
http://www.30stmaryaxe.com/

Eiffel Tower, Paris:
http://www.toureiffel.paris/

Empire State Building, New York:
http://www.esbnyc.com/

The Shard, London:
http://www.the-shard.com/

Burj Khalifa, Dubai:
http://www.burjkhalifa.ae/en/

Pontifica Universidad Católica de Chile:
http://www.uc.cl/ Website in Spanish

Crossing the border from El Chaltén to Villa O'Higgins:
Tane, C. (2014) **Border Crossings: El Chaltén to Villa O'Higgins**. Available online at: http://www.erraticrock.com/information/information-articles-1/border-crossings-el-chalten-to-villa-ohiggins/ [Accessed 15 July 2014]

The 1965 death of Hernán Merino Correa, March 2009:
Emol (2009) **Asesinato del teniente Merino, el episodio más trágico en disputa por Laguna del Desierto**. Available online at:
http://www.emol.com/noticias/nacional/2009/03/31/351631/asesinato-del-teniente-merino-el-episodio-mas-tragico-en-disputa-por-laguna-del-desierto.html [Accessed 15 July 2014]. Website in Spanish.

Academic paper relating to the Laguna del Desierto arbitration:
Santis, H. (1995) **Revisión del laudo arbitral "Laguna del Desierto"**, Revista de Geografía Norte Grande, 22: 3-7. Available online at:
http://www.geo.puc.cl/html/revista/PDF/RGNG_N22/Art01.pdf [Accessed 15 July 2014]. Document in Spanish.

History of the Chile-Argentina border, with mentions of the 1881 Boundary Treaty and the 1902 arbitration of King Edward VII:
Hidden Journeys (date unknown) **The Andes at Ground Level; defining the border**. Available online at: http://www.hiddenjourneys.co.uk/Buenos%20Aires-Santiago/Andes/Lowest.aspx [Accessed 15 July 2014]

Map depicting the Patagonian Chile-Argentina border, according to the 1881 Boundary Treaty:
Hidden Journeys (date unknown) **The Andes at Ground Level; defining the border**. Available online at: http://www.hiddenjourneys.co.uk/Buenos%20Aires-Santiago/Andes/Lowest/hjp.AND.WIKI.018.aspx?mode=image [Accessed 15 July 2014]

Text of the 1881 Boundary Treaty, and the Award by His Majesty King Edward VII in the 1902 Boundary Case:
United Nations (2006) **Reports of International Arbitral Awards; The Cordillera of the Andes Boundary Case (Argentina, Chile)**, VOLUME IX pp. 29-49. Available online at: http://legal.un.org/riaa/cases/vol_IX/29-49.pdf [Accessed 15 July 2014]

Longest two-nation land borders:
Wikipedia (2014) **List of countries and territories by land borders**. Available online

at: http://en.wikipedia.org/wiki/List_of_countries_and_territories_by_land_borders [Accessed 15 July 2014]

The Yerba Mate tree; IUCN Red List:
World Conservation Monitoring Centre (1998) **Ilex paraguariensis**, The IUCN Red List of Threatened Species. Version 2014.3. Available online at: http://www.iucnredlist.org/details/32982/0 [Accessed 08 December 2014]

Yerba mate:
Ma-tea (date unknown) **How to drink Yerba Mate – Traditional Method**. Available online at: http://ma-tea.com/pages/Traditional-Method.html [Accessed 08 December 2014].

Chapter Five

Bird names, descriptions and photographs:
http://www.avesdechile.cl/ Website in Spanish
http://www.avesdechile.cl/aves09.htm English version

From the Avibase website, a comprehensive catalogue of birds in Chile:
http://avibase.bsc-eoc.org/checklist.jsp?region=cl&list=clements scroll down to find the list

The Voyage of the Beagle by Charles Darwin.
Full text chapter by chapter available online at:
http://www.literature.org/authors/darwin-charles/the-voyage-of-the-beagle/
Summary available online at:
http://www.sparknotes.com/biography/darwin/section5.rhtml

Chilean Rodeo:
http://www.chileanhorse.com/index.php?option=com_content&task=view&id=39&Itemid=65

The Cueca dance – history:
Hart, N. (2008) **A brief history of cueca**. Available online at: http://santiagotimes.cl/a-brief-history-of-cueca/

The Cueca dance – description and history:
Don Quijote (date unknown) **Cueca**. Available online at:
http://www.donquijote.org/culture/chile/music/cueca.asp

Match scores for Davis Cup (tennis) World Group Playoff, Chile v Austria, September 2009:
http://www.daviscup.com/en/draws-results/tie/details.aspx?tieId=100013978

Chile Olympic Profile:
http://www.olympic.org/chile

Chapter Six

Servants of Charity:
http://www.servantsofcharity.org/

Luigi Guanella biography:
Servants of Charity (2011) **The Life of Saint Louis Guanella**. Available online at: http://www.servantsofcharity.org/guanella.html [Accessed 16 July 2014]

News report relating the Canonisation of Luigi Guanella to the healing of a man injured while rollerblading:
Wooden, C. (2011) **Healing of US man key to Italian priest's canonization**. Available online at: http://www.catholicnews.com/data/stories/cns/1103915.htm [Accessed 16 July 2014]

Padre Antonio Ronchi biography:
Fundación Obra Padre Antonio Ronchi (date unknown) **Cronologica y datos biográficos**. Available online at: http://www.fundacionronchi.cl/cronologia.htm [Accessed 16 July 2014] Website in Spanish

History of Radio Santa María, acknowledging the role of Padre Antonio Ronchi:
Radio Santa Maria (2012) **Quienes Somos**. Available online at: http://www.radiosantamaria.cl/quienes-somos [Accessed 16 July 2014] Website in Spanish

Description of MADIPRO radio network, acknowledging the role of Padre Antonio Ronchi:
Wikipedia (2013) **MADIPRO**. Available online at: http://es.wikipedia.org/wiki/MADIPRO [Accessed 16 July 2014] Website in Spanish

Thirty years of MADIPRO:
El Diario de Aysén (2013) **Radio MADIPRO de Caleta Tortel: 30 años en el aire acompañando a los Tortelinos**. Available online at: http://diarioaysen.cl/nbreves/radio-madipro-de-caleta-tortel-30-anos-en-el-aire-acompanando-a-los-tortelinos/ [Accessed 08 December 2014] Website in Spanish

Chapter Seven

Fiordo Mitchell Ferry:
http://www.barcazas.cl/barcazas/wp/?lang=en

Caleta Tortel:
http://www.visitetortel.cl/

Guaitecas Cypress; IUCN Red List:
Souto, C., Premoli, A. & Gardner, M. (2013) **Pilgerodendron uviferum**, The IUCN Red List of Threatened Species, Version 2014.1. Available online at: http://www.iucnredlist.org/details/32052/0 [Accessed 16 July 2014]

Chapter Eight

HMS Beagle:
Port Cities (date unknown) **HMS Beagle 1820-1870**. Available online at: http://www.portcities.org.uk/london/server/show/ConFactFile.64/HMS-Beagle.html [Accessed 08 December 2014]

HMS Adventure:
Note: this ship was originally named HMS Aid
Wikipedia (date unknown) **HMS Aid 1809**. Available online at: http://en.wikipedia.org/wiki/HMS_Aid_(1809) [Accessed 08 December 2014]

The 1826-1830 hydrographic survey by HMS Adventure and HMS Beagle:
King, P. P. (1839) **Voyages of the Adventure and Beagle, Volume 1**, (ed: FitzRoy, R), London: Henry Colburn. Available online at: http://darwin-online.org.uk/content/frameset?itemID=F10.1&viewtype=text&pageseq=1 [Accessed 08 December 2014]

History of Tortel:
Ilustre Municipalidad de Tortel (2012) **Historia**. Available online at: http://www.visitetortel.cl/nuestra-comuna/historia.html Website in Spanish [Accessed 16 July 2014]

History of Tortel:
Valdés Baigorria, J. (2009) **Un gran paso para Tortel y para la Patagonia Chilena; La comuna y su epopéyica historia**. Available online at: http://www.surlink.cl/index.php/aysen/4118 Website in Spanish [Accessed 16 July 2014]

Chapter Nine

Reserva Nacional Tamango; CONAF:
http://www.conaf.cl/parques/reserva-nacional-lago-cochrane-o-tamango/ Website in Spanish

Reserva Nacional Tamango:
http://www.visitchile.com/en/tamango-national-reserve/

Thomas Cochrane biography:
Hickman, K. (2014) **Napoleonic Wars: Admiral Lord Thomas Cochrane**, Military History. Available online at: http://militaryhistory.about.com/od/naval/p/Napoleonic-Wars-Admiral-Lord-Thomas-Cochrane.htm [Accessed 16 July 2014]

Thomas Cochrane biography:
Royal Navy Museum (2004) **Biography: Thomas Cochrane**, Information Sheet #5. Available online at:
http://www.royalnavalmuseum.org/info_sheets_thomas_cochrane.htm [Accessed 16 July 2014]

Thomas Cochrane, location of grave:
Westminster Abbey (2013) **Thomas Cochrane, Earl of Dundonald**, History. Available

online at: http://www.westminster-abbey.org/our-history/people/thomas-cochrane [Accessed 16 July 2014]

History of Chilean nitrate mining and exports:
Bermúdez Miral, O. (1987) **Breve Historia de Saltire**, original published in Spanish, Santiago, Ediciones Pampa Desnuda. Excerpt in English available online at: http://www.albumdesierto.cl/ingles/2histori.htm [Accessed 17 July 2014]

Decline of Chilean nitrate mining:
Marr, P. (2007) Ghosts of the Atacama: **The abandonment of nitrate mining in the Tarapacá region of Chile**, Middle States Geographer, 40, pp22-31. Available online at: http://geographyplanning.buffalostate.edu/MSG%202007/3_Marr.pdf [Accessed 17 July 2014]

Humberstone (nitrate mining ghost town); UNESCO:
http://whc.unesco.org/en/list/1178
Click Gallery for photographs

Arturo Prat biography:
Hickman, K. (date unknown) **War of the Pacific: Commander Arturo Prat**, Military History. Available online at: http://militaryhistory.about.com/od/naval/p/War-Of-The-Pacific-Commander-Arturo-Prat.htm [Accessed 17 July 2014]

Arturo Prat biography:
Angel, B. (2011) **Great Chileans: Arturo Prat**. Available online at: http://www.ilovechile.cl/2011/05/21/great-chileans-arturo-prat/21928 [Accessed 17 July 2014]

Lapis Lazuli description and background:
http://www.gemstone.org/index.php?option=com_content&view=article&id=117:sapphire&catid=1:gem-by-gem&Itemid=14

Ten Chilean varieties of nothofagus listed in:
Chester, Sharon R. (2008) **A Wildlife Guide to Chile**, Princeton University Press, Princeton NJ. p45.

Bread types in Chile, with illustraions:
http://www.speakinglatino.com/breads-of-chile-picture-guide/

Chapter Ten

Chilean Huemul; IUCN Red List:
Jiménez, J., Guineo, G., Corti, P, Smith, J.A., Flueck, W., Vila, A., Gizejewski, Z., Gill, R., McShea, B. & Geist, V. (2008) **Hippocamelus bisulcus**. The IUCN Red List of Threatened Species. Version 2014.1. Available online at: http://www.iucnredlist.org/details/10054/0 [Accessed 17 July 2014]

Patagonian Huemul:
Huffman, B. (2013) **Hippocamelus bisulcus**. Available online at: http://www.ultimateungulate.com/Artiodactyla/Hippocamelus_bisulcus.html [Accessed 17 July 2014]

Huemul conservation:
Conservacion Patagonica (date unknown) **Huemul Deer Recovery**. Available online at: http://www.conservacionpatagonica.org/buildingthepark_biodiversity_huemul.htm [Accessed 17 July 2014]

Southern Pudú; IUCN Red List:
Jimenez, J. & Ramilo, E. 2008. **Pudu puda.** The IUCN Red List of Threatened Species. Version 2014.1. Available online at: http://www.iucnredlist.org/details/18848/0 [Accessed 17 July 2014]

Southern Pudú fact sheet:
Huffman, B. (2006) **Pudu puda.** Available online at: http://www.ultimateungulate.com/Artiodactyla/Pudu_puda.html [Accessed 17 July 2014]

Cochrane:
http://www.explorepatagonia.com/eng/cuidades/cochrane.php

Cochrane:
http://www.cochranepatagonia.cl/ Website in Spanish

Chapter Eleven

Worldwide climate averages:
http://www.worldclimateguide.co.uk/

Water shortage in Lima, Peru:
Ortiz, Diego M. (2013) **Peru's impending water crisis**. Available online at: http://www.peruthisweek.com/blogs-perus-impending-water-crisis-50285 [Accessed 17 July 2014]

Distribution of water on earth:
USGS (2014) **The World's Water**. Available online at: http://water.usgs.gov/edu/earthwherewater.html [Accessed 17 July 2014]

HidroAysén:
http://www.hidroaysen.cl/ Website in Spanish

Basic details of the HidroAysén project:
http://www.hidroaysen.cl/?page_id=177 Website in Spanish

Patagonia Sin Represas (Patagonia Without Dams):
http://www.patagoniasinrepresas.cl/ Website in Spanish
http://www.patagoniasinrepresas.cl/final/index-en.php English version

Impact of the dams:
Patagonia Sin Represas (date unknown) **Impacto de las Represas.** Available online at: http://www.patagoniasinrepresas.cl/final/contenido.php?seccion=problema_impactorepresas [Accessed 17 July 2014] Website in Spanish

Impact of the pylons:
Patagonia Sin Represas (date unknown) **Impacto de las Torres.** Available online at:

http://www.patagoniasinrepresas.cl/final/contenido.php?seccion=problema_impactotorres [Accessed 17 July 2014] Website in Spanish

Mistaken economic model:
Patagonia Sin Represas (date unknown) **Modelo Económico Equivocado**. Available online at:
http://www.patagoniasinrepresas.cl/final/contenido.php?seccion=problema_impactorepresas [Accessed 17 July 2014] Website in Spanish

The alternative proposal:
Patagonia Sin Represas (date unknown) **Nuestra Propuesta / Plan Nacional de Desarrollo Energético**. Available online at:
http://www.patagoniasinrepresas.cl/final/contenido.php?seccion=nuestrapropuesta [Accessed 17 July 2014] Website in Spanish

Surface area of the proposed dams and power capacity:
HidroAysén (2011) **Descripción del Proyecto**. Available online at:
http://www.hidroaysen.cl/?page_id=177 [Accessed 17 July 2014] Website in Spanish

Longest transmission lines in the world:
Power Technology (2014) **The world's longest power transmission lines**. Available online at: http://www.power-technology.com/features/featurethe-worlds-longest-power-transmission-lines-4167964/ [Accessed 17 July 2014]

Generating capacity of Chile and anticipated need:
Esposito, A. and Cambero, F. (2013) **Chile needs strong leadership for big projects: HidroAysen**, Available online at:
http://www.reuters.com/article/2013/05/22/us-latam-summit-hidroaysen-idUSBRE94L0ZD20130522 [Accessed 17 July 2014]

Per capita electricity consumption:
World Bank (2014) **Electric power consumption (kWh per capita)**. Available online at: http://data.worldbank.org/indicator/EG.USE.ELEC.KH.PC [Accessed 17 July 2014]

President Piñera's support for HidroAysén:
Crellin, O. (2012) **Chile with 50% hydro power by 2034, but serious energy shortages in 2015**. Available online at: http://en.mercopress.com/2012/01/16/chile-with-50-hydro-power-by-2034-but-serious-energy-shortages-in-2015 [Accessed 17 July 2014]

Chapter Twelve

Puerto Bertrand:
http://www.puertobertrand.com/ Website in Spanish

Making a haybox:
Neville, F. (2008) **Haybox cooking: how to make a haybox and save energy by Huw Woodman**. Available online at: http://www.cottagesmallholder.com/haybox-cooking-how-to-make-a-haybox-and-save-energy-by-huw-woodman-752/

Use of a haybox:
Low Impact Living Initiative (LILI) (date unknown) **Retained heat cooking**. Available online at: http://www.lowimpact.org/factsheet_retained_heat_cooking.htm
Includes printable pdf factsheet

Composting toilets. A range of articles:
http://www.treehugger.com/tag/composting-toilets/

The Leave No Trace Seven Principles:
The Leave No Trace Seven Principles (2012). Available online at:
https://lnt.org/learn/7-principles
The member-driven Leave No Trace Center for Outdoor Ethics teaches people how to enjoy the outdoors responsibly. This copyrighted information has been reprinted with permission from the Leave No Trace Center for Outdoor Ethics: www.LNT.org

Chapter Thirteen

Puerto Guadal:
http://www.puerto-guadal.com/

The story of Saturnino Inayo Treque and the foundation of Mina Silva, taken from:
Danka Ivanoff Wellman (2007) **Lago General Carrera, Temporales de Sueños**, Chile, LOM Ediciones. Book published in Spanish.

Mina Silva and Puerto Cristal:
http://www.turismopuertocristal.cl/en/history.html

Lago General Carrera:
World Heritage Encyclopedia (2013) **Buenos Aires / General Carrera Lake**. Available online at: http://worldheritage.org/articles/Buenos_Aires/General_Carrera_Lake [Accessed 18 July 2014]

Puerto Guadal, including brief history of Mina Escondida:
Caputo, L. (2009) **Puerto Guadal**. Available online at:
http://www.vivatravelguides.com/south-america/chile/carratera-austral-and-southern/puerto-guadal/ [Accessed 18 July 2014]

Settlers in Puerto Guadal:
http://www.puerto-guadal.com/pages_english/eng_7_history.html

Turner Bros Asbestos Company:
Grace's Guide (2014) **Turner Bros Asbestos Co.** Available online at:
http://www.gracesguide.co.uk/Turner_Brothers_Asbestos_Co [Accessed 18 July 2014]

Usnea (Old Man's Beard) depicted in:
Chester, Sharon R. (2008) **A Wildlife Guide to Chile**, Princeton University Press, Princeton NJ. p59.

Use of the honorific title 'Don':
Wikipedia (2014) **Don (honorific)**. Available online at:
http://en.wikipedia.org/wiki/Don_(honorific) [Accessed 18 July 2014]

Chapter Fourteen

Catedral de Marmol photographs:
http://www.atlasofwonders.com/2011/08/marble-cathedral.html

Glaciar Exploradores:
http://chile.travel/en/donde-ir/patagonia-2/aysen-patagonia/exploradores-glacier/

Laguna San Rafael:
http://chile.travel/en/donde-ir/patagonia-2/aysen-patagonia/san-rafael-lagoon/

Northern Patagonian Ice Field:
World Heritage (2013) **Northern Patagonian Ice Field**, (World Heritage Encyclopedia). Available online at:
http://cdn.worldheritage.org/articles/Northern_Patagonian_Ice_Field [Accessed 18 July 2014]

Patagonian Ice Fields:
Further sources listed under Chapter Four.

Ohio State University School of Earth Sciences:
http://www.geology.ohio-state.edu/

Environmental impact of meat production:
Carrington, D. (2014) **Giving up beef will reduce carbon footprint more than cars, says expert.** Available online at:
http://www.theguardian.com/environment/2014/jul/21/giving-up-beef-reduce-carbon-footprint-more-than-cars [Accessed 22 July 2014]

Environmental impact of meat production:
Walsh, B. (2013) **The Triple Whopper Environmental Impact of Global Meat Production.** Available online at: http://science.time.com/2013/12/16/the-triple-whopper-environmental-impact-of-global-meat-production/ [Accessed 22 July 2014]

Environmental impact of meat production; Food and Agriculture Organisation of the United Nations:
FAO (2006) **Livestock impacts on the environment.** Available online at:
http://www.fao.org/ag/magazine/0612sp1.htm [Accessed 22 July 2014]

Impact on the planet of human food choices:
EarthSave (date unknown) **Food Choices and the Planet.** Available online at:
http://www.earthsave.org/environment.htm [Accessed 22 July 2014]

Overgrazing and desertification:
Conservación Patagonica (date unknown) **Overgrazing and Desertification.** Available online at: http://www.conservacionpatagonica.org/whypatagonia_mtp_overgrazing.htm [Accessed 22 July 2014]

Academic paper describing the Leones Valley glacial lake outburst flood (GLOF):
Harrison, S., Glasser, N., Winchester, V., Haresign, E., Warren, C. and Jansson, K. (2006) **A glacial lake outburst flood associated with recent mountain glacier retreat, Patagonian Andes.** The Holocene 2006; 16; 611. Available online at:
http://hol.sagepub.com/content/16/4/611.abstract [Accessed 30 August 2014]

Historical methods for measuring mountain heights:
Cajori, F (1929) **History of Determinations of the Heights of Mountains.** Isis Vol. 12 No. 3, pp482-514. Available online at:
http://penelope.uchicago.edu/Thayer/E/Journals/ISIS/12/3/Determinations_of_Heights_of_Mountains*.html [Accessed 22 July 2014]

How GPS works:
http://www8.garmin.com/aboutGPS/ [Accessed 22 July 2014]

How GPS works; Georgia State University:
Nave, R. (date unknown) **Global Positioning Satellites.** Available online at:
http://hyperphysics.phy-astr.gsu.edu/hbase/gps.html [Accessed 22 July 2014]

Issues of measuring elevation using GPS:
Fraczek, W. (2003) Mean Sea Level, GPS, and the Geoid. Available online at:
http://www.esri.com/news/arcuser/0703/geoid1of3.html [Accessed 22 July 2014]

Accuracy of GPS elevation readings:
How accurate is the GPS elevation reading? Available online at:
https://support.garmin.com/support/searchSupport/case.faces?caseId=%7B66f1b0a0-4cd6-11dc-4733-000000000000%7D [Accessed 22 July 2014]

1991 and 1923 measurement of elevation of Monte San Valentin:
Lliboutry, L. (1999) **Glaciers of the Wet Andes,** USGS. Available online at:
http://pubs.usgs.gov/pp/p1386i/chile-arg/wet/index.html [Accessed 22 July 2014]

2001 measurement of elevation of Monte San Valentin:
Guzmán, E. (2002) **Expedición Invernal al Monte San Valentin (Winter Expedition to Mont San Valentin).** Available online at:
http://www.cumbresaustrales.cl/relato_valentin.htm [Accessed 22 July 2014] Website in Spanish

Triffids:
The Triffids (date unknown). Available online at: http://triffids.wuthering-heights.co.uk/triffids.php [Accessed 22 July 2014]

Gunnera tinctoria (Giant rhubarb); Biological Records Centre:
Pilkington, S. (2011) **GB Non-natives factsheet; Gunnera tinctoria.** Available online at: http://www.brc.ac.uk/gbnn_admin/index.php?q=node/222 [Accessed 22 July 2014]

Ecological impacts of Chilean rhubarb in New Zealand:
Williams, P.A.; Ogle, C.C.; Timmins, S.M.; La Cock, G.D.; Clarkson, J. 2005: **Chilean rhubarb (*Gunnera tinctoria*): biology, ecology and conservation impacts in New Zealand.** DOC Research & Development Series 210. Department of Conservation, Wellington. 27 p. Available online at: http://www.doc.govt.nz/documents/science-and-technical/drds210.pdf [Accessed 22 July 2014]

Chapter Fifteen

Villa Cerro Castillo:
http://www.explorepatagonia.com/eng/cuidades/cerro-castillo.php

Reserva Nacional Cerro Castillo:
http://www.conaf.cl/parques/reserva-nacional-cerro-castillo/ Website in Spanish

Topological prominence:
http://www.peakbagging.com/PromPage.html
Scroll down page for links to list of prominent peaks in Great Britain and various other locations.

A list of the world's ultra-prominent peaks:
http://www.peaklist.org/ultras.html

Chapter Sixteen

Coyhaique:
http://chile.travel/en/donde-ir/patagonia-2/aysen-patagonia/coyhaique-2/

Municipalidad de Coyhaique:
http://www.coyhaique.cl/ Website in Spanish

Monumento Natural Dos Lagunas:
http://www.conaf.cl/parques/monumento-natural-dos-lagunas/ Website in Spanish

Chilean National Curriculum; MINEDUC (Ministerio de Educación):
http://www.curriculumnacional.mineduc.cl/ Website in Spanish

The Chilean Empanada:
http://www.thisischile.cl/2009/11/the-chilean-empanada/?lang=en

Seeking an accepted terminology for indigenous people of the Americas:
Oliver-Johnson, L. N., (2012) **Why are terms such as Aboriginal peoples, American Indian, Indian, Indigenous Peoples, First Nations and Native American all used to describe the original inhabitants of North and South America?** History of the American Indian, American Military University. Available online at:
http://www.academia.edu/1299780/WHY_ARE_TERMS_SUCH_AS_ABORIGINAL_PEOPLES_AMERICAN_INDIAN_INDIAN_INDIGENOUS_PEOPLES_FIRST_NATIONS_AND_NATIVE_AMERICAN_ALL_USED_TO_DESCRIBE_THE_ORIGINAL_INHABITANTS_OF_NORTH_AND_SOUTH_AMERICA [Accessed 19 February 2014]

OECD. Organisation for Economic Co-operation and Development:
http://www.oecd.org/

OECD data:
http://stats.oecd.org/

Categories of school in Chile:
Bravo, D., Mukhopadhyay, S. and Todd, P. E. (2010) **Effects of school reform on education and labor market performance: Evidence from Chile's universal**

voucher system, Quant Econom. Jul 2010; 1(1): 47–95. Available online at: http://www.ncbi.nlm.nih.gov/pmc/articles/PMC3208354/ [Accessed 23 July 2014]

2011 student protests. Short description and photographs, 10 August 2011: http://www.theatlantic.com/infocus/2011/08/student-protests-in-chile/100125/ [Accessed 23 July 2014]

2011 student protests, 5 August 2011:
Franklin, J. (2011) **Chile student protests explode into violence**. Available online at: http://www.theguardian.com/world/2011/aug/05/chile-student-protests-violence [Accessed 23 July 2014]

2011 student protests, 10 August 2011:
The Guardian (2011) **Chile riot police clash with student protesters**. Available online at: http://www.theguardian.com/world/2011/aug/10/chile-riot-student-protest-violence [Accessed 23 July 2014]

School occupations, 7 October 2011:
Franklin, J. (2011) **Chilean girls stage 'occupation' of their own school in education rights protests**. Available online at: http://www.theguardian.com/world/2011/oct/07/chilean-girls-occupation-school-protest [Accessed 23 July 2014]

2011 student protests, 25 October 2011. Includes funding data and types of schools: BBC News (2011) **Chile's student protests show little sign of abating**. Available online at: http://www.bbc.co.uk/news/world-latin-america-15431829 [Accessed 23 July 2014]

University and school students end occupations, 28 December 2011:
Hinchcliffe, J. (2011) **Chilean students end some school occupations but pledge to continue protests**. Available online at: http://en.mercopress.com/2011/12/28/chilean-students-end-some-school-occupations-but-pledge-to-continue-protests [Accessed 23 July 2014]

Salvemos el año escolar, 30 August 2011:
La Tercera (2011) **Mineduc amplía plazo para inscribirse en Plan Salvemos el Año Escolar**. Available online at: http://www.latercera.com/noticia/educacion/2011/08/657-389681-9-mineduc-amplia-plazo-para-inscribirse-en-plan-salvemos-el-ano-escolar.shtml [Accessed 23 July 2014] Article in Spanish

Chapter Seventeen

Puerto Cisnes:
http://www.municipalidadcisnes.cl/ Website in Spanish

Maqui berries:
http://allmaquiberry.tumblr.com/

Santa Teresa de Los Andes:
http://www.corazones.org/santos/teresa_andes.htm [Accessed 23 July 2014] Website in Spanish

Santa Teresa de Los Andes:
http://www.americancatholic.org/Features/Saints/saint.aspx?id=1900 [Accessed 23 July 2014]

Environmental issues relating to the commercial salmon farming:
Lee, J. (2013) **Can the Farmed Salmon Industry Become Sustainable?** Available online at: http://www.triplepundit.com/2013/08/farmed-salmon-sustainable/ [Accessed 23 July 2014]

ISAv Salmon disease in Chile:
Pure Salmon (date unknown) **Infections Salmon Anaemia (ISA) in Chile – Backgrounder**. Available online at: http://www.puresalmon.org/pdfs/ISA-backgrounder.pdf [Accessed 23 July 2014]

Red Tide; Carleton College, Minnesota:
Bruckner, M. (2014) **Red Tide – A Harmful Algal Bloom**, Microbial Life Educational Resources. Available online at:
http://serc.carleton.edu/microbelife/topics/redtide/index.html [Accessed 23 July 2014]

Fiesta de Pescado Frito; report on eldivisadero.cl (regional newspaper based in Coyhaique):
Diario El Divisadero (2012) **Con masiva participación se realizó minga comunitaria en "Fiesta del Pescao Frito.** Available online at: http://www.eldivisadero.cl/noticia-9909 [Accessed 23 July 2014] Website in Spanish

Chapter Eighteen

Puyuhuapi; Cámara de Turismo. Includes some history of the first settlers:
http://www.puertopuyuhuapi.cl/

Puyuhuapi:
http://www.enjoy-chile.org/puerto-puyuhuapi-attractions-chile.php

History of immigration into Chile; Migration Policy Institute:
Doña-Reveco, C. and Levinson, A. (2012) **Chile: A Growing Destination Country in Search of a Coherent Approach to Migration.** The online journal of the Migration Policy Institute. Available online at: http://www.migrationpolicy.org/article/chile-growing-destination-country-search-coherent-approach-migration [Accessed 23 July 2014]

Welsh settlement in Patagonia:
BBC (2008) **The Welsh in Patagonia.** Wales History on BBC Wales. Available online at: http://www.bbc.co.uk/wales/history/sites/themes/society/migration_patagonia.shtml [Accessed 23 July 2014]

Puyuhuapi-style houses:
http://www.elpangue.com/puyuhuapi.html

German immigration in Puyuhuapi:
Chilotes and Germans; a 4-minute video in which a resident of Puyuhuapi explains

some of the history of the village. Available online at:
http://www.livingatlaschile.com/?s=Chilotes+and+Germans

Un Techo Para Chile:
http://www.techo.org/ Website in Spanish; click link for English version

A brief history of Techo:
http://www.techo.org/en/techo/que-es-techo/

Parque Nacional Queulat; CONAF:
http://www.conaf.cl/parques/parque-nacional-queulat/ Website in Spanish

Parque Nacional Queulat:
http://www.interpatagonia.com/paseos/puyuhuapi-ventisquero-colgante-queulat/index_i.html

Termas Ventisquero de Puyuhuapi:
http://www.termasventisqueropuyuhuapi.cl/

Cementario General, Recoleta, Santiago:
http://www.cementeriogeneral.cl/ Website in Spanish

Chapter Nineteen

La Junta:
http://www.interpatagonia.com/lajunta/

Inauguration of the Pinochet memorial on the Carretera Austral in La Junta:
Emol (2000) **Monumento en honor a Pinochet será inaugurado el lunes.** Available online at: http://www.emol.com/noticias/nacional/2000/08/30/31204/monumento-en-honor-a-pinochet-sera-inaugurado-el-lunes.html [Accessed 25 July 2014] Website in Spanish

Some years later, article reflecting on the controversy relating to the Pinochet memorial:
Varas, J. (2009) **Augusto Pinochet, el polémico monumento a un genocida.** Available online at:
http://www.emol.com/noticias/nacional/2000/08/30/31204/monumento-en-honor-a-pinochet-sera-inaugurado-el-lunes.html [Accessed 25 July 2014] Website in Spanish

Timeline of Pinochet's presidency:
The Guardian (1999) **Chile under Pinochet - a chronology.** Available online at:
http://www.theguardian.com/world/1999/jan/15/pinochet.chile1 [Accessed 25 July 2014]

Salvador Allende autopsy:
The Guardian (2011) **Chilean president Salvador Allende committed suicide, autopsy confirms.** Available online at:
http://www.theguardian.com/world/2011/jul/20/salvador-allende-committed-suicide-autopsy [Accessed 25 July 2014]

Timeline of Chilean history:
Timelines (2014) **Chile profile; A chronology of key events**. Available online at: http://www.timelines.ws/countries/CHILE.HTML [Accessed 25 July 2014]

Augusto Pinochet biography:
Biography (2014) **Augusto José Ramón Pinochet Ugarte**. Available online at: http://www.biography.com/people/augusto-pinochet-9441138 [Accessed 25 July 2014]

Legacies of Pinochet's dictatorship; human rights violations and the neo-liberal economic model:
Navia, P. (2013) **Chile, 11 September 2013: death and birth of a nation**. Available online at: https://www.opendemocracy.net/patricio-navia/chile-11-september-1973-death-and-birth-of-nation [Accessed 25 July 2014]

2012 GDP figures:
World Bank (2014) **GDP per capita (current US$)**. Available online at: http://data.worldbank.org/indicator/NY.GDP.PCAP.CD [Accessed 25 July 2014]

UNDP Human Development Index:
UNDP (2014) **Human Development Report 2014**. Available online at: http://hdr.undp.org/en/content/human-development-report-2014 [Accessed 25 July 2014]

Sebastián Piñera biography:
Oficina de Sebastián Piñera (date unknown). **Biography of the president of the Republic Sebastián Piñera Echenique**. Available online at: http://www.sebastianpinera.cl/node/313 [Accessed 26 July 2014]

Impact of Chile's February 2010 earthquake; Earthquake Engineering Research Institute:
EERI (2010) **Learning from Earthquakes; The Mw 8.8 Chile Earthquake of February 27, 2010**. Available online at: https://www.eeri.org/site/images/eeri_newsletter/2010_pdf/Chile10_insert.pdf [Accessed 26 July 2014]

Earthquake during Piñera's inauguration as president:
BBC News (2010) **New Chile quake as Pinera sworn in as president**. Available online at: http://news.bbc.co.uk/1/hi/world/americas/8561340.stm [Accessed 26 July 2014]

President Piñera and the rescue of Los 33:
http://www.sebastianpinera.cl/presidente/rescate-de-los-33-mineros Website in Spanish

Compiled reports relating to Los 33:
BBC News (2012) **BBC News, Chile Mine, Special Report**. Available online at: http://www.bbc.co.uk/news/special_reports/chile_mine/ [Accessed 26 July 2014]

The January 2011 Magallanes protests:
BBC News (2011) **Deal ends Magallanes gas protest**. Available online at: http://www.bbc.co.uk/news/world-latin-america-12222392 [Accessed 26 July 2014]

Piñera's 2011 State of the Nation address interrupted by protestors:
BBC News (2011) **Chile: Valparaiso protesters in clashes with police**. Available online at: http://www.bbc.co.uk/news/world-latin-america-13487338 [Accessed 26 July 2014]

CODELCO copper miners' strike:
BBC News (2011) **Chilean copper miners strike over restructuring plans**. Available online at: http://www.bbc.co.uk/news/world-latin-america-14116015 [Accessed 26 July 2014]

2011 student protests continue Chile.
BBC News (2011) **Chile's student protests show little sign of abating.** Available online at: http://www.bbc.co.uk/news/world-latin-america-15431829 [Accessed 23 July 2014]

Puerto Raúl Marín Balmaceda:
http://www.puertoraulmarin.cl/ Website in Spanish

Puerto Raúl Marín Balmaceda:
http://www.cuencadelpalena-queulat.cl/contenidos/index.php?id=3 Website in Spanish

The rediscovery of the wine grape Carmenère:
Hall, L. S. (2011) **Carmenere a Focus at a Conference on the Anniversary of its Rediscovery.** Available online at:
http://www.winebusiness.com/news/?go=getArticle&dataid=70385 [Accessed 26 July 2014]

Darwin's beetle; University of Nebraska State Museum. Includes remark from Darwin's notes:
http://museum.unl.edu/research/entomology/Guide/Scarabaeoidea/Lucanidae/LUC/CHIA/grantii.html [Accessed 26 July 2014]

Data on Volcán Melimoyu; Global Volcanism Program:
http://www.volcano.si.edu/volcano.cfm?vn=358052

Data on Nevado Ojos del Salado; Global Volcanism Program:
http://volcano.si.edu/volcano.cfm?vn=355130

Map showing the 15 administrative regions of Chile:
http://www.nationsonline.org/oneworld/map/chile-administrative-map.htm

2011 Aysén protests:
Long, G. (2012) **Chile's Patagonia region sees mounting unrest.** Available online at: http://www.bbc.co.uk/news/world-latin-america-17256697 [Accessed 26 July 2014]

Fishermen seize the Puente Presidente Ibañez in Puerto Aysén:
Torres, D. (2012) **Pescadores y organizaciones sociales se toman puente de ingreso a Aysén.** Available online at:
http://www.biobiochile.cl/2012/02/07/pescadores-y-organizaciones-sociales-toman-puente-presidente-ibanez-en-ingreso-a-ciudad-de-aysen.shtml [Accessed 28 July 2014] Website in Spanish

The demands of the Aysén protestors:
González, A. (2012) **Las claves del Movimiento por la Región de Aysén y sus demandas por mejoras sociales.** Available online at: http://www.latercera.com/noticia/nacional/2012/02/680-431148-9-las-claves-del-movimiento-por-la-region-de-aysen-y-sus-demandas-por-mejoras.shtml [Accessed 26 July 2014] Website in Spanish

Occupation of the aerodrome at Villa O'Higgins:
Ayala, L. (2012) **Habitantes de Villa O'Higgins deponen toma en aeródromo de Aysén por emergencia.** Available online at: http://www.emol.com/noticias/nacional/2012/02/23/527692/manifestantes-deponen-toma-en-aerodromo-de-aysen-por-emergencia.html [Accessed 28 July 2014] Website in Spanish

Roads from Coyhaique to Balmaceda Airport, and to Argentina, are blocked:
López, A. and Sierralta, P. (2012) **Camioneros de Coyhaique se toman accesos al aeropuerto y paso hacia Argentina.** Available online at: http://www.latercera.com/noticia/nacional/2012/02/680-431910-9-camioneros-de-coyhaique-se-toman-accesos-al-aeropuerto-y-paso-hacia-argentina.shtml [Accessed 28 July 2014] Website in Spanish

Bishop Luis Infanti of Aysén holds a mass for protestors at Coyhaique cathedral:
López, A. (2012) **El conflicto se agudiza en día crítico por falta de combustible y afecta al turismo.** Available online at: http://diario.latercera.com/2012/02/19/01/contenido/pais/31-101070-9-el-conflicto-se-agudiza-en-dia-critico-por-falta-de-combustible-y-afecta-al.shtml [Accessed 28 July 2014] Website in Spanish

Amnesty International calls for investigation:
Santiago Times. (2012) **Violence escalates in Chile's Aysén region.** Available online at: http://santiagotimes.cl/violence-escalates-in-chiles-aysen-region/ [Accessed 28 July 2014]

Government calls for removal of Aysén Roadblocks:
Hobman, J. (2012) **Roadblocks in Chile's Aysén protests have to go, government says.** Available online at: http://santiagotimes.cl/roadblocks-in-chiles-aysen-protests-have-to-go-government-says/ [Accessed 26 July 2014]

Chapter Twenty
Futaleufú:
http://www.futaleufu.cl/ Website in Spanish

The ghost ship El Caleuche:
http://www.caleuche.com/English/caleuche_legend.php

Pisco Sour. Recipe and background:
http://www.makemeacocktail.com/blog/77/the-pisco-sour-a-history/

Río Futaleufú map of rapids:
http://yelcho.cl/wp-content/uploads/Futaleufu-Rafting-Map.jpg

Top ten whitewater rafting destinations:
National Geographic (date unknown) **Top 10 Whitewater Rafting.** Available online at:
http://travel.nationalgeographic.com/travel/top-10/white-water-rafting/ [Accessed 28 July 2014]

The International Year of Quinoa; Food and Agriculture Organisation of the United Nations:
http://www.fao.org/quinoa-2013/en/

Río Futaleufú rapids:
http://www.exchile.com/ChileRaftingUpperFuta.html

Classification of rapids:
Expediciones Chile (date unknown) **Chile rafting FAQs; How are rapids classified on the Futaleufu?** Available online at:
http://www.exchile.com/KayakSchool_FAQs.htm [Accessed 28 July 2014]

Opening of Puente La Dificultad:
Miranda A. (2009) **Inaugurado Puente Mecano En Futaleufú.** Available online at:
http://futaleufu.cl/noticia.php?not=MzUy [Accessed 28 July 2014] Website in Spanish

Chapter Twenty-One

Data on Volcán Hudson; Global Volcanism Program:
http://www.volcano.si.edu/volcano.cfm?vn=358057

Volcanic Explosivity Index:
USGS (2009) **VHP Photo Glossary: VEI.** Available online at:
http://volcanoes.usgs.gov/images/pglossary/vei.php [Accessed 17 July 2014]

Parque Pumalín:
http://www.parquepumalin.cl/en/index.htm

El Amarillo, Parque Pumalín:
http://www.parquepumalin.cl/en/visiting_elamarillo.htm

History of Parque Pumalín:
Conservation Land Trust (date unknown) **Pumalín Park.** Available online at:
http://www.theconservationlandtrust.org/eng/pumalin.htm [Accessed 28 July 2014]

The Conservation Land Trust:
http://www.theconservationlandtrust.org/

Conservación Patagónica:
http://www.conservacionpatagonica.org/

Downloadable leaflet on Parque Pumalín; includes map showing Camping Grande and Volcán Minchinmahuida, and information on Sendero Ranita de Darwin:
http://www.parquepumalin.cl/download/mapapumalin.pdf

Hantavirus:
Willacy, H. (2013) **Hantavirus Infection.** Available online at:
http://www.patient.co.uk/doctor/hantavirus-infection [Accessed 28 July 2014]

Chaitén:
http://www.camaraturismochaiten.cl/

Data on Volcán Minchinmahuida; Global Volcanism Program:
http://www.volcano.si.edu/volcano.cfm?vn=358040

Data on Volcán Chaitén; Global Volcanism Program:
http://www.volcano.si.edu/volcano.cfm?vn=358041

May 2008 eruption of Volcán Chaitén; includes maps and diagrams:
Ball, J. (date unknown) **Chaitén (Chaiten volcano – Chile).** Available online at:
http://geology.com/volcanoes/chaiten/ [Accessed 29 July 2014]

Report on May 2008 eruption of Volcán Chaitén; Scientific Electronic Library Online:
Lara, L. E., (2009) **The 2008 eruption of the Chaitén Volcano, Chile: a preliminary report.** Andean Geology 36 (1): pp125-129. Available online at:
http://www.scielo.cl/scielo.php?script=sci_arttext&pid=S0718-71062009000100009 [Accessed 29 July 2014]

February 2009 eruption of Volcán Chaitén; includes satellite photograph:
NASA (2009) **Eruption of Chaiten Volcano.** Available online at:
http://earthobservatory.nasa.gov/NaturalHazards/view.php?id=37087 [Accessed 29 July 2014]

Academic paper on the Liquiñe-Ofquei fault and the Peru-Chile subduction zone:
Murdie, R. E., Styles, P., Prior, D. J. and Daniel, A. J. (2000) **A new gravity map of southern Chile and its preliminary interpretation.** Andean Geology 27 (1) pp49-63. Available online at:
http://www.andeangeology.cl/index.php/revista1/article/viewFile/V27n1-a04/691 [Accessed 29 July 2014]

The 9.5Mw earthquake in Valdivia, Chile in 1960:
http://earthquake.usgs.gov/earthquakes/world/events/1960_05_22.php

The 8.8Mw earthquake in Maule, Chile in 2010:
http://earthquake.usgs.gov/earthquakes/eqarchives/poster/2010/20100227.php

Long-tailed pygmy rice rat; IUCN Red List:
Pardinas, U., D'Elia, G., Teta, P. & Patterson, B. (2008) **Oligoryzomys longicaudatus.** The IUCN Red List of Threatened Species. Version 2014.2. Available online at: http://www.iucnredlist.org/details/15250/0 [Accessed 29 July 2014]

Chapter Twenty-Two

The brown rat; University of Michigan Museum of Zoology:
Armitage, D. 2004. **Rattus norvegicus**, Animal Diversity Web. Available online at:
http://animaldiversity.ummz.umich.edu/accounts/Rattus_norvegicus/ [Accessed 29 July 2014]

Santa Bárbara:
http://www.nuevachaiten.cl/ Website in Spanish

Chaitur:
http://www.chaitur.com/

The International Music Festival of Viña del Mar:
Brassea, L. (2014) **Historia y Memoria de Viña del Mar: Orígenes del Festival Internacional de la Canción.** Departamento de Cultura, Municipalidad de Viña del Mar. Available online at:
http://culturaenvina.wordpress.com/2014/02/21/origenesfestival/ [Accessed 29 July 2014] Website in Spanish

Patagonian Cypress; IUCN Red List:
Premoli, A., Quiroga, P., Souto, C. & Gardner, M. (2013) **Fitzroya cupressoides.** The IUCN Red List of Threatened Species. Version 2014.2. Available online at:
http://www.iucnredlist.org/details/30926/0 [Accessed 29 July 2014]

Fascicularia bicolor:
http://www.strangewonderfulthings.com/181.htm

Sendero Cascadas, the trail from Caleta Gonzalo to the waterfall, briefly described at the foot of this page:
http://www.parquepumalin.cl/en/visiting_caletagonzalo.htm

The ferry Tehuelche:
http://www.navierapuelche.cl/f_tehuelche.html

Southern Pudú; IUCN Red List:
Jimenez, J. & Ramilo, E. 2008. **Pudu puda.** The IUCN Red List of Threatened Species. Version 2014.1. Available online at: http://www.iucnredlist.org/details/18848/0 [Accessed 17 July 2014]

Southern Pudú fact sheet:
Huffman, B. (2006) **Pudu puda.** Available online at:
http://www.ultimateungulate.com/Artiodactyla/Pudu_puda.html [Accessed 17 July 2014]

Chapter Twenty-Three

Ferry route Caleta Gonzalo to Hornopirén:
http://www.travelaid.cl/eng/boats/hornopirengonzalo.htm

Map of the northern Carretera Austral. Includes the ferry crossings at Caleta Gonzalo, Leptepú, and Puelche:
http://www.taustral.cl/

The ferry Mailén; specification and photograph:
http://www.navierapuelche.cl/f_mailen.html

Chilean Dolphin; IUCN Red List:
Reeves, R.R., Crespo, E.A., Dans, S., Jefferson, T.A., Karczmarski, L., Laidre, K., O'Corry-Crowe, G., Pedraza, S., Rojas-Bracho, L., Secchi, E.R., Slooten, E., Smith,

B.D., Wang, J.Y.. & Zhou, K. (2013) **Cephalorhynchus eutropia.** The IUCN Red List of Threatened Species. Version 2014.2. Available online at: http://www.iucnredlist.org/details/4160/0 [Accessed 30 July 2014]

Hornopirén:
http://www.hornopiren.net/ Website in Spanish

World Bank data on Chile:
http://data.worldbank.org/country/chile

Chile classified as a high income country by the World Bank:
World Bank (2013) **New Country Classifications.** Available online at: http://data.worldbank.org/news/new-country-classifications [Accessed 30 July 2014]

Income inequalities in OECD countries:
OECD (2014) **Social and welfare issues; inequality.** Available online at: http://www.oecd.org/social/inequality.htm [Accessed 30 July 2014]

Report on rising income inequality in OECD countries; inequality.org is from the Program on Inequality and the Common Good at the Institute for Policy Studies in Boston MA:
Babones, S. (2013) **OECD: Inequality Rising Faster than Ever.** Available online at: http://inequality.org/oecd-report-inequality-rising-faster/ [Accessed 30 July 2014]

Chilean grassroots demands a more equal society:
The Economist (2012) **Progress and its discontents.** Available online at: http://www.economist.com/node/21552566 [Accessed 30 July 2014]

Freemarket capitalism and wealth creation:
Forbes, F. (2009) **Capitalism: A True Love Story.** Available online at: http://www.forbes.com/2009/09/30/fact-and-comment-opinions-steve-forbes.html [Accessed 30 July 2014]

Article suggesting that the role of freemarket economics in Chile's stability and growth has been overstated:
Klein, N. (2010) **Milton Freidman did not save Chile.** Available online at: http://www.theguardian.com/commentisfree/cifamerica/2010/mar/03/chile-earthquake [Accessed 30 July 2014]

The role of capitalism in reducing global poverty:
The Economist (2013) **Towards the end of poverty.** Available online at: http://www.economist.com/news/leaders/21578665-nearly-1-billion-people-have-been-taken-out-extreme-poverty-20-years-world-should-aim [Accessed 30 July 2014]

The shortcomings of neoliberal economics:
Friends of the Earth (date unknown). **Towards Sustainable Economies: challenging neoliberal economic globalisation.** Available online at: http://www.foe.co.uk/sites/default/files/downloads/towards_sust_economies.pdf [Accessed 4 August 2014]

Oxfam briefing paper on economic inequality:
Fuentes-Nieva, R. and Galasso, N. (2014) **Working for the Few: Political capture**

and economic inequality. Available online to download in English or Spanish at: http://policy-practice.oxfam.org.uk/publications/working-for-the-few-political-capture-and-economic-inequality-311312 [Accessed 4 August 2014]

Date on Quintile Income Ratio and Income Gini Coefficient can be found in the 2013 Human Development Report:
UNDP (2013) **Human Development Report 2013, The Rise of the South: Human Progress in a Diverse World.** Available online to download in English or Spanish at: http://hdr.undp.org/en/2013-report [Accessed 4 August 2014]

Gabriel Palma's detailed paper proposing the 'Palma ratio':
Palma, J. G. (2011) **Homogeneous middles vs. heterogeneous tails, and the end of the 'Inverted-U': the share of the rich and what it's all about.** Cambridge Working papers in Economics (CWPE) 1111. Available online at: https://www.repository.cam.ac.uk/bitstream/handle/1810/241870/cwpe1111.pdf;jsessionid=F8ECB56532B6C83855BDA0032A16DAF3?sequence=1 [Accessed 4 August 2014]

A discussion paper on the Palma ratio:
Cobham, C. and Sumner, A. (2013) **Is It All About the Tails? The Palma Measure of Income Inequality.** Working paper 343, Centre for Global Development. Available online at: http://www.cgdev.org/sites/default/files/it-all-about-tails-palma-measure-income-inequality.pdf [Accessed 5 August 2014]

Support for the Palma ratio:
Pizzigati, S. (2014) **A Better Yardstick for Measuring Inequality.** Available online at: http://inequality.org/yardstick-measuring-inequality/ [Accessed 5 August 2014]

News article describing the Palma ratio; includes world map of inequality:
Fisher, M. (2013) **Map: How the world's countries compare on income inequality (the U.S. ranks below Nigeria).** Available online at: http://www.washingtonpost.com/blogs/worldviews/wp/2013/09/27/map-how-the-worlds-countries-compare-on-income-inequality-the-u-s-ranks-below-nigeria/ [Accessed 5 August 2014]

Contao. Brief information:
http://www.turismoruralchile.cl/zones/hornopiren.htm Website in Spanish

Chapter Twenty-Four

Ferry route Puelche to Caleta la Arena:
http://www.navierapuelche.cl/estuario.html Website in Spanish

Detailed discussion of the pre-colonial history of the Americas in this book:
Mann, Charles C. (2005) **1491: New Revelations of the Americas Before Columbus.** New York: Knopf.

Evidence of human habitation near Coyhaique, Patagonia, 8000 years ago:
Mena, R. (2006) **The first inhabitants at the end of the world.** Available online at:

http://www.nuestro.cl/eng/stories/recovery/franciscomena_patagonia.htm [Accessed 5 August 2014]

Evidence of pre-clovis human habitation near Puerto Montt, Patagonia, 12500 years ago; University of Nebraska-Lincoln:
Wilford, J. N., (1998) **Chilean Field Yields New Clues to Peopling of Americas.** Available online at: http://www.unl.edu/rhames/monte_verde/monte_verde1.htm [Accessed 5 August 2014]

Data on GDP per capita (current US$):
http://data.worldbank.org/indicator/NY.GDP.PCAP.CD?page=6 [Accessed 5 August 2014]

Chile population data; United Nations Department of Economic and Social Affairs:
http://esa.un.org/unpd/wpp/unpp/panel_population.htm [Accessed 5 August 2014]

Epilogue

Continuing protests in Aysén region, 24 February 2012:
Emol (2012) **Nueva jornada de disturbios de madrugada en Aysén deja varios heridos.** Available online at:
http://www.emol.com/noticias/nacional/2012/02/24/527737/comienza-nueva-jornada-nocturna-de-disturbios-en-aysen.html [Accessed 5 August 2014] Website in Spanish

Government insists that roadblocks must be removed , 1 March 2012:
Hobman, J. (2012) **Roadblocks in Chile's Aysén protests have to go, government says.** Available online at: http://santiagotimes.cl/roadblocks-in-chiles-aysen-protests-have-to-go-government-says/ [Accessed 5 August 2014]

Leaders of Aysén protests agree to remove blockades , 7 March 2012:
Jarroud, M. (2012) **Protesters Lift Roadblocks in Southern Chile.** Available online at: http://www.ipsnews.net/2012/03/protesters-lift-roadblocks-in-southern-chile/ [Accessed 5 August 2014]

Students march in April 2012, 25 April 2012:
La Segunda (2012) **Marcha estudiantil de este miércoles triplicó la convocatoria que se logró en abril de 2011.** Available online at:
http://www.lasegunda.com/Noticias/Educacion/2012/04/740848/A-las-1100-horas-comienza-primera-marcha-estudiantil-del-ano-en-Santiago [Accessed 6 August 2014] Website in Spanish

Students march in June 2012, 28 June 2012:
La Segunda (2012) **Encapuchados protagonizan saqueos y barricadas en marcha estudiantil.** Available online at:
http://www.lasegunda.com/Noticias/Nacional/2012/06/759159/Universitarios-marchan-por-la-capital-para-exigir-gratuidad-y-fin-al-lucro [Accessed 6 August 2014] Website in Spanish

Education minister caps student loan interest rate at 2%, 23 April 2012.
Crelling, O. (2012) **Chilean minister presents university funding plan to president.**

Available online at: http://santiagotimes.cl/chilean-minister-presents-university-funding-plan-to-president/ [Accessed 6 August 2014]

Student leaders reject new university finance plan, 24 April 2012.
Crelling, O. (2012) **'No small print in education reform,' Chilean minister says.** Available online at: http://santiagotimes.cl/no-small-print-in-education-reform-chilean-minister-says/ [Accessed 6 August 2014]

2012 education reforms, 30 August 2012.
Gribney, E. (2012) **The mañana project.** Available online at: http://www.timeshighereducation.co.uk/features/the-maana-project/420981.article [Accessed 6 August 2014]

Occupation of school sites, 15 August 2012:
The Guardian (2012) **Chile student protesters occupy high schools.** Available online at: http://www.theguardian.com/world/2012/aug/15/chile-student-protesters-high-schools [Accessed 6 August 2014]

Carabineros evict students, 16 August 2012:
La Segunda (2012) **139 detenidos deja masivo desalojo de colegios en Santiago.** Available online at: http://www.lasegunda.com/Noticias/Nacional/2012/08/772993/78-detenidos-deja-masivo-desalojo-de-colegios-de-Santiago [Accessed 6 August 2014] Website in Spanish

Commission of Inquiry into Higher Education denounces seven universities, 30 August 2012.
Gribney, E. (2012) **The mañana project.** Available online at: http://www.timeshighereducation.co.uk/features/the-maana-project/420981.article [Accessed 6 August 2014]

Justice Minister resigns, 19 December 2012:
Franklin, J. (2012) **Victory for Chilean students as minister resigns over corruption scandal.** Available online at: http://www.theguardian.com/world/2012/dec/19/victory-chilean-students-minister-resigns [Accessed 6 August 2014]

Michelle Bachelet's pre-election proposals for education reform, 29 October 2013.
Douchez-Lortet, C. and Steefel, K. (2013) **Bachelet releases policy platform 21 days ahead of election.** Available online at: http://santiagotimes.cl/bachelet-sends-first-education-bill-congress-students-plan-protest/ [Accessed 6 August 2014]

President Piñera outlines an eight-point energy plan for Chile, 16 January 2012:
Crellin, O. (2012) **Chile with 50% hydro power by 2034, but serious energy shortages in 2015.** Available online at: http://en.mercopress.com/2012/01/16/chile-with-50-hydro-power-by-2034-but-serious-energy-shortages-in-2015 [Accessed 5 August 2014]

HidroAysén. Timeline of events relating to the HidroAysén proposals, 10 June 2014:
Emol (2014) **Las fechas más importantes que han marcado el polémico proyecto HidroAysén.** Available online at:

http://www.emol.com/noticias/economia/2014/06/09/664442/se-define-el-futuro-de-hidroaysen.html [Accessed 5 August 2014] Website in Spanish

Chilean government subcommittee gives preliminary approval for the HidroAysén dams, 9 May 2011:
Emol (2011) **Comisión aprueba HidroAysén pero exige medidas en favor de la zona.** Available online at:
http://www.emol.com/noticias/economia/2011/05/09/480621/comision-aprueba-hidroaysen-pero-exige-medidas-en-favor-de-la-zona.html [Accessed 5 August 2014] Website in Spanish

Supreme Court rejects appeals against HidroAysén approval, 4 April 2012:
Emol (2012) **Corte Suprema rechaza recursos de protección y da luz verde a proyecto HidroAysén.** Available online at:
http://www.emol.com/noticias/nacional/2012/04/04/534308/fallo-de-la-corte-suprema-por-los-recursos-de-proteccion-presentados-contra-hidroaysen.html [Accessed 5 August 2014] Website in Spanish

Protesters march in Santiago in response to Supreme Court decision, 1 June 2012:
Los Angeles Times (2012) **Controversial dam project in Chile's Patagonia region on hold.** Available online at: http://latimesblogs.latimes.com/world_now/2012/06/dam-project-chile-patagonia-suspended.html [Accessed 5 August 2014]

Colbún SA suspend work on environmental impact study, 30 May 2012:
Emol (2012) **Colbún pide frenar EIA de proyecto de transmisión de HidroAysén.** Available online at:
http://www.emol.com/noticias/economia/2012/05/30/543190/colbun-suspende-el-estudio-de-impacto-ambiental-de-hydroaysen.html [Accessed 5 August 2014] Website in Spanish

Endesa Chile remove HidroAysén from list of active projects, 7 January 2014:
Emol (2014) **Endesa Chile retira a HidroAysén de su cartera de proyectos en América Latina.** Available online at:
http://www.emol.com/noticias/economia/2014/01/07/638370/hidroaysen-endesa-chile-retira-proyecto-de-documento-que-presenta-a-inversionistas.html [Accessed 5 August 2014] Website in Spanish

Cancellation of the HidroAysén proposals, 10 June 2014:
Howard, B. C. (2014) **Chile Scraps Huge Patagonia Dam Project After Years of Controversy.** Available online at:
http://news.nationalgeographic.com/news/energy/2014/06/140610-chile-hidroaysen-dam-patagonia-energy-environment/ [Accessed 5 August 2014]

Cancellation of the HidroAysén proposals, 12 June 2014:
Tompkins, K. (2014) **Victory Against HidroAysén: Dam Project is Cancelled.** Available online at: http://www.conservacionpatagonica.org/blog/2014/06/12/victory-against-hidroaysen-dam-project-is-cancelled/ [Accessed 5 August 2014]

Declaration on hidroaysen.cl, 11 June 2014, following the Chilean government decision:
http://www.hidroaysen.cl/?p=1937 Website in Spanish

Copper trading prices, past 25 years:
http://www.infomine.com/investment/metal-prices/copper/all/ [Accessed 5 August 2014]

Hantavirus deaths, 6 February 2012:
The Guardian (2012) **Chile on health alert over hantavirus outbreak spread by rats.** Available online at: http://www.theguardian.com/world/2012/feb/06/chile-hantavirus-outbreak-spread-rats [Accessed 5 August 2014]

Sustainability of salmon farming, 26 August 2013:
Lee, J. (2013) **Can the Farmed Salmon Industry Become Sustainable?** Available online at: http://www.triplepundit.com/2013/08/farmed-salmon-sustainable/ [Accessed 6 August 2014]

Global Salmon Initiative (GSI):
http://www.globalsalmoninitiative.org/

WWF welcomes the Global Salmon Initiative, 15 August 2013:
WWF (2013) **WWF welcomes "game changer" initiative in salmon farm sustainability.** Available online at:
http://wwf.panda.org/who_we_are/wwf_offices/chile/?209717/WWF-welcomes-game-changer-initiative-in-salmon-farm-sustainability [Accessed 6 August 2014]

WWF supporter page on farmed salmon:
http://www.worldwildlife.org/industries/farmed-salmon

Transportes Aéreos Don Carlos cease operating flights between Coyhaique and Villa O'Higgins, 30 April 2013:
Radio Santa María (2013) **Transportes aéreos "Don Carlos" dejó de realizar vuelos subsidiados a Villa O'Higgins.** Available online at:
http://www.radiosantamaria.cl/regional/1133-transportes-aereos-don-carlos-dejo-de-realizar-vuelos-subsidiados-a-villa-o-higgins [Accessed 15 July 2014] Website in Spanish

SERNAGEOMIN, Servicio Nacional de Geologia y Mineria:
http://www.sernageomin.cl/ Website in Spanish

SERNAGEOMIN Red de vigilancia volcánica (Vigilance network for volcanoes):
http://www.sernageomin.cl/volcanes.php Website in Spanish

May 2013 evacuation around Volcán Copahue; Video, 30 May 2013.
Pinto, R. (2013) **Chile and Argentina evacuate after Copahue volcano alert.** Available online at: http://www.bbc.co.uk/news/world-latin-america-22722825 [Accessed 6 August 2014]

Data on Volcán Copahue; Global Volcanism Program:
http://www.volcano.si.edu/volcano.cfm?vn=357090

Sebastián Piñera sits at Oval Office desk (amongst other blunders) 16 March 2014.
Edwards, S. (2014) **An ode to Piñera, a satirist's dream president.** Available online at: http://santiagotimes.cl/ode-pinera-satirists-dream-president/ [Accessed 6 August 2014]

Michelle Bachelet sworn in as President, 11 March 2014.
BBC News (2014) **Michelle Bachelet sworn in as Chile's president.** Available online at: http://www.bbc.co.uk/news/world-latin-america-26528923 [Accessed 6 August 2014]

May 2014 Education Bill introduced by government of Michelle Bachelet, 19 May 2014.
Malthouse, E. (2014) **Bachelet sends first education bill to Congress, students plan protest.** Available online at: http://santiagotimes.cl/bachelet-sends-first-education-bill-congress-students-plan-protest/ [Accessed 6 August 2014]

Chilean Minsitry of Works meets with representatives of Parque Pumalín to discuss Carretera Austral route between Hornopirén and Caleta Gonzalo, 17 August 2011:
Argandoña, C. (2011) **Golborne acuerda mesa de trabajo con Tompkins por Carretera Austral.** Available online at: http://diario.latercera.com/2011/08/17/01/contenido/pais/31-80438-9-golborne-acuerda-mesa-de-trabajo-con-tompkins-por-carretera-austral.shtml [Accessed 5 August 2014] Website in Spanish

Discussion of the Hornopirén to Caleta Gonzalo route:
Proyecto y Parque Pumalín (2013) **Conectividad Para Palena.** Available online at: http://www.parquepumalin.cl/en/conectividad_para_palena.htm [Accessed 5 August 2014]

Government announces decision to favour an 'interior coastal route', 4 October 2006:
Emol (2006) **Carretera austral pasará por terrenos de Douglas Tompkins.** Available online at: http://www.emol.com/noticias/nacional/2006/10/04/231799/carretera-austral-pasara-por-terrenos-de-douglas-tompkins.html [Accessed 5 August 2014] Website in Spanish

Extension of the Carretera Austral from Puerto Yungay to Puerto Natales:
Ministerio de Obras Públicas (2004) **Plan de Inversiones para la Conectividad Austral.** pp24 onwards. Available online at: http://www.conectividadparapalena.cl/descargas/Plan_de_Inversiones_Conectividad_Autral.pdf [Accessed 5 August 2014] Document in Spanish

Made in the USA
Middletown, DE
22 September 2018